The Doctrine
of God

The Doctrine of God

A Global Introduction

Veli-Matti Kärkkäinen

Baker Academic
Grand Rapids, Michigan

© 2004 by Veli-Matti Kärkkäinen

Published by Baker Academic
a division of Baker Publishing Group
P.O. Box 6287, Grand Rapids, MI 49516-6287
www.bakeracademic.com

Printed in the United States of America

Library of Congress Cataloging-in-Publication Data
Kärkkäinen, Veli-Matti.
    The doctrine of God : a global introduction / Veli-Matti Kärkkäinen.
        p.   cm.
    Includes bibliographical references and indexes.
    ISBN 0-8010-2752-7
    1. God. 2. Theology, Doctrinal. I. Title.
BT103.K37 2004
231'.09—dc21   2003028166

Contents

Preface

This volume brings to completion the three-part textbook series on God, Christ, and the Holy Spirit. *Pneumatology,* highlighting the rich theological and biblical traditions of the Holy Spirit, started the trilogy and was followed by *Christology.* The present book, which focuses on interpretations of what in trinitarian language is called Father, has the same format and goal as the previous two books in the series.

My teaching experience in Europe, Asia, and the United States has taught me as much as has continual reading of theologies written by men and women from various parts of our shrinking global village. It is to my students that I dedicate this book. They continue to teach me and challenge me to offer limited thinking about God, and this they do without requesting I pay tuition!

To Susan Wood of the Fuller Faculty Publications Department, who labored with me on all three volumes by painstakingly checking my English, I owe heartfelt thanks. Melinda Van Engen of Baker Academic similarly deserves a big thank you for editing these three books. She helped me in so many ways to clarify expressions and to make the books more user-friendly. Robert N. Hosack of Baker Academic was instrumental in giving shape to and providing enthusiastic support for this trilogy.

Introduction

God-Talk Then and Now

The Obligation—and Impossibility—of God-Talk

The great theologian and philosopher of the Christian church, Augustine of the fifth century, set the tone for any inquiry into the mystery of God. In his celebrated *De Trinitate (On the Trinity)*, the bishop of Hippo penned:

> Let me ask of my reader, wherever, alike with myself, he is certain, there to go with me; wherever, alike with me, he hesitates, there to join with me in inquiring; wherever he recognizes himself to be in error, there to return to me; wherever he recognizes me to be so, there to call me back; so that we may enter together upon the path of charity, and advance towards Him of whom it is said, "Seek His face evermore." And I would make this pious and safe agreement, in the presence of our Lord God, with all who read my writings . . . because in no other subject is error more dangerous, or inquiry more laborious, or the discovery of truth more profitable.[1]

As theologians, we are bound to talk about God, not only because *theology* as talk/speaking *(logos)* about God *(theos)* inevitably deals with God but primarily because essential "to every religious system is the belief that reality is more than what is perceived, that sensory experience communicates only a superficial appearance of what is really real." Thus, "underneath or above

---

1. Augustine, *On the Holy Trinity,* vol. 3 of *A Select Library of Nicene and Post-Nicene Fathers* (Grand Rapids: Eerdmans, 1956), 1.3.5.

what we see and hear is a transcendent yet present reality that is suprasensory, supranatural, spiritual, divine, or all of these."[2]

We are confronted, therefore, with the obligation to speak of God while at the same time acknowledging the impossibility of that kind of discourse. No one expressed this dilemma more powerfully than Karl Barth, the church father of the twentieth century: "As ministers we ought to speak of God. We are human, however, and so cannot speak of God. We ought therefore to recognize both our obligation and our inability and by that very recognition give God the glory. This is our perplexity."[3]

We could avoid this challenge simply by pulling together biblical materials relating to God. Theology, however, by its nature goes beyond the Bible and addresses questions that the Bible does not address (even though the practice of theology involves looking at the biblical materials and assessing to what extent biblical guidelines were honored in the theological discourse). The premier North American evangelical theologian Donald G. Bloesch puts the matter in proper perspective:

> In the awesome attempt to define God, theology must do more than simply repeat the mainly figurative language of the biblical narrative. It must also draw upon the conceptual language of philosophy in order to illuminate the mystery of the God who revealed himself in biblical history and most of all in Jesus Christ. The Bible is not a treatise on metaphysics, but its affirmations have ineradicable metaphysical implications. It does not present us with a full-blown ontology, but its depictions of God have an unmistakable ontological cast.[4]

Thus, theology is left with the virtually impossible task of speaking about God. How do we do this at the beginning of the third millennium?

New Horizons for God-Talk

Living as we do at the beginning of the third millennium, we are faced by a most creative paradox. On the one hand, there is no denying the insurmountable problems associated with talk about God following the Enlightenment and especially the advent of postmodernism. If any discourse is highly suspect, it is certainly talk about God. On the other hand, ironic as it may sound, there is no denying the fact that toward the end of the second millennium the doctrine of God, in both philosophical theology and systematic theology, took on new

2. Ted Peters, *God—The World's Future: Systematic Theology for a Postmodern Era* (Minneapolis: Fortress, 1992), 83.

3. Karl Barth, *The Word of God and the Word of Man* (New York: Harper & Brothers, 1957), 186.

4. Donald G. Bloesch, *God the Almighty: Power, Wisdom, Holiness, Love* (Downers Grove, Ill.: InterVarsity, 1995), 31.

relevance. Numerous exciting developments are still taking place, many of which are highlighted in this book.

At the beginning of the twentieth century, the Scottish theologian James Orr, in his celebrated *Progress of Dogma*,[5] made the claim that various doctrines were at the forefront of discussion in different times and contexts. Students of the history of theology know that christological and trinitarian debates, coupled with a growing interest in aspects of the doctrine of salvation, took the upper hand during the first centuries. In medieval times, the doctrine of atonement was in vogue. The doctrine of the church lay dormant until the Reformation. Toward the end of the second millennium, the doctrine of the Holy Spirit took on a new significance, and a resurgence took place concerning various aspects of the doctrine of God, especially the relationship between God and the world (whether God is affected by what happens in history). New proposals for understanding the God-world dynamic were suggested, such as those coming from process theology. The boundaries of God-talk began to be challenged by new interpretations ranging from secular to death-of-God to political to—most recently—ecological or green theology. Women joined the discourse about God with the emergence of feminist movements and challenged the sexist, as they saw it, talk about God as "Father."

A growing body of literature from non-Western contexts came into focus beginning in the early 1970s. Latin American liberation theology talked about God in relation to social, political, and economic issues; African theologies rooted God-talk in the culture of ancestors, spirits, and communalism; and Asian interpretations of God took their departure in the mystical, aesthetic, and pluralistic context of Asia.

So here we are in the midst of a most exciting, challenging, perhaps even disturbing renewal of discourse about God. This book offers a survey—or takes stock—of most of the important developments regarding the doctrine of God. But how do current developments relate to what has come before? In other words, what is the relationship between Christian tradition and current interpretations of God? This question is crucial for the following survey and also guided the selection of materials.

Classical Theism under Attack

In systematic theology, it has become customary to use "classical theism" as a generic term designating traditional approaches to discourse about God. The meaning of this widely debated term will become evident later in the discussion, but for now, a tentative description can be given. Classical theism denotes those post-biblical developments of early Christian theology as it sought to

---

5. James Orr, *The Progess of Dogma* (Grand Rapids: Eerdmans, n.d.).

express faith in the biblical God with the help of Greco-Roman philosophical categories. These developments reached a peak in the highly philosophical, speculative systems of medieval scholasticism and were further refined, for example, by post-Reformation Protestant orthodoxy.

The picture of God that emerged from that philosophical and speculative gristmill, while suited for the purposes of early apologetic and later speculative philosophical theologies, has, since the Enlightenment of the eighteenth century, come under criticism by a number of theological movements. Complaints have been many: The God of classical theism as an Unmoved Mover, while enjoying his own perfect fullness of being, is distanced from the world, unaffected by the happenings of history, unrelated to Christian life (let alone social and political struggles), and so on. Furthermore, say critics from a wide variety of traditions, that kind of God is also far removed from the dynamic, narrative, life-related discourse of the Bible, especially in the Old Testament.[6]

There is no denying that much of the energy for the contemporary resurgence of interest in discourse about God—whether in the West or in the third world—has its source in the desire to radically revise the classical approach:

> Much of the reinterpretation of the doctrine of God can be traced to a rising reaction against classical theism—the legacy of Hellenism that has left an indelible imprint on Christian theology. Here God is depicted as immutable, self-contained, all-sufficient, impassible, supremely detached from the world of pain and suffering. How can this kind of God be reconciled with the biblical God who earnestly cares for his people—even to the extent of taking their pain and guilt upon himself in the incarnation and atoning death of his Son?[7]

Consequently, the present book has two main purposes: first, to survey interpretations of God throughout Christian history, including the biblical testimonies, and second, to let the classical theistic tradition and its challengers converse with one another.

There is a plurality of testimonies concerning God and God's relationship with humans, beginning even in the Bible. Rather than suppressing that plurality, we need to listen carefully to the rich symphony of voices. This survey, therefore, attempts to be comprehensive by including all major interpretations, whether biblical, historical, or contemporary (both mainline and contextual, such as the voices of women and other minorities). It follows the exciting and winding developments of the doctrine of God in Christian theology by highlighting the sometimes radically contrasting views.

The plan of the book is as follows: It begins by delving into biblical testimonies concerning God in light of recent scholarship. The Old Testament

---

6. Some theologians have made a distinction between "classical" and "biblical" theism; see Bloesch, *God the Almighty,* 14; see also pp. 22, 29, 109.

7. Ibid., 21.

receives more attention than the New Testament, since the first part of the Christian canon sketches the main ideas of the doctrine of God. Jesus and the early church accepted the Yahweh of the Old Testament as their God.

Following the biblical survey, the book traces the development of the Christian doctrine of God from the early fathers to the beginning of the twentieth century. The main purpose is to highlight the various—often creative—ways biblical materials were cast into the thought forms appropriate to the context. The historical survey, while paying proper attention to the dominant motifs, also highlights the contributions of marginal voices.

Contemporary interpretations of God, the main focus of this book, is divided into two main sections. Western theologies of God are discussed in both their European and North American varieties. Beginning with Karl Barth and Paul Tillich, the two precursors of much twentieth-century theology, the book examines interpretations of God among leading European theologians such as Jürgen Moltmann and Wolfhart Pannenberg. In regard to North American interpretations of God, the book considers challenges to classical theism such as death-of-God theology, process theology, and Open theism. A lengthy section follows that focuses on contextual approaches such as feminist and black theologies and theologies among immigrant communities (African, Asian, and Hispanic American) and Native Americans.

During a time when the majority of Christians lives outside Europe and North America, it is scandalous that African, Asian, and Latin American theologies are hardly mentioned in textbooks, let alone given fair treatment. The last part of this book, contemporary interpretations of God outside the Western academy, attempts to correct the tragic neglect of third world voices in almost all works of systematic theology by discussing African, Latin American, and Asian understandings of God.

Part 1

Classical Theistic Traditions

Biblical Orientations

Who is God according to the Christian faith? What characteristics does God possess? What distinguishes the Christian God from other gods? The simplest way to address these questions is to guide the inquiring person to the Bible. After all, Christian churches at all times have claimed to found their faith on the biblical revelation. Yet declaring that the Bible is *the* guide to the doctrine of the Christian God—as if a careful reading of the biblical text coupled with a thorough and systematic classification of relevant passages would answer all questions about God—is a claim needing qualification. First of all, the Bible is not a collection of ready-made doctrines, even though preachers and teachers of the church since ancient days have often handled the Bible as though it were. Rather, the Bible is a compilation of testimonies about God from various contexts and various perspectives. Most of the Bible, and certainly the Old Testament, is in the form of stories, testimonies, chronicles, worship hymns, questions to God, and so on. In other words, it is only through carefully listening to the narrative of the Old Testament that we gain a perspective on who God is. This issue has not always been acknowledged by Christian theologians. The reminder of John Goldingay, an Old Testament theologian, merits attention:

> Christian theology has not regularly talked about God in narrative terms. The creeds, for instance, are structured around the persons of Father, Son, and Spirit, and systematic theology has often taken God's trinitarian nature as its structural principle. Before the revival of trinitarian thinking in the late twentieth century, systematic theology often emphasized the fundamental significance of attributes of God such as omnipotence, omniscience, omnipresence, and perfection.

Second, as a book written and edited by a number of people over many centuries, the Bible cherishes a plurality of voices. It is not a homogenous book, nor is it supposed to be read in a univocal way. Take, for instance, the existence of four Gospels or two sets of historical books covering basically the same material (Samuel-Kings and Chronicles). The Christian church, again, claims that there is a common core, a set of shared convictions among the legitimate plurality. There is, therefore, not a cacophony of disconnected voices but a symphony with numerous melody and harmony variations. Thus, we should not listen to any one tone to the exclusion of the others.

Third, God's revelation in the Bible has a developing, growing, emerging nature. When we open the Bible and start reading about God the Creator in Genesis, we do not have all the perspectives we have at the end of Revelation. To do justice to the Bible's view of God, we need to be patient and follow the various rivers that run through the canon.

For our purposes here—a book about systematic rather than biblical theology—the task of looking at the biblical data is even more demanding. Systematic theology should always take a hard look at the biblical data, but by nature its task is to go beyond—hopefully not against—the biblical revelation and then, at the end of the day, to double-check whether theological ideas are in harmony with biblical orientations. Systematic theology asks many questions about which the biblical revelation is silent. With regard to the doctrine of God, take these for example: How do we address God the Father in an inclusive way? What is the influence of particular worldviews and philosophies on the doctrine of God? How can we speak of the Christian God in a way that relates to other living faiths?

This inquiry into the biblical orientations of the doctrine of God begins by looking first at various testimonies and pointers in the Old Testament. Rather than ignoring or paying scant attention to what the Old Testament has to say about God in order to hasten to the New Testament—the favorite part of the canon for most Christians—we will spend some quality time in the first part of the Bible. We do so for two reasons: First, the Old Testament is part—and a much larger part for that matter—of the canon of the Christian church; therefore, what it has to say about the topic matters. In addition, the first part of the Bible lays the foundation for the second part, the New Testament. In fact, when it comes to the doctrine of God, the main motifs of the symphony are composed in the Old Testament. The apostolic church basically adopted the God of Abraham, Isaac, and Jacob as its God. In regard to some doctrines, the doctrine of the church or salvation, for example, the New Testament makes a major contribution. With the doctrine of God, however, the Old Testament is of critical importance. Following the discussion of the perspectives on God found in the Old Testament, chapter 2 considers the ways the New Testament shapes and adds to the foundation laid by its predecessor.

1

The Old Testament

The Rise of Jewish Monotheism

God as the Theme of the Old Testament

The Old Testament is a good starting point for considering the doctrine of God because, in the words of the leading American Old Testament theologian Walter Brueggemann, the "primal subject of an Old Testament theology is of course God."[1] Having said this, Brueggemann hastens to add:

> But because the Old Testament does not (and never intends to) provide a coherent and comprehensive offer of God, this subject matter is more difficult, complex, and problematic than we might expect. For the most part, the Old Testament text gives us only hints, traces, fragments, and vignettes, with no suggestion of how all these elements might fit together, if indeed they do. What does emerge, in any case, is an awareness that *the elusive but dominating Subject of the Old Testament cannot be comprehended in any preconceived categories.* The God of the Old Testament does not easily conform to the expectations of Christian dogmatic theology, nor to the categories of any Hellenistic perennial philosophy. . . . The Character who will emerge from such a patient study at the end will still be elusive and more than a little surprising.[2]

1. Walter Brueggemann, *Theology of the Old Testament: Testimony, Dispute, Advocacy* (Minneapolis: Fortress, 1997), 117.
2. Ibid., italics in text.

15

To do justice to the biblical theology of God, we need to keep in dynamic tension two foundational affirmations: On the one hand, God is the theme of the Old Testament. On the other hand, no doctrine of God per se is found in the Bible, at least not in the sense of systematic theology. As a general rule, one can say that "in Hebraic religion, God is known by what God does. What God does is remembered and recollected as history—the history of God's encounter with humanity. In these encounters, God is remembered as having a definable, discernible character by those whom God has met."[3]

Brueggemann's *Theology of the Old Testament* provides a paramount example of this rule. Utilizing court terminology, Brueggemann maintains that "Israel's Core Testimony" (the title of part 1) comes in three forms, all of them directly or indirectly related to what God does: testimonies in verbal sentences (testimonies to God's mighty deeds), testimonies in adjectives (testimonies to what God is like when one considers his actions), and testimonies in nouns (testimonies concerning how to name the God who acts and saves). In addition, a forthcoming work titled *Old Testament Theology: Israel's Gospel* by John Goldingay is outlined entirely in terms of God's actions:

- God set in motion (created)
- God started over
- God promised
- God delivered
- God sealed
- God gave
- God accommodated
- God wrestled
- God preserved
- God sent
- God exalted[4]

3. Thomas C. Oden, *The Living God: Systematic Theology*, vol. 1 (San Francisco: Harper & Row, 1987), 40.

4. John Goldingay, *Old Testament Theology: Israel's Gospel* (Downers Grove, Ill.: InterVarsity, 2003), 13. I am fully aware that Brueggemann's and Goldingay's methodological and philosophical approaches to the study of the Old Testament are not identical. Brueggemann's is a typical postmodern "rhetorical" approach in which the student of the biblical text dares not inquire into the historical ("factual") basis of its statements, only its verbal form (see Brueggemann, *Theology of the Old Testament*, 65, 118–19). Goldingay uses an "evangelical" approach. While fully acknowledging the rhetoric of the Old Testament and its narrative form and the dubious nature of trying to ascertain historical basis in so many instances in the story, he is not, however, ready to lay aside the question of historicity. In that sense, Goldingay's approach, while otherwise very different from the "modernism" of Gerhard von Rad and other giants of the former generation, is closer to their agenda. Aware of this basic difference in approaches, I believe I can confidently borrow from both authors for the purposes of this book.

This exposition and consideration of Old Testament perspectives on God and their relevance for later theological reflection follow in the footsteps of these two premier biblical scholars. After inquiring into the roots and emergence of the Hebraic view of God and the rise of Jewish monotheism, the chapter looks at how the Old Testament initially names God by focusing on the two principal names *Elohim* and *Yahweh*. It then looks at what God does (God's actions) and what God is like. This prepares us to go back to the business of naming God. In other words, as the Israelites came to know about God's actions and his characteristics, they began to apply various designations to God. Finally, the chapter discusses how the Old Testament God relates to other gods.

The Emergence of Jewish Monotheism

The term *monotheism,* from two Greek words, *monos,* "one," and *theos,* "God," characterizes Old Testament belief. This monotheistic faith is best illustrated in the famous Shema, Israel's "confession of faith": "Hear, O Israel: The LORD our God, the LORD is one" (Deut. 6:4). Quite early, the Israelites left behind henotheism—the belief that other gods exist but that only their God is to be worshiped (if ever henotheism existed)—and embraced monotheism. How did this happen? What was the origin of Israelite monotheism, the view adopted by the Christian church?

According to a recent textbook, there is "no doubt that the great monotheistic religions, including Islam, owe their theological understanding primarily to the witness of the biblical texts."[5] This statement holds even if we admit with many scholars that the ancient Israelites were, at the beginning, henotheists. According to this view, Abraham and his descendants specialized in the cult of Yahweh, originally a tribal god of the Semites. Their belief in Yahweh soon made their faith unique. By the time of the monarchy, beginning around 1000 B.C., the existence of rival gods was seen as a threat to the unity of the nation and its worship. Later on, so the theory goes, Jewish monotheism developed through dialogue with Greek and mystery religions and was eventually adopted by the Christian tradition.

This outline of the emergence of monotheism, which is not without scholarly challenges, has variations. One of the most disputed questions is whether early Israelites were ever polytheists, believers in several gods. At present, most scholars of religion accept the early existence of monotheism among the Israelites, seeing it not as the result of a long development but as a distinguishing mark of the Jewish faith. In the confines of this book, we cannot enter into a complicated discussion of this point. For our purposes, we can safely say that the Old Testament faith is based on the idea of monotheism, belief in one God, and that this conviction was held by Jesus and the apostles as the pioneers of the Christian church.

5. Gerald Bray, *The Doctrine of God* (Downers Grove, Ill.: InterVarsity, 1993), 112.

At first glance, it seems that Israel was not so different from the surrounding nations, whose own gods guaranteed the unity of their people. The Hittites, the Edomites, and many others worshiped their own gods. Israel's uniqueness, however, lay in the worship of one God. True, many other nations also recognized one supreme God, a "high God." But Israel worshiped the one true God. Moreover, the Israelites were from the beginning cautious about erecting statues of their God or conceiving of their God in sexual terms, as did many surrounding nations. These features not only distinguished Israel's monotheism but also protected the Israelites from practices such as cultic prostitution, an activity not alien to Israel's history but one always rejected by its mainstream religious leadership.

The Israelites also thought of God's activity in a unique way:

> Other nations of course described their goddesses or gods as acting in history; Marduk, for instance, helped the Babylonians secure prosperity and defeat their enemies. And Israel saw Yahweh at work in the world of nature and the cycle of the seasons. But Yahweh acted *primarily* in the great events of the nation's history, while the deities of neighboring nations generally had *more* to do with safeguarding the repeated annual cycle of vegetation. That meant that, in contrast to divinities whose function was to guarantee that the same thing would keep happening—Yahweh made *new* things happen. His people escaped Egypt, they settled a new land, and so on.[6]

In other words, Israel's religion took a particular interest in historical changes and world events. Israel's God, unlike most other gods, was not only the guarantor of moral norms but could also guide and criticize the monarchy. God was not in the service of the people; the people were subject to God.

Of course, Jewish monotheism "had to go through many stages of development before it reached the concept of a transcendental and spiritual god. It was necessary first that the Decalogue and the Book of the Covenant prohibit most stringently polytheism and every form of idolatry."[7] But that comment takes us ahead of our story. The following discussion focuses on the various Old Testament testimonies concerning God.

How to Name God

The first testament—the first part of the Christian canon—introduces its main character's name abruptly: "In the beginning God [*Elohim*]." No apologies, no apologetics, just plain talk. Genesis begins with God. It does not start

---

6. William C. Placher, *A History of Christian Theology* (Philadelphia: Westminster, 1983), 20, italics in text.

7. Edmund J. Fortman, ed., *Theology of God: Commentary* (New York: Bruce Publishing, 1968), 8.

like a modern legal document, with a preamble defining key terms. It begins in the middle of things, like the narrative that it is. "God" is a fully realized character, but we discover what this character is like only through following the story. The first readers of Genesis, of course, knew this God, and their knowledge of this God's character was taken for granted. But stage by stage, modern readers of Genesis discover who this person is, and by the end of the story they are in a position to reread "In the beginning God . . ." with greater comprehension.[8]

In fact, many names are applied to this God in the first part of the Bible. The two most significant for later theology are *Elohim,* rendered "God" in most English translations, and the tetragrammaton YHWH, usually transliterated "Yahweh" or "Jehovah" and translated "LORD" in English Bibles. Perhaps the fact that the first page of the Bible presents God as *Elohim,* a common name for "god" in the ancient world, is a clue to who this God is: *Elohim* is someone people without special revelation can relate to. God is known in some way in the world he created.

Elohim is a plural form. "Elsewhere the plural can be a numerical plural, referring to gods. But applied to the one God, it is an intensive plural suggesting that this God embodies all the deity there is."[9] *Elohim* and its root, *'el,* are generic designations of God common to all Semitic languages. The root *'el* occurs as a common noun ("the god," "god") and also as the proper name for a particular god. The Pentateuch also illustrates this wider usage of the generic term. Since *El* did not necessarily denote the highest god, the patriarchs used the name *El Elyon,* "God Most High" (Gen. 14:18–22), to point to *the* God.

In line with the narrative nature of the Old Testament, many of the names given to God emerge from concrete life situations. In the patriarchal narratives, Hagar coins the name *El Roï,* "the God who sees me," after God speaks to her in the desert (Gen. 16:13). Abraham calls God *Yhwh yireh,* "Yahweh will provide," when God sends a ram to take the place of his son Isaac (Gen. 22:14). Jacob names God *El Bethel,* "the God of Bethel" (35:7), and so on.

Other names for God include *El Shaddai,* "God Almighty," and *Yahweh Sabaoth,* "Lord of Hosts." The special name *Adonai,* rendered in most English Bibles as "Lord" (not in small caps) arose in roughly 300 B.C. out of the Jewish reluctance to pronounce the tetragrammaton. This name was later translated into Greek as *Kyrios* (literally, "lord," "master," or "sir"), the name used in the New Testament to refer to God the Father, Jesus Christ, or the Godhead in general.

The origin and meaning of the divine name *Yahweh* have been the subjects of much debate. Attempts to derive it from an outside religion are not convincing. Not much more promising is the suggestion that the name derives from *ya-huwa,* meaning "O he." The current scholarly consensus is that the

---

8. Goldingay, *Old Testament Theology,* 51.
9. Ibid.

name is connected with the verbal root *hwy* or *hwh,* meaning "to be." This is strongly supported by the observation that the Exodus 3 theophany (divine self-manifestation) is the only interpretation the Old Testament gives for the name *Yahweh.* In Exodus 3, Moses is confronted by the burning bush and is told, "I am the God of your father, the God of Abraham, the God of Isaac and the God of Jacob" (v. 6), identifying God with the past faith of Israel. As John Goldingay comments:

> God's self-identification further indicates the actuality of personal meeting. *I am the God of your father, the God of Abraham, the God of Isaac, the God of Jacob* is no revelation in the sense that it proffers no new information for systematic theology, but it is a revelation of the identity of the person who speaks. It is a crucial such revelation. It indicates that the person who speaks can be identified with the one who has related to Moses and to his people in the past. This is no new God, even if this is a new revelation as far as Moses and his contemporaries are concerned.[10]

As the exchange between God and Moses continues, Moses asks what he should say if asked the name of the God who sent him. Then comes the passage that has intrigued expositors for centuries: "I AM WHO I AM" (Exod. 3:14).

Not only is the origin of the name *Yahweh* debated but so is the proper translation of Exodus 3:14: *'ehyeh asher 'ehyeh.* The New Revised Standard Version reflects this uncertainty by offering two alternative translations in the margin: "I AM WHAT I AM" and "I WILL BE WHAT I WILL BE." No less than five lines of interpretation have been suggested:

> (i) The reply is intentionally evasive, because it is God's nature to remain hidden, or because to know God's name might give man power over him. But against this is the fact that the name is revealed to Moses in v. 15. (ii) God is the eternally existent one. (iii) "I am because I am." This suggests that there is no cause for God's existence outside himself. (iv) "I will be what I will be," or "I will be what I intend to be." (v) "I am he who is," or "I am the one who is." He is the God who alone has real existence.[11]

All of these renderings can be justified linguistically. In light of Old Testament theology, however, the most probable interpretation is that the name YHWH reveals the constancy and dependability of God. It conveys the idea that God is always the same. Whether it has related meanings such as "I am he who exists," referring to the one who really exists and/or is eternal, cannot be ascertained in light of this early revelation in the Old Testament. The fact that later Jewish and Christian theology came to that understanding seems

10. Ibid., 205, italics in text.
11. C. Brown, "God, Gods, Emmanuel," *New International Dictionary of New Testament Theology,* ed. C. Brown, 4 vols. (Grand Rapids: Zondervan, 1975–85), 2:68.

inevitable, but at this point in salvation history the Old Testament does not press the issue.

Moses' question about the name of the one sending him does not arise as a detached philosophical query but reflects a most natural and expected reaction to the revelation of the divine Actor. The verbal form *'ehyeh,* an imperfect tense form in Hebrew, denotes a *kind* of action, not primarily a *time* of action—in this case an action yet to be completed. This might be another clue to the main orientation of the name *Yahweh:* a being whose activity "could have begun in the past, or begins in the present or will begin in the future, but will take some time to be completed."[12]

Whatever the precise meaning, it is clear that God does not identify himself as Yahweh to answer a philosophical inquiry into the nature or the attributes of the divine Being but rather to state "what God will be in relationship to his people. . . . This comports nicely with the fact that the Israelites' reason for asking about the name has to do with a great need. They need to know not merely that God exists, but that God does and will soon act on their behalf."[13] Israel's God is the one to be trusted, to be depended on. Thus, the way God is identified in the Old Testament makes clear God's desire to be known in what he is doing and will yet do.

The God Who Acts

The God Who Creates

The foundational statement about God in the Old Testament is that God is the Creator.[14] The narrator of Genesis, the book of beginnings, opens with, "In the beginning God created the heavens and the earth." A previous generation of Old Testament theologians maintained that creation did not play a major role in Israel's relationship with Yahweh; rather, their relationship was based on the hope for redemption.[15] Those days are gone now, and Old Testament scholarship unanimously affirms the centrality of the doctrine of creation to the Israelite faith.[16] Yet it is in the context of exile that this doctrine receives its fullest articulation. Facing the threat of total abandonment by God, the Israelites hold fast to their faith in Yahweh, the Creator of heaven and earth and

12. Ben Witherington III and Laura M. Ice, *The Shadow of the Almighty: Father, Son, and Spirit in Biblical Perspective* (Grand Rapids: Eerdmans, 2002), 11.

13. Ibid., 11–12.

14. In this and the following two subsections, I am following the broad outline of Brueggemann's *Theology of the Old Testament,* with frequent references to Goldingay.

15. This view was almost canonized by the influential work of Gerhard von Rad, "The Theological Problem of the Old Testament Doctrine of Creation," in *The Problem of the Hexateuch and Other Essays,* trans. E. W. Trueman Dicken (New York: McGraw-Hill, 1966), 131–43.

16. For a brief synopsis, see Brueggemann, *Theology of the Old Testament,* 159–64.

all its inhabitants. The God who creates is stronger than the host of Babylonian gods. Therefore, Isaiah proclaims confidence in Yahweh's power based on the fact that Yahweh is the creating God:

> It is I who made the earth
>   and created mankind upon it.
> My own hands stretched out the heavens;
>   I marshaled their starry hosts.
> I will raise up Cyrus in my righteousness:
>   I will make all his ways straight.
> He will rebuild my city
>   and set my exiles free,
> but not for a price or reward,
>   says the LORD Almighty.
>
>   Isaiah 45:12–13

The fact that God is able to guide the course of Cyrus, a pagan king, is attributed to God's capacity to create the heavens and their hosts.

Goldingay points out an emphasis in the creation narrative that is often overlooked by expositors: It took special insight and wisdom for Yahweh to bring about all that he created.[17] The Book of Proverbs provides wonderful examples of this emphasis:

> By wisdom [insight] the LORD laid the earth's foundations,
>   by understanding he set the heavens in place;
> by his knowledge the deeps were divided,
>   and the clouds let drop the dew.
>
>   3:19–20

In the spirit of Genesis 1, Psalm 33:6–9 attributes the creation to God, who with the help of his Spirit and Word brought into being the heavens and the earth.

The word that denotes creating both in Genesis 1 and in passages that praise creation, such as Isaiah 42:5–6, is *bara'*, "the most majestic of terms of God's action as Creator, a verb used with no other subject except Yahweh, the God of Israel. It is Yahweh, the God of Israel, who creates the heavens and the earth and all that is, who summons, orders, sustains, and governs all of reality."[18] There are, of course, several Hebrew verbs for God's creative action, such as *yatsar* ("to form," "to shape as a potter"), but *bara'* carries a special meaning. The emphasis of *bara'* is the sovereignty with which God acts.

---

17. Goldingay, *Old Testament Theology,* 30.
18. Brueggemann, *Theology of the Old Testament,* 146.

The most well-known creation passage, found at the very beginning of the Old Testament, rather than being an inquiry into how God creates is a liturgical hymn celebrating the power of God to bring about the heavens and the earth.[19] God is depicted as the sovereign power who not only creates but also puts in their proper places the elements of creation, including the venerated sun, moon, and stars. This is one way the Old Testament affirms God's sovereignty, power, and benevolence. The God who creates is worth trusting. This is also the message of Isaiah:

> In Isaiah 45:9–12, Yhwh designs and shapes like a potter, begets like a father, travails like a mother, creates like an artist, stretches like a sheikh, and commands like a king (44:24 has already pictured Yhwh beating out like a metalworker). Together these images suggest the precision, purposefulness, pleasure, pain, care, effort, sovereignty, and effectiveness of the creator's work.[20]

The God Who Promises

When God affirms his promise to Abraham, the verb expressing God's action is *shaba'*, "to swear." Having no one higher to appeal to, God swears by himself: "I swear by myself, declares the LORD . . . I will surely bless you and make your descendants as numerous as the stars in the sky and as the sand on the seashore. Your descendants will take possession of the cities of their enemies, and through your offspring all nations on earth will be blessed, because you have obeyed me" (Gen. 22:16–18). Several key themes related to Israel's faith in Yahweh are found here: confirmation of God's faithfulness to his promises; a promise about the land and the descendants and more importantly about God's blessing; and an exhortation to shape one's life according to God's commandments. This narrative runs through much of the Old Testament. The God who promises sees to it that his purposes are not frustrated.

Related to God's act of promising is his desire to give; promise and blessing are tied together: "So the LORD gave Israel all the land he had sworn to give their forefathers. . . . Not one of all the LORD's good promises to the house of Israel failed; every one was fulfilled" (Josh. 21:43, 45).

The God Who Delivers

Having made generous promises, God also ensures that these promises are not frustrated by human rebellion. Beginning in the Book of Exodus, which

---

19. In the confines of this book, there is neither space nor need to enter the complicated technical discussion concerning how to translate this passage, either "In the beginning God created (from scratch?)" or "When God began to create," implying that the second verse is the main opening clause, thus saying that God was already at work, with the present reality described as some kind of chaos.

20. Goldingay, *Old Testament Theology,* 42.

becomes the standard reference point for the generations to come of God's faithfulness, God affirms, "I am the LORD, and I will bring you out from under the yoke of the Egyptians. I will free you from being slaves to them, and I will redeem you with an outstretched arm and with mighty acts of judgment. . . . Then you will know that I am the LORD your God, who brought you out from under the yoke of the Egyptians" (Exod. 6:6–7). The twin themes of God as deliverer and redeemer are brought together, anticipating also the teaching of the New Testament.

In subsequent situations of distress, Israel is summoned back to retell the story of the exodus, which celebrates God's role as deliverer. One such occasion is found in the Book of Joshua as the people face the challenge of crossing the Jordan River to enter the Promised Land: "For the LORD your God dried up the Jordan before you until you had crossed over. The LORD your God did to the Jordan just what he had done to the Red Sea when he dried it up before us until we had crossed over. He did this so that all the peoples of the earth might know that the hand of the LORD is powerful and so that you might always fear the LORD your God" (Josh. 4:23–24). Even much later, during the exile, Israel's faith in God is sustained by the living memory of God as their deliverer from Egypt (e.g., Amos 9:7).

The God Who Commands

In its most pervasive testimony, the witness of the Old Testament asserts: "Observe what I command *(swh)* today" (Exod. 34:11). Commandment dominates Israel's witness about Yahweh. Yahweh is a sovereign ruler whose will for the world is known and insisted upon. Israel as the addressee of command exists and prospers as it responds in obedience to these commands.[21]

God is the One who commands; Israel, the people of God, obeys. Brueggemann argues with regard to the main verb denoting commandment *(swh)* that "Yahweh's linkage to this verb is elemental for the Old Testament and is *perhaps Yahweh's defining and characteristic marking.*"[22] Consequently, Yahweh's command dominates the Sinai tradition (Exodus 19–Numbers 10) and the Book of Deuteronomy. A significant portion of Israel's core literature (the Torah) is dedicated to the commandments of Yahweh.

The primal command of Yahweh calls for exclusive loyalty to him; this is the preamble to the Decalogue (Exod. 20:2–3). The giving of the law is accompanied by God's self-manifestation, and the stipulations and contents of the law come from the mouth of God. God's commandments govern all of life for Israel, in relation both to God and to fellow human beings, even strangers.

21. Brueggemann, *Theology of the Old Testament,* 181.
22. Ibid., 182, italics in text.

God's commandments demand that the people be not only obedient but also holy unto God, separated, dedicated, devoted to God. This is the point of the ceremonial legislation in Leviticus and elsewhere. The standard is Yahweh's own character: "Be holy because I, the LORD your God, am holy" (Lev. 19:1). The list of commandments following this foundational statement then spell out what it means to be holy like Yahweh. The priestly and sacrificial machinery of Israel is a God-given means to help the people strive for the holiness and purity demanded of them as God's people.

The God Who Provides

One of the ways Yahweh is celebrated and honored relates to Yahweh's role as the one who provided for and guided the nation of Israel during her long journey: "Remember how the LORD your God led you all the way in the desert these forty years, to humble you and to test you in order to know what was in your heart, whether or not you would keep his commands" (Deut. 8:2). Both the exit out of Egypt and the entrance into the Promised Land are attributed to God, and during the journey, God acted as a loving, disciplining father to the nation (Deut. 8:5). Yahweh provided manna, quail, water, protection, a cloud and a pillar of fire for guidance, as well as his presence.

What God Is Like

In addition to describing God by means of his actions, the Old Testament authors used adjectives to paint a more specific picture of Israel's God. The biblical text contains several lists of adjectives that highlight the most significant features of God. For example, Exodus 34:6–7 reads:

> The LORD, the LORD, the compassionate and gracious God, slow to anger, abounding in love and faithfulness, maintaining love to thousands, and forgiving wickedness, rebellion and sin. Yet he does not leave the guilty unpunished; he punishes the children and their children for the sin of the fathers to the third and fourth generation.

Lamentations, recounting the tragedy of the fall of Jerusalem, moves from despair to confidence by focusing on the characteristics of Yahweh. Having confessed, "My splendor is gone and all that I had hoped from the LORD" (3:18), the author asserts:

> Yet this I call to mind
> and therefore I have hope:
> Because of the LORD's great love we are not consumed,
> for his compassions never fail.

> They are new every morning;
>   great is your faithfulness.
> I say to myself, "The LORD is my portion;
>   therefore I will wait for him."

3:21–24

Sometimes intimate terms are employed to affirm the love and care of Yahweh for his bride, Israel: "And I will take you for my wife forever; I will take you for my wife in righteousness and in justice, in steadfast love, and in mercy. I will take you for my wife in faithfulness; and you shall know the LORD" (Hosea 2:19–20 NRSV).

Based on the characteristics God exhibited in specific situations, the Israelites were able to make generalizations about the nature of God. For example, Yahweh's loving compassion "endures forever" (e.g., Isa. 54:10; Lam. 3:21–23). The biblical descriptions of God are as much a confession of faith as statements based on observation. They point to the future trustworthiness and reliability of God. At the same time, these expressions are highly relational: "They articulate the ways in which Yahweh relates to 'us,' to Israel, to whomever is Yahweh's partner in a particular testimonial utterance."[23] Summarizing these kinds of statements, Brueggemann paints a picture of what God is like:

- There is no one like Yahweh, whose entire existence is committed to a relationship with Israel.
- There is no one like Yahweh, a God marked by tenacious fidelity toward and solidarity with the people under his rule.
- There is no one like Yahweh, who while endlessly faithful sometimes expresses a harshness toward his beloved partner.[24]

Again, How to Name God

Having inquired into God's actions and the characteristics that Israel's testimonies attributed to God, we can take another look at how the Old Testament names God. According to Brueggemann, by using nouns to name and characterize Yahweh, "Israel assigns to (or recognizes in) Yahweh elements of constancy and substance that make Yahweh in some ways knowable and available to Israel."[25] However, these nouns are not to be taken in the fixed sense of later attributes of God, certainly not as God's substance, but rather in a much more dynamic and less settled way. In that sense, they are like metaphors.

23. Ibid., 225.
24. Ibid., 228.
25. Ibid., 229.

These metaphors can be classified as metaphors of governance, wherein Israel witnesses to Yahweh's capacities to govern and order life and to assert authority, and metaphors of sustenance, which convey that God nurtures, cares, and enhances life.

Metaphors of Governance

Metaphors of governance include the following: Yahweh as judge, king, warrior, and father. Each pertains to power and sanctions and reflects God's ability to establish order.

YAHWEH AS JUDGE

The metaphor of judge reveals that Israel's God is committed to a rule of just law and that he is the one to whom those in need of protection and justice can turn. He intervenes on behalf of his people and is said to love justice (Ps. 99:4; Isa. 61:8). Because God is judge not only of Israel but of the whole world, there is order and justice: "Say among the nations, 'The LORD reigns.' The world is firmly established, it cannot be moved; he will judge the peoples with equity" (Ps. 96:10).

Yahweh's role as the judge of the nations is the foundation on which individuals can appeal to Yahweh's righteousness (Psalm 7). The divine judge not only guides the nations into the path of righteousness but also knows the secrets of men's and women's hearts.

YAHWEH AS KING

The image of king is closely related to that of judge because the ruler was the highest guarantor of order and justice. In the Old Testament, Yahweh is depicted as the king not only of Israel, God's people, but of the entire cosmos: "The LORD sits enthroned over the flood; the LORD is enthroned as King forever" (Ps. 29:10). This psalm, like others—"Say among the nations, 'The LORD is king!'" (96:10 NRSV)—acknowledges God's sovereign rule over nature and nations.

YAHWEH AS WARRIOR

The image of God as warrior is linked to the images of king and judge. "Yahweh as warrior is the one who, as a judge committed to a rule of law, acts to stabilize, maintain, or implement that rule, over which the king will preside."[26] In his role as warrior, Yahweh fights against and defeats all illicit claimants to power.[27]

---

26. Ibid., 241.

27. A reliable guide to various aspects of Yahweh as warrior is Patrick D. Miller, *The Divine Warrior in Early Israel* (Cambridge: Harvard University Press, 1973).

In Exodus 15:1–18, in the aftermath of Yahweh's intervention at the exodus, he is celebrated as a warrior ("man of war" in the RSV). The same testimony appears much later at the time of exile: "See, the Sovereign LORD comes with power, and his arm rules for him. See, his reward is with him, and his recompense accompanies him" (Isa. 40:10).

Israel has faith that Yahweh is not merely a man of war in general but a man of war *for* and *on behalf of* Israel. As "Yahweh of Hosts," the divine warrior is the military leader who fights against the enemies of Israel and of Yahweh. "That day the LORD saved Israel from the hands of the Egyptians, and Israel saw the Egyptians lying dead on the shore" (Exod. 14:30). Thus, Israel could be confident that "the LORD your God, who is going before you, will fight for you" (Deut. 1:30).

Yahweh as Father

Because the fatherhood of God, in relation to Jesus Christ primarily and by derivation to believers in Jesus Christ, is one of the main emphases of the New Testament picture of God, it gets more attention in the next chapter. But although the image of Yahweh as father is less visible in the Old Testament than in the New, texts such as Exodus 4:22 and Hosea 11:1, among others, make it clear that Israel is Yahweh's (firstborn) son.

Metaphors of Sustenance

While the images of sustenance are less dominant in the Old Testament, they comprise an important part of Israel's testimony regarding God. Such metaphors include Yahweh as artist, healer, gardener, vinedresser, mother, and shepherd.

Yahweh as Artist

As an artist, Yahweh is portrayed as a skillful potter who shapes humans out of dust (Gen. 2:7) and forms animals and birds (Gen. 2:19). But even as an artist Yahweh is endowed with might and power. This comes to the fore especially in Jeremiah 18, where Yahweh likens himself to a potter who can do what he wants with the clay, in this case Israel.

Yahweh as Healer

Yahweh the healer acts both to prevent and to treat sickness. Exodus 15:26 promises freedom from sickness provided that the people follow the precepts of the divine healer. Deuteronomy promises actual treatment: "I put to death and I bring to life, I have wounded and I will heal" (32:39). Yahweh's healing, in fact, is an alternative to the "diseases of Egypt" (Deut. 28:60). Yahweh not only heals individuals but also restores cities and peoples (Jer. 30:17; Hosea 14:4; etc.).

What is distinctive about the ministry of this healer is that it is coupled with pathos and sympathy. The act of healing is not always an expression of Yahweh's power. At times it is an expression of Yahweh's love and care. For example, in Jeremiah 8:22, Yahweh feels for the suffering of his people:

> Is there no balm in Gilead?
>   Is there no physician there?
> Why then is there no healing
>   for the wound of my people?

YAHWEH AS GARDENER-VINEDRESSER

As the divine gardener, Yahweh plants gardens as part of the work of creation (Gen. 2:8) and enhances the fruitfulness of the land (Num. 24:6). More often, though, the imagery of gardener is applied to Yahweh's dealings with the people of Israel: "The vineyard of the LORD Almighty is the house of Israel, and the men of Judah are the garden of his delight" (Isa. 5:7).

YAHWEH AS MOTHER

Though written in a world of male dominance, the biblical text every now and then refers to God using female and maternal images. The divine father is capable of acting as a divine mother. One of the most famous texts comes from Isaiah: "As a mother comforts her child, so will I comfort you; and you will be comforted over Jerusalem" (66:13).

When Israel, in the midst of feelings of abandonment by God, wonders if Yahweh has rejected her, the response comes in the form of motherly love:

> Can a mother forget the baby at her breast
>   and have no compassion on the child she has borne?
> Though she may forget,
>   I will not forget you!
> See, I have engraved you on the palms of my hands;
>   your walls are ever before me.
>
> Isaiah 49:15–16

While it may be true that "perhaps the image of Yahweh as mother does not include any dimension that is not already available with the image of Yahweh as father," it is also true that "on the whole, the metaphor of mother is positive and reassuring"[28] and, in today's world, relevant for theological responses to sexism.

YAHWEH AS SHEPHERD

The image of Yahweh as shepherd is related to metaphors of governance, for kings were often depicted as shepherds of the flock (Isa. 44:28). "The image

---

28. Brueggemann, *Theology of the Old Testament*, 259.

evokes a wise, caring, attentive agent who watches over, guards, feeds, and protects a flock that is vulnerable, exposed, dependent, and in need of such help."[29] The shepherd imagery, while most familiar from the Psalms (such as the beloved Psalm 23), concentrates on the time of exile, when Israel was in need of the reassurance of a wise, caring, divine shepherd:

> He tends his flock like a shepherd:
> He gathers the lambs in his arms
> and carries them close to his heart;
> he gently leads those that have young.

> Isaiah 40:11

In the same vein, the prophet Jeremiah assures Israel that "he who scattered Israel will gather them and will watch over his flock like a shepherd" (31:10). The fullest Old Testament exposition of the shepherdhood of Yahweh is found in Ezekiel 34, a passage carried over to the New Testament and applied to Jesus (John 10).

Struggling with God

There is a dynamic relationship—even tension—between images such as mother and warrior. A full and balanced account of Israel's testimonies regarding God must not overlook the less than soothing side of Yahweh.

Israel's Yahweh is no local god to be held in a box but a sovereign Lord. Israelite perceptions of and testimonies regarding Yahweh convey not only comfort and affirmation but also awe, fear, and confusion. These feelings arise out of a tension, a dynamic disjunction, between seemingly opposing features of Yahweh's actions and dealings with the people of Israel. Exodus 34 provides a textbook example of this tension. Following a list of affirmations concerning Yahweh's never-ending love, there is an abrupt warning concerning his judgments:

> The LORD, the LORD, the compassionate and gracious God, slow to anger, abounding in love and faithfulness, maintaining love to thousands, and forgiving wickedness, rebellion and sin. Yet he does not leave the guilty unpunished; he punishes the children and their children for the sin of the fathers to the third and fourth generation.

> verses 6–7

29. Ibid.

Israel's God, while loving and caring, is also a sovereign Lord whose actions in dealing with his people are sometimes unexpected. The familiar story from 2 Samuel 6 illustrates this principle: Uzzah, who attempts to steady God's ark, is struck dead.

There is thus a continuous struggle between the people's perception of Yahweh and Yahweh's unpredictable behavior, bringing tension into the Old Testament picture of God. Brueggemann notes that even the above-mentioned metaphors of sustenance, which generally display features of caring, nurturing, and sympathy, are tension-filled. On the one hand, the images of Yahweh as potter, gardener, and shepherd reveal Yahweh's ability to mold, plant, and guide. On the other hand, the potter sometimes smashes an ill-shaped pot (Jer. 19:11); the gardener both plants and uproots (Jer. 1:10); the shepherd scatters the fold (Jer. 31:10); the healer not only restores but also wounds (Job 5:18). But in all his surprising, unexpected actions, Yahweh is still the one to be trusted. The same potter who smashes also shapes again; the gardener is patient in waiting for the fruit; the shepherd regathers the scattered fold; and the doctor goes after the wounded.[30]

Brueggemann deals with this tension by referring to Yahweh's righteousness, which is revealed in three related ways:

- The glory of Yahweh "refers to the claim and aura of power, authority, and sovereignty that must be established in struggle, exercised in authority, and conceded either by willing adherents or by defeated resisters." In other words, Yahweh has a rightful claim to governance. Pharaoh is hardened not only to save Israel but also to establish the name of Yahweh among the nations.[31]
- The holiness of Yahweh "refers to the radical otherness of Yahweh, who may not be easily approached, who may not be confused with anyone or anything else, and who lives alone in a prohibition zone where Israel can enter only guardedly, intentionally, and at great risk." Yahweh, in fact, is known as the Holy One of Israel (Isa. 29:19).[32]
- The jealousy of Yahweh, which is of course linked to his glory and his holiness, refers to "Yahweh's strong emotional response to any affront against Yahweh's prerogative, privilege, ascendancy, or sovereignty." This is made clear already in the preamble to the Decalogue at Sinai (Exodus 20). Indeed, on occasion Yahweh is known as "Jealous" (Exod. 34:14).[33]

These three aspects of Yahweh reveal his desire for Israel to honor him as the only God. Yahweh also makes an eternal commitment to Israel by means

30. See ibid., 277–82.
31. Ibid., 283.
32. Ibid., 288.
33. Ibid., 293.

of a covenant. "The sovereign God, Yahweh, who exhibits glory, holiness, and jealousy is known among the nations as 'the God of Israel.' "[34] Why? Because Yahweh has personally covenanted with Israel. Yahweh, therefore, struggles to keep Israel as his covenant people—"How can I give you up?" (Hosea 11:8)—and Israel struggles to cling to Yahweh's faithfulness even when the odds seem to be against them. No wonder, then, that among Israel's testimonies to Yahweh are those that Brueggemann fittingly calls "countertestimonies." They express ambiguity, confusion, fear, doubt, and complaint. No description of the Old Testament view of God is complete without a discussion of this aspect of Israel's faith in God.

Israel's questions to Yahweh, when the people face the hard side of their God, take several forms:[35]

> Is the LORD among us or not?
>
> Exodus 17:7

> Why, O LORD, do you stand far off?
> Why do you hide yourself in times of trouble?
>
> Psalm 10:1

> How long, O LORD? Will you forget me forever?
> How long will you hide your face from me?
> How long must I wrestle with my thoughts . . . ?
> How long will my enemy triumph over me?
>
> Psalm 13:1–2

These questions—How long? Why? Where is God?—do not arise out of sterile theological inquiry but out of practical struggle with God. Is God to be trusted? Is God what we think he is?

Not only questions but also complaints and accusations are among Israel's testimonies. A genre of literature often called Psalms of Lament occupies a significant portion of Israel's hymnody and is found not only in the Book of Psalms but also elsewhere, such as Jeremiah 10–20. The main reason for their complaints is exile. It seemed that everything the people had hoped for from Yahweh—the everlasting dynasty, the indestructible temple, and the survival of the people of God among idolaters—disappeared with their deportation. So they ask in despair, "Why do you always forget us? Why do you forsake us so long?" (Lam. 5:20). That does not look like faith in God! Many times Yahweh seems to neglect his own covenant people.

34. Ibid., 296.
35. See ibid., 319–24.

Countertestimonies to Yahweh are also expressed in a more subtle way. The wisdom literature, rather than celebrating the greatness of Yahweh, quite practically—yet pointedly—reflects on the mystery of the seeming hidden-ness of Yahweh.[36] Such hiddenness adds to the ambiguity of Yahweh. The Israelites, therefore, ask additional questions of Yahweh, questions that seem too bold for many theologians. For example, Does Yahweh deceive? Jeremiah wonders if the Lord has "enticed" him (20:7). The Hebrew term *patah* has several connotations of deception and enticement. Yahweh indeed confesses to "enticing" false prophets (1 Kings 22:20–22). To the long and growing list of questions to and struggles with Yahweh could be added those of Job and others (such as Asaph in Psalm 73) who not only complain about God's actions but also curse their birth (Job 3). Or take the Book of Ecclesiastes, which—in contrast to much wisdom literature that assumes the goodness and justice of God's world—questions the meaning of life even with God in the picture. The author does not deny the meaning of Yahweh for human life, but he also does not offer the simplistic answers that contemporary Christians sometimes do when defending God.

Yahweh and Other Gods

The final question to consider in regard to the emerging picture of God in the Old Testament concerns the relationship between Yahweh and other gods. Exploring this relationship is, among other things, the task of theology of religions, one of the fastest growing fields of Christian theology. As one might guess, the Old Testament, while speaking to the issue, does not offer a complete picture. Yet no survey of the Old Testament view of God can ignore this issue, especially in light of its urgency for our times.

A good place to begin is to acknowledge the comment made by two biblical scholars who have done extensive research in this area: "No comprehensive solution to this issue [Christianity's relationship with non-Christian religions] can be found in the Bible, but it does offer some leads."[37] What leads do these authors suggest? On the one hand, the biblical religion was deeply rooted in the religions of the cultures surrounding Israel. Judaism did not begin as a fixed and autonomous religion but borrowed from pagan religions. On the other hand, as Israel's self-consciousness sharpened, other religions were judged as worthless idolatries and challenges to the worship of Yahweh.

As already mentioned, the foundational affirmation for everything the Old Testament says about gods is the Shema, Israel's confession of faith: "Hear, O Israel: The LORD our God, the LORD is one. Love the LORD your God

---

36. See ibid., chap. 9.

37. Donald Senior and Carroll Stuhlmueller, *The Biblical Foundations for Mission* (Maryknoll, N.Y.: Orbis, 1983), 345.

with all your heart and with all your soul and with all your strength" (Deut. 6:4–5). In the beginning stages of Israel's history, it was difficult enough to acknowledge that Yahweh was the only God *for Israel*. "You shall have no other gods before me" (Exod. 20:3). As the Old Testament progresses, the people of God acknowledge and embrace that Yahweh's power extends to the entire earth. Not until after the exile, however, does Israel finally realize not only that Yahweh is more powerful than other gods but also that no other gods in fact exist. Appeals to other gods become references to a futile human construction (see, e.g., Ps. 115:3–7). In the Book of Isaiah, derogative sayings about other gods abound (43:10–11; 44:6–9; 45:6–22).

Yet that is not all that is said about other gods and religions in the Old Testament. There is a built-in tension between the exclusivism of belief in Yahweh and a cautious acknowledgment of the values of other religions. The former is the rule, the latter an exception. It is against this background of first downplaying other gods and finally denying their existence that stories indicating a more positive attitude toward the adherents of other religions gain their full force. Stories about the leadership of Cyrus, the pagan king who acted as Yahweh's "anointed" (literally, "Messiah") (Isaiah 44–45); the repentance of Nineveh, a pagan city judged by the prophet Jonah; and others indicate that with all their misgivings about and opposition to false gods, the Israelites still occasionally acknowledged and reached out to other faiths.

Noteworthy also are the many passages that celebrate Yahweh as the king of the universe and even invite other nations to join in the praise of God. Many psalms provide illustrations: 74, 93, 97, 98, and 99. The Isaianic hymn invites all the nations to "sing to the LORD a new song" (Isa. 42:10).

In light of the uncompromising verdict on other nations and their gods, the Old Testament prophesy concerning the future of Egypt is striking: "So the LORD will make himself known to the Egyptians, and in that day they will acknowledge the LORD. They will worship with sacrifices and grain offerings; they will make vows to the LORD and keep them" (Isa. 19:21). Egypt even becomes the "people of God." Equally striking is Malachi 1:11: "For from the rising of the sun to its setting my name is great among the nations, and in every place incense is offered to my name, and a pure offering; for my name is great among the nations, says the LORD of hosts" (NRSV). Many prophets are unambiguous about the universal power and purposes of Yahweh; his dealings are not limited to his chosen people. The pagan king Nebuchadnezzar confessed to having "blessed the Most High, and praised and honored the one who lives forever" (Dan. 4:34 NRSV). Darius likewise acknowledged that Yahweh is the living God and decreed that all his people were to "fear and reverence" this God (Dan. 6:26).

One significant aspect should be added to this discussion of Yahweh's relationship with other gods. According to Goldingay, there is significant overlap between Yahweh's role and that of the gods of the surrounding nations: "In Genesis Yhwh had a similar profile to El, the fatherly creator god at the head of the Canaanite pantheon. In Exodus Yhwh came to behave more like Baal, an aggressive, warrior figure. When the Israelites settled in Canaan, they needed a deity involved with nature, and Baal was also such a god." Therefore, "to say that Yhwh first behaved rather like El, and then more like Baal, implies that there is considerable overlap between First Testament religion and Canaanite religion." Then Goldingay summarizes:

> So what is the difference between Yhwh and El, Baal, and other gods? One difference is that Yhwh is one, whereas it is intrinsic to Canaanite theology that there are a number of gods with some ranking between them but no totally stable pecking order. The First Testament can itself assume the existence of a number of 'elohim, but it also asks *Who is like you among the gods, Yhwh* (Exod. 15:11), asserts that Yhwh is God of gods (Deut. 10:17) and declares that all gods bow down to Yhwh (Ps. 97:7). Thus when it applies 'elohim to beings other than Yhwh, these are subordinate entities whom we might term heavenly beings rather than divinities. Yhwh has an unqualifiedly supreme position in relation to them. Yhwh's power cannot be overcome. Yhwh's sphere of activity covers all reality; divine activity in the world is not divided among various powers.[38]

The people of Israel came to a fuller understanding of their God, Yahweh, through a centuries-long struggle, often vis-à-vis other gods and religions. The foundational conviction in the oneness of God was sharpened and crystalized as the people of God approached the time of the coming of the Messiah. While the New Testament claims that Jesus Christ is the only way to the knowledge of God, it is significant that he is the way to the knowledge of the God of the Old Testament, Yahweh, the God of Abraham, Isaac, and Jacob.

---

38. Goldingay, *Old Testament Theology,* 374.

2

The New Testament

The Christian Trinitarian God

Yahweh Is the God of the New Testament

The following statement about the New Testament background of faith in God also applies to the Old Testament; it also illustrates the New Testament's indebtedness to the Old Testament:

> The NT makes no attempt to prove the existence of God. The theistic proofs belong to the later period of apologetics and systematic theology. NT theology begins with some tremendous assumptions—that God exists, that he created man and continues to maintain interest in man. Indeed, the whole structure of early Christian thought takes this for granted. . . . Whatever the value of attempting to prove philosophically the existence of God, the NT offers no guidance.[1]

The "identity of the God of the New Testament with Yahweh, the God of the Old Testament, is everywhere assumed by New Testament writers, though they never explicitly assign to Him the name Yahweh." Therefore, as A. W. Argyle brilliantly suggests, the God of the New Testament might be described as "a nameless God."[2] The New Testament God has titles, such as King and Father. God is the author of the resurrection and eternal life. But God is not called

---

1. Donald Guthrie, *New Testament Theology* (Downers Grove, Ill.: InterVarsity, 1981), 75.
2. A. W. Argyle, *God in the New Testament* (London: Hodder & Stoughton, 1965), 9.

by personal names such as Zeus (of the Greeks), Chemosh (of the Moabites), or Yahweh (of the Hebrews). This feature of namelessness is in fact already found in the Septuagint, the Greek translation of the Old Testament, in which the personal name of the God of Israel, *Yahweh,* does not appear in any form. As C. H. Dodd has observed, "By merely eliminating the name of God the Septuagint contributed to the definition of monotheism."[3]

So we conclude not only that the roots of the New Testament doctrine of God are found in the Old Testament but also that the New Testament presupposes the teaching about God as explicated in the Old Testament. The New Testament adds some features of God to Old Testament theology and highlights certain aspects, especially God's fatherhood and kingship, and it moves toward a fuller understanding of the plurality in God—the movement toward trinitarian faith—but nowhere does the New Testament begin from scratch or reinvent the view of God. Jesus and his disciples, as well as the apostles, were nurtured in the synagogue, utilizing the categories and thought forms of the Old Testament Yahwistic faith. "Broadly speaking, we may say that the God of the New Testament is the God of the Old Testament reinterpreted and more fully revealed in the light of the Person and Work of Jesus Christ."[4]

Seeing the person of Jesus Christ as the gateway to the idea of God in the New Testament is a decisive move in the New Testament:

> No one has ever seen God, but God the Only Begotten, who is at the Father's side, has made him known.
>
> John 1:18 NIV alternative reading

> I am the way and the truth and the life. No one comes to the Father except through me.
>
> John 14:6

> Anyone who has seen me has seen the Father.
>
> John 14:9

Jesus is the way to know God. But the God of Jesus is none other than the God of the Jewish faith, according to the witness of the Old Testament. He is the God of Abraham, Isaac, and Jacob (Mark 12:26–27), the God whom Israel confesses in her Shema (Mark 12:29; see Deut. 6:4). The God of the Old Testament is the God whom Jesus commanded believers to love wholeheartedly, the first great commandment (Matt. 22:37–38).

3. C. H. Dodd, *The Bible and the Greeks* (London: Hodder & Stoughton, 1954), 3.
4. Argyle, *God in the New Testament,* 10.

Because the God of the New Testament is the God of the Old Testament, known by and through Jesus Christ, the way the doctrine of God emerged in both testaments is similar:

> As the Old Testament idea of God was not achieved by abstract thought or metaphysical enquiry, but was given by gradual and partial Divine self-disclosure in and through the history of Israel, so the fuller conception of God found in the New Testament was not the achievement of philosophical speculation, but was revealed in the historical birth, life, ministry, passion, death, resurrection and exaltation of Jesus Christ, followed by the gift of the Spirit of God through Him to the early church.[5]

Though New Testament faith in God shares the heritage of the Hebraic faith, the early church operated in a Greek culture. The etymology of the standard Greek term for God, *theos,* found everywhere in the New Testament, is not known; the only thing known for sure is that it was originally a title. Besides *theos,* the major designation for God in the New Testament, writers used *kyrios.* "The LXX [Septuagint] is characterized by the Hellenizing of Isra-elite-Jewish monotheism and by the reduction of the designations of God."[6] Thus, the Hebrew word *'el* and its derivatives are generally rendered *theos,* only occasionally as *kyrios.*

The concept of god in Greek cultures was both polytheistic and nonpersonal. The gods were often represented in anthropomorphic form as "personal be-ings who exercised a determining influence on the world and fate of men, but who themselves were dependent on a superior fate." As they were not creator gods, "they were not thought of as outside the universe and transcendent."[7] The Greek gods were not righteous; they at times selfishly pursued their own agendas. The New Testament view of God, which was derived from the Old Testament, challenged the Greek view in significant ways. There were also parallels, and early Christian theologians were quick to make use of them.

As already hinted at, the New Testament makes significant additions to the Old Testament concept of God as Yahweh of Israel. Three have significance for later theological developments: Jesus' intimate relationship with God as Father, Jesus' focus on the kingdom of God and thus on the God of the kingdom, and the emerging trinitarian faith. While none of these concepts is foreign to the Old Testament, in the revelation of God through the person of Jesus Christ these three themes gain a new significance and make the New Testament doctrine of God unique. To these developments we now turn.

---

5. Ibid., 11–12.

6. J. Schneider, "God," in *The New International Dictionary of New Testament Theology,* ed. Colin Brown (Grand Rapids: Zondervan, 1976), 2:70.

7. Ibid., 2:66.

God as Father

Father in the Old Testament

The idea of the fatherhood of God is not unknown to the Old Testament, but neither is it a major theme.[8] There are, of course, instances in which Yahweh is pictured as Father. Several prophets, especially in their desire to call Israel back to faithfulness to Yahweh, make use of father imagery: "I thought you would call me 'Father' and not turn away from following me" (Jer. 3:19). Hosea 11 speaks intimately of Yahweh teaching Israel, his son, to walk, but even there the Hebrew word *'ab* ("father") does not appear. In Psalm 103:13, the actual term *father* is used. Similar passages include Proverbs 3:12 and Deuteronomy 32:6, the song of Moses.

Another context in which God is called Father and that expresses a close father-son relationship are passages that relate to the king of Israel: "He said to me, 'You are my Son; today I have become your Father'" (Ps. 2:7). These passages are important for the New Testament father imagery in the sayings of Jesus.

Addressing God in intimate terms using father language is rare in the Old Testament. Biblical scholars also suggest that there is no clear evidence in early Jewish literature that people prayed to God as *abba,* an intimate Aramaic term, prior to the time of Jesus. As we turn to the New Testament and especially to Jesus' use of the term *Father,* we discover a remarkable proliferation of the term, and new aspects come to the fore.[9]

The Father of Jesus

Jesus' way of addressing God and introducing God focuses completely on God as the Father. At the heart of Jesus' message is his announcement of the nearness of the kingdom of God, but even in these cases, Jesus uses the name heavenly Father in reference to the God whose reign is near:

> God shows himself to be Father by caring for his creatures (Matt. 6:26; cf. Luke 12:30). He causes his sun to shine and his rain to fall on the bad as well as the good (Matt. 5:45). He is a model of the love for enemies which Jesus taught (5:44–45). He is ready to forgive those who turn to him (Luke 15:7, 10, 11ff.), ask for his forgiveness (11:4), and forgive others (Matt. 11:25; cf. 6:15; 18:23–35). He lets himself be invoked as Father, and like earthly fathers, and even more than they, he grants good things to his children when they ask (Matt. 7:11). Thus the prayer

8. Ben Witherington III and Laura M. Ice, *The Shadow of the Almighty: Father, Son, and Spirit in Biblical Perspective* (Grand Rapids: Eerdmans, 2002), 1; for possible reasons behind this scarcity of father imagery in the Old Testament, see pp. 4–6.

9. See ibid., 16, 19–20.

to the Father which Jesus taught his disciples combines the prayer for daily bread, the sum of all earthly needs, with the prayer for forgiveness, which is connected with a readiness to forgive (Luke 11:3–4). This prayer also shows that Jesus' proclamation of God's fatherly goodness is related to his eschatological message of the nearness of the divine rule. For the prayer begins with three petitions that are oriented to the coming of the lordship of the Father God.[10]

In all the Gospels, the theme of God's fatherhood is present, but a curious development is evident. Mark, the earliest Gospel, records only four occurrences. Matthew contains thirty references to this theme. The Gospel of John, however, written a few decades later, contains no less than 120! Even though biblical scholars do not offer a conclusive reason for this, it is evident that use of the term *Father* increased over the years.

What do references to God as Father mean? Marianne Meye Thompson, in her recent study *The Promise of the Father,* suggests three facets:

1. God is father in the sense of the origin of a family of people.
2. God is the father who provides for and protects his children.
3. God as father expects obedience and honor.[11]

Some have recently suggested that the difference between the Old Testament hesitation to use father imagery and the frequency with which it is used in the New Testament has to do with the fact that the Old Testament is seen from the Father's point of view, whereas in the New Testament the Father is seen from the Son's point of view. In other words, Jesus makes the difference.[12] Therefore, it is appropriate to focus on Jesus' use of the term *Father* in his life and ministry as told in the Gospels.

The most intimate term for Father, *abba,* comes to the fore in Jesus' prayers. Jesus not only addressed God as *abba* but also taught his disciples to do so. The basic contention of the classic study by Joachim Jeremias, *The Prayers of Jesus,*[13] is that while Jesus' view of God was not completely new, his mode of addressing God was novel because his relationship with God was distinctive. In Jeremias's words, "the complete novelty and uniqueness of *Abba* as an address to God in the prayers of Jesus shows that it expresses the heart of Jesus' relationship to God."[14] While older scholarship—as well as popular teaching

10. Wolfhart Pannenberg, *Systematic Theology,* vol. 1 (Grand Rapids: Eerdmans, 1991), 259.

11. Marianne Meye Thompson, *The Promise of the Father* (Louisville: Westminster John Knox, 2000), 39.

12. C. Seitz, *Word without End* (Grand Rapids: Eerdmans, 1998), 258; and Witherington and Ice, *Shadow of the Almighty,* 20.

13. Joachim Jeremias, *The Prayers of Jesus* (Philadelphia: Fortress, 1967).

14. Joachim Jeremias, *New Testament Theology: The Proclamation of Jesus* (New York: Scribner's, 1971), 67.

even today—maintains that the address *abba* has a Daddy-like nature based on the language of small children, biblical scholars state that the term was also used in an intimate relationship between an adult son and father.

> The term *abba* is clearly enough an intimate way of addressing God using family language, whether by a child or an adult, and as such is less formal than addressing God simply as God or Lord. . . . [The] main point is that Jesus' choice of this term reveals Jesus' awareness of his special relationship with God.[15]

Several distinctive features can be detected in Jesus' way of using father language.[16] First, whenever Jesus directly addresses God, he always speaks to God as Father.[17] Jesus never addresses God as King or Master. Second, Jesus addresses God as *abba* in his utmost distress in Gethsemane (Mark 14:36). Obviously, *abba* denoted not only intimacy but also complete dependence on God. Third, in the Gospels, Jesus alone uses the intimate expression "my Father." Even outside the Gospels, that phrase occurs only on Jesus' lips (Rev. 2:27; 3:5, 21). Disciples are taught to address God as "our Father." Interestingly enough, not until the reception of the Holy Spirit did early Christians begin to address God as *abba,* suggesting that the Spirit is needed to lead Jesus' followers into the same kind of intimate relationship Jesus had with God the Father (Rom. 8:15–16; Gal. 4:6). But Paul and other early Christians used this expression sparingly, so much so that toward the end of the New Testament it disappears. This is understandable in light of the fact that *abba* prayer was regarded as a distinctive form of Jesus' prayer.[18]

The Father of All

Even though the fatherhood of God in the New Testament relates primarily to Jesus as the Son and by derivation to the relationship between the Father and Jesus' own people, the concept also widens to encompass the rest of humanity. We see this in Jesus' teaching about God's fatherly love to all people. Yet it is also true that "fatherhood is the gift of the kingdom of God,"[19] and therefore its full blessing in the coming of the kingdom of God is reserved for those who have submitted their lives to the rule of God, the King and Father.

As suggested above, the ideas of God as Father and God as the ruler of the kingdom are inseparable. The affinity between these two concepts appears most frequently in eschatological settings.

---

15. Witherington and Ice, *Shadow of the Almighty,* 22.
16. For these observations, see ibid., 22–24.
17. Mark 15:34 is an exception since here Jesus follows Psalm 22: "My God, my God."
18. Thompson, *Promise of the Father,* 65.
19. George E. Ladd, *A Theology of the New Testament,* rev. ed., ed. Donald A. Hagner (Grand Rapids: Eerdmans, 1993), 52.

In this eschatological salvation, the righteous will enter into the Kingdom of their Father (Matt. 13:43). It is the Father who has prepared for the blessed this eschatological inheritance of the Kingdom (Matt. 25:34). It is the Father who will bestow upon Jesus' disciples the gift of the Kingdom (Luke 12:32). The highest gift of God's Fatherhood is participation in God's sovereignty, which is to be exercised over all the world. In that day Jesus will enjoy a renewed fellowship with his disciples in the Father's Kingdom (Matt. 26:29).[20]

God of the Kingdom

God's Rule

One of the few points on which there is universal agreement in contemporary New Testament scholarship is that the kingdom of God was Jesus' central message (Mark 1:15 and parallels).[21] What is the background of this message and its God? Again, recent scholarly consensus is that this background is the Old Testament.[22] While the expression "kingdom of God" does not occur in the Old Testament, the idea of God's rule clearly appears in the Old Testament, mainly in two forms: God is the King of Israel (Exod. 15:18; Num. 23:21; Isa. 43:15) and of all the earth (2 Kings 19:15; Ps. 29:10; Isa. 6:5).

The Hebrew term *malkut* as well as the Greek word *basileia,* which are translated "kingdom," would be more appropriately rendered as "rule." God's kingdom is about God's sovereign rule. The majority of scholarship agrees that Jesus taught that the rule of God was both present ("already") and yet to come in its eschatological fulfillment ("not yet").

As already mentioned, the Old Testament does not use the phrase "kingdom of God," even though the idea of God's rule is evident. The language of Old Testament apocalypticism, related to the end time expectation, comes closest to this expression. Thus, Daniel 2:44 says:

> In the time of those kings, the God of heaven will set up a kingdom [*malkut,* "rule"] that will never be destroyed, nor will it be left to another people. It will crush all those kingdoms and bring them to an end, but it will itself endure forever.

20. Ibid., 83.

21. Matthew also uses the term "kingdom of heaven," honoring the Jewish reluctance to use God's name. There are a few instances of expressions such as "the kingdom of the Father" and "the kingdom of the Son of Man," but scholars classify them as secondary Christian developments.

22. See, for example, Leonhard Goppelt, *Theology of the New Testament,* vol. 1 (Grand Rapids: Eerdmans, 1981), 45–51.

The God Who Rules

What does the kingdom of God reveal about the New Testament view of God? The kingdom is God's kingdom, not humanity's. Furthermore, God's rule belongs to the "essence" of being God. God cannot be God without his rule. Thus, "the presence of the Kingdom is to be understood from the nature of God's present activity; and the future of the Kingdom is the redemptive manifestation of his kingly rule at the end of the age."[23]

George E. Ladd highlights four crucial aspects of the God of the kingdom.[24] First, the God of the kingdom is the seeking God. The novel element in Jesus' proclamation of the kingdom is paralleled by a new element in his teaching about God, namely, that God is a God who seeks. Jesus' message of the kingdom proclaimed that God would finally act and also that God was already acting redemptively in history. God was visiting his people through fulfilling the messianic promises.[25] This truth is illustrated by a number of Jesus' parables, perhaps most clearly by the three parables in Luke 15 that highlight God's desire to recover what was lost.

Second, the God of the kingdom is the inviting God. Jesus pictures the eschatological salvation prepared by the God who rules as a banquet or a feast to which many guests are invited (Matt. 22:1–4).

Third, the God of the kingdom is the fatherly God, an aspect already discussed.

Fourth, the God of the kingdom is the judging God.

> While God seeks the sinner and offers him or her the gift of the Kingdom, he remains a God of retributive righteousness to those who reject the gracious offer. His concern for the lost does not dissipate the divine holiness into a benign kindliness. God is seeking, but he is also holy love.[26]

Outside the Gospels, direct references to the kingdom of God are rare. We read occasionally about preaching the kingdom or about the kingdom (Acts 8:12; 28:31), but the expression is not as frequent as in the Gospels. Even in John's Gospel it is less frequent. Even though the idea of God's rule—based on the New Testament's adoption of the Old Testament view of God—does not disappear (one needs to think only of the last book of the New Testament, Revelation), Jesus' distinctive usage of kingdom terminology is replaced by others that most often refer to the rule of Christ over the church, the world, and powers.

Perhaps the most distinctive way the New Testament shapes the Old Testament view of God is by taking the incipient plurality in the Godhead of the

---

23. Ladd, *Theology of the New Testament,* 79.
24. Ibid., 80–88.
25. Ibid., 80–81.
26. Ibid., 85.

Old Testament more seriously. In the New Testament, a trinitarian conception of the Christian God begins to emerge.

The Roots of Christian Trinitarianism

The Plurality of God in the Old Testament

The first chapter in this book surveyed the rise and consolidation of monotheism among the Jews. We have already seen that the New Testament adopted this monotheistic-Yahwistic God as the God of Christian faith. Yet the Christian God is triune. How do we account for this? For centuries, Christian theology tried to solve this problem either by referring to the underdeveloped nature of Old Testament faith before the coming of the Messiah or, more often, by searching for potential trinitarian proof texts in the Bible. These proof texts run from Genesis 1:26 ("Let *us* make . . ."), which current exegesis regards as an example of plurality of majesty (not unlike the pronouncements of royal individuals in the form of "We declare . . ."), to the famous Isaianic threefold "Holy, holy, holy" exclamation (6:3), to passages such as Genesis 18, in which the theophanies of the "Angel of Yahweh" are seen as preincarnation appearances of the Second Person of the Trinity. In light of contemporary exegesis, however, these and similar examples do not hold. They also raise the question of how to come up with a distinctively trinitarian—why not, for example, binitarian—view of God. It is also problematic to regard the Old Testament view of God as infantile, especially since the New Testament, and Jesus himself, did not.[27]

Contemporary theology has taken a different route to account for the emergence of early Christian faith in a Triune God in light of Jewish monotheism. This has meant revisiting and revising some canons of theological scholarship:

> It used to be the conventional wisdom of New Testament scholars that predication of a divine nature to Jesus came about as a result of the impact of Hellenistic culture outside Israel and the ideas that culture had about the Divine. The assumption was that early Jews in tune with their monotheistic language would not use such language of anyone but Yahweh. The oneness of God ruled out speaking of multiple persons in the Godhead.[28]

One of the most recent counters to this assumption has come from Richard Bauckham, a theologian and New Testament scholar. He has argued that the

---

27. For a classic study, see A. W. Wainwright, *The Trinity in the New Testament* (London: SPCK, 1952).

28. Witherington and Ice, *Shadow of the Almighty*, 68.

early Jewish definition of God could include the person of the Son without violating monotheism.[29] What distinguished Yahwistic faith from polytheistic faiths was the desire not to place Yahweh at the summit of a hierarchy of divinity but to place him in an "absolutely unique category, beyond comparison with anything else."[30] In other words, even the highest angels or heavenly powers so highly appreciated especially in apocalyptic literature, while participating in God's rule over the earth, did not share God's essence. However, distinctions within one Godhead, such as between God's Spirit and God's Word, were not necessarily understood as compromises to divine unity. Consequently, Bauckham concludes—and this is highly significant for a New Testament trinitarian outlook—"the Second Temple Jewish understanding of the divine uniqueness . . . does not make distinctions within the divine identity inconceivable."[31]

Despite the undeniable emphasis on God's unity in the Old Testament, there are also elements that point to plurality.[32] For example, God's "Wisdom," "Word," and "Spirit" sometimes function synonymously and are not always distinguished systematically. According to Gerald O'Collins, all three terms are "vivid personifications," both identified with and distinguished from God, representing "personified agents of divine activity," often operating with personal characteristics.[33] According to Proverbs, "Wisdom" is created by God "at the beginning of his work" (8:22). The "Word" is always active, powerful (Isa. 55:11), and creative (Genesis 1). Sometimes "Spirit" and "Word" are connected, as in the psalmist's interpretation of the creation story (33:6). The term *Spirit* as such (*ruah*, "breath") occurs over four hundred times in the Old Testament.[34]

On the basis of these considerations, contemporary scholars believe the gradual emergence of trinitarian faith is consistent with, though goes beyond, the witness of the Old Testament. How did the New Testament handle this Old Testament dynamic between God's unity and his plurality in unity?

Trinitarian Orientations in the New Testament View of God

Students of Christian theology may be disappointed to hear how a recent textbook on the Trinity summarizes the New Testament's approach to the

---

29. Richard Bauckham, *God Crucified: Monotheism and Christology in the New Testament* (Grand Rapids: Eerdmans, 1998), 13.

30. Ibid., 15.

31. Ibid., 22.

32. A most helpful discussion is offered by Gerald O'Collins, *The Tripersonal God: Understanding and Interpreting the Trinity* (New York: Paulist, 1999), 12–32. For the plurality in unity, see also Peter Toon, *Our Triune God: A Biblical Portrayal of the Trinity* (Wheaton: Victor, 1996), 95–112.

33. O'Collins, *Tripersonal God,* 23.

34. See Veli-Matti Kärkkäinen, *Pneumatology: The Holy Spirit in International, Ecumenical, and Historical Perspective* (Grand Rapids: Baker Academic, 2002), 25–27.

Trinity: "There is no mention of the word 'Trinity' in the New Testament. What we do discover from the New Testament writers, though, is a consistent argument for the filial uniqueness of Jesus Christ in relationship to the Father of the old covenant."[35] Although this summary of current scholarship does not seem to promise much, it is precisely in this binitarianism that we can discern the roots for a more developed trinitarian theology of the New Testament. Clearly, the New Testament introduces its trinitarianism through the person of Jesus Christ, who, according to the early Christians, shares in the divinity of the Father God.

During his life, Jesus claimed to have been sent by God (John 5:37) and, more importantly, to have been given the authority to give life as the Father does (5:21) and to execute judgment as the Father does (5:22). Indeed, Jesus claimed that whoever does not honor the Son does not honor the Father (5:23). According to the Matthean Jesus, "No one knows the Son except the Father, and no one knows the Father except the Son and those to whom the Son chooses to reveal him" (11:27).

Before his cross and resurrection, Jesus claimed to have the authority and the approval of his Father. When, as Romans 1:3–4 maintains, Jesus was raised from the dead by his Father, the early Christians saw this as divine confirmation. Such a belief was crucial for the emergence of the doctrine of the deity of Jesus, a claim that was of course hotly contested during Jesus' lifetime by his Jewish opponents; they accused him of blasphemy (John 5:18).

Furthermore, the New Testament applies to the risen and exalted Son the title *Kyrios*, "Lord," which is reserved for the Father in the Septuagint. The *Kyrios*, Son, could be invoked in prayer (a possible interpretation of 2 Cor. 12:8), and the title was put on par with the term *theos*, "God," in the confession of Thomas (John 20:28). In addition, Paul and the writer of Hebrews argue for the Son's preexistence (Col. 1:15–16; Heb. 1:2–3).[36]

Clearly, there are sufficient grounds for speaking of a binitarian foundation. What about the third member of the Trinity as developed in later theology? The Spirit is presented as the "medium of the communion of Jesus with the Father and the mediator of the participation of believers in Christ."[37] Jesus Christ was raised and his divine sonship declared by the power of the Spirit (Rom. 1:4); the God who raised Jesus from the dead will by his Spirit, who dwells in those who believe in Christ, also give mortal bodies eternal life (8:11). The Spirit of sonship who is given to Christians (8:15) is the Spirit of Christ (8:14). The

---

35. Roger E. Olson and Christopher A. Hall, *The Trinity* (Grand Rapids: Eerdmans, 2002), 6.

36. Even if it could be argued (as Pannenberg, *Systematic Theology*, 265) that early Christians did not believe preexistence established the deity of Christ, there is no denying that the preexistence of Jesus implies deity.

37. Pannenberg, *Systematic Theology*, 266. I am indebted to his careful exposition on pp. 264–69.

Gospels also link Jesus and the Spirit. Mark viewed the miracles of Jesus as the work of the Spirit (3:29–30), Matthew attributed exorcism to the same Spirit (12:28), and Luke depicted Jesus as filled with the Spirit (4:1, 14; etc.).[38]

Wolfhart Pannenberg accurately summarizes the rise of trinitarian orientations in the New Testament:

> The involvement of the Spirit in God's presence in the work of Jesus and in the fellowship of the Son with the Father is the basis of the fact that the Christian understanding of God found its developed and definitive form in the doctrine of the Trinity and not in a biunity of the Father and the Son. . . . The New Testament statements do not clarify the interrelations of the three but they clearly emphasize the fact that they are interrelated.[39]

There are few passages in which all three members of the Godhead are mentioned.[40] The early appearance of the baptismal formula (Matt. 28:19) undoubtedly made a significant contribution to the emerging trinitarian view of God. The baptismal narrative of Jesus himself found in all four Gospels (Matt. 3:13–17; Mark 1:9–11; Luke 3:21–22; John 1:32–34) records the Father speaking from heaven to the Son, on whom the Spirit rests in the form of a dove. Furthermore, trinitarian formulae such as benedictions ("May the grace of the Lord Jesus Christ, and the love of God, and the fellowship of the Holy Spirit be with you all" [2 Cor. 13:14]) and some passages seem to be structured according to a trinitarian pattern (Rom. 15:16; 15:30; 2 Cor. 1:21–22), as are some larger biblical sections such as Ephesians 1:1–14. These are but a few examples of how the appearance of Jesus as the One sent by his Father in the power of the Spirit led New Testament writers to an understanding of God as triune.

The New Testament God and Other Gods

We conclude this examination of the New Testament view of God by looking briefly at the New Testament perspective concerning other gods. The starting point for such a consideration is that

> the question of "boundaries" remained a central concern of the early church, as it had been for Jesus himself. The struggle of the early church to move beyond the confines of Israel, to be open to the Gentiles, was a major theme of the Pauline letters and of much of the Gospel tradition.[41]

38. See Kärkkäinen, *Pneumatology,* 29–30.
39. Pannenberg, *Systematic Theology,* 268–69.
40. First John 5:7–8, once regarded as *the* trinitarian text, has a variant reading that mentions "the Father, the Word, and the Holy Spirit," but this is regarded as a later addition.
41. Donald Senior and Carroll Stuhlmueller, *The Biblical Foundations for Mission* (Maryknoll, N.Y.: Orbis, 1983), 157.

In line with Old Testament faith, the church faced a painful struggle to embrace a more inclusive, welcoming attitude toward the Gentiles. Peter finally came to the conclusion, "I now realize how true it is that God does not show favoritism but accepts men from every nation who fear him and do what is right" (Acts 10:34–35). He came to this conclusion, however, after being prompted by an angel. Apart from passages such as Acts 14:16–17, "In the past, he let all nations go their own way. Yet he has not left himself without testimony," and others such as the famous Areopagite speech of Paul (Acts 17:22–31), very little in the New Testament suggests that the early Christians acknowledged much commonality between their God and the gods of the nations.

What can safely be said is that biblical material concerning the early church's view of other religions and gods is, at best, scarce. The early church adopted Jewish monotheism and held to the universality of God's person and nature. At the same time, the church sought to evangelize all people, both Jews and Gentiles. Paul, the prime apostle to the Gentiles, preached the gospel of Christ "that all nations might believe and obey" (Rom. 16:26), implying little trust in the capacity of other gods to save. Paul had the most extensive exposure to other religions and adherents of other religions, but even he did not tackle the issue of how to relate to other gods, except by saying that people should turn from idols to the true God (1 Thess. 1:9).

Two quotations from a contemporary writer illustrate the main orientation of the New Testament with regard to other gods and religions:

The conclusion to be drawn is that religion may be dark, deceptive, and cruel. It harbors ugliness, pride, error, hypocrisy, darkness, cruelty, demons, hardheartedness, blindness, fanaticism, and deception. The idea that world religions ordinarily function as paths to salvation is dangerous nonsense and wishful thinking.[42]

According to the Bible, there also exists among the nations religious faith which lies at the other end of the spectrum. It recognizes faith, neither Jewish nor Christian, which is nonetheless noble, uplifting, and sound. We came across this faith earlier in the category of pagan saints, believers like Abel, Enoch, Noah, Job, Daniel, Melchizedek, Lot, Abimelech, Jethro, Rahab, Ruth, Naaman, the Queen of Sheba, the Roman soldier, Cornelius, and others. These were believing men and women who enjoyed a right relationship with God and lived saintly lives, under the terms of the wider covenant God made with Noah.[43]

The first quotation gives the rule, the second a blessed exception. The New Testament does not resolve this dynamic. Again, later theological discussions tried to make sense of the exclusivistic faith in God, the God of all who still

42. Clark H. Pinnock, *A Wideness in God's Mercy: The Finality of Jesus Christ in a World of Religions* (Grand Rapids: Zondervan, 1992), 90.
43. Ibid., 92.

seems to acknowledge the relative value of how people outside the covenant community think of him.

From the Biblical Data to Later Theological Developments of the Doctrine of God

At this juncture, before turning to a discussion of the development of the doctrine of God in Christian history, it is appropriate to take a brief look at the territory we have covered and also to revisit the foundational questions raised at the beginning of this biblical survey of God: How does the Bible approach God? What contribution does the Bible make to an understanding of the doctrine of God? We can summarize some main characteristics of the biblical materials in the following way.

First, there is a myriad of pictures of God in both the Old and New Testaments. These pictures or testimonies share a common foundation—God is the origin of all, takes care of all, has the authority to set norms, and most importantly is the only true living God—but they also retain the inevitable dynamic associated with multiple testimonies and stories.

Second, the New Testament adopted the Yahwistic faith of the Old Testament. In other words, the God of the New Testament is the God of the Old Testament.

Third, following the Reformation principle of letting Scripture be both a source and a critic of (systematic) theological constructions, we should be cautious about accusing the Bible of rigidity and dryness. Critics of classical theism often point out that the biblical materials reveal a God who is dynamic, responsive, and living. A full acknowledgment of the narrative, testimonial nature of biblical testimonies regarding God should help us better assess both the classical view and its challenges.

In part 2, when discussing historical developments of the doctrine of God, especially with regard to patristic theologies, we will have an opportunity to continue a dialogue with biblical traditions. Later developments, especially during the first four or five centuries, not only built on biblical materials but also went beyond them in trying to connect with the rich cultural, philosophical, and religious contexts in which the Christian faith found itself.

It is beyond the scope of the present book to offer a final judgment as to how faithfully later developments followed biblical leads; that is a study in itself. Opinions among specialists vary—as the following survey indicates—even though it is commonplace to accuse patristic theologies as well as later theologies of "Hellenizing" Christian theology (i.e., making it too dependent on Greek philosophy and thought modes). The return to biblical materials generation after generation is a needed check to ascertain whether and to what extent later theological constructions faithfully reflect biblical—and thus "authoritative"—traditions.

Part 2

Classical Theistic Traditions
Historical Developments

Part 2 surveys the rich tapestry of historical traditions concerning the doctrine of God. To set the stage for this inquiry, a crucial background issue is discussed in more detail: the meaning of the term "classical theism" and its relation to the rest of the book. Following that, the next four chapters present the history of the doctrine of God in four movements. The aim is to highlight the main orientations—the most significant individual theologians and movements of classical theistic traditions—and to allow differing, sometimes even conflicting voices, to converse.

The historical story comprises four main sections:

1. Patristic views of God and their religious and philosophical backgrounds. The defining issues of the doctrine of God (including the Trinity and Christology) were formulated and debated during the first four or five centuries. These developments, therefore, merit closer attention.
2. Milestones in medieval views of God. This chapter covers the sixth to the fifteen century in a selective way. It highlights the importance of a few significant theologians, such as Anselm of Canterbury and Thomas Aquinas, who built on the traditions laid during the patristic era and made significant contributions to them. This era defined the final canons of classical theism.

3. The Protestant Reformers. Although Martin Luther and John Calvin did not concentrate on the doctrine of God, it played an important role in their thinking.
4. The modern quest for God. The dramatic intellectual changes from the time of the Enlightenment and before (from the latter part of the sixteenth century) mark a dividing line in the history of Christian theology. From then until the twentieth century, the question of the existence of God and the meaningfulness of the traditional concept of God were questioned and reshaped as never before. There is no way to understand the theologies of the twentieth and twenty-first centuries without taking stock of thinkers such as René Descartes, Immanuel Kant, Friedrich D. E. Schleiermacher, and Georg W. F. Hegel.

3

Classical Theism

What Is It?

In Search of a Definition

Thus far we have used the term "classical theism" in a generic sense to refer to the way the Christian theological tradition approached the doctrine of God in the past. The introduction to this book made it clear that its discussions of biblical, historical, and contemporary views of God give attention to how the meaning or meanings of that often-used term were defined and how such theism has been challenged. At this juncture we need to pause and take a closer look at the concept of classical theism. To a great extent, materials in the historical section were selected on the basis of their pertinence to this inquiry into the meaning of classical theism and to an exploration of its potential varieties.

The biblical section already alerted us to the variety of views of God held by various authors in various times. It might be the case—and this question will be revisited at the end of part 2—that even the tradition called classical theism, often caricatured by its opponents as a monolithic, fixed movement, escapes uniformity. Since the present book is not a constructive study but rather a descriptive textbook, it does not seek to establish either the validity or the fallacy of either classical theism or its challengers. Rather, the aim is to help readers formulate the right questions and maintain inquiring minds when approaching the huge task of making sense of Christian theology's smorgasbord of views of God in a way that puts classical and contemporary, Western and non-Western views in a proper perspective.

In his small yet helpful book, *The Concept of God,* the Christian philosopher Ronald H. Nash nicely sets the agenda for this inquiry:

> Much recent philosophical and theological literature reflects the struggle be-
> tween two competing concepts of God. The contrasting theories are known by
> a variety of labels. The older, traditional view is frequently referred to simply as
> theism, often as Christian theism, sometimes as classical theism, and occasion-
> ally as Thomistic theism. The contemporary challenger goes by such names as
> panentheism, neoclassical theism, and Process theology.[1]

What does "classical theism" mean and include? While the voices of critics are usually not the most accurate, let alone balanced, they are often helpful in highlighting the issues. David Ray Griffin, a process theologian, has recently presented what he thinks is a fair and accurate analysis of classical theism. While Griffin's analysis may not be definitive, it can serve as a dialogue partner and a tool for further inquiry. Griffin specifically targets his analysis on a more developed form of theism, namely, that presented by Thomas Aquinas in the thirteenth century during the heyday of Christian scholasticism. Griffin notes that Thomas built on patristic ideas, especially those of Augustine from the fifth century (both Augustine's and Thomas's views of God are discussed in the chapters that follow).

According to Griffin's analysis, classical theism focuses on the following attributes of God:

- *Pure actuality:* According to the philosophy of Aristotle, everything that exists is a combination of form and matter; thus, everything possesses both actuality and potentiality. Potentiality for Aristotle meant a lack of perfection; it implied that something was yet to come. Therefore, to preserve God's perfect nature, Christian thinkers had to deny potentiality in relation to God. Consequently, God is absolute actuality, pure form, and there is no matter to actualize his potentiality.
- *Immutability and impassibility:* While these two attributes are not iden-tical, they are related. The former suggests that God does not change, while the latter refers to the impossibility of God's being acted upon. Often—but not always—immutability was interpreted in the sense that God cannot be "moved" in a true emotional sense; where Scripture seems to suggest that God grieves or rejoices, such passages were considered mere metaphor.

    1. Ronald H. Nash, *The Concept of God: An Exploration of Contemporary Difficulties with the Attributes of God* (Grand Rapids: Zondervan, 1983), 19.

- *Timelessness:* God's eternal existence is timeless, outside of time. While the majority of classical theists beginning with Augustine (according to whom God created time as part of creation) accept this statement as true, it has been and is a disputed issue. This element, therefore, is not a decisive feature of classical theism.[2]
- *Simplicity:* God is not composed of parts as is everything else that exists. This attribute of God is, of course, related to many others, such as his changelessness. If God has no parts, God cannot change, since there are no parts for him to lose or gain.
- *Necessity:* This attribute has two aspects. On the one hand, God's existence is necessary in the sense that it is impossible for God not to exist. Everything except God exists contingently (is dependent on God). On the other hand, necessity means that the divine essence itself—"the particular package of attributes God possesses"[3]—is necessary. It is no accident, and it cannot be otherwise; God cannot be other than as he is.
- *Omnipotence and omniscience:* These attributes follow from what has been said before. Omniscience means that God knows all truths and holds no false beliefs. Omnipotence means that within the "limits" of God's own attributes, God possesses the capacity to do everything.[4]

This is a simple, noncritical presentation of the attributes of God; not only critics but also proponents of classical theism have debated all of them, especially those relating to change, power, and knowledge.[5] As already mentioned, however, this explanation is only a heuristic device for pedagogical purposes, a point of reference. Therefore, we leave the various assessments of this analysis to later parts of the book. What is distinctive about classical theism is that it represents an effort to systematize, with the help of philosophical reasoning, the biblical teaching on God, teaching that appears in the form of stories, narratives, testimonies, experiences, and images. To deepen our understanding of classical theism and its significance for the history of Christian thought about God, we turn now to an examination of how this view emerged after the New Testament era and its main implications.

---

2. For a recent helpful discussion of time/eternity with regard to God, see Millard J. Erickson, *God the Father Almighty: A Contemporary Exploration of the Divine Attributes* (Grand Rapids: Baker, 1998), 114–40.

3. Nash, *Concept of God,* 22.

4. David Ray Griffin, *God, Power, and Evil: A Process Theodicy* (Philadelphia: Westminster, 1976).

5. For starters, see Nash, *Concept of God.*

The Relationship between Classical Theism and New Testament Views of God

A natural opening question in the search for a deeper understanding of classical theism asks, In what ways, if any, is this tradition rooted in the New Testament? Enough has already been said about the nature of the biblical witness to God. It is not systematic nor philosophical, whereas classical theism attempts to be both.

Robert M. Grant's study *The Early Christian Doctrine of God* is of help here. He begins with the affirmation, "We shall not expect to find philosophical teaching about God in what Jesus said about the Father, whose reign he was proclaiming and, indeed, inaugurating."[6] The significance of this starting point must not be missed. But Grant wonders whether there still might be "bridges" that connect the Bible and the philosophical doctrines of God that came into being quite early in patristic theology. There are not many, Grant acknowledges, but there are a few, such as Paul's affirmation in 1 Corinthians 8:6 that "there is but one Lord" (echoing the Shema of Israel [Deut. 6:4]). Another is that "so-called gods, whether in heaven or on earth" do not exist (1 Cor. 8:4–6). Grant argues that Paul is echoing the convictions of some influential Greek thinkers and is using (in verses that follow as also in Rom. 11:36) a typical philosophical structure of argument to make his point: "It is clear enough that God is being described in language at least related to philosophy."[7] Other examples cited by Grant include Acts 14 and 17, where Paul finds parallels between Christianity and existing philosophical and religious thought forms. A passage from the Pastoral Letters (1 Tim. 1:17) talks about God in terms that possess a similarity to philosophical approaches: "Now to the King eternal, immortal, invisible, the only God." Terms such as *immortal* and *invisible* reveal a philosophical orientation.[8] Furthermore, a passage in Galatians contrasts God with the gods "who by nature are not gods" (4:8), utilizing contemporary philosophical distinctions.[9]

Based on the Pauline tradition in the New Testament, Grant summarizes:

> It should be pointed out that in Pauline thought the eternal, imperishable, creative, and living true God is contrasted with temporal, perishable, ineffective, and nonliving idols. This is the case in 1 Corinthians [chap. 8]; it is also the case in 1 Thessalonians 1:9: Christians turn from idols to serve the "living and real God." In Galatians 4:8–10 the contrast is between the Creator and elemental spirits which he has created.[10]

6. Robert M. Grant, *The Early Christian Doctrine of God* (Charlottesville, Va.: University Press of Virginia, 1966), 3.
7. Ibid., 6.
8. These were terms used by contemporary and later philosophers when referring to gods.
9. One of the themes in pagan philosophy was to inquire into the conditions of deity, i.e., what it is that makes a god "god."
10. Grant, *Early Christian Doctrine of God,* 10–11.

Grant continues, with regard to Christian writers such as Aristides, Theophilus, and Clement of Alexandria:

> These early Christian writers, then, while in every instance maintaining the primacy of faith in response to the self-revelation of God, do not hesitate to make use of the points of contact between God's revelation and the modes of expression prevalent in Hellenistic Judaism and in Graeco-Roman philosophy generally.
>   . . . Since Christian faith is not totally alien from rational construction, the New Testament writers make use of terms which they share with some of their contemporaries. For them as for others, God is invisible, powerful, eternal, and imperishable. The popular philosophical terminology of causation can be employed in regard to him. It is fairly evident that all this language is secondary to, and derivative from, the primary affirmations of faith. But the fact that it could be employed at all left room for the development of various kinds of philosophical theologies.[11]

To put these comments in perspective, we need to realize that even though the seeds of what is later called classical theism can be found in the New Testament, the New Testament approach is not philosophical nor systematic. We also need to acknowledge that surprisingly early, as this survey will show, Christian theology took the decisive leap from the salvation-historical, narrative-testimonial style of the New Testament to a systematic, philosophical, and constructive approach. One of the ways classical theism did this was by focusing on the attributes of God. If anything is characteristic of classical theism—up until current times—it is the listing of attributes deemed essential to the Godhead and based on biblical revelation.

The Nature and Attributes of God Defined

The survey of the Old Testament revealed that one way God was characterized was by painting a picture of him in terms of his various features or characteristics—or, in the terminology of later philosophical theology, attributes. For example, Exodus 34:6 reads, "The LORD, the LORD, the compassionate and gracious God, slow to anger, abounding in love and faithfulness." The New Testament occasionally continued this practice, as we saw in the Pauline tradition. But patristic and later theological traditions especially focused on the nature and attributes of God, a practice that rapidly came to characterize classical theism.

It is obvious that as the Hebrew language of the Old Testament gave way to Greek formulations during the Hellenistic period, a more conceptual,

11. Ibid., 12, 13–14.

philosophical, and systematic doctrine of God began to emerge. The heart of the synthesis, so Ted Peters claims, of Hebrew and Greek concepts is the identification of God with the source of being. The Jewish philosopher Philo of Alexandria had already made this move when he identified the "he who is" of Exodus 3:14 with the Greek "that which is" *(to hon)*. Gregory of Nazianzus and John of Damascus followed by referring to God as "an infinite and unbounded ocean of being."[12]

A striking illustration of the move toward classical theism in early theology is offered by George L. Prestige in his *God in Patristic Thought*. His study surveys the earliest patristic views of God and attempts to define "elements of theism." Based on numerous quotations from early writers such as Theophilus, Clement of Alexandria, Dionysius of Alexandria, and many others, he comes to the following understanding:

- Inquiry into the "nature" of God—what makes God God—characterizes this early theology.
- Attributes such as incomprehensibility, impassibility, indivisibility, self-identity, and infinity are ascribed to God.
- God as holy and as spirit are among the basic elements of theism discussed by these patristic writers.[13]

Even though many regard this kind of enterprise as a deviation from a dynamic biblical theology toward fixed categories of Hellenism—and this book will listen to those critics' voices in due time—many classical theists have seen it as not only helpful but also inevitable. In the words of Prestige:

> I must make clear my fundamental outlook. I do not believe that the importation of Hellenic rationalism, to expound and explain the facts of Christian history, was illegitimate. Finite minds can never adequately theorise the infinite. But human reason is a valid instrument for unfolding the implications of human experience. There is nothing particularly Hellenic, still less pagan, about rational method, except that the Greeks had the providential privilege of its discovery and development.[14]

Another example of the move toward classical theism comes from a later age, this time from the Eastern traditions, which are, rightly, deemed more mystical and less analytic. The seventh-century Eastern authority John of Damascus, in his celebrated *Exposition of the Orthodox Faith* (1.8), lists no fewer than eighteen distinct attributes of God. The attributes he lists may

---

12. Ted Peters, *God—The World's Future: Systematic Theology for a Postmodern Era* (Minneapolis: Fortress, 1992), 88.

13. George L. Prestige, *God in Patristic Thought* (London: SPCK, 1952), 1–23.

14. Ibid., xiii.

be further classified according to whether they refer to time (subdivided into time's beginning and end), space, matter, or quality:

Time: without beginning, uncreated, unbegotten (beginning); imperishable, immortal, everlasting (end)

Space: infinite, uncircumscribed, boundless, of infinite power

Matter: simple, uncompound, incorporeal, without flux

Quality: passionless, unchangeable, unalterable, unseen[15]

So decisive was John of Damascus's list that it has been widely used in some form until modern times. Even the *Summa theologiae* of Aquinas does not go beyond it but suffices with a more modest presentation. Thomas lists the divine attributes as follows: simplicity, perfection, goodness, incomprehensibility, omnipresence, immutability, eternity, and oneness.[16]

The fact that a careful attempt to define the attributes of God is no marginal exercise for classical theism and thus the mainstream of almost two millennia of Christian theology is illustrated by two later examples. The Fourth Lateran Council of the Roman Catholic Church held in 1215, repeated much later by Vatican I in 1870, defined the attributes in this way: "We firmly believe and simply confess that there is only one true God, eternal, immense, unchangeable, incomprehensible, omnipotent, and ineffable." Similarly, the Westminster Shorter Catechism asks, "What is God?" The answer is in the form of his attributes: "God is a Spirit, infinite, eternal, and unchangeable, in his being, wisdom, power, holiness, justice, goodness, and truth."[17]

These examples show the general orientation and agenda of classical theism. The task ahead is to delve into the history of theology by looking at the various manifestations of classical theism. The place to begin this chronological survey is with the fathers of the church.

15. For bringing Damascus's list to my attention, I am indebted to Gerald Bray, *The Doctrine of God* (Downers Grove, Ill.: InterVarsity, 1993), 81–82.

16. Thomas Aquinas, *Summa theologiae*, vol. 2, ed. T. McDermott (London: Eyre & Spottiswoode, 1964), IA, q. 1–11.

17. Quoted in Peters, *God—The World's Future*, 88.

4

Patristic Contributions
to Classical Theism

Theological doctrines do not emerge, let alone operate, in an intellectual vacuum. Therefore, this survey of patristic contributions to the doctrine of God begins with a brief look at prevailing influences.[1] It then turns to the Christian apologists' views, other pre-Nicene theologies, and later patristic views in both the East and the West. A helpful beginning comes from the premier historian of theology of the former generation, J. N. D. Kelly: "The world in which the Church made triumphant, if sometimes painful, headway was hungry for religion."[2]

The Philosophical and Religious Background

Syncretism and polytheism were the defining features of the day in the Roman Empire during the formative years of early Christian theology. The gods of one country were identified with those of another, and there was much traffic between religions. Mystery religions played a crucial role in shaping popular piety and faith. Most mystery divinities were of Oriental origin.[3]

1. A helpful and succinct account of major influences is offered by J. N. D. Kelly, *Early Christian Doctrines*, 2d ed. (San Francisco: Harper & Row, 1960), chap. 1.
2. Ibid., 6.
3. Ibid., 7.

One religion, Manichaeism, incorporated Christian, Buddhist, and Zoro-astrian elements and had a wide influence on some leading Christian thinkers, especially Augustine of Hippo during his formative years. According to this dualistic religion, reality is composed of good (that is, God) and evil (identified with matter). Manichaean religion, therefore, encouraged withdrawal from the world. Its god was less than the Christian God, who is the Redeemer, because the Manichaean god was himself in need of redemption. Human beings, while sinful and trapped in the material order, share a spark of divinity.

Amid the syncretism and polytheism of the time, however, there was a growing attraction to monotheistic religion. "More and more the many gods of the pagan pantheon tended to be understood either as personified attributes of one supreme God or as manifestations of the unique Power governing the universe."[4]

In addition to the various religions, philosophy exercised a vast influence within the context of early Christian theology. The philosopher Plato, of the fourth century before Christ, was especially influential.[5] He believed there are two worlds, the visible, which is transient, and the invisible, the world of eternal Ideas, the real world. True knowledge can be obtained only from the transcendent world of Ideas, not from the material world. Christian theology soon adopted Platonic views, including the ethical division of these two worlds. The material world was evil, the immaterial good. Plato's thought also influenced the New Testament idea of the resurrection of the body. Christian theology soon adopted the idea of the immortality of the soul, thus making eternal life not a special gift of God but the natural result of the divine in humans. Plato's idea of "the good" markedly shaped the Christian doctrine of God. In *Timaeus,* Plato derived the existence of the world from the "demiurge," a divine artisan who took formless matter and gave it form that reflected the beauty of the Idea of "the good." Parallels with the Genesis story were easily acknowledged. Yet the Platonic creation narrative led to a dichotomy between the Supreme Being and the Creator, a view foreign to the Bible.[6]

Plato's student Aristotle had an undeniable influence on later Christian theology. Aristotle was interested in logic, the categories of thinking, from which classical theists borrowed many tools for their trade. Unlike his teacher, Aristotle denied the existence of Ideas as separate realities, accepting the reality of the material world as we know it. In regard to God, Aristotle adapted his teacher's ideas and developed a concept of God as the Prime Mover of all that exists. This Prime Mover became the Unmoved Mover of classical theism.

---

4. Ibid., 8.

5. See Richard A. Norris, *God and the World in Early Christian Theology: A Study in Justin Martyr, Irenaeus, Tertullian, and Origen* (New York: Seabury, 1965), chaps. 2, 5.

6. See Justo L. González, *A History of Christian Thought,* vol. 1, *From the Beginnings to the Council of Chalcedon,* rev. ed. (Nashville: Abingdon, 1987), 50–52.

One of the major challengers to Platonism was Stoicism. While both accepted that the world was composed of spirit and matter and that divine reason, *logos,* was at the top of the cosmological hierarchy, Stoicism, unlike Platonism, focused on the material. According to the Stoics, both spirit and matter are material in the sense that their smallest element is a fine, fiery substance. This materialistic system had no room for Plato's idea of a transcendent, intelligible world. According to the Stoics, the visible world is self-contained and is not to be looked down upon.[7] The Stoic outlook was a kind of "pantheistic materialism," a monism that taught that God (or *Logos*) is a finer matter that pervaded the material universe.[8]

Philo, a leading Jewish-Hellenistic philosopher who died around A.D. 50, attempted a noble synthesis of Platonic and Yahwistic views of God. Though not a Christian, he shaped the worldview in which Christians carried on their thinking. A recent commentator goes so far as to say that "Philo claimed in the name of Judaism everything which he took from the gentiles," for he believed that everything—philosophy, ethics, psychology, and religions—went back to Moses.[9] According to Philo, God is absolutely transcendent; therefore, no relationship exists between God and the world. God is essential being and is not found in time or space. Rather, these are found in God. For God to interact with the world, an intermediary is needed, the *Logos.* "This *logos* is the image of the divine, and is God's instrument in creation."[10] Philo believed that human beings cannot understand God, since understanding implies a certain mode of possession, and humans can never possess the infinite. Like Plato, however, Philo had a vision of God as a kind of ecstasy at the end of a long, ascending process. The more a human being purifies himself or herself from sensual passions so that the body as the "prison of the soul" looses its grip, the closer one comes to the vision of God. Philo's view was familiar in Christian piety for centuries, seen in a negative view of the body, asceticism, and the desire for a beatific vision.

Later versions of Platonism are often called Middle and Neoplatonism. Middle Platonism (first century B.C. to second century A.D.), in all its variations, was religiously colored. Its adherents desired a way to attain a likeness to God. Combining ideas from both Plato and Aristotle, the Middle Platonists equated the Supreme Mind (Aristotle) and "the good" (Plato). Middle Platonism was more theistic than its classical forerunner, for "at the summit of the hierarchy of being it placed the unique Divine Mind."[11]

Neoplatonism carried the transcendence of God as far as it could go. This system incorporated not only Platonic and Aristotelian concepts but also

---

7. See Norris, *God and the World in Early Christian Theology,* 27–30.
8. Kelly, *Early Christian Doctrines,* 12.
9. Erwin R. Goodenough, *An Introduction to Philo Judeaus,* 2d ed. (New York: Barnes & Noble, 1963), 75.
10. González, *History of Christian Thought,* 45.
11. Kelly, *Early Christian Doctrines,* 15.

Stoic and even Oriental elements. Its heyday was from the middle of the third century to the end of the patristic era in the fifth or sixth century, and its ablest representative was Plotinus of the third century, a Greek-speaking Egyptian. Plotinus was a monist who conceived of reality as a vast hierarchical structure. His highest principle was God, the One, from whom all that exists emanates. "Itself beyond being, and even beyond mind (with which . . . the Middle Platonism equated God), the One is the source from which being derives, the goal to which it ever strives to return."[12] Two implications for Christian theology are worth noting. First, Neoplatonism represented an optimistic attitude toward the universe. Even though matter in itself is evil, the visible universe reflects the intelligible order. Second, whatever exists emanates from the One, and at the lower levels of reality there is an ardent longing for union with what is higher, eventually with the One itself. Neoplatonism, while exercising influence on several Christian traditions, was especially significant among Eastern theologians such as Dionysius the Areopagite.

The final influence on early Christian theology worth highlighting is Gnosticism.[13] Named for the Greek term *gnōsis,* "knowledge," Gnosticism was a constellation of movements not easily defined. In general, however, these movements championed a division between those who were "enlightened" and those who were still living in darkness, as well as a strict dualism between the material (evil) and the spiritual (good). Gnostics denied that God created the world; rather, in the spirit of Platonism, they assigned creation to an inferior deity, a kind of demiurge. Consequently, mediators were needed between the earth and heaven. Christian theology at various instances, perhaps beginning from the time of the early church, was both drawn to and opposed Gnosticism. It was drawn to the idea of wisdom and knowledge but opposed Gnosticism because its views of God, creation, and salvation were not compatible with Christianity.

Having briefly considered the philosophical and religious background of Christian theology, we are ready to begin a survey of patristic views of God. Two main questions guide this endeavor: First, how did the fathers approach the doctrine of God in light of biblical ideas and in relation to existing religious and philosophical ideas? Second, how did patristic theology attempt to come to terms with the plurality of God evident but not yet defined in the New Testament? This second question is secondary to the present book; trinitarian considerations are examined only as they bear on the development of a distinctively Christian view of God. Yet because from the beginning the view of God as triune was integral to the Christian faith, any discussion of the Christian doctrine of God must touch on the doctrine of the Trinity.

12. Ibid., 16.
13. See Norris, *God and the World in Early Christian Theology,* chap. 3.

God as Creator and Transcendent Being in the Apostolic Fathers

J. N. D. Kelly aptly expresses a starting point for inquiring into the emerging theology of God during the first centuries:

> The classical creeds of Christendom opened with a declaration of belief in one God, maker of heaven and earth. The monotheistic idea, grounded in the religion of Israel, loomed large in the minds of the earliest fathers; though not reflective theologians, they were fully conscious that it marked the dividing line between the Church and paganism.[14]

This orientation is evident beginning with the apostolic fathers, a term coined in the seventeenth century to refer to the earliest Christian writers, not including the writers of the New Testament, of the first part of the second century.[15] Their testimony has always been venerated since—as their name indicates, even though its historical validity cannot be established—they were considered to be closest to the apostles. Their testimony is noteworthy because it represents the first layer of postbiblical developments, even though they lived during the time when the New Testament canon was not yet closed.

According to Hermas, the first commandment is to "believe that God is one, who created and established all things, bringing them into existence out of non-existence."[16] For Clement, God is the "Father and creator of the entire cosmos," and for Barnabas and the *Didache,* he is "our maker." God's omnipotence and universal sovereignty are acknowledged because he is Lord Almighty, the Lord who governs the entire universe.[17]

The writings of the apostolic fathers contain a creative combination of biblical teachings and philosophy. For example, Clement of Rome, a Hellenistic-Jewish-Christian author, describes the harmonious operation of God's world in language based on Stoic models. Such a practice reveals the growing tendency of the earliest Christian writers to venture into the sphere of philosophy to illumine the church's faith. The apocryphal *Preaching of Peter* is perhaps the first document to offer a full philosophical discussion of God. It talks about "one God who made the beginning of all things and has control over their end." God is further described as

---

14. Kelly, *Early Christian Doctrines,* 83.

15. The writers and writings identified as the apostolic fathers include Clement of Rome, the *Didache* (an early Christian manual widely used both in catechesis and as one of the first rules of faith), Ignatius of Antioch, Polycarp of Smyrna, Papias of Hierapolis, the *Epistle of Barnabas,* the Shepherd of Hermas, and the *Epistle of Diognetus.* There are also a number of smaller pieces, but the above-mentioned are the apostolic fathers proper. See J. B. Lightfoot and J. R. Harmer, trans., Michael W. Holmes, ed., *Apostolic Fathers,* 2d ed. (Grand Rapids: Baker, 1989).

16. Hermas, *Mandate* 1.1.

17. Kelly, *Early Christian Doctrines,* 83.

> The invisible, who sees all things,
> Uncontained, who contains all things,
> Without needs, of whom all are in need and
>   Because of whom they exist;
> Incomprehensible, eternal, imperishable;
> Unmade, who made all by the word of his power.[18]

The negative adjectives reflect the popular philosophical theology typical of contemporary writings, both Jewish and Gentile. They also echo New Testament ascriptions such as "invisible," "eternal," and "imperishable."

The Apologists and the God of the Philosophers

"Those who lived by reason are Christians, even though they have been considered atheists,"[19] concluded Justin Martyr, one of the most important second-century apologists. The apologists were Christian thinkers who wanted to offer a reasonable defense for the Christian faith vis-à-vis contemporary culture and philosophy. They also sought to establish a correlation between Greek philosophy and Judaism and, by inference, between Greek and Christian thought. In addition to Justin, the late-second-century apologists included Aristides, Tatian, Theophilus of Antioch, and Athenagoras, among others.

Aristides opened his *Apology*, addressed to the Emperor Hadrian (117–38),[20] with an outline demonstrating God's existence based on Aristotle's argument from motion, a procedure lacking in the biblical canon but later utilized by various Christian theologians, especially medieval scholastics.

> The consideration of the order and beauty of the universe induced him [Aristides] to believe in a supreme Being Who was the prime mover and Who, remaining Himself invisible, dwelt in His creation. The fact that there was a cosmos demanded a divine craftsman to organize it. Sovereign and Lord, He has created everything for man; . . . reality came to be out of nothing at the behest of Him Who is incorruptible, unchanging and invisible. He Himself is created, without beginning or end; He has no form, no limits, no sex. The heavens do not contain Him . . . ; on the contrary, He contains them, as He contains everything visible and invisible.[21]

For Aristides, God is the Aristotelian "unmoved Mover and Ruler of the universe," for "everything that moves is more powerful than what is moved, and

---

18. Quoted in Clement of Alexandria, *Miscellanies* 6.39.2–3.
19. Justin Martyr, *First Apology* 46.1–4.
20. Or possibly to Antoninus Pius (138–61).
21. Kelly, *Early Christian Doctrines*, 84.

that which rules is more powerful than what is ruled."[22] God is beyond gender. He has no emotions such as anger or wrath, for no one can resist him, nor can he ever err or forget. By listing these attributes of God, Aristides attacked the false conceptions of gods found in pagan philosophy and religion. For example, he stated that other gods were subject to suffering and death, whereas the incarnation of the Lord Jesus Christ was a voluntary act of God.[23]

Justin Martyr began his search for God under the tutelage of the Stoics. He chronicled this in the fascinating yet stylized work *Dialogue with Trypho,* addressed to his Hellenistic Jewish teacher. Justin admitted, however, that he learned nothing about God; his Stoic teachers did not possess such knowledge, and they themselves knew it. In his desperation for God, Justin inquired into other contemporary philosophies such as that of the Pythagoreans, followers of the famous philosopher-mathematician, but without satisfaction. Finally, not even Platonism could provide him with a satisfactory answer to the question of God.

After his conversion to Christianity, Justin did not set aside the cloak of the philosopher but focused his intellectual and spiritual skills on producing the most famous apologetic works of the second century, his *First* and *Second Apology.* Justin was convinced that philosophy, the "love of wisdom," was indeed a search for God. Yet whatever truth philosophers know can be attributed eventually to God, for, as he pointedly wrote, "Moses . . . is more ancient than all the Greek authors." Whatever philosophers and poets said about ultimate questions came from taking up the suggestions of the prophets.[24] *First Apology* boldly, almost presumptuously, told the philosophers and rulers of the day that they would follow the Christian faith if they were wise people. Wise people abandon traditions that are not good and follow those that are good. He challenged the elite of his day to reassess their condemnation of the Christian faith as superstitious or inferior to the best philosophies. Justin was no modest defender of his faith in the Christian God:

> Our doctrine surpasses all human teaching, because we have the Word in his entirety in Christ, who has been manifested for us, body, reason [*logos*] and soul. All the right principles that philosophers and lawgivers have discovered and expressed they owe to whatever of the Word they have found and contemplated in part. The reason why they have contradicted each other is that they have not known the entire Word, which is Christ.[25]

For Justin, philosophy "contains only part of the truth, but by itself it cannot even distinguish that part of truth from the great deal of falsehood in which

---

22. Quoted in Robert M. Grant, *The Early Christian Doctrine of God* (Charlottesville, Va.: University Press of Virginia, 1966), 17.

23. See ibid., 18.

24. Justin Martyr, *First Apology* 44.8–9.

25. Justin Martyr, *Second Apology* 10.1–3.

it is enveloped. . . . The Word, who was known in part by the philosophers, is now known as a whole by Christians."[26]

But what about the uniqueness of God in the Christian faith? Even if the Son were the *Logos,* the true revealer of God, what about the Father? The Stoics knew no divine power above the cosmic Reason, and the Mind or the divine craftsman of Middle Platonism could hardly be identified with the dynamic biblical idea of the heavenly Father. Here again, while holding fast to the uniqueness of the Christian God, Justin was not afraid to borrow terms from Platonism and other contemporary philosophies. In a few passages, he dared to use the name "Craftsman of the Universe" as an epithet for the Father. At the same time, Justin criticized those, for example, the heretic Marcion, who assumed that there was another god behind the God of the Bible. Justin also made it clear that his doctrine was not the pantheism of Platonism and that his God was no impersonal divine force but rather the God of Jewish and Christian faith revealed in the Bible.[27]

Many more examples could be given of how the apologists defended the biblical faith in God by utilizing the best tools of contemporary philosophies. Clement of Alexandria went so far as to write, "Philosophy was given to Greeks . . . [as] a schoolmaster to bring the Hellenic mind . . . to Christ."[28] By and large, Christian theology ratified the approach of the apologists in their defense and understanding of the God of the Bible. But not all were enthusiastic about the marriage between philosophy and theology. A few voices, such as that of Tertullian of the late second century, wondered, "What indeed has Athens to do with Jerusalem?"[29] doubting the wisdom of blending faith and philosophy (even though, ironically, Tertullian also wrote apologies). Both Tertullian and Irenaeus, two second-century theologians, advanced the quest for a distinctively Christian doctrine of God.

Irenaeus and Tertullian

Theology of History: Irenaeus

Born before the middle of the second century, Irenaeus of Lyon was the first Christian thinker to develop a comprehensive theology of history. In other words, it did not suffice to defend the plausibility of faith in the Christian God. Irenaeus sought to look at the meaning and goal of all history from God's perspective. In his theology of history, Irenaeus became convinced that

26. González, *History of Christian Thought,* 104.
27. See Norris, *God and the World in Early Christian Theology,* 58. Norris's treatment of Justin Martyr and his view of God in chapter 2 is a most helpful introduction to the topic.
28. Clement of Alexandria, *Miscellanies* 1.5.
29. Tertullian, *Prescription against Heretics* 7.

what began in creation, the revelation of God through the *Logos,* was fulfilled in the revelation of the Father by the Son.

Irenaeus's main opponent was Gnosticism. Perhaps because of his constant fight with Gnosticism, Irenaeus was a far less sympathetic friend of secular philosophy than were many others. In opposition to heresies, Irenaeus laid weight on the unity of God. His first and most important point, as noted in his *Against Heresies,* was that the Creator is the one and only God, maker of heaven and earth, and those who postulated a higher god, as did the Gnostics or the heretic Marcion, were blaspheming God.[30] In stressing the unity of God in terms of his doctrine of creation, Irenaeus pointed out that human beings were created in the image of God. Therefore, all human life, including the material and the physical, is not to be seen in a negative light.

Interestingly enough, while critical of many philosophies, Irenaeus did not eschew philosophical terminology when defining his views. For Irenaeus, natural knowledge of God (knowledge that comes from the created cosmos) and personal knowledge of God (knowledge based on the revelation of the Word) should not be distinguished but belong to one and the same category. Irenaeus firmly believed that "by means of the creation itself, the Word reveals God the Creator; and by means of the world the Lord, the Maker of the world."[31]

One of the lasting contributions of Irenaeus to the Christian doctrine of God was his twofold approach to God and knowledge about God. He divided the approach to the doctrine of God into investigation of God as he exists in his own inner being and of God as he manifests himself in the world, in the "economy."

The God of Revelation: Tertullian

Tertullian, the North African well educated in classical arts, including Stoic philosophy and Scripture, was the architect of Latin theology.[32] Tertullian is best known as the inventor of a number of key terms in theology, such as *person* (Latin, *persona*), especially with regard to early christological and trinitarian disputes.

Tertullian was not against reasoning per se, but he wanted to avoid futile speculation on the one hand and on the other make sure that Christian faith was based on divine revelation. According to Tertullian, Christianity is a religion of revelation. God is not so much the god of the philosophers to be searched for with intellectual helps but rather the God of the Bible who revealed himself in Christ. A "wise man" is not necessarily one with great learning but one who "acts in accordance with, not in opposition to, the divine dispensation."[33]

---

30. Irenaeus, *Against Heresies* 2.1.1.
31. Ibid., 4.6.5.
32. A helpful introduction to Tertullian's doctrine of God is Norris, *God and the World in Early Christian Theology,* chap. 4.
33. Tertullian, *The Resurrection of the Flesh* 3.1.

According to Tertullian, the ground of certainty is the "rule of faith," whose content is simple: belief in one God, the Creator of the universe; belief in Jesus Christ, born of the virgin Mary and Son of the Creator God; and belief in the resurrection of the flesh.[34] On the basis of divine revelation, people know the God who is Creator and sovereign Ruler: "What we worship is the only God, who by his Word . . . drew out of nothing, for the glorification of his majesty, this whole immense system."[35]

The Creator God of Tertullian, while preserving and guiding the world, is a transcendent God. The mark of the true God, Tertullian argued, is that he is eternal, ingenerate, uncreated, and without beginning or end.[36] Tertullian was an untiring defender of the majesty and transcendence of God, using the traditional Greek contrast between stable, immortal existence and existence that is unstable and possesses nothing permanent or in its own right.[37] Tertullian affirmed that God is timeless and impassible, themes that were heavily debated in later theologies, especially in the twentieth century.

Even with all his emphasis on biblical revelation as the rule of faith, it is evident that Tertullian adopted many elements from surrounding philosophies. Not all agree with the conclusions of Richard A. Norris that Tertullian basically affirmed the Platonized doctrine of God and creation as well as the Stoic concept of deity as "material," "as an impalpable corporeal substance which in some sense occupies space."[38] But there is no denying the heavy contribution of secular philosophies to Christian theology of God even among those who maintained a critical spirit toward philosophy.[39]

The Formulation of the Trinitarian Doctrine and Its Challengers

The Doctrine of the Trinity in the Making

Before examining the views of the fathers during the third and fourth centuries and beyond, we will look briefly at second-century developments toward trinitarian dogma and how it was first challenged by so-called monarchian views. The biblical survey already concluded that the Old Testament contains the idea of plurality in one God and that the New Testament conveys the no-

34. Tertullian, *Prescription against Heretics* 36.4.
35. Tertullian, *Apology* 17.1.
36. Tertullian, *Against Hermogenes* 4.1.
37. See Norris, *God and the World in Early Christian Theology,* 111–12.
38. Ibid., 112. Interestingly enough, one of the emerging topics in systematic and philosophical theology of God is the concept of space in God. The relation of time to God has been discussed since Augustine, and it will be interesting to see how much the current discussion benefits and borrows from that tradition.
39. Ibid., 112.

tion of God as Father, Son, and Spirit, albeit without defining this notion in any fixed theological terms.

The apostolic fathers, of course, acknowledged the Trinity, even if they had not yet defined the doctrine. Clement of Rome, writing at the turn of the second century, repeatedly referred to the Father, Son, and Holy Spirit. He linked the Father to creation, "the Maker of the whole world" (*1 Clement* 19:2). He stated that through "his beloved servant Jesus Christ," the Creator of the universe keeps the elect of God "intact" (59:2). He saw the Holy Spirit as the inspirer of Scripture (45:2) through whom Christ speaks (22:1).[40]

The apologists were the first to try to come to a tentative understanding of the relationship between Christ and God. They used, for example, analogies such as the sun and sunlight, pointing out the impossibility of distinguishing the light from the sun, which is its source. According to Kelly, "The solution they proposed, reduced to essentials, was that, as pre-existent, Christ was the Father's thought or mind, and that, as manifested in creation and revelation, He was its extrapolation or expression."[41]

A fuller account of the relationship between Father and Son can be found in a famous passage by Athenagoras. Having stated that the unoriginate, eternal, and invisible God created and adorned the universe, which he governs by his Word, Athenagoras went on to identify the Word as the Son of God. In reply to the objection that there is something ridiculous about God's having a son, he stated that God's Son is not like a human son. Instead, he is the "Father's Word in idea and in actualization."[42]

Irenaeus's theology, while sometimes open to various interpretations, left no doubt about the divinity of the Son: "The Father is God, and the Son is God, for whatever is begotten of God is God."[43] Although Irenaeus nowhere expressly called the Spirit God, he clearly ranked the Spirit as divine for the simple reason that the Spirit was the Spirit of God.

Tertullian contributed significant terminological advancements to the doctrine of the Trinity. He used the Latin term *trinitas* ("Trinity") for God, who is not a "simple unity." The threeness of God consists of the Father, Son, and Spirit, each of whom is a *persona,* "person." They share or are a single *substantia,* "substance."

The images and terms used by the early fathers demonstrate that from early on Christian theologians realized the difficulty inherent in a trinitarian orientation: If Jesus is God, how can Christians claim to worship only one God? How is Jesus different from or similar to the Father? How can Christians call Jesus Christ God if the Father is God? Yet as Roger E. Olson and Christopher A.

---

40. Roger E. Olson and Christopher A. Hall, *The Trinity* (Grand Rapids: Eerdmans, 2002), 16–17.
41. Kelly, *Early Christian Doctrines,* 95.
42. Athenagoras, *A Plea for the Christians* 10.
43. Irenaeus, *Proof of the Apostolic Preaching* 47.

Hall state, "We will be disappointed if we expect to find developed trinitarian reflection in the early post-apostolic writers. It is simply not there. More time will be needed for the implications of early Christian thought and practice to ferment and mature."[44] An impetus for the development of trinitarian doctrine came from various controversies. The first major challenge to the doctrine was in the form of a set of movements usually called monarchianism.

The "Monarchy" of the Father

The term *monarchianism* literally means "sole sovereignty." Monarchianism questioned how Christians could maintain Christian-Jewish monotheism while believing in two gods, Jesus Christ and the Spirit, in addition to the Father. While this view was deemed heretical, its motive seemed biblical: It sought to assure the supremacy of God the Father in the tradition of the Shema of Israel (Deut. 6:4) and the affirmation of that faith by Jesus and the apostles.

There are two subcategories of monarchianism: dynamic and modalistic. Both emerged in the late second and early third centuries and stressed the uniqueness and unity of God in light of the Christian confession that Jesus is God. Dynamic monarchianism[45] preserved the sole sovereignty of the Father by promoting the idea that God was dynamically present in Jesus, making Jesus higher than any other human being but not God. In other words, God's power (Greek, *dynamis*) made Jesus *almost* God. Thus, the Father's uniqueness was secured. Modalistic monarchianism[46] defended God's sole sovereignty by seeing the three persons of the Trinity not as self-subsistent "persons" but as "modes" or "names" of the same God. Father, Son, and Spirit do not stand for real distinctions but are merely different ways God presented himself at different times.

In presenting an orthodox response to these views, Tertullian first noted that preservation of the "monarchy" of God, the main concern of monarchianism, did not necessarily require that God be only one person. As Justo González explains:

> The "monarchy," that term which is so cherished by Praxeas and his followers, means simply that a government is one, and does not prevent the monarch from having a son or from managing his monarchy as he pleases—what Tertullian calls the divine "economy." Furthermore, if the father thus wishes, the son may share in the monarchy without thereby destroying it. Therefore, the divine monarchy is no reason to deny the distinction between Father and Son.[47]

44. Olson and Hall, *Trinity,* 20.
45. A helpful exposition, with references to original sources, is offered by Kelly, *Early Christian Doctrines,* 115–19.
46. See ibid., 119–23.
47. González, *History of Christian Thought,* 178, with reference to Tertullian, *Against Praxeas* 3.

Tertullian was convinced that the threeness revealed in the divine economy was in no way incompatible with God's essential unity. To combat both modalism and polytheism, Tertullian introduced the idea of God as one substance *(substantia)* and three distinct persons *(personas)*. Gerald O'Collins defines Tertullian's term *substance* as "the common fundamental reality shared by Father, Son, and Holy Spirit."[48] Tertullian's view was well received and helped to clarify the issue. Yet his response to monarchianism, and the responses of others, did not settle the issue in a decisive way but rather marked a milestone in the centuries-long development of a distinctively Christian view of God.

From Nicea to Chalcedon

The Third-Century Eastern Fathers on God

Even though the historical division between the Christian East and West did not take place until the second millennium (1054), from as early as the end of the second century, two schools began to emerge in Christian theology. The Eastern church was centered in Alexandria, Egypt, an ancient center for learning and, in the beginning of the third century, a melting pot of diverse teachings and movements such as Gnosticism, Neoplatonism, Hellenistic Judaism, and many others. The Eastern tradition expressed itself in Greek, and its distinctive doctrine of salvation was conveyed in terms of deification or divinization (from the Greek term *theōsis,* "denoting God"), which means "becoming like God." The Western wing of the church, with its center in Antioch, used Latin and focused primarily on moral obedience and justification by faith.

The two major figures of the third-century school of Alexandria were Clement (of Alexandria) and Origen. Clement moved Eastern theology in an apophatic direction. The term *apophatic* refers to a kind of theology that proceeds mainly by negations; in other words, such theology reveals aspects about God and God's dealings by conveying what they are *not* rather than what they are. For the Alexandrian theologian, God is transcendent, ineffable, and incomprehensible. God has no attributes and is beyond the category of substance. Nothing can be said directly about God; the divine cannot be defined.[49] Clement also held a trinitarian view of God. Next to the Father and throughout all eternity stands the Word.[50]

Clement further probed the ineffable mystery of God. God is "unity, but beyond unity, and transcending the monad." God can be known only through his Word, who is God's image and inseparable from him, "his mind or rational-

---

48. Gerald O'Collins, *The Tripersonal God: Understanding and Interpreting the Trinity* (New York: Paulist, 1999), 105.
49. See González, *History of Christian Thought,* 200.
50. Clement of Alexandria, *Miscellanies* 5.1.

ity."[51] This triune, transcendent God is also the Creator, and the world is the result of his action. For Clement, therefore, unlike the Platonists from whom he borrowed, the world does not simply emanate from the divinity, nor is it a mere ordering of preexistent matter.[52]

Origen made perhaps the greatest lasting contribution to Eastern theology and beyond. The son of a martyr, he was widely read in the philosophies and literature of his day. In his four-volume *On First Principles,* the doctrine of God is a controlling principle. Norris claims that Origen was the architect of "a new Christian Platonism."[53] Origen did creatively use ideas from pagan philosophies, but he also made clear that knowledge of God is fully known only through revelation in the Bible and especially in the person of Christ.

According to Origen:

> God cannot be comprehended by any human intelligence. God is invisible, not only in the physical sense, but also in the intellectual sense, for there is no mind that is capable of contemplating the divine essence. No matter how perfect our knowledge of God may be, we must constantly be reminded that God is much higher than anything our intelligence can conceive. God is the simple and intellectual nature, beyond every definition of essence.[54]

If anything is crucial to Origen's doctrine of God—and here he agrees with his colleague Clement—it is the principle of unity, absolute unity that is diametrically opposed to the multiplicity of the transient world, the view of Platonism.[55] Origen sought to preserve the transcendence of God and his plurality in unity by maintaining that God is outside time and that the Father begot the Son by an eternal act. Thus, there never was a time when the Son was not.[56]

While Origen, like Clement, affirmed the Trinity, Origen also advanced the discussion. He accepted that the ineffable One is the Triune God and that God is Father, Son, and Spirit. He also affirmed the coeternity of the Son.[57] This eternal Son not only participates in the divinity of the Father, as early theologians often put it, but is also divine "in substance."[58] This is a significant point in light of future developments in trinitarian doctrine: "Only with Origen's doctrine of the eternal begetting of the Son did the concept emerge

51. Ibid., 5.16; see also 3.7.
52. Ibid., 5.14.
53. Norris, *God and the World in Early Christian Theology,* chap. 5.
54. González, *History of Christian Thought,* 216, with reference to Origen, *On First Principles* 1.1.5 and *Against Celsus* 7.38.
55. González, *History of Christian Thought,* 216.
56. Origen, *On First Principles* 1.2.4.
57. E.g., ibid., 1.2.2.
58. Methodius, *Oration on the Psalms* 5.

of an eternal trinity in God."[59] In addition, Origen affirmed the distinct *hypostasis* ("substance," "nature," "essence") of the three persons of the Trinity from all eternity. In line with the growing Eastern tendency to emphasize the three-ness of God—to be fully explicated by the Cappadocian fathers—Origen emphasized more than the Latin fathers the three separate persons in the Trinity.[60] Yet in line with Eastern tradition, Origen recognized the first rank of the Father in the Trinity, so much so that one may wonder whether Origen compromised the full divinity of the Son.[61]

Other theological giants of the Eastern wing of the church during the third and fourth centuries include Athanasius and the three Cappadocian fathers—Gregory of Nyssa, Gregory of Nazianzus (or Nazianzen), and Basil the Great. Their contributions to the doctrine of God, especially the doctrine of the Trinity, receive attention in the following discussion of Arianism, which was tackled first at Nicea and then at Chalcedon.

The fact that this survey does not discuss any third-century Western theologians does not mean there were none. None of their views, however, went beyond those of the beginning of the third century. Theologians such as Hippolytus of Rome and Novatian discussed the doctrine of the Trinity, but they did not produce any distinctive work. Other third-century Latin theologians focused their energies elsewhere. For example, Cyprian of Carthage directed his attention to discussion of the church and salvation.

The Nicene Crisis and the Advancement of the Doctrine of the Trinity

THE CHALLENGE OF ARIANISM

What Kelly calls the "Nicene Crisis"[62] at the end of the third century concerned a right interpretation of the doctrine of God. It was as much about Christology as it was about God, since the burning question was how to maintain Jewish-Christian monotheism in light of the already established doctrine of the divinity of the Son and the emerging doctrine of the divinity of the Spirit. This was the challenge of Arianism. In a sense, the objective of Arianism was merely a version of the monarchianists' objective: to qualify the divinity of the other persons of the Trinity in a way that gives the Father sole divinity, the highest place, so to speak, in the divine hierarchy.

Unfortunately, we do not know exactly what Arius taught, nor if he even taught what is attributed to him. But historical questions aside, either Arius or someone else presented a view that was labeled Arianism.[63] The basic premise was that God

---

59. Wolfhart Pannenberg, *Systematic Theology*, vol. 1 (Grand Rapids: Eerdmans, 1991), 275, with reference to Origen, *On First Principles* 1.2.4.
60. See Kelly, *Early Christian Doctrines*, 129.
61. See González, *History of Christian Thought*, 218–19.
62. Kelly, *Early Christian Doctrines*, chap. 9.
63. Ibid., chap. 9 is a reliable guide to the topic under discussion.

the Father is absolutely unique and transcendent, and therefore, God's essence (the Greek term *ousia* means both "essence" and "substance") cannot be shared by another or transferred to another, even the Son. Consequently, the distinction between Father and Son is one of substance *(ousia)*. If Father and Son are of the same substance, there are two gods. Rather than sharing the same essence with the Father, the Son is the first and unique creature of God. A saying attributed to Arius emphasizes this main thesis about the origin of Christ: "There was [a time] when he was not." Jesus is greater than other creatures, but he is less than God. In a sense, Jesus stands in the middle between divinity and humanity.

The Council of Nicea was called in 325 to deal with the threat of Arianism and related christological issues. Nicea defended the tripartite rule of faith that had already been established:

> We believe in one God, the Father almighty, maker of all things, visible and
>   invisible;
> And in one Lord Jesus Christ, the Son of God, begotten from the Father,
>   only-begotten, that is, from the substance of the Father, God from God,
>   light from light, true God from true God, begotten not made, of one sub-
>   stance [*homoousios*] with the Father. . . .
> And in the Holy Spirit.[64]

According to the Nicene Creed, Christ was not created but was "begotten of the substance of the Father." The key word was the Greek term *homoousios,* which means literally "of the same substance" or "of the same essence." This made Christ equal in divinity to the Father. Not all theologians, however, were happy with the term. The Greek-speaking church would have preferred the Greek term *homoiousios.* The difference is one *i,* which significantly changes the meaning: *Homoi* means "similar to" rather than "the same," *homo.* According to this formulation, Christ is not completely identical with the Father but similar to the Father. Greek theologians had concerns about the stricter formulation because they believed it was not biblical and could be interpreted as indicating numerical identity between the Father and Son, which would lead to modalism. While agreeing on the need to defend the divinity of the Son against Arianism, Eastern theologians also considered it important to preserve the distinctive "personhood" of Father and Son as well as the privileged status of the Father. For Western theologians, however, the *i* seemed to compromise the equal divinity of the trinitarian persons and thus led to a sort of subordinationism.

ATHANASIUS'S ARGUMENTS FOR THE ORTHODOX DOCTRINE OF THE TRINITY

The leading orthodox voice in combating Arianism and affirming the Nicene Creed was that of Athanasius, another celebrated Eastern father from

64. Quoted in ibid., 232.

the fourth century. His concerns were also christological and soteriological: If the Son is a creature, then he is a creature like any other creature and himself in need of salvation rather than capable of helping human beings become deified, become like God. Only God can save. Thus, if Jesus is not God incarnate, he is not able to save humans.[65] Athanasius also wondered whether Arianism undermined the Christian doctrine of God by implying that the divine triad is not eternal, which would lead to a sort of polytheism. Perhaps the most lasting contribution of Athanasius to a genuine trinitarianism is his statement that the Father would not be the Father without the Son, and therefore, he was never without the Son.[66] In other words, to speak of the Christian God is to speak of the trinitarian God. There is no other kind of Christian God.

THE CAPPADOCIANS ON THE TRINITARIAN GOD

The Cappadocian fathers is the name given to three bishops/theologians of the Eastern Greek-speaking church of the second half of the fourth century: Basil the Great, Gregory of Nazianzus, and Gregory of Nyssa. They continued the developments of Athanasius and Nicea but also sharpened the dividing line between the East and the West by focusing even more strongly on the distinctive, separate persons *(hypostaseis)* in the Godhead.

Basil was the first to formulate the standard trinitarian formula for the Greek-speaking church: one essence *(ousia)* and three persons *(hypostaseis)*. For Basil, these two terms are not synonymous and therefore cannot be used interchangeably in referring to the Godhead.[67]

> In the case of the Godhead, we confess one essence of substance [*ousia*] so as not to give a variant definition of existence, but we confess a particular hypostasis, in order that our conception of the Father, Son and Holy Spirit may be without confusion and clear. If we have no distinct perception of the separate characteristics, namely, fatherhood, sonship, and sanctification, but form our conception of God from the general idea of existence, we cannot possibly give a sound account of our faith. . . . The Godhead is common; the fatherhood particular. We must therefore combine the two and say, "I believe in God the Father."[68]

The lasting contribution of Gregory of Nazianzus is the argument that the names "Father," "Son," and "Holy Spirit" are terms of relation. In response to those who claimed that the Father cannot share his essence with anyone and that Christians cannot attribute his action to more than one person in the Trinity, Gregory argued that "Father" is not a term of essence or action. Rather, the term denotes relation, "the relationship of communion of essence

---

65. See ibid., 233.
66. Athanasius, *Defense against the Arians* 1.29; see also 1.14, 36 and 3.6.
67. Basil, *The Letters* 8 is the most comprehensive exposition of these terms.
68. Ibid., 236.6.

which exists between the Father and the Son."[69] The only distinction that can be made between the three persons of the Trinity is related to origin. The Father is the "Unoriginate, for He is of no one." The Son "is not unoriginate, for He is of the Father." The Holy Spirit is "truly Spirit, coming forth from the Father indeed, but not after the manner of the Son, for it is not by the Generation but by Procession."[70] These three distinctions of origin became part of theological orthodoxy in the East.

The third Cappadocian, Gregory of Nyssa, though less a theologian, contributed to the work of the three fathers through his deep knowledge of pagan philosophy and of Origen's thought. His two treatises *On the Holy Trinity* and *On Not Three Gods,* while not breaking new ground, further developed trinitarian doctrine.

Augustine and His Legacy

Moving from the Eastern fathers of the fourth century to their Western counterparts, one could discuss theologians such as Hilary of Poitiers and his twelve-volume *On the Trinity* or Saint Ambrose. But the greatest of the fathers, St. Augustine, bishop of Hippo, occupies the honored last seat in this survey of patristic contributions to classical theism.

The Knowledge of God as Illumination

Even if Augustine never actually joined Manichaeism, at earlier stages he was heavily influenced by it.[71] He was also widely read in the philosophies of his day, especially Neoplatonism. Augustine's theory of knowledge was one of the key themes for his theology. Augustine was troubled by two foundational problems with regard to knowledge: Is knowledge possible? And if so, how? In his *Against the Academics,* directed to his former Skeptic teachers, he stated that even if our senses deceive us, we can at least be certain that we perceive. Similarly, even the radical doubter at least knows that he or she doubts.[72]

The possibility of knowledge, therefore, seemed evident to Augustine, but he still wondered how it was acquired, especially knowledge of eternal and immutable realities. Borrowing from the Platonists, he posited the existence of an intelligible world in which eternal realities exist. He differed from the Platonists, however, by stating that eternal realities exist in God's mind, not in a

---

69. González, *History of Christian Thought,* 314, with reference to Gregory of Nazianzus, *Theological Orations* 16.

70. Gregory of Nazianzus, *Theological Orations* 39.11.12.

71. See Justo L. González, *A History of Christian Thought,* vol. 2, *From Augustine to the Eve of the Reformation,* rev. ed. (Nashville: Abingdon, 1987), 18–20.

72. Augustine, *Against the Academics* 3.1.

realm above the Platonic creator god. According to Augustine, knowledge does not derive from the preexistence of souls (Plato), nor is it innate to God and given to the soul at the moment of its creation. Instead, knowledge is found in "illumination," as the famous passage from *The Trinity* explains:

> But we ought rather to believe, that the intellectual mind is so formed in its nature as to see those things, which by the disposition of the Creator are subjoined to things intelligible in a natural order, by a sort of incorporeal light of an unique kind; as the eye of the flesh sees things adjacent to itself in this bodily light, of which light is made to be receptive, and adapted to it.[73]

In other words, the human mind, which is incapable on its own of knowing eternal truths such as the existence or the nature of God, receives that knowledge through a direct illumination of God. "God the Word places in the human mind the knowledge of ideas that exist eternally in God."[74]

Naturally, Augustine's understanding of knowledge led him to the existence of God. While not ignorant of other kinds of proofs for God's existence, Augustine saw the existence and possibility of truth as foundational for a doctrine of God.

> Our human mind perceives immutable truths that we can neither change nor doubt, and whose existence leads us to the certainty that there must be a perfect truth, one that neither our mind nor all the minds in the universe can have created. This absolute truth, or rather, the foundation of all truth, is God.[75]

Thus, the existence of God is an inescapable reality to be acknowledged.

God as Absolute Being

What kind of God is the Christian God? Augustine never wearied of reminding humans of the limits of their knowledge of the nature of God. As he said, "If you understand, it is not God,"[76] and, "We can more easily say what he is not than what he is."[77]

In the spirit of classical theism, Augustine maintained that God is being, the absolute being, being in its fullness and perfection, "being above which, and without which nothing at all exists."[78] Among the attributes of God, simplicity

---

73. Augustine, *The Trinity* 12.15.24.

74. González, *History of Christian Thought,* 2:36; González's discussion of Augustine's theory of knowledge on pages 34–37 is most helpful.

75. Ibid., 2:37, with reference to Augustine, *Free Will* 2.1–15.

76. Augustine, *Sermons* 117.3.5.

77. Augustine, *Enarration on the Psalms* 85.12.

78. Edmund J. Fortman, ed., *Theology of God: Commentary* (New York: Bruce Publishing, 1968), 120.

was the trait he focused on. Because God is by his essence pure actuality of being and therefore cannot be conceived of as being in potency, he is above all perfection. In fact, Augustine was not satisfied with the term *substance* in regard to God, since it could be misinterpreted as implying a distinction between the essence of being and its accidental qualities (i.e., changeable or nonessential qualities, which God does not have).[79]

For Augustine, God is the Creator of all that exists. God made the universe out of nothing, *ex nihilo*. If God had made the universe out of the divine substance, Augustine reasoned, the result would be divine and would not be a true creation.[80] One of the ways the bishop of Hippo defended the transcendence of the Creator God was with his view of time. Augustine was convinced that God did not create *in* time but rather that God created time. Time is a creation of God. Therefore, God is not bound by time. A corollary is that time is not eternal, while God is.[81]

The Doctrine of the Trinity

Among the many theological themes Augustine brilliantly discussed, few have made as lasting an impression as his doctrine of the Trinity. Even though Augustine's fifteen-volume *De Trinitate* is not only a scriptural and theological exposition but also an intellectual exercise par excellence, Augustine did not see the Trinity as a matter of philosophical speculation. Rather, it is a datum of revelation, which in his view Scripture proclaims on almost every page. Inquiry into this supreme doctrine of Christianity illustrates his principle that faith must precede and illumine understanding.[82]

There is no definite consensus on the starting point—and thus the exact shape—of Augustine's doctrine of the Trinity,[83] but we can trace some highlights in the study of Augustine's doctrine. An older description of Augustine's trinitarian doctrine took his conception of God as "absolute being, simple and indivisible, transcending the categories" as foundational. Therefore, in contrast to those who made the Father the starting point of the Trinity, Augustine began with the divine nature, the Godhead, itself.

Recently, this interpretation of Augustine's view has been criticized because it seems to place Augustine's approach in opposition to the approach of the Cappadocians and Athanasius, who understood the inner relations of the Trinity as ontological (i.e., inherent to the nature of God's essence or being).[84] A middle position recognizes that even though the unity of God was important

---

79. Augustine, *The Trinity* 7.5.10.
80. Augustine, *Confessions* 13.7.
81. Ibid., 11.13.
82. Kelly, *Early Christian Doctrines,* 272.
83. A helpful map is offered by Olson and Hall, *Trinity,* 43–49.
84. Colin Gunton, *The Promise of Trinitarian Theology* (Edinburgh: T & T Clark, 1991).

to Augustine, his approach must not be seen as necessarily contradicting that of the Eastern fathers. Rather, he advanced their quest. His concern was to elaborate on the distinctions among the three persons of the Trinity on the assumption that they are one God. Augustine never used the divine essence per se as his starting point."[85] Whatever the final scholarly judgment regarding Augustine's view, this middle position seems to do justice to his view of God's nature.

Augustine acknowledged that there "is the Father and the Son and the Holy Spirit—each one of these is God, and all of them together are one God; each of these is a full substance and all together are one substance."[86] Then, somewhat surprisingly—yet in line with patristic tradition—he located the unity of the persons not in the divine essence but in the Father. "In the Father there is unity. . . . And the three are all one because of the Father, all equal because of the Son, and all in harmony because of the Holy Spirit."[87] Furthermore, Augustine insisted—and here he agreed with the Cappadocians—that the outward works of the Trinity are always indivisible,[88] even if in terms of "appropriations" some works, such as creation, may be attributed primarily to the Father. In their inner relations, however, the persons can be distinguished but without dividing the absolute unity of the Godhead.

Reflections on the Patristic Theology of God

The canons of classical theism were hammered out during the first four hundred years of Christian thinking. How, then, did the fathers contribute to the doctrine of God?

> They carried on what was perhaps the last great religious argument of the Western world. Certainly in no subsequent argument have the issues been wrought so clearly and argued with such amplitude for stakes were incalculably high. In the third, fourth, and fifth centuries, the Christian mind, tutored both in faith and philosophy, clashed in stern encounter with its two deadliest enemies, Gnostic syncretism and Hellenistic rationalism.[89]

85. Phillip Cary, "Historical Perspectives on Trinitarian Doctrine," *Religious and Theological Studies Fellowship Bulletin* (November–December 1995): 9, quoted in Olson and Hall, *Trinity*, 45.

86. Augustine, *On Christian Teaching* (Oxford: Oxford University Press, 1997), 10, quoted in Olson and Hall, *The Trinity*, 46.

87. Ibid.

88. Augustine, *The Trinity* 1.4.7; 4.21.30; Gregory of Nazianzus, *Oratio in laudem Basilii* 31.9; Gregory of Nyssa, *De deitate Filii et Spiritus Sancti* 2.59.

89. Fortman, *Theology of God*, 101.

The fathers took the biblical witness seriously and tried to make sense of it for their times. They also took seriously the contemporary philosophies and the challenge of syncretistic, polytheistic religions. Employing the categories of Greek thought to shape the dynamic, biblical view of God into a more coherent, rational, and apologetic system made sense in their environment. It was but another way of contextualizing the gospel.

While some of the dynamic nature and diversity of the biblical *narrative* of God was sacrificed for the sake of expressing the theology of God in Greek philosophical terms, it is not clear whether these developments helped to clarify the doctrine of God or introduced strange elements to it. Yet what else could theologians do unless they were ready to write off their cultural background?

Furthermore, as will become evident in the following discussion, the leads provided by patristic theologies were developed in more than one way. For example, both Thomas Aquinas, with his highly analytic and discursive theology, and Eastern theologians, with their mystical orientation, claimed to build on the same biblical and patristic foundations. The acknowledgment of the diversity of medieval and later theological traditions should make one hesitant to pronounce judgments.

As much as patristic theology has been studied, several key issues are still awaiting more light, such as the nature of Augustine's doctrine of the Trinity (whether it is typically "Western," if there ever was a typically "Western" approach) and, consequently, the question of the (alleged) difference between Western (Augustine) and Eastern (the Cappadocians) approaches to God.

The following discussion, as it moves from the sixth century to the eve of the Protestant Reformation, reveals the legacy of the fathers in the works of Anselm of Canterbury, Thomas Aquinas, and others—with a view to how the traditions of classical theism were further developed and what kind of proliferation arose.

5

Milestones in Medieval Theology of God

As the title of this chapter implies, the task at hand is to highlight some key figures and the most critical developments concerning medieval thought on God. The main interest lies in discerning how the central ideas of classical theism, based on the biblical witness and developed by patristic theology, were appropriated and reshaped during the medieval period.

The Vision of God in the Apophatic Theology of the East

The Mystical Theology of the Eastern Church[1]

An appropriate place to begin is by highlighting the contribution of the Eastern wing of Christian theology with its attraction to mystical and apophatic visions of God. A mystical orientation is not limited to the East, of course. It appears in later theologians such as John Scotus Erigena (to be studied below) and the Western mystical tradition of the fourteenth and fifteenth centuries, including Meister Eckhart and Thomas à Kempis. Yet the vision of God in the East is an indispensable testimony to the richness and variety of theistic traditions.

---

1. This subheading is taken from Vladimir Lossky, *The Mystical Theology of the Eastern Church* (Crestwood, N.Y.: St. Vladimir's Seminary Press, 1976).

The apophatic, mystical orientation of the Eastern tradition goes back to the Eastern fathers. Despite their intellectual efforts regarding the doctrine of the Trinity and related topics, the Cappadocians acknowledged that theology can never venture far from personal experience because no words can adequately talk about God. Gregory of Nyssa maintained that true knowledge of God is "the seeing that consists in not seeing, because that which is sought transcends all knowledge, being separated on all sides by incomprehensibility."[2] This view has been appropriately called a tradition of "learned ignorance."[3]

A vision of God begins with celebration of the divine mystery rather than with a rationalistic inquiry into the essence and nature of God.[4] Any knowledge about God—and bearing in mind the truth that God can never be defined, only approached in humble prayer and repentance—requires a combined spiritual and intellectual catharsis, "a purification of the mind that rids us of all false ideas about God."[5] Vladimir Lossky, a recent authority on Eastern theology, describes the process of "ascending" to God with these words:

> The negative way of the knowledge of God is an ascendant undertaking of the mind that progressively eliminates all positive attributes of the object it wishes to attain, in order to culminate finally in a kind of apprehension by supreme ignorance of Him who cannot be an object of knowledge. We can say that it is an intellectual experience of the mind's failure when confronted with something beyond the conceivable.[6]

Symeon the New Theologian—who was not called "theologian" because of his learning or scholarship (he did not exhibit either of these) but rather because of his prayer life and spirituality—compared the divine-human encounter to a blinding flash of light. The vision of God for him was like a man standing at night inside his house and suddenly opening a window just at the moment of a sudden flash of lightning. Unable to bear its brightness, he has to protect himself by closing his eyes and drawing back from the window.[7]

A Mystical Vision of God: Pseudo-Dionysius

The most creative visionary-theologian in the Eastern tradition during early medieval times was Pseudo-Dionysius, an anonymous writer who for

2. Gregory of Nyssa, *The Life of Moses* 2.163.

3. Daniel B. Clendenin, *Eastern Orthodox Christianity: A Western Perspective* (Grand Rapids: Baker, 1994), 55–56.

4. See Timothy Ware, *The Orthodox Way* (Crestwood, N.Y.: St. Vladimir's Seminary Press, 1990), 17.

5. Clendenin, *Eastern Orthodox Christianity*, 56.

6. Vladimir Lossky, *In the Image and Likeness of God* (Crestwood, N.Y.: St. Vladimir's Seminary Press, 1974), 13.

7. Clendenin, *Eastern Orthodox Christianity*, 57.

centuries was believed to have been Paul's disciple. He is also called Dionysius the Areopagite.[8] Church historians agree that, whoever this person was,
his writings—such as *On the Celestial Hierarchy*, a sophisticated treatise into
the nature of angels and other divine beings, and *On the Divine Names* and
Mystical Theology, profound contemplations of God—come from the end of
the fifth century.

In the Eastern tradition of ascending spirituality, Pseudo-Dionysius compared Moses' ascent of Sinai with the ascent of the mind to the knowledge of
God. Moses "reaches the height of the divine ascent. Even here he does not
associate with God, he does not contemplate God (for He is unseen), but the
place where He is."[9] According to Pseudo-Dionysius, the negative way is the
opposite of the affirmative way of "positions," which means descent from
the superior degrees of being to the inferior. In contrast, the negative way of
"detachments" is an ascent toward the divine incomprehensibility.[10]

Pseudo-Dionysius continued the long tradition of Eastern mystical spirituality with his focus on "negative theology." We can describe only what God
is not, not what God is. What God is can be known only when "we worship
with reverent silence the unutterable Truths and . . . approach that Mystery
of Godhead which exceeds all Mind and Being."[11] Maximus the Confessor, a
seventh-century authority on Pseudo-Dionysius's writings, commented on the
nature of the apophatic theology: "The two names of Being and Non-Being
ought both to be applied to God, although neither of them really suits Him. . . .
He possesses an existence that is completely inaccessible and beyond all affirmation and negation."[12] Therefore, the best speech about God is silence, and the
profoundest knowledge of God lies in humble ignorance. "For the ignorance
about God on the part of those who are wise in divine things is not a lack of
learning, but a knowledge that knows by silence that God is unknown."[13]

In a typically Neoplatonic fashion,[14] Pseudo-Dionysius conceived of the
world as a hierarchical structure in which all things come from God and lead
back to God. Every entity has its own specific place in the divinely ordered
universe, God being at the top of everything, covered by an unapproachable
mystery.[15]

8. A helpful introduction is offered by Lossky, *Mystical Theology of the Eastern Church*,
chap. 2.

9. Quoted in Clendenin, *Eastern Orthodox Christianity*, 60.

10. Lossky, *Mystical Theology of the Eastern Church*, 28.

11. Dionysius the Areopagite, *On the Divine Names* 1.3.

12. Quoted in William C. Placher, *A History of Christian Theology* (Philadelphia: Westminster, 1983), 95.

13. Quoted in ibid.

14. Lossky, *Mystical Theology of the Eastern Church*, 29–32, issues a warning not to categorize
the Areopagite too uncritically as a Neoplatonist even if he shares its influences.

15. See Justo L. González, *A History of Christian Thought*, vol. 2, *From Augustine to the Eve
of the Reformation*, rev. ed. (Nashville: Abingdon, 1987), 93.

In this context, the Areopagite introduced his well-known doctrine of three ways of approaching God, a scheme widely used in later mysticism. There is the cathartic or purgative way in which the soul is rid of its impurity, the illuminative way by which the soul receives the divine light, and the unitive way in which the soul is united with God in an ecstatic vision. This vision of God, because of the absolute transcendence of God, is not "comprehensive" but rather intuitive, mystical, uncomprehensive.[16]

Uncreated Energies of God: Gregory of Palamas

As already shown with regard to the fathers, one focus of Eastern thought was the trinitarian doctrine. Lossky states that the apophatic theology of the East was "not an impersonal mysticism, an experience of the absolute, divine nothingness."[17] Yet at the same time, Eastern theologians did not attempt to define the Trinity in too tight of terms. First and foremost, their trinitarian theology was "a theology of union, a mystical theology which appeals to experience, and which presupposes a continuous and progressive series of changes in created nature, a more and more intimate communion of the human person with the Holy Trinity."[18] But the question of the possibility of real union with God poses for Christian theology the antinomy of "the accessibility of the inaccessible nature."[19] During the later medieval period, this question provoked vigorous theological debates in the East, and it finally led to the conciliar decisions on the subject during the fourteenth century. Gregory of Palamas,[20] the leading Orthodox theologian of the first part of the second century, devoted a dialogue titled *Theophanes* to the question of the incommunicable and yet communicable deity. According to Gregory, the archbishop of Thessalonica, "The divine nature must be said to be at the same time both exclusive of, and, in some sense, open to participation. We attain to participation in the divine nature, and yet at the same time it remains totally inaccessible."[21]

How does one resolve this apparent dilemma? Gregory joined the long tradition of the Eastern church by making a distinction between God's "energies," in which humans can participate through deification, and the totally transcendent, unapproachable "essence" of God. Therefore, "to say that the divine nature is communicable not in itself but through its energy, is to remain within the bounds of right devotion."[22] Several church councils embraced this

16. See ibid., 93–95.

17. Lossky, *Mystical Theology of the Eastern Church*, 44.

18. Ibid., 67.

19. Ibid., 69.

20. A basic introduction is John Meyendorff, *St. Gregory Palamas and Orthodox Spirituality* (Crestwood, N.Y.: St. Vladimir's Seminary Press, 1974).

21. Quoted in Lossky, *Mystical Theology of the Eastern Church*, 69.

22. Lossky, *Mystical Theology of the Eastern Church*, 70.

foundational view (for example, Constantinople in 1341 and 1368), and it became the standard teaching of the Eastern church. According to Lossky:

> This distinction is that between the essence of God, or His nature, properly so-called, which is inaccessible, unknowable, and incommunicable; and the energies or divine operations, forces proper to and inseparable from God's essence, in which He goes forth from Himself, manifests, communicates, and gives Himself.[23]

Through the medieval period and beyond, Eastern theology preserved its mystical, apophatic view of approaching God, and the influence of the Eastern wing of the church extended beyond its borders. One of the leading Western thinkers in the early medieval period, John Scotus Erigena, is an example of those who gleaned from mystical theology.

God in Nature: John Scotus Erigena

John Scotus Erigena of the ninth century (not to be confused with John Duns Scotus of the thirteenth century, whose ideas on God are discussed later) was the principal early medieval Western theologian. He belongs to the so-called Carolingian Renaissance, an intellectual revival accompanied by fresh theological work after a period of relative silence.[24] The most distinguishing mark of this intellectual awakening was a return to the classical sources of antiquity. Erigena, an Irish-born genius who moved to France, exemplified this trend with his thorough knowledge of Greek and its philosophy. His acquaintance with Greek helped him to read the Eastern fathers more efficiently, a skill not shared by the majority of Western scholars at that time.

According to Erigena, the fathers had found truth through the use of reason, and therefore later theology should follow the same path. Both reason and authority came from the same God, he concluded.[25] One can label Erigena both a philosopher and a theologian; textbooks usually introduce him primarily as a philosopher. In the spirit of medieval thought, however, these two disciplines are interrelated, often in a way that sees philosophy as the handmaid of theology. Classical theism could not have reached its zenith toward the end of the medieval period without this marriage of the two disciplines regarded as the culmination of all human intellectual endeavors.

Under the influence of Neoplatonism and particularly Pseudo-Dionysius, Erigena emphasized the transcendence and incomprehensibility of God. God is

---

23. Ibid.
24. A helpful introduction to the Carolingian era is offered by González, *History of Christian Thought*, chap. 4.
25. John Scotus Erigena, *On the Division of Nature* 1.66.

above all being, totally unknowable. He can neither be perceived nor conceived. We can know that God is but not what God is. When we declare that God is omnipotent, omniscient, and the like, we are merely trying to say in figurative language that God is greater than what can be said or thought.[26]

Nevertheless—and this distinguishes Erigena from Eastern theologians—he was much more interested in the immanence of God, "immanence amounting to genuine pantheism,"[27] as the title to this subsection implies. For Erigena, the divine nature embraces everything. Apart from God or outside God there is nothing. God is Being unlimited and undifferentiated. The Word is Being circumscribed and divided.[28] "And not only is God in everything, he is identical with all that is, for God and the creature are not two but one and the same."[29]

Perhaps not surprisingly, with his dynamic view of the pantheistic immanence of God, Erigena envisioned a type of evolution. The universe is not static or at rest; rather, it is continually developing.

> Out of God, the great All, all things come and back to him they all find their way. Everything . . . tends naturally to return to its source, and the universe which comes from God tends naturally to return to him. The process of evolution and involution in reality goes on within the divine nature itself, for God is all and the universe is but an expression or manifestation of him. In the unfolding of the divine essence the world comes into existence . . . to return ultimately to the source whence it came.[30]

Erigena posited the eternity of creation. If it is not eternal, it is accidental, external to God. For him, the eternity and immutability of God require that creation be eternal.[31] Yet God is prior to creation, not in the order of time—for God is not in time—but in the order of being. God is the source of the being of creation.[32]

Interestingly, with all his creative speculation, Erigena affirmed the doctrine of the Trinity as foundational to a Christian view of God and followed orthodox doctrine as defined earlier.

The Necessity of God's Existence: Anselm of Canterbury

A different kind of thinker, Anselm of Canterbury of the twelfth century, took for his motto the rule of Augustine, "I believe that I may know," rather

---

26. See Edmund J. Fortman, ed., *Theology of God: Commentary* (New York: Bruce Publishing, 1968), 154.

27. Ibid.

28. John Scotus Erigena, *On the Division of Nature* 1.12, 3.17.

29. Fortman, *Theology of God*, 154, with reference to John Scotus Erigena, *On the Division of Nature* 3.4, 3.17.

30. In Fortman, *Theology of God*, 154–55.

31. John Scotus Erigena, *On the Division of Nature* 3.8.

32. See González, *History of Christian Thought*, 133.

than "I know that I may believe."[33] Anselm joined the long tradition of affirming that all Christian doctrines are true because they are divinely revealed
and that the Christian must accept them on the authority of the church.
Yet at the same time, Anselm insisted on the rational nature of the church's
beliefs; therefore, doctrines could—and should—be proven with intellectual
faculties. The theologian, therefore, has a double task: to explain and elucidate
the truths of revelation for the sake of believers and to prove them true for
the sake of unbelievers. Thus, Anselm developed ontological proof for the
existence of God.

Even though Anselm's ontological argument made him famous, it was not his
starting point. In his early work, the *Monologium* (or *Monologion,* also known
as *Soliloquy*), Anselm sought to demonstrate the existence of God on the basis
of reason alone without appealing to authority. Since there are many goods of
various kinds, he argued, it is necessary to believe that there is one supreme
good through which they all are good. In the same way, we are compelled to
recognize that there is one being greater and higher than all others through
whom they all exist. For Anselm, an infinite regress is unthinkable. We must
assume, instead, an original self-existent being from which all originates. This
is the familiar cosmological argument from contingent to necessary being that
was taken to its logical end by Thomas Aquinas.

Having thus proven to his satisfaction the existence of God, Anselm devoted
the remainder of the *Monologium* to a consideration of God's nature. Here the
canons of classical theism were established with the help of the best intellectual
tools as well as scriptural and traditional resources.[34] The Being behind all that
exists must be the greatest and the best of all. In the words of Anselm:

> It [God] is supreme being, supreme life, supreme reason, supreme safety, supreme
> justice, supreme wisdom, supreme truth, supreme goodness, supreme great-
> ness, supreme beauty, supreme immortality, supreme incorruptibility, supreme
> immutability, supreme blessedness, supreme eternity, supreme unity, which is
> nothing else than to be supremely, to live supremely and the like.[35]

While his argument was profound at the time, the theologian-philosopher of
Canterbury was not yet completely satisfied. He sought to prove the existence
of God with a single proof rather than with several—the aim of his *Proslogion*
(also known as *Address*). This mature work, which took the form of an address
to God following the style of Augustine's *Confessions,* is not only briefer but
also more devotional than the *Monologium.* Anselm put forth the basic idea
of his ontological proof of God in the book's second chapter:

33. Anselm of Canterbury, *Proslogion* chap. 1.
34. For this exposition, I am heavily dependent on the excellent summary in Fortman,
Theology of God, 158–59.
35. Anselm, *Monologium* chap. 15.

Even the fool is convinced that there is something, at any rate in the understanding, than which nothing greater can be conceived, for when he hears this, he understands it, and whatever is understood is in the understanding. And certainly that than which a greater cannot be conceived cannot exist in the understanding alone. For if it be in the understanding alone, it is possible to conceive it as existing in reality, which is greater. If, therefore, that than which a greater cannot be conceived is in the understanding alone, that very thing than which a greater cannot be conceived is one than which a greater can be conceived. But this assuredly cannot be. Without any doubt, therefore, there exists something both in the understanding and in reality than which a greater cannot be conceived.[36]

Even though later critics of Anselm,[37] especially Immanuel Kant, were able to destroy the force of his ontological argument by raising the question as to whether it is really necessary to posit an existence on the basis of an *idea* of an existence, there is no denying the value of Anselm's reasoning for classical theism, especially its combination of philosophy and theology in defense of God. However, even though it took several hundred years for the final criticism to appear, Anselm's proof was not extensively used. The approach of Thomas Aquinas and others, *a posteriori,* "based on experience" (in opposition to Anselm's *a priori,* "apart from experience"), took the upper hand.

What kind of God is "proven" by the ontological argument? This God is absolutely simple; therefore, the divine attributes are not accidents but rather the very essence of God. God is present in every place and time and is not in any place or time, for all times and places are in God.[38] Anselm's God is also Triune,[39] which Anselm believed could be shown by rational means, in the same manner in which he proved the existence of God.[40] Anselm built on not only tradition but also the biblical witness as interpreted by classical theism, for the God of the philosophers would not have been a Triune God apart from biblical revelation and theological tradition.

This brings us to a final point in the discussion of Anselm. Despite his use of logic, it was always the believing mind that undertook to prove the existence of God. Anselm's reasoning was not primarily about apologetics in order to persuade unbelievers—even though evangelistic work was not irrelevant—but about the defense of the faith already received. Furthermore, piety set the tone for his intellectual work. Philosophy served not only theology but also piety, as is evident in his preface to the *Proslogion:*

36. Anselm, *Proslogion* chap. 2.
37. See, for example, Gerald Bray, *The Doctrine of God* (Downers Grove, Ill.: InterVarsity, 1993), 68–69.
38. Anselm, *Monologium* chaps. 16, 17, 20, 21–24; *Proslogion* chap. 12.
39. See, for example, Bray, *Doctrine of God,* 180–82.
40. See Anselm, *Monologium* chaps. 29–65; *Proslogion* chap. 23.

I do not try, Lord, to attain Your lofty heights, because my understanding is in
no way equal to it. But I do desire to understand your Truth a little, that truth
that my heart believes and loves. For I do not seek to understand so that I may
believe; but I believe so that I may understand. For I believe this also, that "unless I believe, I shall not understand."[41]

Before discussing the greatest medieval theologian, the "Angelic Doctor" of
the church, Thomas Aquinas, a short detour to the twelfth-century visionary
Joachim of Fiore is in order. One can hardly find approaches to theology and
faith that differ more than those of Thomas and Joachim; for that reason, both
of them receive a hearing.

The God of Three Ages: Joachim of Fiore

Joachim of Fiore, a twelfth-century Italian monk, exhibited nothing like
the systematic thinking of Anselm. Spending his life in a monastery in con-
templation and study of the Bible, especially the Apocalypse, Joachim sought
the hidden significance of history in the meaning of numbers, visions, and
prophecies. He was an apocalyptic preacher waiting for God's final takeover
of the world, which was estranged from the Creator. When he died in 1202,
he was generally regarded as a saint, even though many of his doctrines soon
fell into disfavor. Though trinitarian in his own way, Joachim was primarily
a pneumatologist, a charismatically oriented student of the Spirit and the
imminent end.[42]

The structuring principle for his theology and faith was a threefold division
of world history. The age of the Father was the Old Testament dispensation;
that of the Son was the New Testament aeon, including the church; and the
age of the Spirit was about to be launched in Joachim's time. It would be
signaled by the rise of new religious movements, which would lead to the
reform and renewal of the church and the final establishment of peace and
unity on earth.

In this unique trinitarian outlook, Joachim assigned to each age a specific
manner of divine administration. The age of the Father was ruled by law, and
in it people were to work and marry. The ideal was the Old Testament patriarch. The age of the Son, in which people were to learn, was ruled by grace,
and the ideal was the priest, who teaches. Finally, the age of the Spirit would
be ruled by love. In this age, people were to praise God, and the ideal would
be the monk filled with the love of God.[43] In line with other apocalyptists of

41. Anselm, *Proslogion* chap. 1.
42. See Veli-Matti Kärkkäinen, *Pneumatology: The Holy Spirit in Ecumenical, International,
and Contextual Perspective* (Grand Rapids: Baker Academic, 2002), 53.
43. See Placher, *History of Christian Theology,* 149–50.

history, the theologian of Fiore offered precise dating: Each age consisted of forty-two generations of thirty years each. The age of the Son was due to end in 1260.[44]

The Zenith of Classical Theism: Thomas Aquinas and Scholasticism

The Background of Later Medieval Theology

Before examining the contribution of the ablest proponent of classical theistic traditions, Thomas Aquinas of the thirteenth century, we look first at the intellectual and spiritual environment at the height of scholastic theology.[45] The twelfth and thirteenth centuries saw the establishment of universities. The medieval mind-set gave theology the honored position of queen of the sciences, with philosophy subservient to it. The university setting gave rise to some of the greatest theological *summas,* for example, the *Sentences* of Peter Lombard. At the same time, emerging mendicant orders such as the Dominicans and the Franciscans also devoted considerable time to the study of Christian theology.

The introduction of Aristotelian, Arabic, and Jewish philosophies to the universities and through educated leaders to the church was one of the most definitive marks of classical theism during these centuries. Among several notable Arabic philosophers, one towered over the rest: the famous Averroës (ibn-Rushd). Having found in Aristotle the "supreme truth," he studied several disciplines, including theology, yet never left behind the Qur'an. What he did was offer a philosophical interpretation of the Qur'an. Struggling with the most profound intellectual issues common to Christians and Moslems, such as the relationship between faith and reason, Averroës finally met his end at the hands of the Moslem establishment.

Two prominent Christian traditions, Franciscan and Dominican, came to dominate theology during the late medieval period. The Augustinian heritage continued to serve as the springboard for all major topics of theological study and debate. This legacy brought with it the influence of Neoplatonism. Theologians associated with the Franciscan school, most notably Bonaventure, relied heavily on the Augustinian model. At the same time, Aristotle was reintroduced to the theological guild. Theologians differed in the extent to which they were

44. The major recent study on Joachim is Christopher Walsh, *The Calabrian Abbot: Joachim of Fiore in the History of Western Thought* (New York: Macmillan, 1985). See also Bernard McGinn, "The Abbot and the Doctors: Scholastic Reactions to the Radical Eschatology of Joachim of Fiore," *Church History* 40 (1971): 30–47.

45. Scholasticism was the highly intellectual, philosophical, and rational approach in Christian theology, as represented by Aquinas and others in the late medieval period. González, *History of Christian Thought,* chap. 8 is a helpful guide to the topic.

willing to employ the Aristotelian system. Aquinas, of course, critically used Aristotle while at no time leaving Augustine behind, thus producing a new kind of synthesis of these seemingly rival schools of thought. This synthesis became a hallmark of the Dominican school headed by Aquinas.

The growing influence of Aristotle challenged the Augustinian-Anselmian ontological approach to the question of God and championed instead a more experience-based, cosmologically oriented approach in line with the slowly rising sciences. Soon, it became clear that the mere idea of God was not enough to convince theologians and philosophers of the existence of God. The grounds for the existence of God had to be sought in the world God had created. This was the approach of Aquinas and his followers.

God as the Subsistent Being: Thomas Aquinas

ARISTOTELIAN METAPHYSICS IN THE BACKGROUND

Most of the philosophical works of Thomas Aquinas are commentaries on Aristotle, though he also wrote some original philosophical works such as *On Being and Essence* and *On the Principles of Nature*. In the field of theology, his three most significant works are *Commentary on the Sentences* (of Lombard), *Summa contra gentiles,* and *Summa theologiae.*

Following his teacher Albert the Great, Aquinas distinguished between truths grasped by human reason and those revealed by God. These truths are not in opposition, since both derive from God, but they have their own spheres of operation. Thus, the division between "nature" and "grace" emerged and rose to its full force. Aquinas maintained that grace does not nullify but rather fulfills what is in nature. In order for this to happen, there must be a correspondence between earthly and heavenly realities. This correspondence was achieved by the use of analogy: Divine things could be described in terms reserved for the natural order.[46] For example, in light of the existence of earthly fathers, the idea of God as Father is understandable.

An examination of Aquinas's philosophical orientation regarding the question of God requires an explanation of terminology. Aquinas's metaphysics was basically Aristotelian, though it included some Neoplatonic and Augustinian features as well. First, to define the concrete form of "being," Aristotelian-Thomist metaphysics makes a distinction between *substance* and *accident.* Substance is that which exists in itself; an accident (or accidental property) exists

---

46. Aquinas distinguished among three ways of speaking: (1) univocal: The same term and meaning are used in exactly the same sense, as when *animal* refers to both a human being and a donkey; (2) equivocal: The same term is used but with a different meaning, as when *dog* refers both to an animal and a star; (3) analogical: The common meaning of a term is used to show some similarity or corresponding characteristic of a different entity, as when *father* is used to speak of God. See Thomas C. Oden, *The Living God: Systematic Theology,* vol. 1 (San Francisco: Harper & Row, 1987), 42–43.

only in a substance. Any substance, which is always concrete and individual (not an "eternal" Idea that exists apart from an individual being),[47] possesses several accidents or qualities. Second, there is a distinction between *matter* and *form.* Form makes a thing (matter) what it is. The term *form,* therefore, means more than "shape." Third, there is a distinction between *act* and *potency.* "That which can be, but which is not, exists in potency; that which already is, exists in act."[48] Everything that can change is still in potency; a perfect being, in no need of becoming (either for better or for worse), is pure act. Finally, this system distinguishes between *essence* and *existence,* between the "whatness" of a thing and its "thatness." This distinction does not mean that there are essences apart from concrete existence or that existence is a mere predicate of essence; it means, rather, that existence is the act that makes essence real.

Before applying this conceptual apparatus to Aquinas's articulation of God's nature and essence, we discuss the more foundational issue of how to posit God's existence in the first place. This takes us to the famous five ways of Thomism.

FIVE WAYS OF PROVING GOD'S EXISTENCE

The first thesis of the *Summa theologiae* states that the proposition "God exists," while evident in itself, is not evident for humans. Thus, Aquinas rejected the thesis of Anselm according to which the existence of God is a self-evident truth because the *idea* of God is a necessary thought. Thomism added to the canons of classical theism the conviction that the existence of God can be proved by arguments drawn from the universe, from creation. These arguments can be seen as a logical extension of the principle of analogy.

According to Aquinas, the first way to prove the existence of God begins with the fact of movement.[49] Everything in motion has to be moved by something; in the technical language of Thomism, it has to go from potency to act. Only one mover behind all others is not moved by another. Such a being, which may properly be called the prime or unmoved mover or pure act, is God.

The second way is that of causality. All things in the world have causes, and so there needs to be a final cause. If a first cause did not exist, the others would be nonexistent too. The first cause is God.

The third way is based on the distinction between the contingent and the necessary. All things in the world are contingent, dependent on something outside themselves. In a sense, they receive their existence from another being.

47. This distinction illustrates the competing philosophical schools of (Aristotelean) nominalism and (Platonic) realism. Realism believes in the existence of some "Idea," "form," or "universal" for each type of concrete thing (e.g., the Idea of chair in contrast to the countless number of different examples of chairs). Nominalism contends that such universals do not actually exist; they are just "names." Only concrete things (such as the chairs that we actually have in the world) exist. Aquinas sought a synthesis of these two views.

48. Quoted in González, *History of Christian Thought,* 265.

49. The five ways can be found in Thomas Aquinas, *Summa theologiae* I, q. 2, a. 3.

A being necessary in itself is needed to give existence to all other beings. For Aquinas, that being is God.

The fourth way builds on the idea of various degrees of perfection in beings. The being that is totally perfect and is the cause for the various degrees of perfection in all other beings is God.

The fifth way relates to the order evident in the world. All things seem to move toward an end proper to them. That could not happen without a purpose. This is the traditional teleological (Greek, *telos,* "end," "purpose," "goal") argument. That which leads things to their proper end or purpose is God.

It is easy to see that all five ways—sometimes Aquinas classified them differently[50]—follow the same logic. Each takes its departure from things known through the senses. Then it discovers in the known some good that is incomplete in the sense that it is not self-sufficient, be it movement, existence, degree of perfection, or something else. Each way, then, finds in God the final reason or perfection. Clearly, this way of "proving" God's existence presupposes at least some kind of idea of god.[51] As already mentioned, classical theists did not start as atheists or agnostics doubting the existence of God and trying to persuade themselves or others of God's existence. Rather, they were believers who wanted to demonstrate the reasonableness of the faith. It should also be noted that this kind of reasoning, apart from an appeal to biblical revelation, does not give evidence for the Christian God but for a general concept of God.

God's Nature and Attributes

What kind of God was Aquinas's God? Following his metaphysics, Aquinas affirmed that God is a substance, analogous to (but not identical with) other substances, and that like them God has properties, usually called attributes. For Aquinas, God is not a non-being but the supreme being, an ever active power. According to Edmund Fortman:

> The leading idea running through his [Aquinas's] whole system is that every finite being is made up of act and potency, essence and existence. Existence brings the potency of an essence into act, but is itself limited by that potency. This distinction between essence and existence is vital; it is the shibboleth of Thomism. It is because God alone is subsistent being, without distinction between his essence and existence, that he is all-perfect. And it is ultimately from contingent being that we deduce the existence of God.[52]

In one way or another, Aquinas deduced all the attributes of God from the being of God. These attributes concern the nature and operations of God in himself and *ad extra,* in relation to the world. The attributes relating to the

---

50. Aquinas, *Summa contra gentiles* 1.13 contains another kind of classification that gives preeminence to the first way, that is, the idea of the Prime Mover.

51. See the helpful discussion in González, *History of Christian Thought,* 266–67.

52. Fortman, *Theology of God,* 175.

being of God are first the properties of being in general, raised to their supreme perfection: simplicity or oneness, truth, goodness or perfection. Then come infinity, which excludes all limitations of essence; immensity and ubiquity, which exclude all limitations of space; and eternity, which excludes temporal limitations. "Lastly, with regard to our natural knowledge, the Being of God is invisible and incomprehensible, yet nevertheless knowable by analogy."[53]

To gain insight into how God and his attributes are viewed in the Thomistic system, we can take as an example God's knowledge. It is universal. Its primary object is the divine essence inasmuch as this explicitly contains all the attributes and the relations of the Trinity. But it also extends to every other object, both all possible beings and all beings actually called into existence in the past, present, and future.[54] God perceives the latter not in themselves but in himself, in that he decrees these things to exist long before they come into actual existence. They are present to him for all eternity.[55] In Aquinas's opinion, to say that God's knowledge of things derives from things themselves would be to ascribe imperfection to God: Infinite intelligence would depend on the finite.[56] God's perfection is not dependent on anything outside of God. God is completely self-sufficient in his being.

One of Aquinas's most debated contributions to the doctrine of God is his insistence on divine impassibility, an attribute closely related to God's immutability. Because God is perfect, he is immutable: Neither his knowledge nor his will changes.[57] In line with Aristotelian metaphysics, Aquinas maintained that the divine being must be "pure action without the admixture of any potentiality, because potentiality itself is later than action. Now everything which in any way is changed is in some way in a state of potentiality, whence it is obvious that God cannot be changed."[58] God cannot be acted upon, being completely perfect. But what about emotions? Scripture seems to suggest that God feels emotions. In response, Aquinas made a distinction between two kinds of emotions: Love and joy truly exist in God. Sadness and anger, however, can be attributed to God only metaphorically, since they imply imperfection. Once again, whatever is in God internally does not compromise God's absolute perfection; whatever is a result of God being acted upon is impossible according to Aquinas's notion of God.[59]

Aquinas joined the tradition of attributing blessedness to God. To say that God is eternally blessed means that God rejoices in the outpouring of goodness, mercy, and love on creatures. The blessedness of God, or the divine beatitude,

53. Ibid., 183–84.
54. See, for example, Aquinas, *Summa theologiae* I, q. 14, a. 2, 9.
55. Ibid., I, q. 14, a. 8.
56. See Fortman, *Theology of God,* 185.
57. Aquinas, *Summa theologiae* I, q. 14, a. 5.
58. Ibid., IIA, q. 22, a. 1.
59. See Millard J. Erickson, *God the Father Almighty: A Contemporary Exploration of the Divine Attributes* (Grand Rapids: Baker, 1998), 147–48.

means that God's life is full of joy, both within the Godhead and in relation to creatures. Aquinas defines God's blessedness in this way: God "has whatever he wills and . . . wills nothing evil."[60]

When listing attributes of God, Aquinas makes use of the analogical way of speaking. There is a scale of degrees of excellence. When speaking of God, therefore, Aquinas attributes to him the height of goods and perfections. They are analogous to what is known in part but are beyond complete knowing.[61]

ON THE TRINITY

In regard to the doctrine of the Trinity, Aquinas followed in the footsteps of Augustine. He also widely discussed Anselm's trinitarian proposal. On the one hand, Aquinas affirmed the Augustinian insistence on the unity of the Godhead as the starting point for his doctrine. For Aquinas, the unifying divine nature (God's substance) is a rational-intellectual essence, that is, an eternal mind without temporal thought. However, an intellectual nature requires some degree of multiplicity in the same way that love does. And, indeed, God is both intellect and love. This is the gateway for Aquinas to affirm, on the other hand, plurality in the Godhead:

> The intellectual love of the Father gives rise to the eternal begetting of the Son who is distinct from the Father only in being generated (begotten) by him from all eternity. The love between the Father and Son gives rise to the eternal procession of the Holy Spirit from both of them as their "bond of love" which is distinct from them only in proceeding forth from them eternally.[62]

God as Being: John Duns Scotus

Another giant from the thirteenth century is John Duns Scotus. Without doubt he represents the zenith of the Augustinian-Franciscan tradition, the other mainstream movement during the later medieval era.

While John Duns Scotus, the "Subtle Doctor," never reached the heights of scholarship of the "Angelic Doctor," Thomas Aquinas, his contribution to Christian theology of God cannot be dismissed.[63] His somewhat ambiguous way of writing, coupled with serious textual problems in his works, makes him a challenging theologian to study. Basically a Franciscan theologian, he focused on practical piety. While continuing the Augustinian tradition, he wanted to revise its epistemology. He also found Aquinas's approach less than satisfactory. According to Scotus, the

---

60. Quoted in Oden, *Living God*, 128.
61. See ibid., 47–48.
62. Roger E. Olson and Christopher A. Hall, *The Trinity* (Grand Rapids: Eerdmans, 2002), 64.
63. In my exposition of Scotus, I am heavily indebted to a helpful discussion in González, *History of Christian Thought*, 307–11.

Augustinian doctrine of illumination could easily lead one to consider God the proper object of human intelligence, while the Aristotelian-Thomist position seemed to suggest that the human intellect has as its proper object the essence of material things. Both are problematic. Even at its best, human knowledge of God is neither direct nor primary. On the other hand, even if Aquinas's approach of gaining knowledge of God through knowledge of the world is correct in principle, it cannot give a satisfactory answer to how to move beyond material objects. Thus, Scotus was not content with the doctrine of analogy.

How did Scotus resolve this dilemma? For him, the proper object of the human intellect is being, being as being, without qualification. The fact that "being" is known to humans implies that "being" can be predicated of all beings without distinction. Here, of course, Scotus differs from Aquinas, who suggested that God's being and the being of the rest of creation are analogous, not identical kinds of being.

In contrast, Scotus's univocal predication of being lays the foundation for his proof of the existence of God on the basis of being itself. Since being is always predicated univocally, it must be predicated of God in the same sense as of creatures. Scotus identified pairs of characteristics of being—necessary and contingent, infinite and finite, uncreated and created, and so on—and stated that one characteristic in each pair must apply to every being. He then reasoned that because beings exist that possess the imperfect characteristics of these pairs, a being must exist that possesses the perfect characteristics of the same pairs. One can see that Scotus's reasoning uses some aspects of both Anselm's ontological and Aquinas's cosmological approaches. It resembles the Anselmian view in its starting point: reflections on the notion of being rather than on the created world. Yet Scotus basically uses *a posteriori* reasoning (based on observed facts), as did Aquinas, in that he begins with the existence of concrete beings.[64]

The God of Scotus shares all the traditional attributes such as simplicity, immutability, omniscience, and so on. Yet a feature in Scotus's doctrine of God distinguishes his system from Thomism. Aquinas, in line with his Dominican orientation, focused on God's intellect. For Scotus, the emphasis is on God's will. Scotus, unlike Aquinas, did not spend much time trying to figure out the reasons for God's actions. His answer was simple: "There is no reason except that will is will."[65] Yet this God was not a capricious God: In God, who is absolutely simple, reason and will are the same.

The Rise of the Social Model of the Trinity

Theological work on the Trinity declined in creativity and depth after the patristic era (around A.D. 500 to 600). Many theologians, especially in the Latin

---

64. See ibid., 310–11.
65. John Duns Scotus, *Ordinatio* 1, dist. 8, part 2, q. 1.24.

West, regarded Augustine's *Trinity* as the last word. High and late medieval thinkers, however, built on the tradition and also advanced the discussion.[66] Based on the groundbreaking work of the Cappadocians, a social model of the Trinity arose, an idea recently embraced by many (e.g., Jürgen Moltmann).

For Hugh of St. Victor, a mystically oriented theologian of the eleventh century, the doctrine of the Trinity was not only a matter of intellectual speculation but also a divine mystery to be celebrated. While affirming both Augustine's view of the unity of the Godhead as the starting point of the doctrine and Anselm's basic views, Hugh reintroduced to medieval theology the importance of the doctrine of the attributions. This doctrine holds that, while all the works of the Trinity in relation to the world are indivisible, distinctive works can be appropriated to each member in the Trinity. This principle helps Christians contemplate the grace of a particular person of the Trinity and praise him for it without implying a separation of the being of God.[67]

Richard of St. Victor, Hugh's student, shared his teacher's desire to approach the Trinity not merely from a logical viewpoint but also from a more mystical and spiritual one. Richard found a personalist orientation in Augustine's doctrine of the Trinity that allowed him to highlight the distinctiveness of the Father, Son, and Spirit yet without compromising their underlying unity. In his *On the Trinity* (never fully translated into modern English), Richard began with the persons of the Father, Son, and Spirit and with human persons in community. He attempted to demonstrate that unity of essence is required by the perfect love that exists between persons who are distinct from one another in some way. He suggested a new understanding of "person" as "an incommunicable existence of the divine nature." There must be three such "persons" in God, he then argued. Why? Because God is love, as the Bible affirms:

> That is because perfect love is always directed toward what is distinct from and in some sense outside the self. Self-love is imperfect love. God's love must be perfect *and* not in any way dependent upon the creation. Thus, God's love must be other-directed within God himself. This is why there must be at least two persons (incommunicable existents) within God: the lover and the beloved.[68]

Richard's main insight, which focused on God's intratrinitarian love, provided an alternative to the dominant Augustinian/Thomistic interpretation. So far so good, but naturally a question arises: Might there be only two persons in the Godhead? Richard reasoned that love between two is less perfect than love between three. There is always an element of selfishness in the mutual love of only two persons. To make love perfect, yet another member has to

---

66. An up-to-date, concise introduction to the doctrine of the Trinity in the Middle Ages, strongly recommended as an introduction to key figures and movements, is Olson and Hall, *Trinity,* 51–67.

67. Ibid., 58.

68. Ibid., 59.

be added to the circle. Richard concluded that perfect love "cannot be had without a Trinity of persons."[69] Of course, this answer does not eliminate further questions, such as, would yet another member, or several more, in the circle make the love even more perfect? Despite these logical problems, Richard of St. Victor's idea of sociality in God has been enthusiastically embraced among thinkers as diverse as liberation theologians, feminists, and Jürgen Moltmann.

Reflections on Medieval Theology of God

This selective survey of approaches to the doctrine of God from the sixth century to the eve of the Reformation in the sixteenth century is a testimony to the dynamic and force of classical theism. Building on the foundational developments of the fathers, the Western wing of the church drew out the full implications of a doctrine of God in the philosophical-theological atmosphere of the times. One of the key concerns was to begin with proving the existence of God, not so much to convince unbelieving minds as to encourage believing hearts to have full confidence in the truth of the Christian message.

The rise of scholasticism welded philosophy and theology. Distinct, but never in opposition, these two disciplines served the common cause of Christendom, which in the high medieval period achieved an incomparable earthly status. For us today, living in fragmented, postmodern times, it is almost impossible to envision a world in which not only theologians but also the best of the academy sharpened their tools to establish the truth of Christian doctrine based on the biblical witness and patristic tradition.

Nevertheless, there is no homogeneity in classical theism. Undoubtedly, the major strand of theism, as advanced by Thomas Aquinas and his school, reached almost a canonical status with its highly speculative yet tradition- and Bible-based approach, utilizing both Platonic and Aristotelian philosophies. It is an example of a highly contextualized approach to the doctrine of God. At the same time, however, both in the Latin West and especially in the Christian East, divergent movements arose within classical theism. The mystical, apophatic theology of the Eastern church and the mystical strand in the West represent traditions of classical theism that differed widely from the orientation of the Dominicans. Even the two leading schools of high scholasticism, Dominican and Franciscan, had profound differences. In addition, even the views of authorities such as Augustine received various hearings: The social model of the Trinity offered a new reading of Augus-

69. Edmund J. Fortman, *The Triune God: A Historical Study of the Doctrine of the Trinity* (London: Hutchinson & Co., 1972), 193.

tine that complemented the established view, which focused on the unity of the Godhead.

As we move next to the Protestant Reformers' views, the proliferation of Christian doctrines of God becomes even more evident. Martin Luther and John Calvin, the main figures in the next section, while standing on the shoulders of Augustine, other fathers, and the entire medieval tradition, reappropriated the heritage of classical theism in different ways.

6

The Reformers on God

Changing Foci

In both the ancient and the medieval eras, discussions of God for the most part emphasized the metaphysical. In other words, theology had to do with God as he is in himself, the absolute, changeless, and eternal being. Things began to change, however, during the Protestant Reformation as focus shifted from metaphysics to a "God-for-us" emphasis.

For example, even though John Calvin emphasized the sovereignty of God, he focused on the implications of God's sovereignty for salvation rather than God's sovereignty in and of itself. While Martin Luther struggled with the problem of God's will, he did not merely discuss the superiority of God's will to God's intellect. Rather, he focused on the connection between God's will and sin and justification.[1]

The Crucified God: Martin Luther

Martin Luther is known as the theologian of justification by faith. What is less known is that the structuring principle of Luther's theology is the idea of two kinds of theology: theology of glory and theology of the cross. This

1. See Gerald Bray, *The Doctrine of God* (Downers Grove, Ill.: InterVarsity, 1993), 105; see also pages 199–201 for the differences between the Reformers' approach to God and that of their predecessors.

distinction goes back to the formative years of Luther's spiritual and theological career.

In April 1518, Luther presided over the disputation of the chapter of his Augustinian order at Heidelberg. The disputation concerned a series of theses Luther had drawn up for the occasion. The result was a new phrase, namely, *theologia crucis,* "theology of the cross." Most recent Lutheran scholars agree that *theologia crucis,* far more than being just *a* topic among others, is *the* programmatic theme underlying all of Luther's theology.[2] For Luther, a true theologian approaches the question of God from the perspective of the cross: "That person does not deserve to be called a theologian who looks upon the invisible things of God as if they were clearly perceptible in those things which have actually happened. . . . He deserves to be called a theologian, however, who comprehends the visible and manifest[3] things of God seen through suffering and the cross."[4]

The Heidelberg Disputation culminated in a thesis that may be regarded as the key theme for Luther's theology and doctrine of God: "The love of God does not find, but creates, that which is pleasing to it. . . . Rather than seeking its own good, the love of God flows forth and bestows good."[5] Human love is oriented toward something inherently good. God's love, however, is directed toward something that does not exist in order to create something new. According to Luther, "This is the love of the cross, born of the cross, which turns in the direction where it does not find good which it may enjoy, but where it may confer good upon the bad and needy person."[6] God's love is not found where one would assume it to be, namely, in heaven among the powerful, religious, good. On the contrary, God's love—and therefore the possibility of any kind of true knowledge of God—is found "hidden under its opposites."[7] God seemingly conceals himself in lowliness to reveal the greatness of his love.

Luther at times describes the works of God with biblical imagery. By citing the verse "The Lord kills and brings to life; he brings down to Sheol and raises up,"[8] Luther introduces a major aspect of his "theology of paradoxes": God's alien work *(opus alienum Dei)* and God's proper work *(opus proprium*

---

2. For a helpful guide, see Alister E. McGrath, *Luther's Theology of the Cross* (Oxford: Oxford University Press, 1985). My exposition is heavily indebted to Kari Kopperi, *Paradoksien teologia: Lutherin disputaatio Heidelbergissä 1518* [*Theology of Paradoxes: Luther's Disputation in Heidelberg 1518*], (Saarijärvi: Gummerrus, 1997).

3. Surprisingly, here the English translation is not only inadequate but also misleading, as it gives almost the opposite idea from the original: The term *posteriora (Dei)* means literally "rearward," i.e., God's back (referring to Luther's exposition of Exodus 33, where Moses is allowed to see only God's back instead of his face).

4. *Heidelberg Disputation* [= *HDT*], 19, 20; *Luther's Works* [= *LW*] 55 vols., ed. Jaroslav Pelikan (St. Louis: Concordia, 1955–1986), 31:52.

5. *HDT* 28; *LW* 31:57.

6. *HDT* 28; *LW* 31:57.

7. *HDT* 20; *LW* 31:52; see also *HDT* 17; *LW* 31:44.

8. 2 Samuel 2:6 (Luther mistakenly refers to 1 Kings 2:6).

Dei). God's alien work involves putting down, killing, taking away hope, even leading to desperation. God's proper work is the opposite: forgiving, giving mercy, taking up, saving, encouraging, and so on.[9] Luther calls the alien work "the works of the left hand" and the proper work "the works of the right hand." It is important to understand that, while these two kinds of works seem to be the opposite of each other, they result from the same love of God. Luther in fact says that God's proper work is veiled in his alien work and takes place simultaneously with it.[10] The purpose of the alien work of God is not to scare human beings but to help them recognize the true God, a God of love and care. God's love is directed toward the sinful, weak, and "nothing" to make them holy, strong, and wise.[11]

To show the paradoxical nature of his theology of the cross, Luther goes so far as to say that God's works are not just veiled in their opposite but also sometimes create bad results.[12] To illustrate his point, Luther compares the working of God in the world to a worker with a bad axe: Although the worker himself is skillful, because of the tool the results are bad. Furthermore, Luther argues that at times God uses even Satan for his *opus alienum* in order to work out his *opus proprium.*[13]

The God who acts in this way is a hidden God. Whereas the theologian of glory looks for God in majesty and glory, the theologian of the cross observes God in the shame and lowliness of the cross.[14] In Exodus 33:18–23, when Moses asks God to show his face, God responds, "But . . . you cannot see my face, for no one may see me and live" (33:20). Instead, Moses is allowed to see God's back. On the basis of this event, Luther differentiates between God's visible properties, such as the humility and weakness shown in the cross, and God's invisible properties, such as virtue, divinity, wisdom, justice, and benevolence.[15] A theology of glory goes astray in that it "calls evil good and good evil" (it calls wisdom, power, and glory "good" but the weakness and death of the cross "bad"), whereas, "a theology of the cross calls the thing what it actually is."[16] For Luther, there is a great difference between knowing that there is a God and knowing what or who God is. "Reason knows only that God is, not who he is and who is the true God."[17]

What was Luther's contribution to the doctrine of the Trinity? Here as elsewhere he wanted to be in the first place a faithful student of the patristic

9. *LW* 14:95.
10. *HDT* 16; *LW* 31:50.
11. *HDT* 16; *LW* 31:50–51.
12. *HDT* 5, 6; *LW* 31:45.
13. *HDT* 6; *LW* 31:45.
14. *HDT* 20; *LW* 31:52.
15. *HDT* 20; *LW* 31:52.
16. *HDT* 21; *LW* 31:53.
17. Wolfhart Pannenberg, *Systematic Theology,* vol. 1 (Grand Rapids: Eerdmans, 1991), 348.

and later Christian tradition. He gladly affirmed the unity of God as one eternal, undivided, divine essence and the threeness of the persons as eternal distinctions within that one shared essence. Yet he appealed to an incomprehensibility within God beyond which reason must not go: "How this intertrinitarian relation is carried on is something we must believe; for even to the angels, who unceasingly behold it with delight, it is unfathomable. And all who have wanted to comprehend it have broken their necks in the effort."[18] Thus, Luther eschewed speculation into the inner life of God. Yet at the same time, he insisted, against those who wanted to discard the doctrine, that it is necessary for salvation.[19]

Several distinctive aspects of Luther's view of the Trinity are worth mentioning. First of all, he maintained that the Trinity is not part of the hiddenness of God. The trinitarian God is revealed in Jesus Christ. Luther found testimony to the unity of the hidden and revealed God in biblical statements such as John 14:9: "Anyone who has seen me has seen the Father."[20] Second, Luther insisted on the distinctness of the three persons, not unlike the Cappadocians. Third, his trinitarian doctrine echoed some of the key themes of the social model of Richard of St. Victor: The three persons of God can be seen as distinct persons of love in community. According to authors Roger E. Olson and Christopher A. Hall, "It would be misleading to claim Luther as an example or advocate of the 'social analogy' of the Trinity, but he certainly was not locked into the Augustinian psychological analogy that tended to reduce the persons of God to mere relations of origin."[21]

The Sovereign God: John Calvin

Luther's younger Reformed colleague of Geneva, John Calvin, opens his magnum opus, the *Institutes of the Christian Religion* (which underwent several extensive revisions before taking its final form in 1559) by asserting that knowledge consists of two parts: knowledge of God and knowledge of self.[22] A look at our sinful nature and insufficiency shows our need for true knowledge of God. Yet one should start with knowledge of God and then move to knowledge of self, for "it is clear that man never achieves a clear knowledge of himself unless he has first looked upon God's face, and then descends from

18. Quoted in Ewald M. Plass, ed., *What Luther Says: A Practical In-Home Anthology of Luther for the Active Christian* (St. Louis: Concordia Publishing, 1959), 1385.

19. Roger E. Olson and Christopher A. Hall, *The Trinity* (Grand Rapids: Eerdmans, 2002), 69.

20. Quoted in Pannenberg, *Systematic Theology,* 340.

21. Olson and Hall, *Trinity,* 69.

22. John Calvin, *Institutes of the Christian Religion,* trans. Henry Beveridge (Grand Rapids: Eerdmans, 1972), 1.1.1.

contemplating him to scrutinize himself."[23] Knowledge of God is given through two means: creation and Scripture.

Calvin affirmed a general knowledge of God apart from special revelation. Within every person is a natural awareness of divinity, as even the practice of idolatry testifies.[24] General knowledge of God is based on the *sensus divinatis,* a God-given means of awareness of God's existence. The three effects of *sensus divinatis* are the universality of religion, which because of sin manifests itself in idolatry, "the servile fear of God," and the troubled conscience.[25] For Calvin, creation as the "theatre of God" points to God: God's power is manifested through the beauty of creation and its order.[26] This knowledge, however, apart from special revelation, does not bring about true knowledge of God.[27]

The limitations of general knowledge of God are due, on the one hand, to sinfulness. On the other hand, they are the result of the great distance between Creator and creature. We cannot know God, not only because we are sinners but also because we are finite creatures and God is infinite. This means we must not seek to know God in his highest glory but only as he is revealed, mainly through Scripture.[28] The revelation in Scripture goes beyond what can be learned from creation by providing knowledge of the Trinity; creation, including angels and demons; the original state of human beings; and God's particular providence.[29]

Revelation of God, even though indispensable for true knowledge of God, does not make the divine essence known to us, since that is too much for limited humans: "Those who propose to enquire what the essence of God is, only delude us with frigid speculations, it being much more our interest to know what kind of being God is, and what things are agreeable to his nature."[30] Yet God makes sure that the Bible reveals enough so that we can sort out true knowledge of God from falsehood. Scripture talks about God through "anthropomorphism" and "accommodation," adapting the language of God so that it is suitable for our limited understanding.[31] Calvin divides knowledge of God into two distinct yet related spheres: knowledge of God as Creator and knowledge of God as Redeemer.[32]

Interestingly, Calvin devotes a great deal of attention to the doctrine of demons, much more than to angels. However, his interest is not the kind of

23. Ibid., 1.1.2.
24. Ibid., 1.3.1.
25. Ibid., 1.5.15.
26. Ibid., 1.5.1–3.
27. Ibid., 1.5.4, 12–14.
28. Justo L. González, *A History of Christian Thought,* vol. 3, *From the Protestant Reformation to the Twentieth Century,* rev. ed. (Nashville: Abingdon, 1987), 138; Calvin, *Institutes* 1.13.21.
29. See Edmund J. Fortman, ed., *Theology of God: Commentary* (New York: Bruce Publishing, 1968), 231.
30. Calvin, *Institutes* 1.2.3.
31. See González, *History of Christian Thought,* 138.
32. Calvin, *Institutes* 1.14.1–2.

speculation of Pseudo-Dionysius or other medieval figures. Rather, it arises out of a practical concern related to the Christian life and is part of his view of God as sovereign. The existence of the devil and his troops is related to the divine will and predestination.

Calvin is well-known for his doctrine of predestination, and many scholars have declared it the center of his theology. It is not the center of his theology, however, but one of its key themes. The doctrine grew and developed as Calvin revised the *Institutes*, finally occupying a place among his doctrine of salvation and the Christian life.[33] According to Calvin, "We call predestination God's eternal decrees, by which he determined with himself what he willed become of each man."[34] Calvin is always primarily an expositor of the Bible, and so he sees the doctrine of election running through the pages of the Old Testament and the New. To defend the sovereignty of God and God's transcendence, Calvin makes it clear that

> God's decree of election does not depend on divine foreknowledge. Predestination is not simply God's decision to deal with a person according to what God foreknows regarding that person's future actions and attitudes. On the contrary, the fact that election is a sovereign decree means that it does not depend on any human action, past, present, or future. It is an independent decision on God's part.[35]

In contrast to the sophisticated medieval inquiries into the meaning and role of the divine will in the Godhead, Calvin's interests lie in its relation to the Christian life. It is part of his doctrine of justification by faith, assuring the elect of the power of God to save them, and it lays the foundation for Calvin's doctrine of the church, the community of the elect.

Another key motif in Calvin's doctrine of God is the glory of God. God's mighty works in creation and providence testify to his glory and sovereignty. One's free surrender to the providence and sovereignty of God, rather than being a burdensome duty, should appeal to one as a way to add to God's glory. Those who refuse such surrender seek to rob God of glory and thereby show their own rebelliousness.

> Therefore, let all the glory be to God. God's is the glory, not only in the elect, but also in the reprobate, who are also fulfilling the divine will. For even the evil and reprobate are doing the *hidden* will of God. Their evil is in resisting God's *revealed* will, and for this they will be punished. But they are still in the hands of God, who uses their evil for justice and for the divine glory.[36]

33. Ibid., 3.21–24.
34. Ibid., 3.21.5.
35. González, *History of Christian Thought*, 158, with reference to Calvin, *Institutes* 3.22.1–7.
36. González, *History of Christian Thought*, 143, italics in text, with reference to Calvin, *Institutes* 1.17.5, 1.18.1.

Despite his insistence on God's sovereignty and glory, Calvin does not champion a capricious God. God is never merely sovereign. He is sovereignly good, sovereignly just, and sovereignly merciful and gracious. "The dimension of sovereignty or gratuitousness is never permitted to condition or to control the mercy of God, so that he might become suddenly and arbitrarily not merciful, not just, and not good."[37]

A related question concerns the way Calvin deals with the topic of God's emotions. He deals with the issue in his extensive biblical commentary writings. In commenting on Genesis 6:6, he writes:

> The repentance which is here ascribed to God does not properly belong to him, but has reference to our understanding of him. . . . That repentance cannot take place in God easily appears from this single consideration, that nothing happens which is by him unexpected or unforeseen. The same reasoning, and remark, applies to what follows, that God was affected with grief.[38]

Calvin then goes on to deny that God can be sorrowful or sad; rather, God "remains for ever like himself in his celestial and happy repose." When the Bible implies otherwise, it is using anthropomorphism.[39]

The Trinity is one of the aspects of knowledge of God that is revealed in the Bible. For Calvin, this knowledge is not available elsewhere. Calvin follows the orthodox tradition, even though he is aware that the terminology used is not found in Scripture. He accepts it, however, as a means of expressing clearly the doctrine of the Bible against heretics.[40]

The theology of the Protestant Reformers was consolidated over two centuries, and then the doctrine of God faced new challenges from the Enlightenment and subsequent intellectual movements such as classical liberalism, which transformed the canons of theology. The last chapter of this historical survey inquires into the developments that took place in post-Reformation times, roughly the time of modernity to the second half of the twentieth century.

37. Fortman, *Theology of God,* 236.

38. John Calvin, *Commentaries on the First Book of Moses Called Genesis* (Grand Rapids: Baker, 1979), 1:248–49.

39. Millard J. Erickson, *God the Father Almighty: A Contemporary Exploration of the Divine Attributes* (Grand Rapids: Baker, 1998), 148–49.

40. See González, *History of Christian Thought,* 140.

7

The Modern Quest for God

Before discussing the leading philosophical, theological, and religious developments that transformed the intellectual world after the Reformation, this chapter inquires into the ideas of René Descartes, often dubbed "the father of modern philosophy," and his younger colleague Blaise Pascal. They were the forerunners of the modern approach to the doctrine of God.[1]

From the Certainty of the Self to the Certainty of God: René Descartes

The seventeenth-century French philosopher René Descartes, a pupil of the Jesuits, devoted his extraordinary intellectual skills to finding a sure foundation and method for human knowledge. Having been trained as a mathematician, he desired to find the kind of unconditional, absolute certainty in philosophy and theology that seemed to be available in the sciences. These rules he presented in his famous *Discourse on Method* (1637).

To accomplish his ambitious task, Descartes claimed to leave behind every dogmatic starting point and every presupposition. He, as a thinking subject,

1. The massive study by Philip Clayton, *The Problem of God in Modern Thought* (Grand Rapids: Eerdmans, 2000) puts all students in its debt. An older but more accessible source for beginning students is the careful survey offered by Hans Küng, *Does God Exist? An Answer for Today* (Garden City, N.Y.: Doubleday & Doubleday, 1980). I consulted both of these works for this book.

found himself "as if forced to become my own guide."[2] Thus, the essence of the Cartesian method—Descartes's name in Latin is Cartesius, and therefore his philosophy is often called Cartesianism—is to doubt all knowledge derived from one's senses. The only thing one can assume is the certainty of purely rational knowledge. Descartes's method, however, does not involve skepticism about the possibility of knowledge, nor does it involve agnosticism regarding the existence of God. Descartes was convinced of the possibility of absolute truth, and therefore he set out to find the true method to attain it. In addition, he was a believer, not a denier of God.[3]

According to Descartes, before attempting to prove the existence of God or the world, one has to find a foundation for knowing one's own existence. Descartes has been credited with proposing "a method by which the human self establishes the existence of itself and of reality by its own process of thinking."[4] Descartes's classical ontological reasoning is based on the principle of doubt as set forth in his *Discourse on Method*. He notes that he was ready to "reject as absolutely false anything of which I could have the least doubt, in order to see whether anything would be left after this procedure which could be called wholly certain." Then comes the kernel of his method:

> Thus, as our senses deceive us at times, I was ready to suppose that nothing was at all the way our senses represented them to be. . . . Finally, as the same percepts which we have when awake may come to us when asleep without their being true, I decided to suppose that nothing that had ever entered my mind was more real than the illusions of my dreams. But I soon noticed that while I thus wished to think everything false, it was necessarily true that I who thought so was something. Since this truth, *I think, therefore I am (or exist),* was so firm and assured that all the most extravagant suppositions of the sceptics were unable to shake it, I judged that I could safely accept it as the first principle of the philosophy I was seeking.[5]

This is the famous *cogito ergo sum* ("I think, therefore I am"). With this premise, Descartes was certain he had established the foundation of knowledge in the mind's own experience of certainty.

From this point, before proving the existence of the world, he set out to prove the existence of God. He did not follow the Thomistic approach, which takes as its starting point the existence of contingent beings, from which it argues for the existence of God. Descartes was not willing to start from the

---

2. Quoted in Kung, *Does God Exist?* 7.
3. See Justo L. González, *A History of Christian Thought*, vol. 2, *From Augustine to the Eve of the Reformation,* rev. ed. (Nashville: Abingdon, 1987), 322–23.
4. Catherine Mowry LaCugna, *God for Us: The Trinity and Christian Life* (San Francisco: HarperSanFrancisco, 1992), 251.
5. René Descartes, *Discourse on Method and Meditations,* trans. Laurence J. Laufleur (Indianapolis: Bobbs-Merrill, 1960), 24.

world but only wholly and entirely from the self. His ontological orientation, therefore, leans toward that of Anselm of Canterbury (and Augustine before him). The difference between Descartes and Anselm, however, is that Descartes does not attempt to show that the idea of God makes the existence of God necessary. Descartes instead wants to know the origin of the idea of God that is in the thinking subject's mind. He concludes that within his mind is the idea of an infinite and perfect being. He attempts to doubt this idea, but he finds he cannot. He must, therefore, explain its existence. The only way he could have the idea of a perfect being is if it had been placed in his mind by such a being. His finite mind certainly could not of itself have conceived of such an idea, which is clearly greater than his mind. He could not have produced the idea of perfection and infinity. God himself planted it in him. Thus, Descartes regards the idea of God as an innate idea in human beings. But can we be sure that we are not deceiving ourselves or that we are not being deceived by an evil spirit? Descartes's response is simple: If God were a deceiving spirit, he could not be the most perfect being. "The concept itself or the idea of the perfect being therefore includes not only the existence but also the truthfulness and goodness of God. A deceiver-God is impossible."[6] From this point, the step to the material world is no longer difficult. The truthfulness and goodness of God guarantees the existence of the world.

Descartes did not see himself in opposition to theological tradition, even though many after him have interpreted his contribution in that way. Unlike many later modernists with their ideas of a "natural religion," Descartes never held such a thought and remained a faithful Catholic.[7] He affirmed that a consideration of God's attributes helps us investigate the truth of other things, since God is their cause. He spoke of God's omnipotence, immutability, and immensity (omnipresence). He conceived of God both as Creator and Sustainer. As Philip Clayton succinctly notes, "All of these factors make it somewhat ironic that Descartes has been credited by history with supplying the major impulse toward deism,"[8] let alone natural religion or atheism.

From the Risk of Faith to Trust in God: Blaise Pascal

Blaise Pascal, a younger contemporary of Descartes, had a radically different approach to the doctrine of God. Hans Küng sets the scene for Pascal's approach:

---

6. Küng, *Does God Exist?* 14; see also Clayton, *Problem of God in Modern Thought,* 63–65.
7. For the centrality of theology to Descartes, see Clayton, *Problem of God in Modern Thought,* 61–63.
8. Ibid., 72.

Certainty of knowledge is a long way from security of life. Not that we need to be always looking death in the face. By thinking, by clear and distinct thinking, it is possible—perhaps—to gain conceptual certainty, but never existential security. And "pure" mathematics in particular, with its absolute certainty, often contributes—as soon as it is "applied"—as much to the insecurity as to the security of human life.[9]

Pascal, a multitalented mathematician, physicist, engineer, as well as a widely read philosopher, was not content with the precision of Descartes's method but searched all his life for the "logic of the heart."[10] He acknowledged the value of the ideal of certainty in mathematics and sciences, but he seriously doubted if any such certainty could be attained in the humanities. He was also troubled by the dual nature of the human person, the greatness and the wretchedness, either of which could take the upper hand.

When looking for a foundation for his primarily existential questions, Pascal was confronted by two basic positions, either skepticism or dogmatism, neither of which appealed to him. Yet he knew he had to decide, for nondecision is a choice as well. His choice was this: to take the risk of believing in God, "in whose light both the greatness of man . . . and the wretchedness of man . . . can be explained."[11] How did a premier scientist come to this conclusion? The "God of Jesus Christ . . . can only be found by the ways taught in the Gospel. . . . He can only be kept by the ways taught in the Gospel."[12]

In contrast to Descartes, Pascal believed the ultimate ground of certainty, on which there can be no doubt, was not one's own self-awareness, not even an idea of God—whether acquired by reasoning or innate—but the God of the Bible.

The guiding methodological principle for Pascal, if there was one, was to avoid "two excesses: to exclude reason, to admit nothing but reason."[13] With a profound critical mind, Pascal noticed that certainty is lacking not only in questions of religion but also in most ordinary affairs. Life is full of uncertainties, yet we dare to take risks. Who can guarantee, he asked, one's safety at sea or in battle? To wait for full certainty would paralyze human life. What we can look for is a "rule of possibility." Applying the rules of the calculation of probabilities to the question of the existence of God, Pascal concluded that supposing God's existence is not a groundless dream, even though it can never be proved. And after all, choose one must. So one must make a responsible choice.[14]

Pascal had little interest, therefore, in the tradition of philosophical theology, which attempted to prove the existence of God. According to Küng, "What

9. Küng, *Does God Exist?* 42.
10. Ibid., 46.
11. Ibid., 56–57.
12. Ibid., 57–58.
13. Ibid., 60.
14. Ibid., 61.

is important to him [Pascal] is *not* the path *from conceptual certainty of the self to conceptual certainty of God,* but the path *from existential certainty* of God *to existential certainty of the self.*"[15]

What both Descartes and Pascal anticipated and prepared for, each in their own way, was a new intellectual era known as modernism. It broke through the homogenous culture of the medieval and Reformation eras with the emergence of the Enlightenment. To this intellectual watershed we now turn.

The Enlightenment as the Catalyst for a Radical Transformation of Theology

Immanuel Kant's remark "Have courage to use your own reason"[16] reflects the emerging worldview of the Enlightenment (from the German word *Aufklärung,* "clearing up") of the late seventeenth and eighteenth centuries. Belief in God was still possible—the Enlightenment was not necessarily a clarion call for atheism—but it was no longer possible on the basis of divine revelation in the Bible but on the basis of natural religion. This change is best illustrated in the provoking work by M. Tindal, *Christianity as Old as Creation, or, the Gospel a Republication of the Religion of Nature,* written in 1730. This book put Christianity on par with natural or "rational religion" and argued that there is no need for divine revelation. An earlier work by the leading English empiricist John Locke, *Reasonableness of Christianity* (1695), similarly argued for a religion that could be defined within the limits of reason and common sense. When Locke looked at the Bible, he found a simple faith and the call to a moral life, with nothing much contrary to reason. In Locke's reading of the Bible, Jesus exposed the errors of polytheism and idolatry, established a clear and rational morality, and reformed the worship of his time, freeing it of superstition. Locke could not find in Jesus' message any mention of the doctrine of the Trinity or many other traditional doctrines that had come to occupy major roles in Christian theology.

What makes the Enlightenment mentality different from that of previous eras (many of which also emphasized reason) is the *independent* use of reason, free from church authorities, divine revelation, and other people's tutelage. The Enlightenment concept of rationality and knowledge had already been anticipated by Descartes's faith in the capacity of human reasoning to attain undisputed truths. By replacing ancient superstitions, traditional religious convictions, and authorities, whether secular or ecclesiastical, the new methods of science promised to reveal the mysteries of the world and to remove the conditions of ignorance, poverty, and perhaps even war.

15. Ibid., italics in text.
16. Cited in William C. Placher, *A History of Christian Theology* (Philadelphia: Westminster, 1983), 237.

The most decisive turn for Christian theology was the rise to prominence of biblical and historical criticism. Whereas in the past the biblical text had been seen as a trustworthy historical account, now doubts and denials began to mount. Enlightenment theologians demanded that the Bible be studied as a historical document using the same methods and principles applied to the study of any other historical work. No traditional dogma escaped the critical eye of this new science. Hand in hand with biblical criticism came what is often called "doctrinal criticism." The seventeenth-century historian of theology J. F. W. Jerusalem noticed that several traditional dogmas, such as the two natures of Christ and the Trinity, were not found in the New Testament but were later products of the church. He believed, therefore, that these doctrinal aberrations should not be regarded as binding or legitimate but should be abandoned.

One of the stepchildren of the Enlightenment was classical liberalism, whose influence on the enterprise of Christian theology has been unsurpassed. Liberalism followed the new scientific and philosophical mind-set and, like the Enlightenment, championed the freedom of the individual thinker to criticize and reformulate beliefs free of authorities. The focus of theology was soon placed on the ethical dimension of Christianity rather than on metaphysical doctrines such as the essence of God or the Trinity. Along with confidence in the human ability to establish the truth of the Christian message, there was also a drift toward God's immanence at the expense of God's transcendence. Whereas orthodoxy posited a radical discontinuity between the natural and the supernatural, between God and humanity, liberalism suggested a continuity. This also meant a continuity between religions. In addition, religious truths were no longer conceived of as fixed formulae to be received by the faithful from the divine and ecclesiastical authorities but as learned human opinions that were constantly in need of revision and reshaping.

How all these changes translated into new conceptions of God beginning in the eighteenth century is the topic of the following discussion. The rest of this chapter discusses views of God in the philosophies and theologies of three intellectual giants: Immanuel Kant, Georg W. H. Hegel, and Friedrich D. E. Schleiermacher. This necessarily limited and selective discussion takes us to the beginning of the twentieth century.

God in the Realm of Practical Reason: Immanuel Kant

Any discussion of modernity must at least briefly consider Immanuel Kant, a philosopher who, on the one hand, destroyed all grounds for affirming the existence of God through metaphysical and scientific speculation yet, on the other hand, found God necessary for ethics and morality. Kant denied neither God nor God's existence. Instead, he pointed his critique at cheap metaphysical talk about God. In *Critique of Pure Reason* (1781), he did not find it possible to talk about God. However, he found God-talk possible in another context, what he defined as the realm of "practical reason." In his subsequent work, *Critique of Practical Reason* (1788), Kant located God in the area of ethics and morality. Consequently, he had to split reality into two spheres: the factual and the ethical. Kant located faith in the moral experience and claimed that we do not have knowledge of things in themselves *(noumena)* but only of their appearance *(phenomena)* or effects on us.[17]

To understand this fatal split of reality—later resisted forcefully by another giant of modern Western thought, Hegel—we need to look at Kant's epistemology, his theory of knowledge. Before Kant, the human mind was thought to be more or less a passive receptor of sensory and other experiences. Kant turned the tables around and maintained that the mind actively processes and shapes the raw material provided by the senses. The mind does this with the help of formal concepts present in human consciousness, such as space and time. This explains the distinction between things in themselves, outside of human knowledge, and their effects on the knower. With this subjectivistic turn, Kant limited knowledge to the realm of personal experience. There is no going back to metaphysical speculations apart from personal experience. Kant, of course, did not deny that metaphysical ideas such as God may really exist; what he denied was the possibility of knowing whether or not they exist. In complete contrast to Aquinas and other champions of cosmological proofs for the existence of God, Kant argued that there is no way to read transcendent realities such as God, the immortal soul, and human freedom from sensory experience. Any reality that lies beyond the categories lodged within the human mind, especially space and time, cannot be known through the senses.[18]

Based on Kant's views, one would assume that Kant joined the growing number of Enlightenment thinkers to whom God was no real entity at all. Kant did not. Instead, his motto stated, "I have therefore found it necessary to deny knowledge, in order to make room for faith."[19] The goal of human intelligence is to inquire into not only "theoretical knowledge," the knowledge of how things are, but also "practical reason," the realm of duty and morality, what "ought" to be. Human beings are not only thinkers but also actors. Thus, the goal of human life is to become "practically" as rational as possible, in Kant's words, to live according to duty. Echoing Jesus' maxim, Kant's "categorical imperative" was: "Act as if the maxim of thy action were to become by thy will a Universal Law of Nature."[20] It is the job of religion to assist one in living a better moral life. However, the source of Kant's categorical imperative is not

---

17. Stated as a rule in Immanuel Kant, *Critique of Pure Reason,* trans. Norman Kemp Smith (New York: St. Martin's, 1929), 27.

18. See Stanley J. Grenz, *The Social God and the Relational Self: A Trinitarian Theology of the Imago Dei* (Louisville: Westminster John Knox, 2001), 75.

19. Kant, *Critique of Pure Reason,* 75.

20. Immanuel Kant, *Fundamental Principles of the Metaphysics of Morals,* trans. Thomas K. Abbott (Indianapolis: Bobbs-Merrill, 1949), 38.

religion. Rather, the categorical imperative is universally known. Therefore, nonreligious people are not excused.

This opens the way for Kant's affirmation of the existence of God. Nobody in this life will attain to the good life. Therefore, an afterlife is assumed that provides time for maturation. God is needed to provide such an afterlife. Thus, by reasoning about practical morality, Kant established the existence of God. Yet Kant was not a theologian, and he did not contribute to a coherent doctrine of God, even less the Trinity.

But what about the God of the Bible? Kant admitted that even though Christianity is an expression of natural religion, it is also a historical, particular religion. As a natural religion, it is not founded by anyone, not even Jesus Christ; Jesus was the one who taught this religion. This is the view of Kant's *Religion within the Limits of Reason Alone* (1793). It appealed to Enlightenment thinking in that it did not take revelation as its starting point but rather the use of reason.

God and the Absolute Spirit: Georg W. F. Hegel

Georg W. F. Hegel built on the foundation laid by Kant and others, but for him denying metaphysics was far too high a price to pay for meaningful God-talk. Hegel argued that if we cannot know or talk about things in themselves, how can we even say with Kant that they exist? Hegel's starting point was to locate religion, and thus God, in the realm of reason. Unlike Kant, Hegel joined theology with philosophy and by doing so gave speculative reason a crucial role in religion. However, he did this by anchoring his world-embracing philosophy in history. He maintained that what is most distinctive about history is its dynamic, developing nature. Therefore, according to Hegel, truth is a process and a dialectic, a view that is in harmony with his dynamic view of reality. Truth, rather than being a static concept, is the process of reasoning itself. Actually, for Hegel, truth is history.[21]

Hegel's main methodological idea is simple yet profound: There is an integral connection between the structure of thought and the structure of reality. As Stanley Grenz explains, "Rather than being the rational conclusions reached from the use of the proper reasoning pattern, . . . according to Hegel, truth is the process itself; truth is the whole, the ebb and flow, the twists and turns of the process of reasoning that eventually leads to resolution."[22] Furthermore, Hegel maintained that the reasoning process, a process that he appropriately called "conception," does not view its object as external to itself but as contained within itself. This process leads finally to the gathering of all conceptions into a connected whole, the Absolute.

21. See W. H. Walsh, *An Introduction to the Philosophy of History* (London: Hutchinson's University Library, 1951), 137ff.
22. Grenz, *Social God and the Relational Self,* 26.

On this basis, one can see that, for Hegel, there is an intrinsic connection between the historical process and the divine. Unlike the Enlightenment thinkers who looked to nature to find God as its Creator, Hegel sought the divine in "the Idea," the meaning lying behind the world process. Thus, he viewed all processes in nature and history as forming a "unified whole and thereby as the manifestation of an underlying spiritual principle, which he referred to as Spirit." The German term *Geist* has a wider meaning than "spirit" in English. It means both spirit and mind. This dual meaning of the concept helps to explain the rationalism of Hegel's system. The Spirit also denotes mind. "Reality for Hegel is Spirit: The universe is, in a sense, the product of mind and therefore intelligible to mind."[23] And so, the entire world process is the activity of the Spirit: "Through that process Spirit takes on objective form and comes to full awareness of itself."[24]

This takes us to the doctrine of God. God is not a transcendent creator of the world but rather a Spirit permeating everything.[25] God and the world are not two separate entities but belong together.[26] To be God, God has to create a world, but that world is God's creation and therefore not ultimately separate from God: "We define God when we say that He distinguishes Himself from Himself, and is an object for Himself, but that in this distinction He is purely identical with Himself, is in fact Spirit."[27] In fact, even God as Spirit is in the process of becoming. According to Clark H. Pinnock, Hegel had

> the vision of a God, present in all of history, becoming who God is, realizing God's own potentialities of being, through all the changes and contradictions. He viewed the world as God in God's development, as God externalizing God's own self in history and leading the world onward and upward in stages to God's own divine fullness. Reality itself is the history of God, God going out from and returning to God's own self.[28]

This concept of God, in turn, leads to Hegel's distinctive "trinitarian" view.[29] In the Godhead, there are three moments of divine reality. The Essential Being, pure, abstract being, resembles the role of the Father. The Explicit Self-Existence refers to the entrance of the abstract Spirit into existence through the creation

23. Walsh, *Introduction to the Philosophy of History,* 137.

24. Stanley J. Grenz and Roger E. Olsen, *Twentieth-Century Theology: God and the World in a Transitional Age* (Downers Grove, Ill.: InterVarsity, 1992), 33.

25. Even though Hegel rarely uses the term *God,* it is clear that for him Spirit is equivalent to the divine/God. See Robert C. Solomon, *From Rationalism to Existentialism: The Existentialists and Their Nineteenth-Century Backgrounds* (Lanham, Md.: Littlefield Adams, 1992), 52.

26. Hegel represents a kind of pantheism in which a clear line of demarcation between God/God's Spirit and the world/world spirit cannot be drawn.

27. Georg W. F. Hegel, *Hegel's Lectures on the Philosophy of History* (London: George Bell & Sons, 1890), 78, quoted in Placher, *History of Christian Theology,* 276.

28. Clark H. Pinnock, *Tracking the Maze: Finding Our Way through Modern Theology from an Evangelical Perspective* (Dallas: ICI University Press, 1996), 103.

29. A helpful, succinct exposition is offered in Grenz, *Social God and the Relational Self,* 26–29.

of the world (Son). God becomes part of that which is not God (creation). The Self-Knowledge is the Spirit passing into self-consciousness. God becomes fully conscious of himself through the historical process. The final goal of all historical happenings and the process of the Spirit is God returning to himself in humanity. This takes place in the religious life, in which humanity comes to know God as God knows himself. This is the final reconciliation within reality. In the incarnation of Christ, the idea of the unity of God and humankind was made explicit in history. The universal philosophical truth of the divine-human unity was actualized in a particular historical individual.[30]

God and the Feeling of Absolute Dependence: Friedrich D. E. Schleiermacher

With the blossoming of Romanticism, a movement of modernism that cherished emotions, beauty, and aesthetics over but not necessarily at the expense of pure rationality, many thinkers looked for new ways of appropriating their belief in God. Because Kantian and Cartesian rationalism were not dismissed, rationalism was coupled with and guided by aesthetics. The most transformative figure in this enterprise, the repercussions of which are still felt in Christian theology, was Friedrich D. E. Schleiermacher, routinely called "the father of modern theology." While Kant placed the locus of religion in ethics,[31] and Hegel placed it in reason, Schleiermacher suggested that the proper locus of religion is in *Gefühl*, "feeling," a subjective experience or intuition, or, as he put it, the "feeling of absolute dependence."[32] God is the ultimate ground for this feeling. It is important to note that in German, Schleiermacher's language and the language of theology at that time, *Gefühl* is a broader term than the English word *feeling*. It also means intuitive, pre-reflexive, and has to do with piety.

The central component in Schleiermacher's theology is the experience of "God-consciousness," the acknowledgment of being totally dependent on something outside oneself. Therefore, redemption for Schleiermacher involves the development of God-consciousness, the feeling of absolute dependence. This must pervade "the whole life, so that one's entire being is directed through the God-consciousness to the Kingdom of God."[33]

---

30. See Grenz and Olsen, *Twentieth-Century Theology,* 36–37.

31. By making this distinction between Kant and Schleiermacher, I am not denying the fact that Schleiermacher was also deeply in debt to Kant. He shared with Kant the refusal to connect religion with speculative reason and science and the desire to connect it with the practical realm. For this see Schleiermacher's opening comments in *The Christian Faith,* 2d ed., ed. H. R. Mackintosh (Edinburgh: T & T Clark, 1928), §2.

32. Ibid., §4.

33. Quoted in Gary D. Badcock, *Light of Truth and Fire of Love: A Theology of the Holy Spirit* (Grand Rapids: Eerdmans, 1997), 115.

Consequently, for Schleiermacher, religious experience is primary, theology secondary. Doctrinal formulae are historical and bound to a particular time and context and thus can never be absolute. Schleiermacher had no interest in metaphysical questions concerning the Spirit. The decisive focus was the Spirit's role with regard to human beings and Jesus' relationship with the Father.

> What this means, however, is that the Holy Spirit is the presence of God in the Christian community in awakening and animating the life of faith, discipleship of Christ, and therefore devotion to the kingdom of God. The same God present in Christ is present in the church, in other words, the only difference being that in the one case his presence was particular, while in the other case it is general and corporate in the ecclesial sense.[34]

The Spirit for Schleiermacher is effectively the spiritual influence left behind by Jesus that gives coherence to the life of the church as a spiritual entity and therefore to the life of Christian faith.[35] Schleiermacher ruled out metaphysical definitions of older trinitarian theology in favor of ethical and experiential ones. In Jesus' life, the absolute God-consciousness was mediated by the Spirit of God. The Holy Spirit is also the union of the divine essence with the human nature in the form of the common Spirit that exists among believers or among those who have been regenerated by Christ.[36]

By now it should be obvious that the doctrine of the Trinity as developed by Christian tradition held no interest for Schleiermacher. In fact, in his major systematic work, *The Christian Faith,* in almost eight hundred pages, the doctrine of the Trinity receives only fourteen pages. At the end of this book, Schleiermacher notes:

> We have only to do with the God-consciousness given in our self-consciousness along with our consciousness of the world; hence, we have no formula for the being of God in Himself as distinct from the being of God in the world, and should have to borrow any such formula from speculation, and so prove ourselves disloyal to the character of the discipline [theology] at which we are working.[37]

In other words, Schleiermacher did not delve into speculation about the doctrine of God in general and the Trinity in particular apart from the world and salvation history.

---

34. Ibid., 116.
35. Schleiermacher, *Christian Faith,* §§121–25.
36. Ibid., §123.
37. Ibid., §748.

Denial of the Existence of God: The Challenge of Modern Atheism

While it lies outside the scope of this book to give a detailed history of philosophical ideas of God, a brief discussion of the growing atheistic forces that came out of the Enlightenment are in order before summing up the historical survey. Once the view of the Bible as the provider of divine truth had been set aside, communication with other religions had begun to increase, and prospects for an earthly paradise had begun to appeal to the developers of science, what place was there for God? Kant was able to find a place for God through his rational reasoning, and Hegel championed a pantheistic idea of God with his Spirit interpretation. Schleiermacher pulled God down from the heavens and placed him within human consciousness. Others, however, found no place for God. The leading challenges from various atheistic movements[38] included the following:

- Friedrich Nietzsche pronounced God's death in the name of total human freedom. Any concept of a personal God would make freedom impossible.
- Ludwig Feuerbach saw God's existence as only an image projected into the skies by human consciousness.
- Sigmund Freud opposed belief in God because of its negative effects on the world and the individual.
- Karl Marx turned the Hegelian idealistic system upside down and opposed all notions of God as cheap escapes from facing the problems of real life. According to Marx, religion was the "opium of the masses" and a way for the rich to dominate.
- A final death blow, so it was supposed, to any idea of God was dealt by the powerful intellectual movement called logical positivism. All talk about God and other nonsensory topics was not only unfounded but totally senseless. Once philosophy becomes an exercise in analyzing language, no grounds for belief in metaphysics can be allowed.

38. In theological schools, it belongs to the realm of philosophy to tackle the issues of atheism in more detail. A good starter, written by a theologian-philosopher, is Küng, *Does God Exist?*

8

Reflections on the Historical Developments of Classical Theism

Now that this historical survey concerning the growth of traditions about God in both Western and Eastern theology has come to an end, it is time to reflect on the question, What is the shape of classical theism in light of historical developments?

Theologians agree that "the conventional doctrine of God [classical theism] has a double origin, in the Bible and in Greek thinking."[1] However, agreement stops there. Many theologians, especially process theologians and more recently Open theists (also known as free will theists, to be discussed later), see the connection of the classical doctrine of God to Greek philosophy as a major obstacle. They maintain, with various nuances, that deterioration—even perversion—of the doctrine as a whole began at that junction. Thus, there have been titles such as "The Pagan Dogma of the Absolute Unchangeableness of God"[2] or "Overcoming a Pagan Inheritance."[3] Once again, it is not the task of the present book to argue either for or against the validity of classical theism but simply to raise the question as to whether classical theism is what it has been claimed to be and whether the caricature often painted by its theological

1. Gerald H. O'Hanlon, *The Immutability of God in the Theology of Hans Urs von Balthasar* (Cambridge: Cambridge University Press, 1990), 1.
2. By R. B. Edwards in *Religious Studies* 14 (1978): 305–13.
3. Clark H. Pinnock, *Most Moved Mover: A Theology of God's Openness* (Grand Rapids: Baker Academic, 2001), title of chap. 2.

opponents is accurate. Several observations can be made on the basis of the historical data.

First, the dynamic, relational, narrative, diverse biblical testimonies concerning Yahweh of the Old Testament, the God of Jesus Christ and the early church, were expressed by early Christian theology using the categories and concepts of existing Greco-Roman philosophies. In line with the strict monotheism of the Old Testament, the fathers combated the polytheistic (and often pantheistic) conceptions of God in the surrounding religions, which they saw as contradictory to the biblical testimony. However, despite their caution not to baptize Christianity into any human philosophies—since for them Christianity was a religion of revelation—they were quite open to constructing the doctrine of God using Greek metaphysical and ontological categories. How could Christian theology defend its distinctive view of God apart from using terms understandable to the public? At the same time, early theology faced a struggle in trying to hold on to both the monotheism of Yahwehism and the emerging trinitarianism. In regard to trinitarian developments, Greco-Roman philosophical ontology was less successful than it was in the defense of monotheism.

Second, there is no doubt that subsequent theology throughout the Middle Ages and beyond, especially in post-Reformation Protestant orthodoxy and Catholic theology even after Vatican I at the end of the nineteenth century, took the views of the fathers as legitimate interpretations of the Bible and thus as normative. This survey has shown that the patristic traditions—themselves dynamic and varied—were not adopted indiscriminately but were further contextualized, especially by the skillful work of the scholastics. No doubt, much of the plurality of the biblical dynamic view of God was lost. Yet the canons of theism were developed in a way appropriate to the medieval hierarchic, nonegalitarian feudal society.

Third, from the beginning there was more than one interpretation of how to translate the doctrine of God into contemporary language. Eastern apophatic, mystical theology approached God quite differently than did the Latin-speaking West. The mystical strand, isolated geographically and in terms of mind-set, continued vigorously in the East. In the beginning centuries of the second millennium, this tradition reentered Western theology through medieval mysticism. The various approaches are a living testimony to the capacity of classical theism to incorporate a wide variety of influences.

Fourth, among classical theists, even those who wanted to stand in the ancient tradition going back to the fathers, there were some such as Martin Luther who almost turned the tables with their dynamic views of God. How can Luther's theology of the cross be reconciled with Anselm's and the scholastics' views? In reality, the term "classical theism" is a scholarly construction existing only in the minds of theologians, a generic concept drafted in hindsight to point out some dominant features in the development of the doctrine of God among Christian theologians.

Fifth, with the rise of the Enlightenment and subsequent developments, especially classical liberalism, the canons of Christian theology came under critical—albeit often hopelessly naïve—reappraisal. Though neither Georg W. F. Hegel's nor Friedrich D. E. Schleiermacher's view of God stands in the tradition of classical theism, both sought to express something contextually relevant on the basis of traditional Christian theology. Process theologians, Open theists, death-of-God theologians, liberationists, and feminists, among others, gained inspiration for their work by going back into history, especially the last three hundred years. Radical revisions of classical theism were underway long before A. N. Whitehead or P. T. de Chardin appeared in the twentieth century. Perhaps theologians would do well to consider the often creative ways both Eastern and Western Christianity attempted to speak to its context. Contextualizing is a risky business, and the short history of contextual theologies displays the difficulty of maintaining a balance between one's context and the biblical message. Contextualization as such is not a new phenomenon. Though it may be new as an acknowledged enterprise, in reality it has always been the approach of the Christian faith, whether in Greco-Roman, medieval, or Enlightenment culture.

On that note, we now move from a consideration of biblical and historical traditions concerning the doctrine of God to the contemporary scene. The next part continues the story of the rich, variegated, even conflicting testimonies concerning God, who is revealed as Yahweh in the Old Testament and the Father of Jesus Christ in the New Testament.

Part 3

God in Contemporary European Theologies

While Europe is no longer the world center for Christian theology, as it was until the first part of the twentieth century,[1] any survey of the doctrine of God must pay attention to European theologies, which, with all their limitations, have helped to shape global theology. Moreover, almost without exception, all non-Western and other contextual theologians have been trained in European or North American academies. Much contextual theology is still a response to and a dialogue with leading European theologians such as Karl Barth and Jürgen Moltmann.

This survey covers eight theologians who have written extensively on the topic of God and have interacted with the biblical and historical foundations of theistic traditions. They are representative both theologically and ecclesiastically. Karl Barth and Paul Tillich, two radically different thinkers who have roots in the classical liberalism of the turn of the twentieth century, represent the first part of the century. John Zizioulas, the most well-known and widely discussed theologian of the Eastern Orthodox tradition, represents the mystical, apophatic tradition of the East. Two Roman Catholic thinkers, Hans Küng and Karl Rahner, who both came to international fame as a result of

---

1. For changing trends at the global level with regard to the shape of Christianity, see Philip Jenkins, *The Next Christendom: The Coming of Global Christianity* (New York: Oxford University Press, 2001). We will come back to the implications of these changes when discussing non-Western theologies.

Vatican II (1962–65) but subsequently took dramatically different routes in their pilgrimage, respond to two interrelated challenges of late modernity in the West: How to speak meaningfully about God in light of secularism (Rahner) and atheistic/agnostic forces (Küng). Two leading Protestant theologians, the Lutheran Wolfhart Pannenberg and the Reformed Jürgen Moltmann, both desire to dialogue with and go beyond the intellectual challenges that began with the Enlightenment, especially those of Hegel, Schleiermacher, Kant, and others. Yet their theologies of God are markedly different. Pannenberg desires to do scientific theology, apparently free from contextual influences and based on reasoning and historical foundations, that could appeal to both Western and non-Western worlds. Moltmann seeks to speak to the political, social, and ecological challenges facing today's world. Finally, the British pluralist John Hick, who later established his residence in North America, exemplifies the most radical departure from classical theism: As a result of several moves from Christocentric to God-centric to reality-centric views, he by and large left behind the biblical and historical tradition of Christianity and works from a universalist worldview.

Any survey must necessarily be selective. Therefore, the following chapters do not cover many significant thinkers such as Søren Kierkegaard, the precursor to Christian existentialism; Rudolf Bultmann, the New Testament theologian who wanted to write a "demythologized" theology that would go beyond the ancient worldview of the Bible and would speak to the challenges of modernity; Eberhard Jüngel, the German theologian who envisioned "God-in-Becoming," thus paving the way for several orientations in the theologies of the latter part of the twentieth century, from process theology to the panentheism of Moltmann and others; Thomas F. Torrance, the Scottish theologian who focused on the relationship between science and faith and attempted to create a doctrine of God that built on both tradition and the challenges of (post-) modernity; and, among others, Helmut Thielicke of Germany, whose *Evangelical Faith* in three volumes aimed for a middle course between Cartesianism and existentialism in his desire to build on the Word of God. This book does not survey their views, but the following discussions do refer to some of these names.

9

Karl Barth

God as Wholly Other

The Struggle with the Immanentism of Classical Liberalism

Both thematically and chronologically, it is appropriate to begin with Karl Barth, who, according to one author, in 1918 ushered in a "contemporary revival of theology" with his highly influential *Epistle to the Romans*.[1] Barth was thoroughly immersed in the tradition of nineteenth-century classical liberalism. In the spirit of liberalism, the great church historian Adolf von Harnack contended that all Christian dogmas, especially trinitarian and christological doctrines, were later Hellenizations of the simple gospel of Christ, a kind of "deterioration of dogma." In Barth's view, classical liberalism turned "God-talk" into "man-talk," which dissatisfied him. His scolding remark of Friedrich D. E. Schleiermacher, whom he saw as the backbone of the era's pervasive immanentism, reveals Barth's anguish: "To speak about God meant to speak about humanity, no doubt in elevated tone, but . . . about human faith and works. Without doubt human beings were magnified at the expense of God—the God who is sovereign Other standing over against humanity."[2]

---

1. Claude Welch, *In This Name: The Doctrine of the Trinity in Contemporary Theology* (New York: Charles Scribner's Sons, 1952), 45.
2. Karl Barth, "The Humanity of God," in *Karl Barth: Theologian of Freedom,* ed. Clifford Green (London: Collins, 1979), 48.

Barth's clash with liberalism began with his *Epistle to the Romans,* first published in 1918 (revised in 1922). In that work, Barth denies the principle of continuity that liberalism had taken for granted and argues for a radical discontinuity between God and humanity as well as between nature and grace. Barth's view of God is exposited in the first volume of his monumental *Church Dogmatics* (1932–67).

Knowledge of God in Jesus Christ

According to Barth, there is absolutely no way of knowing God apart from revelation:

> Revelation is God's self-offering and self-manifestation. . . . In revelation God tells man that he is God, and that as such he is his Lord. In telling him this, revelation tells him something new, something which apart from revelation he does not know and cannot tell either himself or others.[3]

Where do we find this revelation? This is the second axiom of Barth's view of knowledge of God: Jesus Christ.

> When Holy Scripture speaks of God, it concentrates our attention and thoughts upon one single point. . . . And if we look closer, and ask: who and what is at this point upon which our attention and thoughts are concentrated, which we are to recognize as God? . . . From its beginning to its end the Bible directs us to the name of Jesus Christ.[4]

What about the possibility of having knowledge of God apart from the revelation in Christ? Barth is skeptical. His thinking shifted from an extreme denial of knowledge of God apart from revelation[5] to a less vehement position,[6] but his main views did not change.[7] The basic reason Barth so adamantly opposed any notion of natural theology was that for him revelation of God—to be revelation in the first place—is of a redemptive nature. Revelation is more than a vague knowledge of God. Only knowledge of God that helps us know God as Savior can be called Christian revelation.

---

3. Karl Barth, *Church Dogmatics,* vol. 1, part 2 (Edinburgh: T & T Clark, 1956), 301.

4. Karl Barth, *Church Dogmatics,* vol. 2, part 2 (Edinburgh: T & T Clark, 1957), 52–54.

5. The most radical denial of the value of other religions and natural religion is the famous paragraph 17 (over eighty pages!) in "The Revelation of God as the Abolition of Religions," *Church Dogmatics,* vol. 1, part 2.

6. Barth, *Church Dogmatics,* vol. 4, part 3 (Edinburgh: T & T Clark, 1961), 97. See Carl Braaten, *No Other Gospel? Christianity among the World's Religions* (Minneapolis: Augsburg Fortress, 1992), 53–59.

7. See further Paul F. Knitter, *No Other Name? A Critical Survey of Christian Attitudes toward the World Religions* (Maryknoll, N.Y.: Orbis, 1985), 80–87. The problem with Knitter's exposition is that he makes Barth an exclusivist.

The Christian God Is a Trinitarian God

Barth can be hailed as the pioneer of the revival of trinitarian theology for the twentieth century. His *Church Dogmatics* is based on the trinitarian view of God, a particular Christian God. "The doctrine of the Trinity is what basically distinguishes the Christian doctrine of God as Christian, and therefore what already distinguishes the Christian concept of revelation as Christian, in contrast to all other possible doctrines of God or concepts of revelation."[8]

Changing the pattern of systematic theology, Barth begins his *Dogmatics* with the doctrine of the Trinity and thus makes it foundational. His starting point is his famous formula: "God reveals himself. He reveals himself through himself. He reveals himself."[9] Thus, for Barth, God's revelation and God's being are identical. God is who God is revealed to be.[10] Only after discussing the doctrine of the Trinity does Barth venture into topics that are usually treated prior to it: the knowledge of God; the reality of God (his being and attributes), and the doctrine of election. Historically, discussion of the oneness of God preceded that of his triunity. Barth reversed this order.

How, then, does Barth formulate his trinitarian doctrine? Whereas classical theology freely used the term *person* with reference to the three members of the Trinity, Barth is not happy with that term because its modern usage differs so much from its earlier usage. The modern use of the term *person* implies the existence of three members of the Trinity with their own wills and minds. Barth prefers the term "mode of Being" (from the German *Seinsweise*).[11] Since God has only one personality, talking about three persons contradicts this principle. To illustrate, Barth says that if Jesus Christ were a personality different from the Father, he could not be the Father's self-revelation.[12] Furthermore, positing a threefold subject makes three gods, tritheism.[13]

God in History

Because of his preference for the term *mode* over *person,* Barth frequently has been accused of modalism, the view that denies real distinctions in the Godhead. If we had only the first part of his *Dogmatics,* that criticism might hold to some extent, but in light of later volumes, it is not valid. In fact, Barth

---

8. Barth, *Church Dogmatics,* 1/1:301.
9. Ibid., 1/1:296.
10. Ibid., 1/1:299.
11. Ibid., 1/1:355.
12. Ibid., 1/1:350–51; for a helpful discussion, see Stanley J. Grenz, *The Social God and the Relational Self: A Trinitarian Theology of the Imago Dei* (Louisville: Westminster John Knox, 2001), 37.
13. Barth, *Church Dogmatics,* 2/1:297.

introduces historicity into the Triune God and in doing so "revolutioniz[es] so-called 'classical Christian theism.'"[14] He does this most dramatically in the last volume of *Church Dogmatics*. Barth describes incarnation as the Son of God's journey into a far land. Acting as the prodigal son of Luke 15, the Son of God effects reconciliation since the journey is that of God himself revealed in the Son. "Barth brought the immanent and economic Trinities together by positing that the Son's journey is God's own journey and that the Son's self-humiliation in birth, life, and death is an expression of God's transcendence. God is exalted in the humility of the Son."[15] In other words, "The Way of the Son of God into a Far Country"—the title of volume 4, part 1—brings history into the triune life of God and clearly reveals the real, ontological distinctions of Father, Son, and Holy Spirit. As Ted Peters succinctly comments, Barth's legacy to the current doctrine of God is showing that "the historical event of Jesus Christ belongs to the becoming of God proper."[16]

Creation as the Self-Giving Love of God

On the basis of his theology of revelation, Barth insists that the "insight that man owes his existence and form, together with all the reality distinct from God, to God's creation" is based on the divine self-witness in Christ.[17] In other words, even the knowledge of God as Creator is not derived from the world but is possible only through faith in Jesus Christ. It is not possible by philosophical argument or by reflection on human experience to demonstrate that the world is a reality distinct from God or that this reality depends on God as Creator.[18]

But why did God create the world in the first place? Barth's answer is simple: Jesus Christ. God "needs" creatures in order that there shall be the one creature Jesus Christ.[19] Because of this God made a covenant. For Barth, creation is the "external basis of the covenant"; it prepares the sphere in which life under the covenant will take place.[20] The covenant relationship is based on grace—thus, "creation is grace"[21]—and the relationship between God and the world is essentially based on God's love. The act of creation is a "free positing

14. Roger E. Olson and Christopher A. Hall, *The Trinity* (Grand Rapids: Eerdmans, 2002), 97.

15. Ibid.

16. Ted Peters, *God as Trinity: Relationality and Temporality in Divine Life* (Louisville: Westminster John Knox, 1993), 82.

17. Karl Barth, *Church Dogmatics*, vol. 3, part 1 (Edinburgh: T & T Clark, 1958), 3.

18. Ibid., 3/1:5–7.

19. Ibid., 2/1:579.

20. Ibid., 3/1:107.

21. Ibid., 3/1:40.

of reality by the omnipotence of divine love."[22] This is the famous Barthian understanding of God as "the one who loves in freedom."[23]

But if God is as he has been revealed to be in Jesus Christ, then it is inevitable that he should create a world distinct from himself.[24] Creation and incarnation flow out of God's self-willed free decision to let the eternal intratrinitarian love extend beyond the triune fellowship. This is the God revealed to us in Jesus Christ, and for Barth there is no other God.

22. Ibid., 3/1:27.
23. Ibid., 2/1:257.
24. Ibid., 3/1:51.

10

Paul Tillich

God as the Ground of Being

Apostle to the Intellectuals

Paul Tillich, a German theologian who moved to the United States because of the Nazi regime, expressed his theological motto in the following way: "My whole theological work has been directed to the interpretation of religious symbols in such a way that the secular man—and we are all secular—can understand and be moved by them."[1] Coming from a liberal training similar to that of his contemporary Karl Barth, Tillich reacted to that legacy in a completely different way. Rather than seeing antithesis between faith (or theology or revelation) and reason (or culture or even secularism), he strove for correlation, if not synthesis, between modern secular philosophy and Christian theology.

For Tillich, the task of theology is to be "apologetic," in the sense of presenting the case for Christian faith in a way so that modern men and women can understand it and relate it to their needs. This apologetic approach presupposes some common ground between the Christian message and the contemporary culture. In Tillich's own words, "Philosophy formulates the questions implied

1. Quoted in D. MacKenzie Brown, ed., *Ultimate Concern: Tillich in Dialogue* (New York: Harper & Row, 1956), 88–89. A most helpful brief introduction to various facets of Tillich's theology is Stanley J. Grenz and Roger E. Olson, *Twentieth-Century Theology: God and World in a Transitional Age* (Downers Grove, Ill.: InterVarsity, 1992), 114–30. My own exposition owes to their succinct, lucid summary, even though I usually give references to Tillich's own works.

in human existence, and theology formulates the answers implied in divine self-manifestation under the guidance of the questions implied in human existence."[2] The entire structure of his three-volume *Systematic Theology* (1951–63) follows this path: First there is a question related to the intellectual and cultural context; this is followed by a theological answer. For Tillich, reason does not resist revelation but rather asks for it; revelation entails the reintegration of reason.

Ontology as the Gateway to the Notion of God

The value of philosophy for Tillich's theology is based on his idea of correlation. Tillich—in the long tradition of Christian theology going back to Augustine, Anselm, and Descartes—sees ontology, of all the fields of philosophy, as his closest dialogue partner. Ontology (from the Greek word meaning "being") is the study of being. According to Tillich, the question of being and its counterpart, the threat of "non-being," is *the* question for the modern person.

Tillich is not naïve about ontology; he does not expect it to provide the ultimate answers. Rather, the value of ontology, and philosophy in general, lies in the questions it proposes for Christian theology.

The crucial question of life, which should also occupy theologians who talk about God, is the question of non-being. For modern, secular men and women, anxiety about non-being is present in everything finite.[3] The threat of non-being raises the question of a power of being that can overcome this threat and maintain being. Such being, Tillich rightly notes, cannot be finite but must be "being-itself," or, as he came to call it, "the Ground of Being." Here is the basis for the notion of God offered by Christian theology: "Only those who have experienced the shock of transitoriness, the anxiety in which they are aware of their finitude, the threat of non-being, can understand what the notion of God means."[4] This brings us to the most controversial yet creative part of Tillich's thinking about God.

The Ground of Being and God above God

To the age-old question of the relationship between the god of the philosophers and the God of the Bible, Tillich has a straightforward answer: "The God of Abraham, Isaac and Jacob and the God of the philosophers is the same God."[5] This conclusion comes from ontological questioning. To do justice to

2. Paul Tillich, *Systematic Theology,* vol. 1 (Chicago: University of Chicago Press, 1951), 61.
3. Tillich, *Systematic Theology,* vol. 2 (Chicago: University of Chicago Press, 1957), 19–24.
4. Tillich, *Systematic Theology,* 1:61–62.
5. Tillich, *Biblical Religion and the Search for Ultimate Reality* (Chicago: University of Chicago Press, 1955), 85.

his foundational premise that "God" cannot be part of finite existence, Tillich expresses the kernel of his view of God in a most ambiguous and potentially misleading way: "God does not exist. He is being itself beyond essence and existence. Therefore, to argue that God exists is to deny him."[6]

To unpack this compact sentence, we need to be aware of the fact that here—as often—Tillich uses terms in a technical sense, specifically, in the technical sense he himself defined. Tillich defines *existence* and *essence* in unique ways that do not correspond to how they are used in philosophy in general. Reality, as we know it, can be divided into these two realms. Essence is the potential, unactualized perfection of things. Something with essence has ontological reality but no actual existence. Existence, on the other hand, describes something that is actual and "fallen" from essence. Because it is cut off from its perfection, while still being dependent on it, it is not itself.[7] In other words, existence refers to what is both finite and fallen, in a sense, divorced from the perfection of essence.

Now we can return to Tillich's controversial definition of God. Tillich is not an atheist denying the existence of God according to the usual meaning of the term, even though this is a contested issue among interpreters of Tillich's thought,[8] but denying that God exists in the same way we do lest God be made part of finite, fallen existence. For God to be the sustaining force behind all being, he cannot be even the highest or the best being. He must be conceived of as the "power of being," "power of resisting nonbeing," "infinite power of being," or ultimately "being-itself."[9] If God were part of existence (in Tillich's meaning of the term), there would be a need for another god, "God above God," which Tillich does not want.

The Transcendence and Immanence of God

What, if anything, can be said of this God of Tillich, the Ground of Being? Tillich struggled with the problem of language. It is more than understandable that in light of his ontological premise, he could not say very much about God. He tried to make God-talk acceptable by resorting to the category of symbolic rather than literal language. Even the term *God* is a symbol for God. We cannot call God "personal," for that would make him limited; we can only symbolically refer to him as "suprapersonal" *(überpersönlich)*.[10] The only thing that can be said of God is that God is "being-itself," the "Ground of Being."[11]

6. Tillich, *Systematic Theology,* 1:205.
7. Grenz and Olson, *Twentieth-Century Theology,* 122.
8. For helpful notes about the discussion, see ibid., 122–23.
9. Tillich, *Systematic Theology,* 1:235–36.
10. See Philip Clayton, *The Problem of God in Modern Thought* (Grand Rapids: Eerdmans, 2000), 467–71.
11. Tillich, *Systematic Theology,* 1:238–39.

How, then, does Tillich talk about transcendence and immanence? Obviously, immanence is no great problem. His view comes close to panentheism: God and the world participate in each other. Everything finite participates in being itself, which is the structure of being in which everything is grounded.[12] God participates absolutely and unconditionally as its ground and aim.[13]

Transcendence is a much more challenging question for Tillich:

> Being-itself is not the universal essence of everything, the underlying substance of the world, because being-itself transcends the essence/existence split to which all things in the world are subject due to their element of nonbeing. Being-itself does not participate in nonbeing and therefore infinitely transcends everything finite.[14]

Many theologians have been left wondering what all this actually means and whether Tillich sees any kind of genuine transcendence in God. That Tillich is a panentheist is clear, but how his panentheism relates to God's transcendence, which he himself claimed, is a continuing issue of contention among his interpreters.[15]

The Christian God and Other Gods

A few years before his death, Tillich paid a visit to Japan. This trip influenced him greatly, as it was the first time he experienced a concrete form of another religion. The third chapter of his *Christianity and the Encounter of World Religions*[16] is an engaging account of this experience. Rather than seeing Buddhism as an underdeveloped religion, Tillich sees it as a dynamic one. This encounter was so powerful that he was no longer able to call Christianity the absolute religion.[17] There are differences between these two religions, Tillich notes, but they can be regarded as complementary rather than as exclusive. The key element uniting these two religions is the Christian concept of the kingdom of God, "a social, political and personalistic symbol" concerned with establishing justice and peace, and its Buddhist equivalent, Nirvana, "an ontological symbol" concerned with providing an answer to finitude, separation, and suffering in the Ultimate Ground of Being. Christianity conceives of the world as the creation of God and in its essence good and the human being as a responsible creature who precipitated the fall by his sinful actions.

12. Ibid., 1:238.
13. Ibid., 1:243–45.
14. Grenz and Olson, *Twentieth-Century Theology,* 125.
15. For starters, see ibid., 126.
16. Paul Tillich, *Christianity and the Encounter of World Religions* (New York: Columbia University Press, 1961).
17. Ibid., 57.

For Buddhism, the existence of the world presupposes "an ontological fall into finitude." The human being is "a finite bound to the wheel of life with self-affirmation, blindness, and suffering."[18]

With regard to the doctrine of the Trinity and its implications for theology of religions, Tillich offers interesting reflections. Operating with the generic category of the "history of religious experience," Tillich argues that trinitarian thinking in some form or another has a foundation in reality. Tillich sees threeness as a universal structure. He points to the threefold manifestation of God as creative power, saving love, and ecstatic transformation. Yet we have to ask why the number three seems to persist. Why not two or four or something else? Tillich's response is that the number "three corresponds to the intrinsic dialectics of experienced life and is, therefore, most adequate to symbolize the Divine Life."[19] Tillich did not live long enough to develop these incipient ideas, but his existentialistically oriented, ontologically based view of God leans toward an inclusive view of other religions' gods.

18. Paul Tillich, *The Future of Religions,* ed. Jerald C. Bauer (Chicago: University of Chicago Press, 1966), 65–66.

19. Tillich, *Systematic Theology,* 2:283; I am indebted to Ted Peters (*God as Trinity: Relationality and Temporality in Divine Life* [Louisville: Westminster John Knox, 1993], 73–74) for finding this remark in Tillich.

11

John Zizioulas

God as Communion

The Ontology of Communion

Both John Zizioulas and Paul Tillich see ontology as the starting point for the doctrine of God. Yet it is difficult to find two twentieth-century theologians who differ more in their approaches to and the implications they draw from ontological considerations. Zizioulas, formerly professor of theology in England and now the bishop of Pergamon, Greece, has in the last two decades established himself as the most well-known interpreter of the mystical, often apophatic, tradition of Eastern Orthodoxy. The work that brought him international fame is fittingly titled *Being as Communion* (1985). In fact, it is not a study about God, even less a systematic presentation of theology as a whole; it is a collection of essays about the church. Yet this book gives a fair introduction to Zizioulas's view of God and the Trinity and thus presents a contemporary Eastern Orthodox perspective.

For Zizioulas, there is no true being without communion; nothing exists as an "individual" in itself.

> From the fact that a human being is a member of the Church, he becomes an "image of God," he exists as God Himself exists, he takes on God's "way of being." This way of being . . . is a way of *relationship* with the world, with other people

and with God, an event of *communion,* and that is why it cannot be realized as the achievement of an *individual,* but only as an *ecclesial* fact.[1]

Communion is an ontological category; even God exists in communion. Zizioulas comes to the conclusion that the most significant contribution of the Greek fathers, especially the Cappadocians, was the construction of a specific ontology, one that contrasted with the ancient Greek ontology, that looks at the "person" as an individual.[2] No individual apart from others can ever be a "person," since personhood is not "an adjunct to a being, a category we add to" a person.[3] Rather, person is itself the essence of being. (Here Zizioulas's use of *essence* takes up the ancient trinitarian and christological language of *hypostasis,* from the Greek term meaning "essence" or "substance.")

Greek ontology was fundamentally monistic: The being of the world and the being of God formed an unbreakable unity. The Platonic conception of the creator God did not satisfy the fathers precisely because the doctrine of creation from preexisting matter limited divine freedom. It was necessary, therefore, to find an ontology that avoided monism as the gulf between God and the world. In the Greek patristic view, communion becomes an ontological concept. Nothing in existence is conceivable in itself, as Aristotle posited.[4] Zizioulas insists that communion is not just another way of describing being, whether individual or ecclesial, but rather belongs to the ontology of being. Thus, we should speak of an actual "ontology of communion."

As already mentioned, with his ontology of communion Zizioulas wants to propose a new understanding of personhood, an "ontology of personhood" over against the Greek "non-personal" view.[5] The Greek term for "person" originally referred to the mask of an actor in the theater. Then it gained the meaning of something added to a being, implying that the "person" is not his true *hypostasis* ("essence"). In that view, personhood does not have an ontological content.[6] It was out of the desire among the fathers to give ontological expression to faith in the Trinity that a new kind of understanding of personhood as communion emerged. In other words, the fathers wanted to address the question What does it mean to say that God is Father, Son, and Spirit without ceasing to be one God? The revolutionary insight of the Cappadocians was the identification of the *hypostasis* ("essence") with the "person." Tertullian's formula, *una substantia, tres personae* ("one substance/essence, three persons") did not meet this requirement, since the term *person* lacked an ontological content.[7] The

---

1. John Zizioulas, *Being as Communion: Studies in Personhood and Communion* (Crestwood, N.Y.: St. Vladimir's Seminary Press, 1985), 15, italics in text.
 2. Ibid., 16.
 3. Ibid., 39.
 4. Ibid., 16–18.
 5. Ibid., 27, the subheading uses this term.
 6. Ibid., 32–33 especially, but see all of chap. 1.
 7. Ibid., 36–37.

following section looks at how this translates to Zizioulas's understanding of God as trinitarian communion.

Trinity as Communion

On the basis of their ontology of communion, the Cappadocians criticized ancient Greek ontology, in which God first is God (his substance) and then exists as Trinity, as three persons, the way Christian theology has approached God.[8] According to the groundbreaking insight of the Cappadocians, which Zizioulas enthusiastically endorses, the "Holy Trinity is a *primordial* ontological concept and not a notion which is added to the divine substance or rather which follows it, as is the case in the dogmatic manuals of the West and, alas, in those of the East in modern times." In other words, the substance of God, "God," has no ontological content, no "true being, apart from communion," a mutual relationship of love.[9]

God cannot be known as "God," only as trinitarian persons in communion: "Man can approach God only through the Son and in the Holy Spirit."[10] Outside the Trinity there is no God. In other words, God's being coincides with God's communal personhood. For Zizioulas, then, "the being of God could be known only through personal relationships and personal love. Being means life, and life means *communion*."[11]

Zizioulas's communion ontology and doctrine of the Trinity have been immensely influential for the doctrine of God during the last two decades and continue to shape the landscape.[12] Several theologians such as Jürgen Moltmann, Wolfhart Pannenberg, the liberationist Leonardo Boff, and the late Catholic feminist Catherine Mowry LaCugna built on the communion idea.

8. The basic philosophical and theological orientation is given in ibid., chap. 2.
9. Ibid., 17.
10. Ibid., 19.
11. Ibid., 16, italics in text.
12. For a recent appraisal, see Stanley J. Grenz, *The Social God and the Relational Self: A Trinitarian Theology of the Imago Dei* (Louisville: Westminster John Knox, 2001), 53.

12

Hans Küng

God and the Challenge of Atheism

Taking the Challenge of Atheism Seriously

Hans Küng of the University of Tübingen, Germany, has been not only one of the most productive and creative post-conciliar theologians of the Roman Catholic Church but also one of the most disputed figures in that church. Officially, he was stripped of his teaching credentials as a Roman Catholic theologian; still, he was able to retain his post at the university until his retirement. His two works on the doctrine of God, *On Being a Christian* and its rejoinder, *Does God Exist?*[1] a monumental philosophical-theological work, are the main focus here. While Küng has moved to interreligious dialogue and global ethics, his work on the doctrine of God is a milestone in twentieth-century Western theology.

Küng has boldly faced two major challenges to the Christian doctrine of God. One is atheism and related movements, which is the focus of his earlier work. The other is other gods and other religions, the focal point of the latter part of his career.

Küng states that all arguments of the eminent atheists "are certainly adequate to raise doubts about the existence of God but not to make God's non-existence unquestionable." Similarly, projections for the end of religion "involve

---

1. Hans Küng, *On Being a Christian* (Garden City, N.Y.: Doubleday, 1976); and idem, *Does God Exist? An Answer for Today* (Garden City, N.Y.: Doubleday, 1980).

an ultimately unsubstantiated extrapolation into the future."[2] Atheism is no neutral position for this theologian; it too lives by an undemonstrable faith, whether in human nature, society, or science.

Consequently, the answer to atheism must tackle with all seriousness two foundational, interrelated questions: "Does God exist? . . . [and] Who is God?"[3] Modern atheism, Küng argues, demands an account of belief in God.[4] Too often, Christian theology has resorted to "a theological withdrawal strategy" that talks about God in terms of need or commitment but overlooks the question of the truth of Christian faith.[5] Küng maintains that much of atheism and other criticisms of religion have been more about rejecting institutionalized religion than about rejecting the idea of God.[6] Thus, we should not be too indiscriminate in morally condemning atheism as deliberate apostasy.[7]

In regard to modern rationality originating from Descartes and Kant, Küng maintains that, fortunately, there are currently prospects for beginning a new dialogue between science and faith, coupled with a rediscovery of transcendence by some secular thinkers and "secular quasi-religiousness."[8] Christian theology should take "a radical course correction"[9] with regard to that opportunity and not resort to a ghetto mentality. Theology and science—which were never supposed to be antagonists—should together acknowledge the complexity and the unity of reality.[10]

Küng also sees positive horizons between theology and philosophy. Philosophy can never again become an exercise in the analysis of language alone, as analytical philosophy maintained in the beginning of the twentieth century. Küng's sympathies lie with Hegel's desire to reconcile faith and knowledge.[11] Modern philosophy has taught theology to take seriously God's historical nature and "secularity." This can be a corrective to classical theism and give more credit to the biblical view of a living and dynamic God who acts in a real way in history.[12]

Yes to God—Yes to the God of the Bible

Even though Küng takes up the challenge of atheism and nihilism, he does not set high hopes on the classical proofs of God. Cartesian reasoning from

2. Küng, *Does God Exist?* 329.
3. Ibid., xxi.
4. Ibid., xxii.
5. Ibid., 327–30.
6. Ibid., 324.
7. Ibid., 334–39.
8. Ibid., 553–59.
9. Ibid., 115.
10. Ibid., 120–25.
11. Ibid., 182; see also 120.
12. Ibid., 181–88.

the greatest Being may be able to prove the existence of the *idea* of God, but it can never prove his existence, and cosmological proofs are always susceptible to more than one reading. Even if God's existence could be proved, it does not lead one to the Christian God of the Bible. That is why the God of the philosophers is not necessarily identical with the God of Abraham, Isaac, and Jacob.[13] Both denial and affirmation of God are possible.[14]

What can we know of that God? The God of religions in general and of Christianity in particular is a God with a name—various religions give God various names[15]—whereas the god of the philosophers is a nameless god. The God of the Bible is the living God, the one and only God, the God of liberation, the God of love, the God Yahweh. This God is a person, a Creator God who intervenes in the affairs of his world and leads it to the final goal.[16] Furthermore, the biblical God is "the God of Jesus Christ."[17] Jesus taught believers to know God as the Father, neither a tyrannical nor a patriarchal God but the One who loves and cares.[18] Finally, since the Spirit is introduced in the salvation history of the Bible, Küng affirms the doctrine of the Trinity, even if he is not happy with the abstract, logical way tradition has often expressed it.[19]

The Christian God and Other Gods: The Challenge of Interreligious Dialogue

The fact that Küng in recent decades has moved from intra-Christian considerations to the field of theology of religions is not surprising in light of even his early theology.[20] For him, it is "perfectly clear that the God of the Bible is not only the God of Jews and Christians but the God of all men."[21] Küng does not naïvely admire world religions; he admits they are wrong and need the revelation of God in Jesus Christ. But that does not make them futile nor necessarily hostile to the idea of the biblical God. Even in their error, the

13. Ibid., 529–35; for his discussion of natural theology, see also 518–28.
14. Ibid., 568–71.
15. See ibid., 587–602.
16. See ibid., 613–66.
17. Title for chapter G.III, in ibid., 667.
18. See ibid., 667–96.
19. See ibid., 696–702.
20. Already during Vatican II, Küng wrote a programmatic article, originally a communication at a conference held in Bombay, India, in 1964, entitled "Christian Revelation and Non-Christian Religions" (first published under the title "The World Religions in God's Plan of Salvation," in *Christian Revelation and World Religions,* ed. J. Neuner [London: Burns & Oates, 1967], 25–66).
21. Hans Küng, "The Freedom of Religions," in *Attitudes toward Other Religions,* ed. Owen C. Thomas (New York: Harper & Row, 1969), 205.

world religions proclaim the truth of God. "Though they are far from God, God is not far from them."[22]

Küng has never significantly changed this basic orientation, which in a rather confusing way he calls "Christian universalism." Yet more recently, his focus has been on global ethics and religions' contribution to building a peaceful, harmonious human society.[23] This has been intensified by his participation in the interreligious forum called the Parliament of the World Religions.

One might think these considerations lead Küng to embrace all religions as equal and their conceptions of God as complementary. This is not the case. According to him, at the innermost level, the specifically Christian criterion is directly applicable only to Christians: faith in and commitment to Jesus Christ. Christians cannot but share this with other people. This criterion, then, is only indirectly applicable to non-Christians, to the extent that Christians faithfully apply it to themselves first.[24] Therefore, Küng is not ashamed of confessing that for Christians Jesus Christ is "*the* way, *the* truth, and *the* life!" and that "Jesus Christ is for Christians the *decisively regulative* norm."[25]

22. Ibid., 210.

23. See Hans Küng, *Theology for the Third Millennium* (New York: Doubleday, 1988); and idem, *Global Responsibility: In Search of a New World Ethic* (London: SCM, 1991).

24. Hans Küng, "What Is True Religion? Toward an Ecumenical Criteriology," in *Toward a Universal Theology of Religion,* ed. Leonard Swidler (Maryknoll, N.Y.: Orbis, 1987), 231–50.

25. Ibid., 246–47, italics in text. Küng has recently tested these affirmations in collaboration with the Chinese J. Ching in the book *Christianity and Chinese Religions* (New York: Doubleday, 1989).

13

Karl Rahner

God as the Mystery of the World

Transcendental Experience of God

The late Karl Rahner is the main figure in contemporary Roman Catholic theology. With Hans Küng, he towers over the twentieth-century theology of the church that claims the membership of roughly half of all Christians. Unlike Küng, however, Rahner's theology is far less accessible to a larger audience, even though all his major works, especially his *Theological Investigations* and *Foundations of Christian Faith,* have been translated into English. His style is highly philosophical, and he created his own theological vocabulary. Whereas Küng's main target in his first major work was atheism and related challenges to belief in God, Rahner's main target throughout his life was widespread secularism, especially in the West.[1]

A helpful place to begin discussion of Rahner's theology of God is with some of the key concepts in his "transcendental method." "Transcendental experiences" reveal that humans are naturally oriented toward the Holy Mystery, called God, first in the form of an "unthematic knowledge of God."[2] A human being is by nature "spirit," which means he or she is open to receive revelation.

---

1. Karl Rahner, *Foundations of Christian Faith: An Introduction to the Idea of Christianity* (New York: Crossroad, 1982), 46.
2. Ibid., 20–21, 53.

God is not alien to human nature but an intrinsic part of it as the necessary condition for human subjectivity. The task of "transcendental reflection" is to discover the necessary preconditions for human experience. Human beings are not only part of nature but are also oriented toward an infinite, mysterious horizon of being that Christians know as God.

On the one hand, ordinary, everyday experiences of life are in a sense orientations to God. On the other hand, they do not ultimately make sense apart from the Holy Mystery. Even though not recognized as such in the era of growing skepticism and secularism, "God," according to Rahner, is the most self-evident reality. Rahner's talk about "mystery" does not denote anything "senseless and unintelligible"[3] but something that transcends humans yet is not outside the realm of intuition or even knowledge in a later stage of encounter and reflection. In fact, paradoxically, this "mystery in its incomprehensibility is what is *self-evident* in human life."[4] Grace is first and foremost God's self-communication and presence through his Spirit to human existence.[5]

What about the need for God's self-revelation? Despite his distinctive approaches and terminology, Rahner is a traditional theologian. He differentiates between two kinds of revelation: First, there is what he calls "transcendental," implicit, unthematic revelation about God, which we have just discussed. This is complemented and fulfilled by "categorical revelation," specific revelation in history through events, words, and symbols. This categorical revelation does not do away with or oppose transcendental revelation. Rather, it discloses the inner reality of God, which cannot be discovered through transcendental revelation alone: the personal character of God and his free relationship with human beings. Thus, universal, transcendental experience of God in the Spirit does not remove the need for historical, special revelation.

God as the Absolute Person

Rahner, as a traditional Catholic theologian and a Jesuit, never wanted to leave behind the canons of classical Christianity. Yet because of his desire to speak to modern men and women, his unbelievably extensive corpus contains little discussion of God's attributes or essence, abstract and speculative topics in which scholastic theology invested so much time. Instead, in addition to writing on the doctrine of the Trinity (his real focus concerning the doctrine of God), he invests much energy on the possibility of speaking about God—conditions in the human person that allow knowing and speaking of God in a meaningful way.

3. Ibid., 12.
4. Ibid., 21.
5. Ibid., 116–26; see also 139.

There are a couple of key points with regard to Rahner's God-talk. As "Absolute Mystery" or "Holy Mystery," God is immanent within human experience—in the realm of how humans receive transcendental experiences—even if he cannot be comprehended. What can be said of God is, first, that God is person.[6] Rahner considers this one of the fundamental assertions about God and approaches this frequent depiction of God with reference to God's infinity. As the infinite, God can never be the object of human inquiry. But that does not make God impersonal; the impersonal could give birth only to impersonal, not to personal. Rahner does not explain precisely what he means when he calls God "person." He implies that as a transcendent, infinite "person," God is a different kind of person than are humans, yet there is some analogy. At the end of the discussion, he says that God is the "Absolute Person" and that therefore God is absolute in his freedom.

With regard to God as Creator, Rahner—who in line with Catholic tradition affirms creation *ex nihilo*—also defends God's freedom.[7] God is free; we are dependent. Our creatureliness makes us radically different from God and radically dependent on him. There is no place for panentheism in Rahner's thought. But more importantly, no dualism is allowed between God and the world: God and the world, even though distinct, are not dualistically opposed. This is Rahner's self-acknowledged corrective to much of classical theism.[8] One way in which Rahner's theology overcomes dualism is through his distinctive view of the Trinity. God's dealings with the world—as the "economic Trinity"—is a reliable and accurate expression of who God is in his "immanent Trinity."

The Economic and Immanent Trinity

What has been called "Rahner's Rule"[9]—"the 'economic' Trinity is the 'immanent' Trinity and the 'immanent' Trinity is the 'economic' Trinity"[10]—has been hailed by many as a watershed in recent development of trinitarian doctrine.[11] But what, in fact, is the importance of this formula? Ted Peters puts Rahner's doctrine of God and the Trinity in a proper perspective:

Rahner proposes this rule in order to advance the thesis that it is God as one or another of the divine persons who relates to the world; it is not God as the

6. Ibid., 71–75.
7. Ibid., 75–81.
8. Ibid., 62.
9. Ted Peters, *God as Trinity: Relationality and Temporality in Divine Life* (Louisville: Westminster John Knox, 1993), 96.
10. Karl Rahner, *The Trinity* (1970; reprint, New York: Seabury, 1997), 22.
11. See Walter Kasper, *The God of Jesus Christ* (New York: Crossroad, 1984), 274; and Stanley J. Grenz, *The Social God and the Relational Self: A Trinitarian Theology of the Imago Dei* (Louisville: Westminster John Knox, 2001), 38.

unity of the divine being. The way we experience God is through God's saving activity within history—through the economy of salvation—and here we know God as the redeeming word in Christ and as uniting love in the Spirit. We do not know God in general. We experience God first in the economy of salvation, and Rahner believes we can trust this experience. In the economy of salvation, God is communicating Godself. God is internally just the way we experience the divine in relation to us, namely, as Father, Son, and Spirit.[12]

This means that the way God relates to the world is discovered in terms of each of the three *hypostaseis,* not in terms of God as a unity.[13] In this view, only Jesus could become incarnated, not the Spirit or the Father. Jesus is not simply God in general but specifically God as Son. The same applies to the other persons of the Trinity.[14] Contrary to Karl Barth, Rahner is ready to call each of these *hypostaseis* "person."[15]

Rahner was concerned that theological tradition had speculated on the being of God and God's triunity apart from salvation history and thus had come to emphasize God's unity, naturally leading to a neglect of the Trinity as well as of the relationship between the Christian life and the Trinity. This divorces God-talk from history and makes it generic in nature. The biblical way of speaking of God involves talking about a particular God, the Old Testament Yahweh who acts as Father, Son, and Spirit in the New Testament. Why then continue talking about the immanent Trinity at all? Talk about the immanent Trinity—God as triune in Godself—was needed to protect God's absolute freedom and to avoid dissolving God into history.[16]

Rahner was the first to notice the implications of his trinitarian doctrine for the classical view of God's immutability. If history is introduced into the Godhead, as Barth had already done, and if the economic Trinity is equated with the immanent Trinity, then God changes in and through his relations with the world. To tackle this issue, Rahner refers to the incarnation. He makes a distinction between God changing within the divine being and God changing outside himself. In other words, he makes a distinction between "internal" and "external" change. Rahner states, "He who is not subject to change in himself can himself be subject to change in something else."[17] God created the human creature in such a way as to be a proper vehicle for "God's own becoming-in-self-expressions. . . . In assuming nature through the incarnation, God 'becomes' while remaining immutable."[18]

12. Peters, *God as Trinity,* 96.

13. Ibid., 97.

14. Ibid., 100.

15. See Rahner, *Trinity,* 44.

16. Roger E. Olson and Christopher A. Hall, *The Trinity* (Grand Rapids: Eerdmans, 2002), 98.

17. Rahner, *Foundations of Christian Faith,* 220.

18. Grenz, *Social God and the Relational Self,* 40, with reference to Rahner, *Foundations of Christian Faith,* 223.

God among Other Religions

Rahner is best known for his controversial term "anonymous Christians." To understand this often misrepresented concept, we must note that for him the categorical revelation of God, the true, thematic revelation, is not confined to the church or to Christian revelation. Wherever people are open to receiving revelation—and in principle they have this capacity by virtue of the grace of God, which elevates them above themselves—such breakthroughs can occur. Rahner is confident that "in all religions there are individual moments of such a successful mediation . . . when the supernatural, transcendental relationship of man to God through God's self-communication becomes self-reflexive [i.e., thematic, conscious]."[19]

This does not mean, of course, that all religions possess equally valid expressions of divine self-revelation. There is error in any religion. Through Christ's death and resurrection, God's gracious self-communication in the Spirit became manifest in history: The "world is drawn to its spiritual fulfillment by the Spirit of God, who directs the whole history of the world in all its length and breadth towards its proper goal."[20]

By virtue of the grace of God, a person, even without hearing explicit preaching about the Christian God, qualifies himself or herself as an "anonymous Christian" by accepting the grace "present in an implicit form whereby [the] person undertakes and lives the duty of each day in the quiet sincerity of patience, in devotion to his material duties and the demands made upon him by the person under his care."[21] According to Rahner, Christ is present and efficacious in followers of other religions (and therefore in non-Christian religions) through his Spirit.[22] In other words, if a non-Christian responds positively to God's grace, for example, through selfless love for another, then that person, even though not knowing it objectively, has accepted the God revealed in Christ. But since salvation cannot be divorced from Christ, the term "anonymous Christian" is more appropriate than "anonymous theist."[23]

19. Rahner, *Foundations of Christian Faith,* 173.

20. Karl Rahner, "The One Christ and the Universality of Salvation," in *Theological Investigations,* vol. 16 (New York: Crossroad, 1983), 203.

21. Karl Rahner, "Anonymous Christians," in *Theological Investigations,* vol. 6 (Baltimore, Md.: Helicon, 1969), 394.

22. Karl Rahner, "Jesus Christ in the Non-Christian Religions," in *Theological Investigations,* vol. 17 (New York: Crossroad, 1981), 43.

23. See Gavin D'Costa, *Theology and Religious Pluralism: The Challenge of Other Religions* (Oxford: Basil Blackwell, 1986), 87.

14

Wolfhart Pannenberg

God as the Power of the Future

Theology in Search of the Truth

The title of the first chapter in Wolfhart Pannenberg's monumental three-volume *Systematic Theology*, "The Truth of Christian Doctrine as the Theme of Systematic Theology,"[1] sets the tone for this theological work by one of the premier theologians of our time. Against all the forces of postmodernism, Pannenberg boldly sets up a coherent, logical presentation of Christian doctrine in defense of truth. According to Pannenberg, the task of systematic theology is the exposition of Christian doctrine in a way that is in harmony with what we know of God and reality as a whole.[2] In that sense, theological claims are by nature hypotheses to be tested and, if possible, confirmed.[3] The truth of Christian claims cannot be presupposed but rather is the goal of theology.[4]

In Pannenberg's search for a coherent truth, his foundational anthropological insight is that faith in God is not something external to and imposed on

---

1. Wolfhart Pannenberg, *Systematic Theology*, vol. 1 (Grand Rapids: Eerdmans, 1991), 1. Pannenberg is a prolific writer, but whenever possible I give references to his *Systematic Theology*, since that represents the *summa* and latest phase of his creative work.
2. For his definition of theology along these lines, see Pannenberg, *Systematic Theology*, 59–60.
3. Ibid., 50.
4. Ibid., 52.

humans but rather something inherent to humanity. In his view, religion is an essential dimension of human life; it belongs to the nature of humanity to be open to God and to search for meaning and truth.[5] Of course, the "incurable" religiosity of humankind[6] does not guarantee the truth of theological claims. Rather, it is necessary but not satisfactory evidence.[7]

The Future Confirmation of Truth Claims by God

In the 1960s, Pannenberg, with Moltmann, came to be known as a "theologian of hope." In his theology of hope, God's transcendence is defined less spatially and more in relation to time: God "comes to us from the future." Pannenberg defines God as the "power on which all finite reality depends."[8] God is the power of the future. This plays into his understanding of truth.

The truth of Christian claims about God—and thus of theological claims— awaits its final confirmation (or lack of confirmation) until the end of time.[9] In the meantime, is there any way for humans to have at least some kind of certainty? According to Pannenberg, the "decision regarding their truth rests with God himself. It will be finally made with the fulfillment of the kingdom of God in God's creation. It is provisionally made in human hearts by the convicting ministry of the Spirit of God."[10] Decisive here is Christ's resurrection, a divine confirmation of Christ's claim to be the Son of God and thus the agent who will usher in the final victory of God in his kingdom.

Finally, what matters in determining the truth of the Christian message—and thus of the existence of and claims about the God of the Bible—is whether "the idea of God corresponds to an actual reality . . . [and is] able to illumine human existence, as well as our experience of the world as a whole."[11] Consequently, if the idea of God must illumine not only human life but also our experience of the world, then theology should also.[12] Therefore, Pannenberg does not shy away from arguing for the truth of the Christian message vis-à-

---

5. For a short statement, see ibid., 154–57. For a full-scale treatment, see his *Anthropology in Theological Perspective* (Philadelphia: Westminster, 1985), which is in fact an attempt to fight the opponents of religion on their own field, namely, psychology, anthropology, sociology, and history.

6. Pannenberg, *Systematic Theology,* 157.

7. Ibid., 93.

8. Wolfhart Pannenberg, *Introduction to Systematic Theology* (Grand Rapids: Eerdmans, 1991), 8.

9. Pannenberg, *Systematic Theology,* 54.

10. Ibid., 56.

11. L. Miller and Stanley J. Grenz, eds., *Fortress Introduction to Contemporary Theologies* (Minneapolis: Fortress, 1998), 132.

12. Wolfhart Pannenberg, "What Is Truth?" in *Basic Questions in Theology,* vol. 2 (Philadelphia: Fortress, 1971), 1.

vis competing truth claims, even if that is not typical of theology at the end of the second millennium.[13]

The God of the Bible and the God of the Philosophers

With Karl Rahner, Pannenberg acknowledges that in modern Western culture the word *God* in public consciousness no longer has factual content. In contrast to earlier cultures in which the term signified something "real," in postmodern secular culture, "the existence of God has not only become doubtful but the content of the concept of God has also become unclear." Ironically, Christian theology has contributed to this plague by relegating God-talk to religious experience and the subjective realm. Therefore, the truth claims about God are not even discussed, let alone confirmed, in the public arena.[14]

Christian philosophy and theology have also encouraged a loss of factual content associated with the term *God* by their reluctance to connect the God of the Bible with the god of the philosophers. According to Pannenberg, Christian theology has missed the fact that in the Bible the term *god* serves not only as a proper name but also as a general designation. The Bible contains both *Yahweh* (proper name) and *Elohim* (a generic term for God). Proper names, Pannenberg notes, make sense only in connection with terms for species. Therefore, to make God-talk intelligible, Christian theology must not cut off this general term as the background for talking about the particular God Yahweh, the Father of Jesus Christ. Christians, if they continue to issue truth claims in their proclamation of the revelation of the one God in Jesus Christ, need to affirm the concept of God in philosophical theology. Otherwise, theology will "involuntarily . . . [regress] to a situation of a plurality of gods in which Christian talk about God has reference to the specific biblical God as one God among others."[15]

One may ask, Is Pannenberg, then, supporting the use of natural theology and classical proofs for God's existence? Not quite. His understanding is innovative. First of all, he thinks that the only "proof" that still has relevance is anthropological, as explained above: Since humans are incurably religious, faith in God is not external to human nature, as atheism has posited. Yet the anthropological perspective can never prove the existence of God; it only makes God-talk reasonable. Cosmological proofs also have some relevance, not in the classical form but in reference to the main task of faith in and doctrine of God: to be able to illumine human experience in the world and reality as a whole.[16]

---

13. See Wolfhart Pannenberg, "Religious Pluralism and Conflicting Truth Claims," in *Christian Uniqueness Reconsidered,* ed. Gavin D'Costa (Maryknoll, N.Y.: Orbis, 1990), 96–116.

14. Pannenberg, *Systematic Theology,* 63–65, quotation on 64.

15. Ibid., 69.

16. Ibid., 92–93.

Second, with regard to natural theology, Pannenberg notes the radical shift in the meaning of the term: While it later came to denote something in "harmony with human nature," originally, in early Christian theology, it meant "something that accrues with the nature of God." God-talk was regarded as "natural," in harmony with who God is. Thus, this shift in meaning opened the way for ontological and other proofs in accordance with human ways of reasoning.[17] Among the fathers, however, the task of natural theology was to guarantee that talk about God was in harmony with the nature of God since "at stake was the truth of the Christian God as not just the national God of the Jews but the God of all peoples."[18]

The Christian God Is a Triune God

The most important way in which Pannenberg revises the traditional discussion of the doctrine of God relates to the order of the topics: While it is customary to treat the unity of God prior to the Trinity, Pannenberg reverses the two.[19] The threeness of God is for him the way to talk about the Christian God. The other distinctive feature in Pannenberg is his explicit grounding of the doctrine in revelation rather than in speculation. Thus, talk about the Trinity is grounded in salvation history. Pannenberg, in the main, follows Rahner's rule. He applies this rule by looking at how the three trinitarian persons appear and relate to one another in the event of revelation in the life and message of Jesus. It is only on the basis of this Triune God that Christian statements about the one God and his essence and attributes can be discussed.[20]

For Pannenberg, the beginning of the trinitarian understanding of God, thus of the Son and Spirit too, lies in Jesus' announcement of the nearness of the rule of God. Jesus taught us to know God as Father. Jesus' differentiation from and service to the Father establishes Jesus' sonship.[21] The Spirit is introduced by virtue of his involvement in God's presence in the work of Jesus and in the fellowship of the Son with the Father. This is the reason Christian theology did not adopt a binitarian view but rather a trinitarian view.[22]

The key to Pannenberg's trinitarian doctrine, then, is "the Reciprocal Self-distinction of Father, Son, and Spirit as the Concrete Form of Trinitarian Relations."[23] Applying Hegel's concept of "self-differentiation," which means

17. Ibid., 76–82.

18. Ibid., 79.

19. A helpful exposition is offered in Stanley Grenz, *Reason and Hope: The Systematic Theology of Wolfhart Pannenberg* (Oxford: Oxford University Press, 1990).

20. See especially Pannenberg, *Systematic Theology*, 200, where Pannenberg summarizes his method of approaching the Trinity.

21. See, for example, ibid., 304–5.

22. Ibid., 268.

23. Subhead in ibid., 308.

that by giving oneself to one's counterpart one gains one's identity from the other, Pannenberg maintains that the Father is "dependent" on the Son for his identity and that the Son and the Spirit are "dependent" on the Father and each other.[24] For example, Jesus, by differentiating himself from the Father yet subordinating himself to the service of the coming of God's kingdom—apart from which God cannot be God[25]—not only gains his status as Son but also establishes the Father's deity. Furthermore, as a result of Jesus' self-humiliation (Phil. 2:5–11), the Father hands over the kingdom to the Son, and at the end the Son hands it back to the Father (1 Cor. 15:24), thus giving room for the eternal lordship of the Father.[26]

God as Spirit

It is only from the threeness of God that Pannenberg moves to the unity of the trinitarian God and God's attributes. Rather than leaving behind the three-ness of God, Pannenberg attempts to tie threeness and unity closely together in the doctrine of the attributes. A foundational insight here, borrowed partly from Hegel and Descartes, builds on the concept of the infinite: "The true meaning of the infinite encompasses both its contradiction to finitude and its immanence in the finite."[27]

Laying aside the typical ways of looking at God as either reason or will, which guided theological reflection since Origen, Pannenberg views God's relational essence as "Spirit."[28] Here Pannenberg sees a potential convergence between science and theology. The field theories of modern physics no longer view field phenomena as bodily entities but as independent of matter and defined only by their relations to space and time. Pannenberg believes the concept of "field"—which he introduces in more detail in the second part of this systemat-ics in relation to the doctrine of creation—could be used to interpret the idea of God as Spirit. Pannenberg is excited about the possibilities of opening up a new understanding of the relations between the trinitarian persons and the divine essence that is common to all of them.

Herein lies, Pannenberg believes, a solution to the ancient problem of the doctrine of the Trinity that makes sense of John 4:24: "God is Spirit." On the one hand, the Spirit has been conceived of as the divine essence common to all three persons. On the other hand, the Spirit is the Third Person alongside the Father and the Son. As a divine field, of course, the Spirit would be impersonal,

---

24. See Stanley J. Grenz, *The Social God and the Relational Self: A Trinitarian Theology of the Imago Dei* (Louisville: Westminster John Knox, 2001), 48.

25. Pannenberg, *Systematic Theology*, 313, among others.

26. Concerning the Spirit, see ibid., 315.

27. Grenz, *Reason and Hope*, 54; see Pannenberg, *Systematic Theology*, 349–59.

28. Pannenberg, *Systematic Theology*, 370–74.

a view alien to Christian theology. It is also clear that the Spirit as person can be thought of only as a concrete form of the one deity, just like the Father and the Son. Pannenberg explains how to view the Spirit both as person and as the essence of the common deity:

> But the Spirit is not just the divine life that is common to both the Father and the Son. He also stands over against the Father and the Son as his own center of action. This makes sense if the Father and the Son have fellowship in the unity of the divine life only as they stand over against the person of the Spirit. Precisely because the common essence of the deity stands over against both—in different ways—in the form of the Spirit, they are related to one another by the unity of the Spirit.[29]

In other words, although both the Father and the Son are differentiated from the essence of the Godhead, which is Spirit, they are bound together through the Spirit, the Third Person of the Trinity. Likewise, in that the personal Spirit glorifies the others, that is, differentiates himself from them, he too knows himself to be connected to the Father and the Son.[30] This survey of Pannenberg's doctrine of God concludes with a brief discussion of two main attributes he assigns to God, namely, infinity and love.

The Infinity and Love of God

Pannenberg notes that there are only two ways the Bible defines God: "God is Spirit" (John 4:24) and "God is love" (1 John 4:8, 16). Paul joins them together by saying that the love of God is poured out in our hearts through the Spirit (Rom. 5:5).[31] On the basis of sayings in 1 John 4:8, 16, Pannenberg understands God's love as the power that manifests itself in the mutual relations of the trinitarian persons and is identical with the divine essence. The two statements "God is Spirit" and "God is love" denote the same unity of essence by which Father, Son, and Spirit are united in the fellowship of the one God.[32]

Pannenberg admits that the term *infinity* is not a biblical term for God. Yet it is implied in biblical descriptions of God, especially in the attributes of eternity, omnipotence, and omnipresence, as well as holiness, one of the most crucial designations. In the concept of infinity, freedom from limitation is not the primary point. Strictly speaking, the infinite is not that which is without end but that which stands opposed to the finite. Therefore, from this basic

29. Ibid., 383–84.
30. Grenz, *Reason and Hope,* 61.
31. Pannenberg, *Systematic Theology,* 424.
32. Ibid., 427.

idea of infinite as the antithesis of the finite—which is the core of the idea of the holiness of God: separation from everything profane—follows a crucial implication, namely, that the infinite also embraces, includes in itself, the finite. Thus, Pannenberg sees God not primarily as the "first cause," as theological tradition has most often seen him, but as the "Infinite":

> Thus the holiness of God both opposes the profane world and embraces it, bringing it into fellowship with the holy God. We see here a structural affinity between what the Bible says about the holiness of God and the concept of the true Infinite. The Infinite that is merely a negation of the finite is not yet truly seen as the Infinite, . . . for it is defined by delimitation from something else, i.e., the finite. Viewed in that way, the Infinite is something in distinction from something else, and it is thus finite. The Infinite is truly infinite only when it transcends its own antithesis to the finite. In this sense the holiness of God is truly infinite, for it is opposed to the profane, yet it also enters the profane world, penetrates it, and makes it holy. In the renewed world that is the target of eschatological hope the difference between God and creature will remain, but that between the holy and the profane will be totally abolished (Zech. 14:20–21).[33]

Pannenberg also applies this same principle of finite-infinite to related attributes of God such as eternity, omnipresence, and omnipotence.

Pannenberg notes that love, the other basic designation of God, is likewise not a separate subject apart from the three persons. "As the one and only essence of God it has its existence in the Father, Son, and Holy Spirit."[34] The coming forth of the Son from the Father is the basic fulfillment of divine love. Therefore, it is only under the Trinity that love can be fathomed.[35] The love of God also includes attributes such as goodness, mercy, righteousness, patience, wisdom, and faithfulness.

33. Ibid., 399–400; see also 397–401, 349–52.
34. Ibid., 428.
35. Ibid., 422–32.

15

Jürgen Moltmann

The Crucified God

The God of the Future

The book that brought the young German theologian Jürgen Moltmann to international fame in the mid-1960s was his *Theology of Hope*,[1] a book that interacts with atheism and secular philosophies. Though *Theology of Hope* is not primarily about God, both chronologically and thematically, it is an appropriate place to begin a discussion of Moltmann's theology.

In response to atheists, Marxists, and Ernst Bloch, who in his *Principle of Hope*[2] suggested the idea of "transcending without transcendence"—maintaining hope while denying the metaphysics of transcendence, whether religious or philosophical—Moltmann based Christian hope firmly on a historical ground, namely, the cross and resurrection of Jesus Christ. By suffering the death of his Son and raising him from the dead, the God of the Bible confirmed his promises to bring new life and hope to the dying world. The biblical designation of "the

---

1. Jürgen Moltmann, *Theology of Hope: On the Ground and the Implications of a Christian Eschatology* (London: SCM, 1967). A useful exposition is offered by Richard Bauckham, *The Theology of Jürgen Moltmann* (Edinburgh: T & T Clark, 1995), 29–46. Unlike Wolfhart Pannenberg, whose theology was summarized on the basis of his latest work, *Systematic Theology*, the study of Moltmann has to follow a chronological path since Moltmann has not attempted a summa. His thinking developed and shifted over four decades and is still evolving.
2. Ernst Bloch, *The Principle of Hope* (Oxford: Blackwell, 1986), 210.

God who raises the dead" (Rom. 4:17) is key for Moltmann.[3] Thus, revelation of God, the way to know God, is not an epiphany event coming straight from above, as Karl Barth had suggested, but a promise event.[4] The praxis of hope is in the confidence that history "is open to God and to the future."[5]

The God who raised Jesus from the dead, and therefore showed his faithfulness, is the God with "future as the essence of his being" (a designation Moltmann borrowed from Bloch). The God of the Bible is different from the god of the philosophers. He is the God declared first to the Jewish people as the God of the promise.[6] This God has given "the promise of life as a result of the resurrection from the dead, and the kingdom of God in a new totality of being."[7] This God of the future is the powerful One who overcomes death, which is remoteness from God.

The Suffering God

Moltmann's first major treatise on God is his widely acclaimed *Crucified God,* whose subtitle expresses its basic idea: *The Cross of Christ as the Foundation and Criticism of Christian Theology.*[8] This book represents another side of Moltmann's theology: Whereas *Theology of Hope* focuses on the anticipation of the future, *The Crucified God* focuses on the memory of Christ's death.[9] Borrowing from Martin Luther and his theology of the cross, Moltmann denies the divine impassibility of classical theistic traditions.[10] "How can Christian faith understand Christ's passion as being the revelation of God, if the deity cannot suffer?"[11] The Christian God is revealed in the suffering and shame of the cross. The cross distinguishes God from other gods. God is different from the passionless god of Greek metaphysical notions, Moltmann argues.[12] This means that God is revealed as God in his opposite: godlessness and abandonment by God. In concrete terms, God is revealed in the cross of Christ, who was abandoned by God.[13]

3. Moltmann, *Theology of Hope,* 30.
4. Geiko Müller-Fahrenholz, *The Kingdom and the Power: The Theology of Jürgen Moltmann* (Minneapolis: Fortress, 2001), 47.
5. Moltmann, *Theology of Hope,* 93.
6. Ibid., 141.
7. Ibid., 203.
8. Jürgen Moltmann, *The Crucified God: The Cross of Christ as the Foundation and Criticism of Christian Theology* (1972; reprint, London: SCM, 1974).
9. See Müller-Fahrenholz, *Kingdom and the Power,* 63.
10. See Bauckham, *Theology of Jürgen Moltmann,* chap. 3.
11. Jürgen Moltmann, *The Trinity and the Kingdom of God: The Doctrine of God* (London: SCM, 1981), 21.
12. Ibid., 22.
13. Moltmann, *Crucified God,* 27.

Besides the passion of Christ, another reason for talking about the suffering God is the nature of divine love. According to Moltmann, classical theism eliminates from the notion of God's love for the world any element of reciprocity. God cannot be affected by the objects of his love. For Moltmann, however, God's love is twofold: It is activity for others and also involvement with others.[14] Therefore:

> A God who cannot suffer is poorer than any man. For a God who is incapable of suffering is a being who cannot be involved. Suffering and injustice do not affect him. . . . But the one who cannot suffer cannot love either. So he is also a loveless being.[15]

Furthermore, human suffering penetrates to the heart of the question of whether God exists and also raises the theodicy question. God does not shy away from suffering but makes it his own and so overcomes it and brings about hope. All suffering becomes God's so that God may overcome it.[16] This brings us again to the cross of Christ. Moltmann takes the words of Psalm 22, "My God, my God, why have you forsaken me?" on the lips of the dying Jesus as both an expression of the utmost suffering and anguish of the innocent victim[17] and a cry of the Father, who deserts his Son: "The grief of the Father is here as important as the death of the Son."[18] In other words, the Son suffers dying in abandonment, and the Father suffers in grief over the death of his Son. Thus, God not only feels sympathy or empathy with the ones who suffer but "also accepts and adopts [suffering] in himself, making it part of his own eternal life."[19]

Moltmann believes that it is only when one sees the suffering of God on the cross as the foundational principle of the doctrine of God that the perils of atheism and classical theism can be avoided. Theology is then liberated from the contradiction between God and suffering, and one can boldly confess that "God's being is in suffering and suffering in God's being itself," because God is love.[20]

In his subsequent works, especially *Trinity and the Kingdom of God,* which contains his doctrine of God proper, Moltmann develops the basic ideas presented in these earlier works and draws implications for the God-world relationship and the Trinity.

14. See Bauckham, *Theology of Jürgen Moltmann,* 49–50.

15. Moltmann, *Crucified God,* 222.

16. Ibid., 246.

17. Ibid., 146–47.

18. Ibid., 243.

19. Moltmann, *Trinity and the Kingdom of God,* 119.

20. Moltmann, *Crucified God,* 72; see also Müller-Fahrenholz, *Kingdom and the Power,* 72–73.

Trinitarian Panentheism

How are God and the world related to each other in Moltmann's theology? An answer requires a brief look at his theology of creation, a topic that emerged later in his career. Not until the emergence of his unique view of creation did Moltmann come to a view of the God-world relationship that is appropriately called "trinitarian panentheism."[21] Unlike classical theism, which often depicts God as the transcendent one detached from the world, and pantheism, which equates the world and the divine, Moltmann sees a genuine mutual relationship between God and the world. Both influence and condition each other, but God affects the world more than the world affects God because God is the Creator and Sustainer. The title of Moltmann's doctrine of creation illustrates this principle: *God in Creation.*

Moltmann maintains that the world was created by God's free will.[22] Unlike Barth, who sees freedom and love as complementary ("the One who loves in freedom"), implying that God could have decided not to create the world if he had so wished because he is self-sufficient in himself, Moltmann believes creation "out of freedom" means creation "out of love."[23] God's freedom is the freedom of love; love and freedom are synonymous.[24] Yes, God could have chosen not to create, but that was not what he did, because God chooses only that "which corresponds to his essential goodness, in order to communicate the goodness as his creation and in his creation."[25] This brings us to the starting point of Christian panentheism, which starts from the divine essence:

> Creation is a fruit of God's longing for his Other and for that Other's free response to the divine love. That is why the idea of the world is inherent in the nature of God himself from eternity. . . . And if God's eternal being is love, then the divine love is also more blessed in giving than in receiving. God cannot find bliss in eternal self-love if selflessness is part of love's very nature. God is in all eternity self-communicating love.[26]

This is the paradoxical notion of the "divine necessity" (to create) of God's love together with God's freedom.

Moltmann assumes a "self-limitation of the infinite, omnipresent God." Distinguishing between "an act of God outwardly" and "an act of God inwardly," Moltmann states, "Before God issues creatively out of himself, he acts inwardly on himself, resolving for himself, committing himself, determining

---

21. For this designation, see Bauckham, *Theology of Jürgen Moltmann,* 17.

22. Jürgen Moltmann, *God in Creation: An Ecological Doctrine of Creation* (London: SCM, 1985), 75.

23. Ibid.

24. Ibid., 130.

25. Ibid., 76.

26. Moltmann, *Trinity and the Kingdom of God,* 138.

himself."[27] To create something "outside" himself, "the infinite God must have made room for this finitude beforehand 'in himself.'"[28] This is the famous idea of "self-limitation," Moltmann's creative recasting of the classical view of *creatio ex nihilo:* Through the self-withdrawal of the omnipotent "within Godself," the *nihil* comes into being.[29] Moltmann refers to the Jewish cabalistic doctrine of *zimzum,* which means concentration and contradiction and signifies a withdrawal of oneself into oneself, to describe this "shrinkage process in God," which makes the existence of the universe possible. God withdraws into himself in order to go out of himself.[30]

In his later book on eschatology, *The Coming of God,*[31] Moltmann speaks of the "cosmic Shekinah of God" as a way to express God's desire to be with the world he created out of his free love: "God desires to come to his 'dwelling' in his creation, the home of his identity in the world, and in it to his 'rest,' his perfected, eternal joy."[32] This is the eschatological hope for Christians. In this eschatological Shekinah, the entire creation will be new. The eschatological indwelling of God is the presence of God in the space of his created beings.[33] When God comes to inhabit creation, the "Creator becomes the God who can be inhabited."[34] This is the fulfillment of Moltmann's long-standing eschatological vision, the panentheistic vision of God's being "all in all" (1 Cor. 15:28).[35] Yet Moltmann's panentheistic view of God is thoroughly trinitarian.

Trinitarian History of God

Moltmann is a key figure in the recent renaissance of trinitarian doctrine.[36] Like Wolfhart Pannenberg, he is not interested in abstract speculations about the Trinity. Rather, he sees it as a natural conclusion based on the history of God in the world. For Moltmann, the doctrine of the Trinity is not a departure from the God of Jewish monotheism. In fact, few Christian theologians have tried as hard as Moltmann to build bridges between the Christian doctrine of the Trinity and the Jewish Shema of Yahweh.[37]

27. Moltmann, *God in Creation,* 86.
28. Moltmann, *Trinity and the Kingdom of God,* 109.
29. Ibid.; and Moltmann, *God in Creation,* 86ff.
30. Moltmann, *God in Creation,* 86–87.
31. Jürgen Moltmann, *The Coming of God: A Christian Eschatology* (Minneapolis: Fortress, 1996).
32. Ibid., xiii.
33. Ibid., 265.
34. Ibid., 299.
35. Ibid., 307.
36. See Stanley J. Grenz, *The Social God and the Relational Self: A Trinitarian Theology of the Imago Dei* (Louisville: Westminster John Knox, 2001), 41–46.
37. See Müller-Fahrenholz, *Kingdom and the Power,* 138–40.

The starting point for Moltmann's exposition of the doctrine of the Trinity is Jesus Christ and his suffering on the cross, a suffering within God himself. Here, of course, he follows the lead of Barth. The major difference is that Moltmann starts with three different persons rather than with the substantialist unity of God.[38] The cross is not merely an event between God and humanity. "What happened on the cross was an event between God and God. It was a deep division in God himself, in so far as God abandoned God and contradicted himself, and at the same time a unity in God, in so far as God was at one with God and corresponded to himself."[39] Thus, the cross belongs to the inner life of God. It does not occur only between God and estranged humanity, the way classical theism has approached the topic.[40]

Based on the cross of Christ as the foundation of the Trinity, Moltmann develops his distinctive idea of the "trinitarian history of God": The histories of the Son and the Spirit are in the process of bringing about the glorification of the Father and thus bringing all into eschatological unity. Moltmann does not regard the Father as only the active subject but also as one dependent on the other members of the Trinity. The cross and the resurrection of the Son, the sending of the Spirit, and the consequent rise of the church are the critical stages in which the Father's fatherhood is constituted in the divine Trinity. The final goal is the eschatological unity of the Trinity: "When everything is 'in God' and 'God is all in all,'" then the economic Trinity will be raised into and transcended in the immanent Trinity.[41]

Out of his trinitarian doctrine, Moltmann draws implications for political and social life, advocating equality and friendship in his harsh criticism of "abstract monotheism," which often supports oppression and totalitarian regimes, whether in the church or in society. The Trinity is not a hierarchical entity but rather a fellowship of persons: "We understand the scriptures as the testimony to the history of the Trinity's relations of fellowship, which are open to men and women, and open to the world."[42] According to Moltmann, the church is "a fellowship of equal persons" patterned according to the Trinity.[43]

---

38. See Ted Peters, *God as Trinity: Relationality and Temporality in Divine Life* (Louisville: Westminster John Knox, 1993), 103.

39. Moltmann, *Crucified God*, 244.

40. Ibid., 249.

41. Moltmann, *Trinity and the Kingdom of God*, 175.

42. Ibid., 19; see also 17–18, 191–92.

43. See Veli-Matti Kärkkäinen, *An Introduction to Ecclesiology: Ecumenical, Historical, and Global Perspectives* (Downers Grove, Ill.: InterVarsity, 2002), 128–29.

16

John Hick

A Pluralistic View of God

The Copernican Revolution of Religions

The most heated discussion today concerning the doctrine of God is not about atheism, rationalism, or postmodernism but religious pluralism. The theologian who has been at the forefront of this discussion, beginning in the early 1970s, is John Hick, an Englishman who moved to the United States in the 1980s but has retained close ties with England.[1] His moves from a conservative evangelical Christian to an inclusivist and finally to a pluralist compose an interesting pilgrimage that echoes much of what is going on today in the debate concerning theology of religions.

Hick compares his pluralistic theology of religions to Copernicus's astronomical model. God, the Ultimate Truth, is the center of all religions, which revolve around God like the planets:

> The needed Copernican revolution in theology involves an equally radical transformation in our conception of the universe of faiths and the place of our own religion within it. It involves a shift from the dogma that Christianity is at the center to the realization that it is God who is at the center,

---

1. My exposition owes to Matti T. Amnell, *Uskontojen Universumi: John Hickin uskonnollisen pluralismin haaste ja siitä käyty keskustelu* (Helsinki: STK, 1999).

and that all the religions of mankind, including our own, serve and revolve around him.[2]

It is on this basis that Hick defines his view of pluralism: There is "both the one unlimited transcendent divine Reality and also a plurality of varying human concepts, images, and experiences of and responses to that Reality."[3] Thus, all religions, whether Christian or Hindu[4] or Buddhist,[5] are challenged to move from a "Ptolemaic" view, in which a particular religion stands at the center and other religions are judged by the criteria of that center, to a genuinely pluralistic view of God.[6] To accomplish this task, Hick contends that the views of adherents of religions cannot be taken at face value. Rather, each religion has to be confronted by the challenge of deemphasizing its own absolute and exclusive claims.[7] Hick illustrates his point by referring to an allegory from Buddhist sources according to which ten blind men are touching an elephant and each is describing what an elephant is like on the basis of his limited experience. Various conceptions of God/god(s)/divine such as Yahweh, Allah, Krishna, Param Atma, or the Holy Trinity are but aspects of the divine,[8] like colors of the rainbow.[9]

What is the starting point for Hick's Copernican revolution? Hick builds on the phenomenological similarity of religions.[10] He also notes the self-evident fact that one's religion usually correlates with where one lives.[11] On the basis of these considerations, he calls for "the basic common ground of the world religions." The very same divine Reality is present in various religions and cultures.[12] Thus, rather than assuming opposition between religions, Hick believes all religions have the same basic orientation and share the same hope for salvation. The main biblical-theological basis for pluralism is God's love.[13]

2. John Hick, *God and the Universe of Faiths: Essays in the Philosophy of Religion* (London: Macmillan, 1973); see also, for example, John Hick, *The Second Christianity*, 3d ed. (London: SCM, 1983), 82.

3. Hick, *Second Christianity*, 83.

4. John Hick, *God Has Many Names: Britain's New Religious Pluralism* (London: Macmillan, 1980), 83; and Hick, *God and the Universe of Faiths*, 131.

5. John Hick, *Problems of Religious Pluralism* (London: Macmillan, 1988), 48; see also idem, *The Metaphor of God Incarnate: Christology in a Pluralistic Age* (London: SCM, 1993), 134.

6. See Hick, *Metaphor of God Incarnate*, 135; idem, *The Rainbow of Faiths: Critical Dialogue on Religious Pluralism* (London: SCM, 1995), 44; and Amnell, *Uskontojen Universumi*, 36–37.

7. John Hick, *An Interpretation of Religion: Human Responses to the Transcendent* (London: Macmillan, 1989), 2–3; idem, *Metaphor of God Incarnate*, 135; and idem, *Rainbow of Faiths*, 48.

8. Hick, *God and the Universe of Faiths*, 140–41.

9. Hick, *Problems of Religious Pluralism*, 80; and idem, *Rainbow of Faiths*, ix–x.

10. See Hick, *Rainbow of Faiths*, 13; and idem, *God Has Many Names*, 4–5.

11. John Hick, "Is Christianity the Only True Religion?" *Theology* 101 (1998): 326.

12. John Hick, *Death and Eternal Life* (London: Collins, 1976), 30; idem, *God and the Universe of Faiths*, 141; idem, *God Has Many Names*, 27, 35, 44; and Amnell, *Uskontojen Universumi*, 47.

13. Hick, *God and the Universe of Faiths*, 122–23.

The Mythical Nature of God-Talk

To understand Hick's theology of religions, one has to consider the way he understands talk about religion and the divine. Hick does not deny the cognitive function of religious language (that religious language has a reference to something real or true as opposed to mere metaphorical talk), as many other contemporary pluralists do, but rather uses two approaches to deal with the existence of competing truth claims.

In his first approach, Hick divides the differences among seemingly contradictory claims of various religions into three levels. The first level relates to historical conceptions, such as the Christian belief in the death of Jesus on the cross versus the view of the Qur'an, according to which it only seemed actual. The only way to resolve a conflict at this level is to appeal to historical evidence, which, of course, is lacking.[14] The second level is that of suprahistorical claims, or, as Hick also calls them, "quasihistorical" claims, such as the doctrine of reincarnation. Obviously, there is no way to reconcile the differences between religions that support the idea (Buddhism and Hinduism) and those that do not (Islam, Judaism, and Christianity). Consequently, the only sensible way to deal with this level of conflict is to adopt an attitude of mutual respect and acceptance.[15] The third level concerns conceptions about the Ultimate Reality. Ideas about personal God/gods such as Yahweh, Siva, Visnu, and Allah and impersonal gods such as Brahma, Sunyata, and Dharmakaya cannot be easily reconciled. Thus, according to Hick, these seemingly contradictory descriptions of the divine should be seen as complementary.[16]

Hick's second approach to dealing with contradictory truth claims is to appeal to the mythical nature of religious language. Myth is based on metaphor, which means that people speak in a way "suggestive of another."[17] According to this understanding, metaphors, which are not meant to be taken at face value, convey meaning, but they do so by eliciting emotions and associations familiar to a group that shares a common context of meanings. In an important sense, myth is an expanded metaphor. Even though it is not literally true, it "tends to evoke an appropriate dispositional attitude."[18] Its purpose is to change one's attitude and thus influence one's thinking in a real way. The story about Buddha's flight to Sri Lanka, the creation story of the Old Testament, and the legend of the dance of Siva all function in this way.[19] Rather

14. John Hick, "On Conflicting Religious Truth Claims," *Religious Studies* 19 (1983): 485–91; and idem, *Interpretation of Religion,* 363–65.

15. Hick, *Problems of Religious Pluralism,* 89–95; and idem, *Interpretation of Religion,* 365–72.

16. Hick, *Problems of Religious Pluralism,* 90–95; and idem, *Interpretation of Religion,* 374.

17. Hick, *Metaphor of God Incarnate,* 99.

18. Ibid., 105. See also Hick, *Interpretation of Religion,* 99–104, 348; and Amnell, *Uskontojen Universumi,* 79–81.

19. Hick, *Interpretation of Religion,* 103, 347–72.

than inquiring into the truth of a myth, one should ask how it functions in the life situation and context for which it was created. When myths are treated in this way, Yahweh and Krishna are not antitheses because they operate in their own distinctive spheres.[20]

On the basis of his understanding of language, Hick divides the basic elements of religions into two categories: essentials and superficial elements. Although religions seem to have dramatic differences at the surface, deep down, Hick believes, they have a common foundation. For Hick, the differences at the surface level, even when to some extent cognitive in nature, do not create insurmountable conflicts. For instance, Hick maintains that Jesus' divinity has to be understood metaphorically.[21] A mythological interpretation of Christology has the potential of serving a pluralistic theology of religions. In such a view, Christ is depicted as the embodiment of divine love, complementary to what is revealed about the divine in Buddhism or in Hinduism.[22]

Hick often compares this kind of language to that of lovers. Even though expressions such as "I love you more than anybody else" seem to be absolutist, they are not exclusive. Other lovers freely use them as well, and they are true in various contexts and for the purpose they were meant.

The Ultimate Reality

Later in his career, to do justice to his understanding of the nature of religious language, Hick shifted from speaking about "God" to "the Ultimate Reality." This term is more flexible than the personal "God." For Hick, the great religions of the world are different—and complementary—ways of approaching this Reality, which exists beyond human comprehension. The Sanskrit term *sat* and the Islamic term *al-Haqq* are expressions of this Reality, as is *Yahweh* and the Christian *God*.[23]

Here Hick builds on the Kantian distinction between *phenomena* (the way we see things) and *noumena* (the thing in itself, which is unknown to us) and maintains that part of the divine/Reality is unknown to us, while we can know at least something about another part. The Hindu concept of *nirguna Brahma,* distinguished from *saguna Brahma,* refers to something that cannot be fathomed by human means of knowledge. Similarly, the "eternal Tao" of Taoism, about which we know nothing, is distinguished from the "expressed Tao."[24] Regardless of the differing names

20. Ibid., 267–68.
21. Hick, *God Has Many Names,* 74; and idem, *Second Christianity,* 9.
22. Hick, *God Has Many Names,* 75; and idem, *Rainbow of Faiths,* 22–23.
23. Hick, *Interpretation of Religion,* 10–11.
24. John Hick, "Religious Realism and Non-Realism: Defining the Issue," in *Is God Real?* ed. Joseph Runzo (New York: St. Martin's Press, 1993), 6.

of and approaches to the Reality, in Hick's view, there is only one Reality, the ultimate divine. Consequently, he posits a unified soteriological structure in all religions,[25] which he calls a move from self-centeredness to reality-centeredness.[26]

25. Hick, *Metaphor of God Incarnate,* 136; idem, *Problems of Religious Pluralism,* 69; and idem, *Interpretation of Religion,* 5–6.
26. Amnell, *Uskontojen Universumi,* 148–49.

17

Reflections on Contemporary European Views of God

The twentieth-century European theologies of God were generally responses to and dialogues with both the classical theistic tradition and—perhaps more importantly—the modern search for God begun by Descartes and continued by post-Enlightenment thinkers such as Kant, Hegel, and Schleiermacher.

Without doubt, Karl Barth is the bridge person between classical liberalism's naïve optimism and the shattered reality of the twentieth century with its two world wars. It is easy to judge Barth prematurely for his one-sided reaction to liberalism and his insistence on the transcendence of God. Working in his own context, however, Barth, with all his limitations, helped Christian theology move out of classical liberalism yet continue the program of the Enlightenment. The lasting contribution of Barth was refocusing reflection on the doctrine of God by seeing the Trinity as the constitutive element of theology. Barth not only rehabilitated the Trinity but also helped to recast the doctrine of God in general by pointing to history as the arena in which we get to know God and where God is involved in a real way. Barth was also instrumental in guiding theologians to see revelation as the starting point for the doctrine of God, even if few have followed his dialectical view of Scripture.

Paul Tillich came from the same camp as Barth, yet his way of constructing the doctrine of God for the "secular man" turned out to be diametrically opposed to Barth's. Immersed in existentialist philosophy and to a great extent leaving behind the contours of classical Christian tradition, Tillich, ironically, both prepared for the emerging death-of-God theologies (to be discussed in part 4) and helped to make Christian theology more reasonable to Western culture at the heyday of secularism. Tillich's approach was highly contextualized, and after roughly two decades of unprecedented interest, it did not redeem its promises for a continuing movement.

The two Roman Catholic theologians Hans Küng and Karl Rahner, while vastly different from these two Protestant thinkers from the right and the left of the theological spectrum, share much of the mind-set of Tillich. The early Küng took the challenges of atheism and agnosticism in their various forms (religious, psychological, philosophical, and political) seriously. His *Does God Exist?* is a milestone in Christian theology in advancing a genuine dialogue between believers in God and those who either do not want to or cannot believe. What makes Küng an interesting theologian is that despite his insistence on the reality of the Christian God, he later shifted to theology of religions and more recently to global ethics. As a genuine Catholic inclusivist, he never shared the Barthian exclusivist approach to challenges to faith in God.

Küng's colleague Rahner, while deeply steeped in classical Christian traditions, shared the passion—though not the method—of Tillich in trying to make God-talk reasonable for the secular person living in the latter part of the twentieth century. Unlike Tillich, however, and in spite of his use of philosophy and contextualization, he remained more or less orthodox throughout his career. His genuine inclusivism toward other religions emerges from his insistence that religion is a natural, "innate" part of humanity.

Wolfhart Pannenberg and Jürgen Moltmann, the two contemporary giants of Protestant theology in Europe and the leading figures on the international scene, are bridges to the third millennium. While once dubbed theological colleagues (they were colleagues in the early 1960s in their homeland), they pursued different theological careers. Pannenberg's approach to the question of God began in a way similar to Küng's in that he interacted with atheism. Out of that encounter emerged, for example, his massive study *Anthropology in Theological Perspective.* Such interaction helped him to focus, like Rahner in his own way, on theological anthropology as the gateway to defending the reasonableness of faith in God. Pannenberg was convinced that God-talk can be made rational, even if the existence of God cannot be proved, with the help of the insight that religion—and thus faith in God—belongs to the constitutive element in the human person. With atheism, science and secular philosophy have always been Pannenberg's major challengers. Thus, he spent the better part of his life developing a theological method in relation to these fields. In his *Systematic Theology,* he sets out his entire system in critical dialogue with the post-Enlightenment intellectual ethos as well as with modern science and philosophy. Pannenberg, unlike so many theologians living in the postmodern era, is fully convinced that talk about God, always in painstakingly detailed dialogue with biblical and historical theistic traditions, not only has the right but is also compelled to issue truth claims. Pannenberg's contribution to the doctrine of God also lies in his trinitarian approach in which the Trinity is discussed prior to the unity of God. In addition, all talk about the Trinity is based on revelation. The beginning of the doctrine of the Trinity lies in the way the trinitarian persons come to the fore in the biblical text. Thus, Pannenberg takes seriously the Barthian idea of introducing history into the divine life.

Moltmann's approach to the doctrine of God differs from that of Pannenberg, even though Moltmann also began his work by reacting to atheism. Taking eschatology as his main guide and the cross of Christ as the criterion of theology, he developed a new approach to viewing God and his relationship with the world. It differs from classical theism in that God's involvement with the world is mutual and that suffering is constitutive of divine life; it is also different from pantheism in that God still remains God. It differs from process theology (to be discussed in part 4) for the very same reason. According to Moltmann's panentheism, God and the world influence each other, while the world is dependent on God. Moltmann not only advances Barth's program and, with Pannenberg, introduces history into the life of God but also makes the "trinitarian history of God" the focal point of his doctrine of the Trinity, so much so that the unity of the Godhead can be found only in the coming of the eschatological *perichōrēsis* of God. Moltmann has always sought to speak to real-life issues from a theological perspective. Therefore, his doctrine of God speaks to political, social, gender, and ecclesiastical concerns.

John Zizioulas, the representative of the Eastern Orthodox tradition who has influenced Moltmann, represents a breakthrough in the contemporary doctrine of God with his insistence on communion as the proper mode of God's existence. This is a key to the issue of personhood, much debated throughout history, and the issue of community, both in and outside the church.

As we move next to North American perspectives on God, we will refer to many of these European thinkers.

Part 4

God in North American Perspective

A Dialogue with Classical Traditions

Reflection on God in North America, the United States and Canada, under-standably shares much in common with European traditions and could be, quite justifiably, discussed under the heading of Western theologies. Yet it is becoming clear that a shift is taking place. Europe is loosing its status as the world's theological center, and the center of gravity is moving to North America. Several factors are currently shaping talk about God in North America. The two that follow are the most formative.

First, North America provides fertile soil for the rise of contextual theologies because of its multicultural population. What makes North America distinctive is that it currently includes people from all continents and virtually all nations and languages. Thus, there has been the rise of "immigrant" theologies: Asian American and Hispanic American. Large Asian and Hispanic populations exist in various parts of North America, with growing churches and emerging theological traditions.

Second, North America's ecclesiastical scene differs from Europe's. Theo-logical currents in North America include not only evangelical churches with massive theological schools and growing theological productivity but also various kinds of free churches. In Europe, most churches are declining, even if culturally they continue to occupy a significant role in society, and outside traditional churches very little academic theology is produced. Not so in North

America. Theological and ecclesiastical traditions that are almost unknown in Europe are quite visible across the Atlantic.

The following survey of North American doctrines of God attempts to do justice to these distinctive features. It first examines challenges to classical theism such as the death-of-God theologies of the 1960s, the highly influential process theology, and a recent debate mainly among evangelicals over Open theism (a debate virtually unknown in Europe). The survey also examines the views of mainline evangelical theologians who stand firmly in the tradition of classical theism and therefore criticize those who have challenged the classical tradition.

Because the North American survey includes many approaches and movements, theologies of individual thinkers cannot be exhaustively studied. In that sense, this treatment differs methodologically from the European section, which focused on the contributions of individual theologians.

18

Challenges to Classical Theism

Secular and Death-of-God Theologies

Mapping Out Theological Responses to Secularization

The most radical and controversial challenge to the doctrine of God on the North American scene is a constellation of ideas called secular and death-of-God theologies. These movements, which emphasize the immanence of God, the absence of God from the world, or the nonexistence of God (or at least the idea[s] of God), share a background in the secularism of the Western world culminating in the 1960s.

"Secular theology" here refers to an orientation to the doctrine of God in which secularism is not seen as a threat but rather as an opportunity for Christianity. This view is not limited to Protestantism; it is also found among some Jewish and Roman Catholic thinkers.[1] Harvey Cox is the most notable North American proponent of this view along with the British bishop John T. Robinson. Much of the impetus for a "Christian" version of secularism came from the highly influential thinking of the German martyr Dietrich Bonhoeffer.

The much contested phrase "death of God" made the headlines in an October 1965 *Time* magazine cover story entitled "Is God Dead?" and produced neologisms such as "theothanatology" (from the Greek words meaning the

1. See Eric C. Meyer, C.P., "Death of God," in *God in Contemporary Thought: A Philosophical Perspective,* ed. Sebastian A. Matczak (New York: Learned Publications, 1977), 793–805.

death of God). It also describes various movements and thinkers. Eric C. Meyer helps orient us:

> Now, most Jewish and Christian theologians would not deny that there has long been a progressive fading away of faith in God . . . ; nor would many deny that this development seems to be climaxing in the modern process of radical secularization; but relatively few are willing to affirm this situation in a radical way. Radical or death-of-God theologians are those relatively few who do "talk about God" in various ways that *more or less* radically affirm what has happened to faith in God in the extremely secular situation of modern man; and so it is that they speak positively about the disappearance or absence, eclipse or hiddenness, or even demise or death of God. What one must emphasize, however, is the *more or less*.[2]

Death-of-God theologies can be divided into two main camps: "soft" (theistic and panentheistic views) and "hard" (agnostic and atheistic views).[3] In the first category, thinkers do not believe that God has actually died but that the particular kind of God associated too closely with Judeo-Christian religion and culture is passing away due to the process of radical secularization. They also believe that the God who is wholly transcendent has died, and they focus instead on God as an immanent entity. Harvey Cox is the most noted theologian of the first category. Only the second category, "hard" agnostic and atheistic thinkers, therefore, denotes death-of-God theologies proper. The most famous thinkers in this camp are Thomas J. Altizer and William Hamilton. No doubt, theological movements that take very seriously the secularism of the last centuries of the second millennium represent a distinctive challenge to classical theism, which has taken the existence of God for granted and has described God as the transcendent, all-powerful, all-knowing Other.

A Secular Interpretation of the Christian God

The "Beyond in the Midst of Our Life": The Legacy of Dietrich Bonhoeffer

While Dietrich Bonhoeffer, the martyred German pastor-theologian, was not a "secular" theologian, his emphasis in relating the gospel to the secular

---

2. Ibid., 775.

3. I am adapting here the somewhat ambiguous terminology used in ibid., 776–78. Meyer's terminology in general goes back to the definition by one of the proponents of radical death-of-God theologies: William Hamilton, "The Shape of a Radical Theology," *The Christian Century* 82 (6 October 1965): 1220.

realm was indirectly influential on secular theology. The following discussion briefly highlights his contribution to the doctrine of God.[4]

Like Karl Barth, Bonhoeffer regards God's revelation as coming "straight from above." Yet this does not suggest to Bonhoeffer a separation of faith from the world; in fact, he believes that the world has "come of age." The Christian church finds itself in a world in which humans operate autonomously, without a particular need to refer to divine truth or to God. Earlier, God was needed to "fill in the gaps," to explain things unknown to the human mind. In the secular age, God is no longer needed as a working hypothesis, to be postulated as long as no better explanation is available.[5] Bonhoeffer is happy to do away with this "God of the gaps," who is no longer needed.[6] Thus, Christian theology, rather than trying to oppose "the adulthood of the world," should speak of God in terms that make sense to the secular age.[7]

To speak meaningfully of the God of the Bible, Bonhoeffer suggests "religionless Christianity." This concept opposes both the liberal notion of religion as a natural human commodity and the pietistic privativism in which God is relegated to the inner chambers of the individual heart, which leads to a "magical" view of God. Bonhoeffer also rejects a well-meaning notion of God as the completion of human life; in that view, God is needed as the frosting on the cake. What is needed is a "non-religious interpretation of biblical terminology."[8]

The God Bonhoeffer sees in the Bible and who can speak to the secular age is "the Beyond in the midst of our life." Thus, we are to find God in what we know, not in what we do not know.[9] Furthermore, we are to view God as weak and powerless in the world, the God who "allows himself to be edged out of the world and on to the cross." This is the God who "conquers power and space in the world by his weakness."[10] The end result is what Bonhoeffer calls "holy worldliness": Christians love God in the midst of their everyday lives and share in the suffering of God in the life of the world. This is the culmination of Bonhoeffer's theology and idea of God.[11] The meaning of the transcendence of God is thus reinterpreted by Bonhoeffer: It does not mean finding God "out there" but in the midst of the ordinary. Ordinary life is more than "ordinary" because God can be found there.

---

4. A helpful brief introduction to Bonhoeffer's main theological ideas is offered in Stanley J. Grenz and Roger E. Olson, *Twentieth-Century Theology: God and the World in a Transitional Age* (Downers Grove, Ill.: InterVarsity, 1992), 146–56.

5. Dietrich Bonhoeffer, *Letters and Papers from Prison* (London: Collins, Fontana Books, 1953), 107.

6. Ibid., 114–15.

7. Ibid., 108; see also 117.

8. Ibid., 120.

9. Ibid., 93, 104.

10. Ibid., 122.

11. See Grenz and Olson, *Twentieth-Century Theology,* 153–54.

The Secular City: Harvey Cox

With Bonhoeffer, Harvey Cox believes that secularization represents not a threat to Christianity but rather an authentic consequence of biblical faith, especially in the Jewish/Old Testament tradition. Creation disenchants nature, the exodus desacralizes politics, and the Sinai covenant deconsecrates value, especially in the prohibition of idols. Cox's leading thesis is that secularization is "the legitimate consequence of the impact of biblical faith in history."[12] He makes an important distinction between secularization and secularism. The latter denotes an ideology or a closed worldview that functions like a new religion. Secularization, however, is not something to be opposed by those who take biblical faith seriously; it is an almost irreversible process. The task of Christian theology is to make sure that secularization does not harden into secularism.[13] A similar analysis of secularization is offered by Erich Fromm in his *Art of Loving*.[14]

The value of the process of secularization for Cox is that it helps Christian faith claim the two cardinal virtues of liberty and responsibility. As Bonhoeffer called Christians to embrace the "adulthood of the world," Cox urges theology to welcome the "adult responsibility" of the secular person.[15]

One of Cox's most controversial theses is that politics now plays the role that religion and faith in God once played. Politics unifies society and provides meaning to human life. Consequently, theology should speak to and take part in political life (such as democracy and human rights).[16] For Christian theology to talk more meaningfully to politics and secular society, it must give up the term *God* and find a more suitable designation.

Others followed in the footsteps of Cox to construct an authentically secular interpretation of God. One of the most formative voices was that of Paul van Buren, who wrote *The Secular Meaning of the Gospel*.[17] The most visible figure in Europe was the Anglican bishop John A. T. Robinson. In his controversial book *Honest to God*, Robinson contends that God is not to be seen as "up there" or "out there," whether in spatial or metaphysical and spiritual terms, but rather as something that gives meaning and direction to the world, especially to human relationships in the world. Following Paul Tillich, Robinson speaks of God as "in here," in the depth of being and personal relationships.[18]

---

12. Harvey Cox, *The Secular City: Secularization and Urbanization in Theological Perspective* (New York: Macmillan, 1965), 17.

13. Ibid., 17–37.

14. Erich Fromm, *The Art of Loving: An Enquiry into the Nature of Love* (New York: Harper & Row, 1956).

15. Cox, *Secular City*, 121.

16. Ibid., 255; see also 241–69.

17. Paul van Buren, *The Secular Meaning of the Gospel* (New York: Macmillan, 1963).

18. John A. T. Robinson, *Honest to God* (Philadelphia: Westminster, 1963).

Despite its popularity in the 1960s, secular theology came to an abrupt end. This is not to say that its influence stopped. Rather, the challenges it posed to Christian theism, while not sustaining a life of their own as a movement, were assimilated and adapted in various ways by other theologies. The same fate was experienced by the even more radical responses to secularism, namely, death-of-God theologies.

Death-of-God Theologies

God Is Dead: The Legacy of Friedrich Nietzsche

The leading death-of-God thinker, Thomas J. Altizer, frequently pays tribute to Friedrich Nietzsche, the leading denier of God in the nineteenth century. However, whereas for Nietzsche the cry "God is dead" was a bold, liberating exclamation, for most Christian theologians of the death-of-God movement it was a cry of an anguished, desperate seeker of God.[19]

In *The Gay Science,* Nietzsche depicts a madman running through the streets in search of God crying out:

> God is dead. God remains dead. And we have killed him. . . . Is not the greatness of this deed too great for us? Must not we ourselves become gods simply to seem worthy of it? There has never been a greater deed; and whoever will be born after us—for the sake of this deed he will be part of a higher history than all history hitherto.[20]

Nietzsche titles the fifth book of *The Gay Science* "We Fearless Ones," and it contains a section on "the meaning of our cheerfulness." There he admits that the implications of the "good news" of the death of God can already be seen in Europe and beyond.[21] Now that God is not the one to be trusted, someone else, the human being, the "Superhuman" must take responsibility. Because of the "decline of the faith in the Christian God," Nietzsche concludes that people must welcome "the ungodliness of existence . . . as something given, palpable, indisputable."[22]

---

19. There is no lack of documentation of an earnest search for God among those who ended up being more or less atheistic, radical death-of-God thinkers. See, for example, William Hamilton, *The New Essence of Christianity* (New York: Association Press, 1961), 63–65; and idem, "The Death of God," *Playboy* 13 (August 1966): 84.

20. Friedrich Nietzsche, *The Gay Science,* in *Portable Nietzsche* (New York: Viking, 1974), no. 125, 95–96.

21. Hans Küng, *Does God Exist? An Answer for Today* (Garden City, N.Y.: Doubleday, 1980), 369.

22. Quoted in ibid., 370.

On Taking God out of the Dictionary: William Hamilton

William Hamilton's first major contribution to the topic is *The New Essence of Christianity,* written in 1961, in which he builds on the ideas of Nietzsche, Albert Camus, and Paul Tillich. His main target is less the actual death of God and more a criticism of classical theism's view of providence as an all-powerful God. In the spirit of Bonhoeffer and Tillich, Hamilton issues a call to get rid of expectations of God and to take responsibility for our own lives and the world.

Subsequently, Hamilton begins to talk about the actual death of God, a discussion that culminates in 1966 when he coauthors with Thomas Altizer *Radical Theology and the Death of God.* Having left his teaching post in a theological school, Hamilton focuses more on themes related to the demise of God in English literature. In 1974, he produces a book entitled *On Taking God out of the Dictionary.*

The Gospel of Christian Atheism: Thomas Altizer

The main representative of the death-of-God movement is Thomas Altizer, who struggled to find a theological basis for the claim that God is dead. In his theology, the forces of secularization come to full expression.

What brought Altizer to public notice was the publication in 1966 of his magnum opus, *The Gospel of Christian Atheism.* Altizer's style of writing, anticipating many postmodern theologies to come, is eclectic and not easily followed. The same year also saw the publication of *Radical Theology and the Death of God,* coauthored with Hamilton. This work, significantly, is dedicated to Paul Tillich, whom Altizer named the "modern father of radical theology."[23] Bonhoeffer's influence is also visible in Altizer.

The leading idea of Altizer's theology is the absolute immanence of God in humanity, which "dissolv[es] even the memory or the shadow of transcendence" of God.[24] Altizer regards this dissolving of the transcendence of God into radical immanence as the benchmark of twentieth-century secularism and a new outlook on God. This is the proper Christian response to the call of Sigmund Freud, Nietzsche, existentialist philosophers such as Jean-Paul Sartre and Martin Heidegger, and many others who called Christian theism to revise (or negate) itself to adapt to modernism. For Altizer, Christian theology ought "simply to share the universal condition of man" by taking for "oneself a life without God."[25]

---

23. Thomas Altizer, *The Gospel of Christian Atheism* (Philadelphia: Westminster, 1966), 10.

24. Ibid., 22.

25. Ibid., 23.

Altizer explains the idea of the death of God based on the famous *kenōsis* ("emptying") passage Philippians 2:5–11 (v. 7 especially). Altizer's interpretation, which goes well beyond the literal meaning of the biblical text—or the orthodox interpretation—maintains that the Godhead "emptied" itself thoroughly into Jesus in his *kenōsis,* thus divesting itself of transcendence; this is the "self-annihilation of God." God became identical with humanity by negating his own objective existence through finite life and death.[26] In Altizer's own words:

> The God who acts in the world and history is a God who negates himself, gradually but decisively annihilating his own original Totality. God is that Totality which "falls" or "descends," thereby moving ever more fully into the opposite of its original identity. God or the Godhead becomes the God who is manifest in Christ by passing through a reversal of His original form: thus transcendence becomes immanence just as Spirit becomes flesh.[27]

The end result is that the "death of God abolishes transcendence, thereby making possible a new and absolute immanence, an immanence freed of every sign of transcendence."[28]

As liberating and joyful as the death of God is—and from God's perspective, it is an act of grace for the sake of the creatures in that it overcomes all forms of no to reach a life-affirming yes[29]—it also brings about uneasiness and nostalgia for the once real God. Thus, Samuel Beckett's *Waiting for Godot,* a "god" who never arrives but whose return is waited for, became famous in the wake of death-of-God popularity.

How "Dead" Is God?

The crucial question here is whether Altizer's and Hamilton's ways of speaking about the death of God should be taken literally or symbolically. Paul M. van Buren's title, *The Secular Meaning of the Gospel: Based on an Analysis of Its Language,* reveals that many continued to speak of God's death more or less symbolically (or metaphorically). Van Buren did not actually speak about the death of God literally or symbolically. He wanted to do away with the whole idea of talking about God, including God's death, in a meaningful way. This is the approach of analytic philosophy, which focuses on analyzing language and regards as meaningful only words that have an empirical (however that disputed term is defined) referent. The term *God* hardly meets that criteria and therefore has to be dismissed as meaningless. The book *The Death of God*

26. For a brief, accurate exposition, see Meyer, "Death of God," 778.
27. Altizer, *Gospel of Christian Atheism,* 89–90.
28. Ibid., 154.
29. Ibid.

by Gabriel Vahanian, who is often classified among the death-of-God theologians, is another example of the symbolic approach. Vahanian does not deny the existence of God but points to the "death" of Christian culture in the form understood in classical theism.

In contrast to these thinkers, "hard" death-of-God theologians Altizer and Hamilton do speak about the death of God in a literal sense. To avoid all misconceptions, Hamilton wrote in *Radical Theology and the Death of God*:

> This is more than the old protest against natural theology or metaphysics; more than the usual assurance that before the holy God all our language gets broken and diffracted into paradox. It is really that we do not know, do not adore, do not possess, do not believe in God. It is not just that a capacity has dried up within us; we do not take all this as merely a statement about our frail psyches, we take it as a statement about the nature of the world and we try to convince others. God is dead. We are not talking about the absence of the experience of God, but about the experience of the absence of God.[30]

Yet Hamilton and others regard this as a truly Christian form of theology.[31]

Like secular theology, death-of-God theology could not sustain itself. It was criticized not only by churchgoers and the general public for introducing atheism and paganism into the Christian faith but also by serious theological critics such as Langdon Gilkey for taking the term *God* out of the sphere of Christian theology and Christian tradition.[32]

---

30. Thomas Altizer and William Hamilton, *Radical Theology and the Death of God* (Indianapolis: Bobbs-Merrill, 1966), 27–28.

31. Altizer, *Gospel of Christian Atheism*, 12.

32. See Langdon Gilkey, *Naming the Whirlwind: The Renewal of God-Language* (Indianapolis: Bobbs-Merrill, 1969), 148.

19

God in Process Theology

A Dynamic View of Reality

Much of the modern quest for God has been an exercise in discrediting or abandoning the idea of metaphysics. This was the dominant trend from the Enlightenment to classical liberalism to analytic philosophy to secular theology and the death-of-God movement. Process philosophy and theology are notable exceptions to this rule and the most powerful attempts to build a (post)modern worldview on metaphysics. This is all the more significant given the fact that the originator of process thought was a mathematician from the school of analytic philosophy. Alfred H. Whitehead, about the time of his retirement, moved from Great Britain to the United States to begin a new career as a philosopher.[1]

The decision to build on metaphysics was not motivated by a desire to oppose science. On the contrary, Whitehead sought an understanding of reality that fit the new scientific outlook. Science had abandoned static Newtonian metaphysics with its idea of causality and "concrete" building blocks of reality. With many others, process philosophers envisioned a dynamic metaphysical understanding of reality. Owen Sharkey summarizes the basic ethos of process thought with a description of process theology: "Process Theology is not a col-

---

1. On the relationship between his role as a mathematician and a philosopher-theologian, see Ralph M. Martin, "On the Whiteheadian God," in *God in Contemporary Thought: A Philosophical Perspective,* ed. Sebastian A. Matczak (New York: Learned Publications, 1977), 615–18.

lection of vague and isolated affirmations about the mystery of God but a vision of reality as an organic whole marked by activity, movement, change, life."[2]

The formative work of process thought was done by Whitehead, whose philosophical work was picked up by theologians. The leading process theologians are Charles Hartshorne, Paul Griffith, Schubert Ogden, W. Norman Pittenger, John B. Cobb Jr., and Marjorie Hewitt Suchocki. A reliable self-exposition is offered by Cobb and David Ray Griffin in their *Process Theology: An Introduction*.[3] Lumping these theologians together should not suggest that they speak with a unanimous voice. For an introductory survey of the various contemporary challenges and additions to classical theism, however, it is legitimate to treat them as parts of one movement.

The World in Process: Alfred Whitehead's Metaphysics and View of God

Metaphysical Concepts

In line with Whitehead's dynamic understanding of reality, he posits that the subjective experience (which he calls "feeling") is present not only in humans but in all reality. Here he is following Kant but going beyond him in not limiting this "feeling" to human persons.[4] For Whitehead, everything has meaning and significance within the framework of a whole. There are no bare facts without meaning and significance, and that significance is related to the significance of every other moment and the total movement.[5]

Whitehead proposes a radically new concept of "subject" that he calls "actual entity." The term *entity* usually suggests something solid and enduring; here it means the opposite. An actual entity (also called an "occasion of experience") is not a permanently enduring thing, not an objective, primarily material substance of classical metaphysics.[6] These entities or building blocks of reality, also called "drops of experience," make up reality. Each drop of experience is an activity, a "becoming" that comes into existence and then quickly disappears. Reality, then, is a successive sequence of actual entities succeeding one another with a rapidity that escapes conscious attention; reality is not static but a process. Each actual entity is value-oriented, striving toward the realization of a value, and self-creative and connected to the whole.

2. Owen Sharkey, "The Mystery of God in Process Theology," in *God in Contemporary Thought*, 683.

3. John B. Cobb Jr. and David Ray Griffin, *Process Theology: An Introduction* (Philadelphia: Westminster, 1976).

4. Alfred Whitehead, *Adventures of Ideas* (Cambridge: Cambridge University Press, 1933), 252–53.

5. See Sharkey, "Mystery of God in Process Theology," 686–88.

6. Alfred Whitehead, *Process and Reality* (New York: Free Press, 1978), 28.

Actual entities have two sides; they are dipolar. First, there is what White-head calls the "physical pole," that is, the sense data entering one's conscious-ness.[7] Second, for human consciousness to experience the data received as "something," there needs to be a "mental pole." This dipolarity can also be expressed in terms of the physical pole representing the past and the mental pole the achievable future.[8]

Actual entities are not isolated; each is embedded in a stream of occasions on which it is dependent.[9] Each is related to both the past and the future, as already mentioned. Whitehead's term for past experiences is *prehension*.[10] Each actual entity may accept or reject prehensions from the past. Each actual entity is also related to the future, to "becoming," the potential. In the process of becoming, each entity is confronted by and either accepts or rejects its "initial aim," the best possible way it can contribute to subsequent occasions.[11]

Each actual entity is fleeting; it comes and goes. There is, however, a kind of continuity that Whitehead calls "objective immortality." Once an entity arises and immediately perishes, it is not totally lost, not only because it is the predecessor for the next entity but also because it adds to God's "experience." In that sense, God is the final repository of each entity once it perishes.[12]

God as an Entity in the World Process

What, then, is Whitehead's understanding of God? Whitehead's God is not an exception to all metaphysical principles, relegated to the role of being an explanation as long as no better explanation is available. God is, rather, "their chief exemplification." Whitehead takes for granted that humankind has a common religious experience. Religion, for him, is "the longing of the spirit that the facts of existence should find their justification in the nature of existence."[13] There is no doubt that despite Whitehead's philosophical notions, the

God of Whitehead is the God of the Christians. He believed God to be a personal, transcendent, yet immanent Actuality. He believed the divine Logos had become incarnate and was immanent in Jesus. He believed there is a third divine Person in the Godhead. He believed God to be a loving Actuality. He knew this from reading the epistles of John.[14]

---

7. Ibid., 49.
8. Ibid., 38.
9. Ibid., 309.
10. Ibid., 35.
11. Ibid., 130, 374.
12. Ibid., 373.
13. Alfred Whitehead, *Religion in the Making* (1926; reprint, New York: Meridian Books, 1971), 85.
14. Sharkey, "Mystery of God in Process Theology," 690.

He developed these ideas for the first time in his *Religion in the Making.* Yet at the same time he was a philosopher, and therefore it is difficult to say whether he envisioned himself first as a philosopher and then as a Christian or vice versa.[15]

The foundational idea in his process view of divinity is that "God is an actual entity, and so is the most trivial puff of existence in far-off empty space."[16] Since God is part of the whole of reality, like any other entity, God is also subject to its conditions. As an actual entity, God has two sides: "He has a primordial nature and a consequent nature."[17] "Viewed as primordial," Whitehead notes, God "is the unlimited conceptual realization of the absolute wealth of potentiality."[18] The primordial nature can also be viewed as the nontemporal "mental pole" of God. As such, God is the one who lures all actual entities in their process of becoming.[19] God as primordial is thus the ultimate source of creativity and novelty. The other dimension of God is the "consequent," the temporal, the "physical pole." As such, God prehends the temporal world and functions as the location of all perishing actual entities. In doing so, God experiences "a fullness of physical feeling,"[20] which makes God "the great companion," the "fellow-sufferer."[21] These two poles of God are bound together and presuppose each other.[22]

Several North American process theologians have developed Whitehead's philosophical metaphysics into a theological system and have presented a powerful critique of classical theism. A title by Norman Pittinger, "Process Thought as a Conceptuality for Reinterpreting Christian Faith,"[23] illustrates their main goal.

God as Creative-Responsive Love

Process theology has not been particularly interested in offering proofs for God's existence; rather, Whitehead's and others' focuses have been on the development of a philosophical framework that makes God's existence reason-

---

15. Ibid.

16. Whitehead, *Process and Reality,* 28.

17. Ibid., 524; see also 519–33, which gives a detailed discussion of the dipolar nature of God. Charles Hartshorne has named these two poles "the abstract essence" and "the concrete actuality" (*The Divine Relativity: A Social Conception of God* [New Haven: Yale University Press, 1964], 82–83).

18. Whitehead, *Process and Reality,* 521.

19. Ibid., 287.

20. Ibid.

21. Ibid., 532.

22. Ibid., 529.

23. Norman Pittinger, "Process Thought as a Conceptuality for Reinterpreting Christian Faith," *Encounter* 44, no. 2 (1983).

able and meaningful.[24] John B. Cobb Jr. has attempted a *Christian Natural Theology Based on the Thought of Alfred North Whitehead*,[25] but even that is nothing like the Thomistic or Anselmian attempts to prove the existence of God. Cobb's aim, in line with his mentor's intentions, is to build bridges between religion and science and secular philosophy. Cobb believed he was able to build on the Whiteheadian foundation a view of God that took seriously the personalism of the biblical faith and the evolutionary and dynamic view of contemporary science.

The process view of God places emphasis on God as a dynamic act. This is an alternative to classical theism, about which Whitehead writes, "Undoubtedly, the intuitions of Greek, Hebrew, and Christian thought have alike embodied the notions of a static God condescending to the world."[26] Process theologians criticize what they see as classical theism's various notions of God. They include:

1. God as cosmic moralist, the worst image of which is God as divine lawgiver and judge
2. God as unchanging and passionless absolute, unaffected by anything external to him and lacking emotions
3. God as controlling power, determining every detail of what occurs in the world
4. God as sanctioner of the status quo, primarily interested in order
5. God as male, implying dominance and strength at the expense of emotions and feelings[27]

Process theologians deny the existence of this God and regard classical theism as "an incorrect translation of the central religious idea into philosophical categories."[28]

The God of process theology is creative-responsive love and relates to the world through persuasion, not through power and coercion.[29] In process theology, then, God is not coercive power but rather the one who provides a "lure," what Cobb calls a "teleological pull." Cobb sees this as the focus of Jesus' message about the kingdom of God, "the One who calls."[30]

Yet it is important to notice that "subjects" do not necessarily take up the initial aim offered by God. They have the freedom to choose. God certainly

24. See Cobb and Griffin, *Process Theology*, 42.
25. John B. Cobb Jr., *Christian Natural Theology Based on the Thought of Alfred North Whitehead* (Philadelphia: Westminster, 1965).
26. Whitehead, *Process and Reality*, 526; see also Charles Hartshorne, "Whitehead's Idea of God," in *The Philosophy of Alfred North Whitehead*, The Library of Living Philosophies 3 (Evanston, Ill.: Northwestern University Press, 1941), 515.
27. Summarized from Cobb and Griffin, *Process Theology*, 8–10.
28. Hartshorne, *Divine Relativity*, vii.
29. Cobb and Griffin, *Process Theology*, 41–62.
30. John B. Cobb Jr., *God and the World* (Philadelphia: Westminster, 1965), 42–66.

desires that subjects choose and actualize the aim given to them, but there is no coercive power. In that sense, God takes risks.

This also has implications for the concept of evil: "The obvious point is that, since God is not in complete control of the events of the world, the occurrence of genuine evil is not incompatible with God's beneficence toward all his creatures."[31] Furthermore, there is no certainty that God will finally overcome all evil. Process theologians have not written much on eschatology. What is clear is that no final overcoming of evil and death can be looked for in history. The hope for a better world refers in an ambiguous way to the overcoming of powers that resist the divine experience. This "accomplishes our redemption from evil." Resurrection in process theology means that people are "taken up into God's life."[32]

According to process theology, God is still independent from the world—there is, for example, independence in the ethical sense[33]—but he genuinely affects and is affected by the world. In that sense, God is subject to change, yet he does not lose his nature as God. For process theology, change is not necessarily an indication of a lack of perfection, as the classical tradition has often assumed.[34]

A Major Challenge to Classical Theism

To sum up the contribution of process theology, it is helpful to contrast it with classical theism.

> Process theologians see their view as in contrast to and superior to the orthodox or classical view of God. On that view, God was beyond time and beyond any need of humans. He is totally unmoved by anything in their situation—impassible. Independence or absoluteness are, for the classical theist, positive qualities, while dependence or relativity are thought of as negative qualities. Since God is considered perfect, he must not possess this dependence or relativity.[35]

Ronald H. Nash, in his small yet important book *The Concept of God,* summarizes the process view of God by contrasting it with classical theism:

1. The notion of God's being (classical theism) is replaced by a stress on becoming (process theology).

31. Cobb and Griffin, *Process Theology,* 53.

32. Both quotations are from Stanley J. Grenz and Roger E. Olson, *Twentieth-Century Theology: God and the World in a Transitional Age* (Downers Grove, Ill.: InterVarsity, 1992), 141.

33. Hartshorne, *Divine Relativity,* 47.

34. Ibid., 45–46.

35. Millard J. Erickson, *God the Father Almighty: A Contemporary Exploration of the Divine Attributes* (Grand Rapids: Baker, 1998), 57.

2. The God of process thought is an interdependent cooperator in contrast to the independent God of classical theism.
3. The classical doctrine of divine immutability is replaced by the notion of a changing God.
4. Over against classical theism's stress on the personal nature of God, process theology entertains both personal and impersonal orientations.
5. Process thought rejects the timelessness doctrine of classical theism (not all classical theists support that view, but most do).
6. Whereas for classical theists, God's perfection means that nothing can be added to God's being, for process theologians, God's perfection (a tenet process thought also embraces) is being attained successively; God is growing and evolving.
7. Process theologians view classical theism as having an "absolute" view of God in the sense that God cannot be involved in any real relationship with the world. Process theologians regard their view as "relative."
8. Whereas for classical theists, God's omniscience is unqualified, process theologians understand God's knowledge as perfect with regard to the past and the present but still evolving with regard to the future.
9. Whereas classical theists emphasize God's role as the efficient cause of the world, process theologians stress God's role as the final or ultimate cause.
10. The monopolar view of God in classical theism is replaced by the dipolar view.
11. Process theology does not posit an ultimate victory over evil, whereas classical theism does.[36]

Process theology—against the odds that secularism and the scientific worldview would make metaphysics obsolete—reaffirmed the importance of the quest for God and what lies beyond the visible world. While much of its energy derives from a critique of classical theism, with the help of Whitehead and his theologian disciples, process thought has also offered a highly creative constructive proposal. Mainline Christian theology continues to question whether process theology has been too contextual in succumbing to the framework of a panentheistic worldview, but the movement has been successful in inspiring theological debate. Theological traditions, especially Open theism, to which we turn next, have found it to be a challenging dialogue partner.

36. Ronald H. Nash, *The Concept of God: An Exploration of Contemporary Difficulties with the Attributes of God* (Grand Rapids: Zondervan, 1983), 24–30.

20

Open Theism

A Debate within Evangelicalism

An Attempt to Revise Classical Theism from Within

The most recent challenge to classical theism has arisen within the evangelical movement and attempts to state in contemporary terms the essence of orthodox Christianity and thus classical theism. During the past decade, the left wing of evangelicalism proposed an understanding of God that many within the movement believe owes more to process theology and related views than to classical orthodoxy. This new view, whose reverberations already extend outside the movement itself, is called either Open theism or free will theism. Its most notable proponent is Clark H. Pinnock, whose recent book on the topic, *Most Moved Mover,* purports to present a summary of *A Theology of God's Openness* with responses to criticism.[1] Other evangelical theologians who have contributed to the topic are Richard Rice, John Sanders, William Hasker, David Basinger, and Gregory A. Boyd.[2] The first systematic exposition of the

1. Clark H. Pinnock, *Most Moved Mover: A Theology of God's Openness* (Grand Rapids: Baker Academic, 2001).
2. Richard Rice, *God's Foreknowledge and Man's Free Will* (Minneapolis: Bethany, 1985); John Sanders, *The God Who Risks: A Theology of Providence* (Downers Grove, Ill.: InterVarsity, 1998); William Hasker, *God, Time, and Knowledge* (Ithaca, N.Y.: Cornell University Press, 1989); David Basinger, *The Case for Freewill Theism: A Philosophical Assessment* (Downers Grove, Ill.: InterVarsity, 1986); and Gregory A. Boyd, *God of the Possible: A Biblical Introduction to the Open View of God* (Grand Rapids: Baker, 2000).

view was offered by a symposium in 1994 called "The Openness of God."[3] In the preface of the resulting book, the authors express their desire to offer a new understanding of God from within orthodox Christianity.

Not surprisingly, the starting point for Open theism is a criticism of the classical view of God. Open theists are not happy with the way God's sovereignty, majesty, and glory have been depicted. In their interpretation, classical theism regards God as the final explanation of everything that occurs. God sovereignly created the universe to fulfill his eternal purposes and receive glory. Because God's will is irresistible, everything that happens in the world is a result of his will and working.[4] The proponents of Open theism often caricature what they call the "perfect being theology" of classical theism that derives from Anselm and others.[5] This "unchanging God" of classical theism does not appeal to them.[6] Theirs is "the God who faces a partially open future."[7] According to Sanders, Open theism embraces four guiding principles. First, God loves us and desires for us to enter into reciprocal relations with him. Second, God has sovereignly decided to make some of his actions contingent on our requests and actions. Third, God chooses to exercise a general rather than a meticulous providence, allowing space for us to operate and for God to work resourcefully within it. Fourth, God granted us the relative freedom necessary for genuine give-and-take relationships.[8]

Loving Fatherly God as Open to the Future

The main focus of Open theism is God as love.[9] God as a loving, caring parent is a more suitable image than, for instance, God as a king. God acts in relation to human beings and is affected and moved by human action.[10] Open theism claims to make God's actions real and human freedom count.[11]

Open theism supports its views by reference to the Bible, history, and contemporary systematic considerations. While acknowledging classical theism's connection to a number of isolated passages,[12] Open theists claim to offer a

3. Clark Pinnock, Richard Rice, John Sanders, and William Hasker, *The Openness of God: A Biblical Challenge to the Traditional Understanding of God* (Downers Grove, Ill.: InterVarsity, 1994).

4. See Millard J. Erickson, *God the Father Almighty: A Contemporary Exploration of the Divine Attributes* (Grand Rapids: Baker, 1998), 69–70.

5. See, for example, Rice, *God's Foreknowledge and Man's Free Will,* 14–15.

6. See Boyd, *God of the Possible,* chap. 1.

7. Title of chapter 2 in ibid.

8. Sanders, *God Who Risks,* 282.

9. Richard Rice, "Biblical Support for a New Perspective," in *Openness of God,* 15.

10. Erickson, *God the Father Almighty,* 71, in reference to Rice, "Biblical Support," 15–16.

11. See, for example, Rice, *God's Foreknowledge and Man's Free Will,* 38.

12. For a critical scrutiny of those passages, see, for example, Boyd, *God of the Possible,* 24–51.

coherent, integrated picture of the entire sweep of the biblical text. Gregory Boyd lists a number of examples showing why his view does justice to the biblical story more than classical theism:

- God regrets how things turn out: pre-flood humanity (Gen. 6:6); Saul's kingship (1 Sam. 15:35).
- God asks questions about the future (Num. 14:11; Hosea 8:5).
- God confronts the unexpected: His vineyard produced wild grapes rather than good fruit (Isa. 5:2–4); God "thought" something would happen that did not (Jer. 3:6–7, 19–20).
- God gets frustrated: God seemed not to be able to convince Moses of his ability to be God's messenger (Exodus 4).
- God tests people to know their character (Genesis 3; 22).
- Christians can hasten the Lord's return, implying that the future is open to a certain extent (2 Peter 3:12).[13]

Why, then, did historical Christian theology miss this Open view if it is so overwhelmingly represented in the Bible? Sanders responds that Greek metaphysics quickly came to dominate Christian thinking about God and changed the dynamic biblical perspective on God.[14] The most recent exposition and defense of Open theism, as already mentioned, is offered by the Canadian professor emeritus Clark Pinnock.

Most Moved Mover: Clark Pinnock

The Perils of Conventional Theism

Over the years, Pinnock has clarified both Open theism's basic understanding of God and how it differs from what he calls "conventional" theism. Speaking of the rejection of God by atheists such as Sigmund Freud and Friedrich Nietzsche, Pinnock notes, "What strikes one is not their denial of God's existence, but the fact that not a single one of them had the faintest idea of who God really is as a loving and relational person. When they speak about the God whom they reject, I see little resemblance to the God of the Bible, though I do see a resemblance to the God of conventional theism."[15]

Pinnock denounces the Greek metaphysical tradition of classical theism, "a pagan inheritance" to be overcome. "Jesus spoke Aramaic, not Greek, and the Bible was written in Jerusalem not Athens. The Christian doctrine of God was,

13. Ibid., 55–75.
14. John Sanders, "Historical Consideration," in *Openness of God*, 59–98.
15. Pinnock, *Most Moved Mover*, 2.

however, shaped in an atmosphere influenced by Greek thought."[16] Pinnock mentions a number of evangelicals such as Nicholas Wolterstorff, Hendrikus Berkhof, and Donald G. Bloesch who have been concerned about revising the orthodox view of God.[17]

Pinnock laments that conventional theism does not leave enough room for relationality and communion in God's essence. He quotes Walter Kasper's pointed caricature of classical theism's God as "a solitary narcissistic being, who suffers from his own completeness."[18] Thomism emphasizes God's immutability and thus threatens real relationships, while Calvinism so guards the absolute sovereignty of God that the notion of human freedom easily becomes an empty word. Thus, Pinnock's newest book, *Most Moved Mover,* is a response to the Aristotelian-Thomistic God as the Unmoved Mover.[19]

The Open Nature of God

What modifications need to be made to conventional theism's picture of God? Pinnock lists a number of them:[20]

- God is a personal rather than an "absolutist" God.
- God is a loving person. Love is the very essence of God's being.
- God is communal. The trinitarian God is a loving community of persons.[21]
- God possesses "changeable faithfulness." "As loving communion, God is characterized by changeable faithfulness, a better term for God's immutability. God is completely reliable and true to himself and, at the same time, flexible in his dealings and able to change course, as circumstances require."[22]
- God has an intimate relationship with the world. God as loving parent is involved with the world and affected by his creatures.
- God's sovereignty is "sharing power." The world depends on the Creator, but God exercises sovereignty by sharing power, not by domination. God uses omnipotence to free, not to enslave.[23]
- God's omniscience: "Everyone agrees that God is omniscient and knows everything that any being could know. He knows everything that has

---

16. Ibid., 68. Chapter 2 is titled "Overcoming a Pagan Inheritance."

17. Ibid., 68–79.

18. Ibid., 6, quoting Walter Kasper, *The God of Jesus Christ* (New York: Crossroad, 1986), 306.

19. Pinnock, *Most Moved Mover,* 7–8.

20. Ibid., 79–104.

21. See Clark Pinnock, *Flame of Love: A Theology of the Holy Spirit* (Downers Grove, Ill.: InterVarsity, 1996), chap. 2.

22. Pinnock, *Most Moved Mover,* 85.

23. Ibid., 95.

existed, everything that now exists, and everything that could exist in the future. . . . He also knows what he will do. Thus God can respond in creative ways to everything that happens in the world. But no being, not even God, can know in advance precisely what free agents will do, even though he may predict it with great accuracy."[24]

• God is a wise and resourceful person.

The Open view sees God as a triune communion who seeks relationships of love with human beings, having bestowed on them genuine freedom for this purpose. Love, rather than freedom, is the leading motif in Open theism's view of God. This is what Pinnock sees reflected in Jesus' intimate address of God as *abba* (Mark 14:36). It is also depicted in the parable of God as a father longing for a loving relationship with his sons (Luke 15:11–32).[25]

Open Theism under Attack

Pinnock and other Open theist theologians have faced severe criticism from their evangelical colleagues. Charges against this view include too great a polarization between sovereignty and freedom, too close a relationship to process theology, denial of God's ultimate power, ignorance of the biblical teaching, a diminishing of God's glory, and so on.[26] Some of the harshest critics from the conservative wing of the evangelical movement have bluntly accused proponents of Open theism of heresy, seeing it as a "neo-theism" that denies the Christian doctrine of God.[27] Some serious appraisals have questioned, for example, whether Open theism goes too far in the direction of making revealed mysteries too transparent and leaving the meaning of God's foreknowledge too vague.[28]

Open theists respond that they and their opponents share the fundamentals of orthodox theism: the immanent Trinity; the God-world distinction; God's actions in history; the goodness, unchangeableness, omnipotence, and omniscience of God; and the atoning death and resurrection of Jesus Christ. According to Pinnock, differences are "real" but not necessarily dividing or irreconcilable and should fall in the area of mutual acceptance.[29] Understandably, Open theism has received a more favorable hearing among Arminians and

---

24. Ibid., 99–100.

25. Ibid., 3.

26. For an up-to-date review of criticism and response to it, see ibid., 10–18.

27. Norman L. Geisler, *Creating God in the Image of Man?* (Minneapolis: Bethany, 1997), 11–12; see also Donald A. Carson, *The Gagging of God: Christianity Confronts Pluralism* (Grand Rapids: Zondervan, 1996), 215.

28. See, for example, Donald G. Bloesch, *God the Almighty: Power, Wisdom, Holiness, Love* (Downers Grove, Ill.: InterVarsity, 1995), 254–60.

29. Pinnock, *Most Moved Mover*, 11.

others for whom free will has been a concern in light of Augustinian/Calvinistic determinism, as they have seen it.

Many ask about the relationship between Open theism and process theology. Some critics even wonder if Open theism is a thinly disguised version of process theology. Obviously, they share many commonalities: love of God as the primary way of speaking about God; an emphasis on human freedom; criticism of conventional theism; a dynamic understanding of God; and a focus on the real relationship between God and the world. As a result of such commonalities, a common study was produced in 2000 by process theologians and Open theists.[30] Richard Rice concludes:

> The openness concept of God shares the process view that God's relation to the temporal world consists in a succession of concrete experiences, rather than a single timeless perception. It too conceives God's experience of the world as ongoing, rather than a once-for-all affair. It also shares with process theism the twofold analysis of God or dipolar theism. It conceives God as both absolute and relative, eternal and temporal, changeless and changing. It assigns one element in each pair to the appropriate aspect of God's being—the essential divine character or the concrete divine experience.[31]

But there are also radical differences between these two theologies. Process theology is a natural theology based on Alfred Whitehead's metaphysics, whereas the Open view is based on biblical-historical Christianity. Process theology denies, while the Open theist view affirms, certain crucial Christian doctrines such as creation out of nothing, the final victory of God over evil, and God's love as free love (rather than metaphysically necessary). Most important is the issue of the transcendence of God—the ontological difference between God and the world. Thus, the Open view holds to a view of the relationship between God and the world that is asymmetrical: God, while related to the world, is ontologically independent of it. Despite some similarities, therefore, Open theism and process theology possess theological and philosophical differences.[32]

---

30. John B. Cobb and Clark H. Pinnock, *Searching for an Adequate God: A Dialogue between Process and Free Will Theists* (Grand Rapids: Eerdmans, 2000).

31. Rice, *God's Foreknowledge and Man's Free Will*, 33; see also his "Process Theism and the Open View of God: The Crucial Differences," in *Searching for an Adequate God*, ed. John B. Cobb and Clark H. Pinnock (Grand Rapids: Eerdmans, 2000), chap. 4.

32. See Pinnock, *Most Moved Mover*, 140–50.

21

Evangelical Theology

Revisiting Classical Theism

The Emergence of Evangelicalism as a Theological Force

The discussion of Open theism expressed the left-wing voices of evangelicalism. While Clark Pinnock and other champions of Open theism claim a strong evangelical commitment, the two theologians studied in this chapter—Carl F. H. Henry and his younger colleague Millard J. Erickson—represent the more moderate and, many would say, majority voice. Before delving into their views of God, we need to reflect on the meaning of this widely used term *evangelical(ism)*.[1]

The term *evangelical* currently has two meanings. In its original meaning, *evangelical* denoted Protestant theology as opposed to Catholic theology, thus, for example, the Evangelical-Lutheran Church or evangelical theological faculty. Another meaning was added in the twentieth-century English-speaking world, mainly in the United States but also in Great Britain. According to this meaning, *evangelical* refers to those Protestants who adhere to the more orthodox version of Christianity as opposed to the liberal left wing. In recent decades, the evangelical movement, which is transdenominational, global, and represents not only all sorts of Protestants from Lutherans to Presbyterians

---

1. See Derek J. Tidball, *Who Are the Evangelicals? Tracing the Roots of Today's Movement* (London: Marshall Pickering, 1994).

to Baptists to Pentecostals but also Anglicans, has distanced itself from the more reactionary fundamentalism (even though most fundamentalists claim they are the "true" evangelicals). In this book, the term *evangelical* follows the established English-speaking world's usage.

The choice of Carl F. H. Henry as a leading evangelical theologian of the first generation of contemporary American evangelicals is fairly undisputed. To date, no other evangelical has produced such a summa of the doctrine of God based on an orthodox view of revelation. From the younger generation of evangelicals, Millard J. Erickson was selected because he is a prolific writer with a long teaching career and has established himself as a contemporary spokesperson for a more conservative evangelicalism. His three-volume *Christian Theology* is by far the most widely used textbook in evangelical seminaries and faculties. Also, for Erickson, as for Henry, the doctrine of God is both the leading theme of theology and a topic on which he has written extensively.

God, Revelation, and Authority: Carl F. H. Henry

Back to the Sources

As a professor and long-time editor of the highly influential *Christianity Today,* Carl Henry epitomizes the theological mind of evangelicalism's first generation.[2] Henry's theological program steers a middle course between reactionary fundamentalism, on the one hand, and process theology and what he regards as neo-orthodox liberalism, on the other. Henry attacks Friedrich D. E. Schleiermacher as one of the theologians among the originators of "all that is wrong in theology."[3]

Henry's theology comes to maturity in his massive six-volume work, *God, Revelation, and Authority.* The purpose of this work is to rehabilitate the doctrine of God, based on the revelation of God, as the supreme norm for Christian theology, thus helping theology return to classical theism and classical Christianity. The line from the church fathers to the Protestant Reformation to Protestant orthodoxy of the seventeenth century to American revivalism of the nineteenth century marks the family tree for Henry and his fellow evangelicals.

Henry's rehabilitation project requires rigorous apologetic work. Therefore, he starts with philosophical apologetics to show that Christianity can be rationally defended. This Henry attempted in his earlier work *Remaking the Modern Mind.* In that work, Henry was guided by several considerations:[4]

2. See Bob E. Patterson, *Carl F. H. Henry* (Waco: Word, 1983).
3. Ibid., 28; for Henry's relationship to the theological left and right, see 38–50.
4. As summarized in ibid., 58–59.

1. He felt that striking reversals had taken place in modern philosophy because it had given non-Christian answers to the main problem of humanity, namely, the search for God.
2. He was convinced that evangelicalism's biblical theism could fill the void left by philosophy's retreat. "Contemporary philosophy's extremity is historic Christianity's opportunity."[5]
3. For him, theological liberalism seemed to be inconsistent, disunited, and void of authoritative revelation; it had become an analysis of experience.
4. The option of theological fundamentalism was equally unappealing because it paid no respect to science and philosophy and could not offer reasonable apologetics.

Henry's approach to theology and apologetics has been rightly dubbed "neo-Augustinian": Faith leads to understanding on the basis of light given by God, and understanding in turn strengthens faith and makes it reasonable.

The Revelation of God Based on the Authority of God

The rational, apologetic approach in Henry's doctrine of God, based on his view of the supreme authority of Scripture, is best illustrated by the following formula:

> Divine revelation is the source of all truth, the truth of Christianity included; reason is the instrument for recognizing it; Scripture is its verifying principle; logical consistency is a negative test for truth and coherence a subordinate test. The task of Christian theology is to exhibit the content of biblical revelation as an orderly whole.[6]

Among the fifteen theses that Henry sets forth as the foundation of theology and the doctrine of God, the following are the most important: (1) Revelation is "a divinely initiated activity, God's free communication by which he alone turns his privacy into a deliberate disclosure of his reality."[7] (2) Revelation does not completely erase God's transcendent mystery, inasmuch as God the revealer transcends his own realities.[8] (3) The way God reveals himself is primarily seen in the names applied to God, especially Yahweh.[9]

5. Carl F. H. Henry, *Remaking the Modern Mind* (Grand Rapids: Eerdmans, 1946), 7.
6. Carl F. H. Henry, *God, Revelation, and Authority,* 6 vols. (Waco: Word, 1976–1983), 1:15.
7. Ibid., 2:8.
8. Ibid., 2:47.
9. Ibid., 2:167–73.

God's revelation, which includes general revelation, culminates in his saving acts of redemption in history.[10] Revelation in Christ, therefore, is at the center of Henry's theology. The "climax of God's special revelation is Jesus of Nazareth, the personal incarnation of God in the flesh; in Jesus Christ the source and content of revelation converge and coincide."[11]

The Doctrine of God in the Tradition of Classical Theism

For Henry, the starting point of theology is clear: "From a certain vantage point, the concept of God is determinative of all other concepts; it is the Archimedean lever with which one can fashion an entire world view."[12] His nine-hundred-page presentation of the doctrine of God sets forth a defense and exposition of a classical theistic view in light of the challenges of modernity, such as liberalism, naturalism, process theology, and atheism. He begins with a discussion of the relationship between the essence and existence of God and then presents a classical understanding of the Trinity. Following that is a detailed discussion of the attributes of God, such as eternality, omniscience, immutability, omnipotence, holiness, and love. Finally, Henry ventures into the topics of creation, providence, and evil.

A central affirmation for Henry is that God's reality and existence are the foundation for the existence of the world.[13] This affirmation targets criticism against neo-orthodoxy for turning God into a divine subject and against logical positivism for denying in principle God's existence. Henry summarizes God's essence as "being, coming, and becoming":

> As being, the biblical God is the transcendent ground of being, self-sustaining and complete within himself, living his inner triune life of resplendent self-sufficiency. As coming, God the eternal Sovereign voluntarily came to create, judge and redeem the world and man. When God created the world out of nothing he condescended to be-for-others. As becoming, God fulfilled his plan of salvation by becoming what he was not, namely, the God-man of Nazareth.[14]

God the Father Almighty: Millard J. Erickson

A Restatement of the Classical Doctrine of God

Millard J. Erickson first set out his doctrine of God and revelation in his three-volume *Christian Theology*. In that work, he follows in the footsteps of

---

10. Ibid., 2:247.
11. Ibid., 3:9.
12. Henry, *Remaking the Modern Mind*, 232.
13. Henry, *God, Revelation, and Authority*, 5:40.
14. Patterson, *Carl F. H. Henry*, 129–30.

Henry and classical orthodoxy, affirming revelation as authoritative and inerrant.[15] Even though Erickson acknowledges the possibility of knowledge of God apart from special revelation, such knowledge is always partial and incomplete. Special revelation culminates in Christ and is available to us in Scripture, the dependable and inerrant Word of God.[16]

Having established the authority of divine revelation, Erickson discusses the attributes of God without first considering the relationship between God's essence and existence or between his attributes and essence, themes often discussed in orthodox theologies.[17] Erickson places the attributes of God in two categories:

1. attributes of greatness: spirituality, personality, life, infinity, and constancy
2. attributes of goodness: moral purity (holiness, righteousness, justice), integrity (genuineness, veracity, faithfulness), and love (benevolence, grace, mercy, persistence)[18]

Here Erickson follows the lead of Louis Berkhof's *Systematic Theology*, the most widely used textbook in conservative schools in the first part of the twentieth century, which speaks of "natural" and "moral" attributes of God.[19]

Erickson's systematic theology[20] ends with a consideration of the doctrine of the Trinity. Erickson sets forth the typical orthodox doctrine of the Trinity by building on the unity of God. Usually Erickson dialogues extensively with voices outside the evangelical movement such as those of Karl Barth, Wolfhart Pannenberg, and Jürgen Moltmann. In his treatment of the Trinity, however, he looks only at the Bible and the history of the dogma and does not attempt any kind of constructive work.

Dialogue with Non-Evangelical Views of God

Since completing his *Christian Theology*, Erickson has devoted his energy to producing a number of works that defend evangelical theology against other theologies,[21] define evangelicalism vis-à-vis other evangelical proposals[22]

---

15. See Millard J. Erickson, *Christian Theology* (Grand Rapids: Baker, 1985), chaps. 9–11.

16. See, for example, ibid., 241.

17. Erickson only briefly considers the nature of the attributes and how they are to be understood in relation to the Godhead; see ibid., 265–66.

18. Ibid., chaps. 12–13.

19. Louis Berkhof, *Systematic Theology* (Grand Rapids: Eerdmans, 1953), 55.

20. Erickson, *Christian Theology*, chap. 15.

21. See, for example, Millard J. Erickson, *Where Is Theology Going? Issues and Perspectives on the Future of Theology* (Grand Rapids: Baker, 1994); and idem, *Truth or Consequences: The Promise and Perils of Postmodernism* (Downers Grove, Ill.: InterVarsity, 2002).

22. See, for example, Millard J. Erickson, *The Evangelical Left: Encountering Postconservative Evangelical Theology* (Grand Rapids: Baker, 1997).

(championing a more conservative outlook), or focus on particular doctrines. His doctrine of God has received much attention at both the popular[23] and scholarly levels. In his recent *God the Father Almighty* (1998), Erickson interacts with pluralism (John Hick), process theology, and Open theism, revealing where Erickson, a leading spokesperson for current North American evangelicalism, locates the doctrine of God.

Erickson has serious problems with the pluralistic doctrine of God presented by John Hick and others. He does not believe that the ideas of God as personal deity and impersonal Ultimate Reality can be considered species of a common genus; rather, they are so different that they cannot live together. Erickson also criticizes Hick's tendency to ignore the real differences among religions and their ideas of God. Erickson also laments that revelation is given no role in pluralism and that pluralism neglects the truth question and therefore is not able to argue for the truth of either a religion or a religion's idea of God.[24]

Process theology holds some worthy ideas for Erickson, even if the problems clearly outweigh them. The attempt to construct a genuine metaphysics receives strong support, and he commends process theology's attempt to relate to current life and science. In Erickson's estimation, however, process thought rejects the idea of an underlying substance and thus makes talk about the human person and God extremely difficult. Erickson also wonders how process theologians envision the active relating of God to all events in the world if God is in some way tied to the structures and thus the limitations of the world process. He also questions the basis for their concept of human freedom—in reaction to classical theism's all-powerful God—the way process theology constructs the relationship between divine and human activity, and the unanswered questions about overcoming evil and the "final victory."[25]

Turning next to Open theism, which he prefers to call free will theism, Erickson finds several things to commend it, even though he is eventually quite critical of the project. Positive features include the desire to be biblical and to do justice to the dynamic picture of God in biblical revelation, to relate to the contemporary context, to discern the influence of Greek metaphysics on classical theism, and to make the doctrine of God relevant to Christian living.[26] However, he accuses his Open theist colleagues of selective use of Scripture. Second, Erickson thinks they have misconstrued the relationship between divine foreknowledge and human freedom. His own proposal is compatibilism, which "contends that foreknowledge requires only the certainty of a given

23. See, for example, Millard J. Erickson, *Making Sense of the Trinity: Three Crucial Questions* (Grand Rapids: Baker, 2000); and Millard J. Erickson, *Does It Matter If God Exists? Understanding Who God Is and What He Does for Us* (Grand Rapids: Baker, 1996).

24. Millard J. Erickson, *God the Father Almighty: A Contemporary Exploration of the Divine Attributes* (Grand Rapids: Baker, 1998), 46–48.

25. Ibid., 60–66.

26. Ibid., 84–85.

event, not its necessity."[27] In sum, Erickson concludes that Open theism needs much more work to be persuasive.[28]

To further evangelical and ecumenical exploration into the attributes of God, the second part of Erickson's *God the Father Almighty* offers an engaging dialogue concerning topics such as God and change, eternity, God's power, God's goodness, and God's immanence and transcendence.[29]

Reflections on Evangelical Theology of God

The last two chapters have shown evidence of the growing proliferation of theologies of God among evangelicals. On the one hand, there is a continuing debate (on the North American scene) about Open theism; on the other hand, there is a desire among evangelical theologians to dialogue with non-evangelical views and to define more clearly a distinctively evangelical approach.

Evangelicalism as a theological movement faces the tension—one could also call it an asset—of trying to hold on to the best of classical Christianity, as expressed in a more conservative reading of the Bible, the historical creeds, and the contributions of the Protestant Reformation, while at the same time adjusting to the postmodern context of the third millennium. Unlike many other contemporary movements, such as process theology and death-of-God theology, evangelicalism anchors itself in the biblical traditions and the early creeds. This commitment, however, brings about a tension concerning the relationship between biblical and historical interpretations of God. Is there continuity between the biblical narrative of God and more philosophically oriented interpretations (of classical theism)? This questioning has, of course, birthed the Open theism movement, which many evangelical opponents see as approaching process theology and a more "liberal" interpretation of Christianity.

Another dimension of evangelical reflection on God that needs to be noted is the rapid growth of the movement in the two-thirds world. Many believe that the future of evangelicalism lies in non-Western churches and their theologies. At this point, it is too early to say in what way, if any, evangelical interpretations of God will be shaped by Asian, African, and Latin American contexts and their respective cultures and religions.

27. Ibid., 89.
28. Ibid., 84–92.
29. Ibid., part 3.

Part 5

God in North American Perspective

Contextual Approaches

The same conviction that guided the first book of this trilogy, *Pneumatology: The Holy Spirit in Ecumenical, International, and Contextual Perspective,* is as urgent with regard to the doctrine of God:

> In our contemporary world, theology has the burden of showing its cultural sensitivity. Theology can no longer be the privilege of one people group. Instead, it must be context specific as it addresses God and God's world in specific situations and in response to varying needs and challenges.[1]

No doctrine of God operates or arises in a vacuum. While talk about "contextual theologies" is a recent phenomenon,[2] Christian theology has always been contextual. What makes talk about contextual theologies relevant today is the extent to which theologians *acknowledge* theologies to be contextually shaped, if not determined. For example, the classical creeds from the fourth century, in which faith in the Triune God was cast mainly in Greek metaphysical categories, are highly contextualized forms of presenting Christian faith. Likewise, Anselm of Canterbury's twelfth-century attempt to address the burning question *Cur Deus homo?* ("Why did God become man?") used the thought forms of the hierarchic medieval feudal society. Friedrich D. E. Schleiermacher's theology, based on a subjective God-consciousness, followed post-Enlightenment romanticism. All of these—and many others could be added—are examples of how the context of Christian theology both shapes and inspires talk about God and related topics. This in itself is, of course, not a limitation to theology; it is a wonderful asset, a means of making sense of God-talk. The challenge, however, is to face

---

1. Veli-Matti Kärkkäinen, *Pneumatology: The Holy Spirit in Ecumenical, International, and Contextual Perspective* (Grand Rapids: Baker Academic, 2002), 147.
2. A helpful *theological* orientation to contextual theologies is Robert J. Schreiter, *Constructing Local Theologies* (Maryknoll, N.Y.: Orbis, 1985).

openly and honestly the reluctance Christian theology has shown—and still shows in a more subtle, unacknowledged way (such as when theological studies are carried on as if Western theology were *the* Christian theology)—to expose the limitations of its mainly white, Western interpretations.

The late Hans Frei, in his posthumous work *Types of Christian Theology,* classified contemporary theologies in a continuum of five approaches.[3] The first lies at one end and encompasses those who are completely ignorant of context and build solely on Christian tradition (Karl Barth is a prime example, even though some would put him in the second category). At the opposite end are those who take the surrounding context so seriously that little of the distinctive Christian message is left. In the latter, elements of Christian tradition are used only if they fit the context (death-of-God theologies are examples). Several options fall in the middle. The second approach, while it takes Christian tradition as the norm, tries to make it understandable to the surrounding culture. Right-wing evangelicalism may fall in this category. The third position attempts to correlate culture and Christianity (Paul Tillich may be an ideal example of this position). The fourth option takes a particular philosophy or worldview as its primary guide and interprets Christian faith in that light while still holding on to Christian faith as much as possible (process theology may be a candidate here). Although the value of such models is heuristic, together they alert us to the power and influence of context.[4]

The latter part of this book discusses non-Western global doctrines of God, theologies in Africa, Asia, and Latin America. This part focuses on contextual approaches to God in North America, which with its rich cultural, ethnic, linguistic, and religious diversity provides fertile soil for novel interpretations of God. Thus, here we encounter yet more challenges to classical theism.

The following survey includes several North American voices. First is the understanding of the Christian God among Native Americans. Second, views of God among African Americans and various immigrant theologies of Asian and Hispanic Americans are surveyed. These people groups represent a rapidly growing segment of American society with emerging academic theological work. Third, this part addresses various interpretations of God among women, including feminist, womanist (African American), and Hispanic American *mujerista* theologies.

A word of warning is in order at this point. I write this survey as an outsider to these cultures: I am non-Indian, non-black, non-Asian, non-Hispanic, and non-woman. I cannot write from within the particular context of each of these interpretations of God. I am a white European male, and despite my rich cross-cultural background of living and teaching in Europe, Asia, and North America, my approach is limited.

3. Hans Frei, *Types of Christian Theology,* ed. George Hunsinger and William C. Placher (New Haven: Yale University Press, 1992). This scheme is used, for example, in David F. Ford, "Introduction to Modern Christian Theology," in *The Modern Theologians: An Introduction to Christian Theology in the Twentieth Century,* 2d ed., ed. David F. Ford (Cambridge, U.K.: Blackwell, 1997), 1–15.

4. See Stanley J. Grenz, *Theology for the Community of God* (Grand Rapids: Eerdmans, 1994), 19–20.

22

Native American Theologies

Native American Christian Theology?

During his 1984 visit to the Shrine of the Canadian Martyrs in Midland, Ontario, Pope John Paul II declared that "not only is Christianity relevant to the Indian peoples, but *Christ, in the members of his Body, is himself Indian.*"[1] On the other hand, a pointed question was asked in a poster produced by the Episcopal Church of the U.S.A. to address the concerns of various native peoples: "Can I be Indian and Christian?" The poster acknowledged that the "story of Christianity among our Indian people is often a sad, confusing story." Finally, however, the response to the question was yes.[2]

Native American theology has not yet gained the public's attention, even though there is, and has been, a rich tradition of Christianity among the more than four hundred native peoples of America. Whenever the dominant culture refers to the spirituality of Native Americans, *native* spirituality has been the focus at the expense of a specifically *Christian* native spirituality. Steve Charleston (Choctaw), speaking of "theological supermarkets," comments on this:

> Well-intentioned shoppers may have simply thought that this talk about spirituality was the voice of Native America in the religious dialogue. . . . Still, the spirituality section alone does not complete the supermarket. It is still not an expression of a Native Christian viewpoint. As good (or bad) as these works

1. Quoted in Achiel Peelman, *Christ Is a Native American* (Maryknoll, N.Y.: Orbis, 1995), 13.
2. (New York: Episcopal Church Center, 1989), 26.

may be at articulating Native tradition, they do not offer a clear voice for Native American Christianity. They are not a Native People's Christian theology.[3]

This is not to deny the close connection between native spirituality and Christian faith among Native Americans but rather to warn against equating them.

But what about the entire concept of Native American Christian theology? Many Native American Christians have recognized the potential dangers in attempting to express native religious experiences and perceptions using the language of the dominant society (be it English or French) and the formalized style of academic theology. James L. West (Cheyenne) calls theology a "non-Indian concept" and prefers to describe native religious traditions as a "spiritual way-of-life." He admits that Indian people have a long tradition of words about *Maheo,* "God," but that "theology as an intellectual discipline, sometimes very separated from the everyday life of people, is a very foreign concept to most Indian tribal experience."[4]

The Native American Theological Association was founded in 1977 to promote leadership among native Christians in mainline Protestant churches. Around that time, Steve Charleston (Choctaw), William Baldridge (Cherokee), and Robert Allen Warrior (Osage), among others, began to develop a distinctive Native American theology. Of the earlier generation, the most well-known are Vine Deloria Jr. (Sioux) and George Tinker (Osage/Cherokee).[5]

As mentioned above, native spirituality and native Christian spirituality cannot be equated. But neither can they be torn apart. Understanding the distinctive contribution of Native American theology and spirituality to an understanding of God calls for some background.

The Background of Native Spirituality

For an outsider to say anything valid and accurate about Native American religiosity and culture is a risky business for several reasons.[6] First, there are

3. Steve Charleston, "The Old Testament of Native America," in *Life Every Voice: Constructing Christian Theologies from the Underside,* ed. Susan Brooks Thistlethwaite and Mary Potter Engle (San Francisco: Harper & Row, 1990), 52.

4. James L. West, "Indian Spirituality: Another Vision," *American Baptist Quarterly* 5, no. 4 (1986): 350. See also Rosemary McCombs Maxey, "Who Can Sit at the Lord's Table? The Experience of Indigenous Peoples," in *Theology and Identity: Traditions, Movements, and Polity in the United Church of Canada,* ed. Daniel L. Johnson and Charles Hambrick-Stowe (New York: Pilgrim, 1990). See also James Treat, "Introduction: Native Christian Narrative Discourse," in *Native and Christian: Indigenous Voices on Religious Identity in the United States and Canada,* ed. J. Treat (New York: Routledge, 1995), 1–26; and M. Shawn Copeland, "Black, Hispanic/Latino, and Native American Theologies," in *The Modern Theologians: An Introduction to Christian Theology in the Twentieth Century,* ed. David F. Ford (Cambridge, Mass.: Blackwell, 1997), 376–82.

5. See Treat, "Introduction," 14–15.

6. A helpful, concise discussion of the background of native spirituality can be found in Peelman, *Christ Is a Native American,* chap. 2.

many tribes—over four hundred peoples. Second, there is no denying the lack of sensitivity shown to native cultures and religions by white Christians, both Protestant and Catholic.[7] Third, even today, native people are often regarded as a "social other" who live in their own land.[8]

With these considerations in mind, let us try to say something worthwhile about native culture and religiosity as a context for reflection about God. In general, Native American culture, like most non-Western cultures, embraces a deep spiritual way of life, a kind of holistic web, because

> the concepts and rituals of this experience are not generally confined or even kept by an institution whose existence is defined for this purpose or in any way separated from other institutions. Traditional leaders of Indian tribes do not just play political, social, or legal roles, but are seen as leaders with spiritual power. Traditional understanding of health and medicine do not separate physical health from social, psychological, or spiritual health. Tribal ritual is not governed or controlled by a church. . . . Therefore, the vision or revelation of Maheo [God] is a potential experience for any member of the tribe. Yet, to be born into the life of a certain tribe is to be born into the spiritual life of that people as revealed to them by Maheo or God.[9]

It might be more fitting to talk about a spiritual journey or a religious process than a religion because of the experiential relationship native people have with the supreme being and the spiritual world. Strictly speaking, Native Americans do not believe in God. "They know God as an intrinsic dimension of all their relations. All the living beings of the universe are mystically related to each other and receive their substance from God or from the Great Mystery, their vital center and source of energy."[10] Therefore, religion is not a separate institution but is woven into the web of life. There is a vital connection between God, human beings, and the earth.

Therefore, as ironic as it may sound, the specific term *God* is often missing in Indian languages, not because of a lack of faith in God but because spirituality embraces all of life and is not easily relegated into a separate object. The various designations of God are related to an all-embracing spirituality; God is part of life. The word *Maheo* comes from the Cheyenne and means "Great Mystery"; it is an attempt to describe a transcendent being who is both within this world and yet beyond it and thus supernatural.[11] The Lakota people's *Wakan Tanka* also means "Great Mystery." In the Muscogee (Creek) language, the name of the creator-spirit deity is *Hesaketvmese,* literally "Breath Holder." Other

---

7. For a balanced statement, see Webster Grant, *Moon of Wintertime: Missionaries and the Indians of Canada in Encounter since 1543* (Toronto: University of Toronto Press, 1984).

8. See Copeland, "Black, Hispanic/Latino, and Native American Theologies," 376.

9. James L. West, "Indian Spirituality: Another Vision," in *Native and Christian,* 31.

10. Peelman, *Christ Is a Native American,* 41.

11. West, "Indian Spirituality," 31.

meanings for *Hesaketvmese* include Creator, Sustainer, Redeemer, Intervener, Lover, Intimate Confidant, and Fun-Loving Friend. The deity is accessible and present throughout the entire cosmos.[12]

The Catholic specialist on Native American Christianity, Achiel Peelman, notes that what is most characteristic of the Amerindian religious experience is its "sacramental (concrete) and mystical (relational) quality." This means that "the concrete universe in which the Amerindians make their spiritual journey is already perceived as a sacred or mystical reality."[13] God-experience occurs in the ordinary elements of daily life and is a matter of internal and external harmony because "the entire universe is perceived as a sacred reality filled with spiritual powers."[14]

Peelman maintains that native spirituality's view of God, which can be compared with the Hindu understanding of God, is impersonal because it is suprapersonal. God is the totally Other, but "its (her, his) otherness cannot be placed outside us."[15]

Yahweh and the God of Native Peoples

In an insightful article, Steve Charleston (Choctaw) shares the impact of the Old Testament picture of Yahweh in relation to his own religious background as an Indian Christian. As a seminary student, Charleston began to be impressed by many similarities between the worldview and faith in God in the Old Testament and his own native religiosity. He compiled a list of the connections between his people's tradition and the Old Testament view of God:

God is one.
God created all that exists.
God is a God of human history.
God is a God of all time and space.
God is a God of all People.
God establishes a covenant relationship with the People.
God gives the People a "promised land."
The People are stewards of this land for God.
God gives the People a Law or way of life.
The People worship God in sacred spaces.
God raises up prophets and charismatic leaders.

12. Rosemary McCombs Makey, "Who Can Sit at the Lord's Table? The Experience of Indigenous Peoples," in *Native and Christian*, 45.
13. Peelman, *Christ Is a Native American*, 43.
14. Ibid., 46.
15. Ibid., 49.

God speaks through dreams and visions.

The People maintain a seasonal cycle of worship.

The People believe God will deliver them from their suffering.

God can become incarnate on earth.[16]

These points suggest that the religious worldview and focus of religion of ancient Israel have much in common with those of Native America.

The need for liberation is a key theme for Native American Christianity and thus for faith in God. While Native American theologians have not embraced uncritically the agenda of Latin American or feminist liberation theologies,[17] theologians such as Robert Allen Warrior of the Osage Nation have applied the biblical narratives of the exodus and the covenant to the Indian situation. It is the God of liberation who acts on behalf of the oppressed. Warrior, however, urges Christians to consider the perspective of others, such as the Canaanites, in the exodus story so as to avoid embracing a God of conquest.[18] He also wonders whether Native American liberationists should look elsewhere for their visions of liberation, justice, and peace, leaving the gods of "this continent's real strangers to do battle among themselves."[19]

God Is Red: Vine Deloria Jr.

The most well-known work among Native American theologians is that of Vine Deloria Jr. titled *God Is Red*. Deloria is the son and grandson of Episcopal priests and graduated from a Lutheran seminary. A prolific writer of titles such as *Custer Died for Your Sins: An Indian Manifesto*[20] and *Behind the Trail of Broken Treaties: An Indian Declaration of Independence*,[21] he has been a powerful spokesperson on both political and religious issues.

In *God Is Red*, Deloria looks critically at various Christian doctrines and beliefs in light of native beliefs and finds that they are in direct opposition. In his analysis, Christianity and native religions differ not only in beliefs but also in regard to thought forms, such as concepts of time and space,[22] and history.[23]

16. Steve Charleston, "The Old Testament of Native America," in *Native and Christian*, 76.

17. See Copeland, "Black, Hispanic/Latino, and Native American Theologies," 376–78.

18. Robert Allen Warrior, "Canaanites, Cowboys, and Indians: Deliverance, Conquest, and Liberation Theology Today," *Christianity and Crisis* (11 September 1989): 261–65.

19. Quoted in Peelman, *Christ Is a Native American*, 186.

20. Vine Deloria Jr., *Custer Died for Your Sins: An Indian Manifesto* (New York: Macmillan, 1969).

21. Vine Deloria Jr., *Behind the Trail of Broken Treaties: An Indian Declaration of Independence* (New York: Dell, 1974).

22. Vine Deloria Jr., *God Is Red* (New York: Grosset & Dunlap, 1973), chap. 5.

23. Ibid., chaps. 7–8.

Deloria argues that the most dramatic difference in how Christianity and native religions envision God relates to the question of creation: "Christianity has traditionally appeared to place its major emphasis on creation as a specific event while the Indian tribal religions could be said to consider creation as an ecosystem present in a definable place."[24] A related issue has to do with how to define deity: The majority of Amerindians refuse to describe God in anthropomorphic terms, even if they use designations such as "grandfather" in prayers. Native faith does not demand a "personal relationship" with the Great Spirit, while popular Christianity emphasizes a personal relationship with God.[25]

Deloria never tires of criticizing the manifestations of Christianity in America in general and in conservative/fundamentalistic circles in particular. But what is disappointing is that he fails to give an account of a Christian interpretation of God from a native perspective. The new generation of Native American theologians, pastors, and elders will need to produce a theology of God that does justice to their sacramental, holistic, prophetic interpretation of Christianity.

24. Ibid., 91.
25. Ibid., 92–93.

23

African American
and Immigrant Theologies

African American and Black Theologies

A Black Theology of Liberation

The title of the celebrated classic of black theology, *A Black Theology of Liberation,* written by James H. Cone, illustrates the core of black or African American theology: "Black theology is a theology of black liberation. It seeks to plumb the black condition in the light of God's revelation in Jesus Christ, so that the black community can see that the gospel is commensurate with the achievement of black humanity."[1]

For Cone, Christian theology is a theology of liberation. Therefore, its sole reason for existence is to put into "ordered speech the meaning of God's activity in the world" for liberation. Christian theology must be identified "unreservedly with those who are humiliated and abused." Cone, in fact, goes further by stating that "theology ceases to be a theology of the gospel when it fails to arise out of the community of the oppressed. For it is impossible to speak of the God of Israelite history, who is the God revealed in Jesus Christ,

---

1. James H. Cone and Gauraud S. Wilmore, eds., *Black Theology: A Documentary History, Volume One: 1966–1979* (Maryknoll, N.Y.: Orbis, 1979), 101; see also James H. Harris, *Pastoral Theology: A Black Church Perspective* (Minneapolis: Fortress, 1991), 59–60.

without recognizing that God is the God *of* and *for* those who labor and are over laden."[2]

According to Cone, the sources of black theology and thus "black-talk" about God are the following: black experience, black history, black culture, revelation (as an event always in relation to the context), Scripture, and tradition. The starting point for all God-talk is the black-talk that arises out of the experience of the black community.[3]

The Development of Black Theology

Black theology did not fall from heaven but is a result of the struggle the black community has shared with other minority communities. According to James H. Evans, another senior theologian in that community, black theology differs from traditional theology in much the same way that African American Christianity differs from the Christianity of Europe and the North Atlantic. Since the first Africans set foot on this soil, people of African descent have had a singularly unique experience in the New World.[4]

An important background to the rise of black theology was provided by the appearance of Joseph R. Washington's *Black Religion* in 1964. In this controversial book, Washington, himself an African American, made a distinction between "faith" and "religion." Faith, as represented by white orthodoxy in its traditional form, is belief in God, while religion, at that time represented in underdeveloped Negro spirituality, is a "perverted" version of Christianity, a "folk religion."[5] According to Washington, for true faith to become part of the black community (and thus replace Negro spirituality), black religious organizations had to join white churches. It is no wonder that black leaders responded negatively to this book, which inadvertently helped to bring about a distinctively black theology.

The first stage[6] of black theology in the United States began in 1966 when the National Committee of Negro Churchmen published a black manifesto in the *New York Times*.[7] Three years later, Cone published his classic *Black Theology and Black Power*,[8] which combined Martin Luther King Jr.'s call for

2. James H. Cone, *A Black Theology of Liberation,* Twentieth-Anniversary Edition (Maryknoll, N.Y.: Orbis, 1990), 1, italics in text. Unless otherwise indicated, all page references are to this edition.

3. Ibid., 23–35.

4. James H. Evans, *We Have Been Believers: An African-American Systematic Theology* (Minneapolis: Fortress, 1992), 2.

5. Joseph R. Washington, *Black Religion* (Boston: Beacon, 1964), 22, 38–39.

6. I am following here the analysis of Dwight N. Hopkins, *Introducing Black Theology of Liberation* (Maryknoll, N.Y.: Orbis, 1999), 7–12; chaps. 1–3 give a detailed historical and theological treatment of these stages.

7. Reprinted as "Black Power: Statement by the National Committee of Negro Churchmen," in *Black Theology,* 19–26.

8. James H. Cone, *Black Theology and Black Power* (New York: Seabury, 1969).

the church to be a radical instrument for liberation and Malcolm X's call for African Americans to love themselves as blacks. The second stage was inaugurated by the emergence of the Society for the Study of Black Religion in 1970, as a result of which black theology soon became an academic discipline. In the third stage, the most formative event was the Black Theology Project (started in 1975) made up of church persons, community activists, and scholars with strong ties to African, Asian, Caribbean, and Latin American liberationists. The fourth and present stage, which began in the mid-1980s, has widened the sphere of black theology to include theologies by black women (womanist theology) and has gained an established status in a number of leading theological schools.[9]

Cone and Evans are the leading theologians of the first generation of black theologians. Others have also contributed to the black concept of God. William R. Jones's *Is God a White Racist? A Preamble to Black Theology* considers the problem of theodicy in relation to God's nature as a benevolent God.[10] Major J. Jones's *Black Awareness: A Theology of Hope*[11] is a dialogue with Jürgen Moltmann's theology of hope for the black community and a moderate critique of Cone's too limited view of God as being solely on the side of the oppressed black. Henry H. Mitchell's *Black Belief* is a study of the African roots of the black concept of God and the Holy Spirit.[12]

God of the Oppressed: James H. Cone

James H. Cone's 1975 book, *God of the Oppressed,* is a fascinating theological interpretation of black spirituality and a conception of God as reflected in African American sermons, songs, proverbs, and folktales. Based on these resources, Cone finds support for his foundational insight that all theology is conditioned by the social and historical contexts of a particular people. His starting point is God's preference for the oppressed: "God not only fights for them but takes their humiliated condition upon the divine Person and thereby breaks open a new future for the poor, different from their past and present miseries."[13] From the perspective of "black experience," the doctrine of God focuses on Jesus' death and resurrection, through which "God has freed us

9. The best guide and source for original documents, with annotated bibliographies, is the two-volume work edited by Cone and Wilmore: *Black Theology: A Documentary, Volume One: 1966–1979;* and *Volume Two: 1980–1992* (Maryknoll, N.Y.: Orbis, 1993).

10. William R. Jones, *Is God a White Racist? A Preamble to Black Theology* (Garden City, N.Y.: Anchor Books/Doubleday, 1973).

11. Major J. Jones, *Black Awareness: A Theology of Hope* (Nashville: Abingdon, 1971).

12. Henry H. Mitchell, *Black Belief* (New York: Harper & Row, 1975). A classic study, now outdated but still interesting, is Benjamin May, *The Negro's God: As Reflected in His Literature* (1938; reprint, New York: Athenaeum, 1969).

13. James H. Cone, *God of the Oppressed* (1975; reprint, Maryknoll, N.Y.: Orbis, 1997), 128.

to fight against social and political structures while not being determined by them." The fight is not meaningless because "God is the sovereign ruler and nothing can thwart his will to liberate the oppressed."[14]

In *A Black Theology of Liberation,* Cone presents a comprehensive black theology, including the doctrine of God.[15] Cone begins his doctrine of God not with Genesis 1–3 but with Exodus 1–3, where Israel, a minority people under oppression, cries out to God, and God hears their cries. By delivering this people from Egyptian bondage, God reveals himself as the God of the oppressed.

Even the later stages of Israel's history show that God is particularly concerned about the oppressed within the community. "It is important to note in this connection that the righteousness of God is not an abstract quality in the being of God, as with Greek philosophy. It is rather God's active involvement in history, making right what human beings have made wrong."[16] In Jesus' resurrection, it becomes evident that God's liberating work is not only for Israel but for all who are enslaved.[17]

Some maintain that God is color-blind. Cone contests this view, arguing that it would mean that God is blind to justice and injustice, to right and wrong, to good and evil. The Yahweh of the Old Testament, the God of Jesus Christ, takes sides with the oppressed against the oppressors. Therefore, for Cone, the movement for black liberation is "the very work of God, effecting God's will among men."[18]

This does not mean that only blacks suffer; many others do as well. In this connection, Cone refers to Paul Tillich's concept of the symbolic nature of all theological speech. Since humans cannot describe God directly, we must use symbols that point to dimensions of reality that cannot be spoken of literally. "The focus on blackness does not mean that *only* blacks suffer as victims in a racist society, but that blackness is an ontological symbol and a visible reality which best describes what oppression means in America."[19] Thus, theology is a participation in the passion of the oppressed. Cone states that the sin of American theology is that it has spoken without passion and has thus failed to relate to those at the margins of society. Insistence on a passionate theology is a call for an anthropomorphic point of departure in theology over against Karl Barth and others.[20]

14. Ibid., 145.

15. In the preface to the 1986 edition, he mentions that if he were to write that book anew today, his approach to theology would be less systematic because there is no "abstract" revelation of human experiences; God meets us in the human situation, not as an idea or a concept (Cone, *Black Theology of Liberation,* xix).

16. Ibid., 2.

17. Ibid., 3.

18. Ibid., 6.

19. Ibid., 7.

20. Ibid., 18.

GOD IS BLACK

In contrast to Barth, for whom the Word of God was the point of departure for God-talk, or Tillich, with his method of correlation, the point of departure for Cone is the biblical God as related to the black struggle for liberation.[21] Talk about God, therefore, is never an academic exercise. It is "*dangerous* because the true prophet of the gospel of God must become both 'anti-Christian' and 'unpatriotic.'"[22] Such talk can never affirm the "the white God" of injustice and oppression. Unlike atheists and many existentialists (such as Jean Paul Sartre and Albert Camus), however, Cone is not ready to give up God-language. The primary reason is that every significant black liberation movement has had a religious dimension. True God-talk is needed to expose the "White God . . . [as] an idol created by racists."[23]

Because blacks have come to know themselves as black, and because that blackness "is the cause of their own love of themselves and hatred of whiteness, the blackness of God is the key to our knowledge of God." There is no place for a colorless God in black theology, Cone contends.

> The black theologian must reject any conception of God which stifles black self-determination by picturing God as God of all peoples. Either God is identified with the oppressed to the point that their experience becomes God's experience, or God is a God of racism.[24]

The blackness of God means that God has made the oppressed condition his own condition. This is the essence of the biblical revelation in Cone's analysis. By electing Israelite slaves as the people of God and by becoming the Oppressed One in Jesus Christ, God is known among the humiliated and the oppressed.[25]

The blackness of God is also the key to the doctrine of the Trinity in Cone's black theology:

> Taking seriously the Trinitarian view of the Godhead, black theology says that as Creator, God identified with oppressed Israel, participating in the bringing into being of this people; as Redeemer, God became the Oppressed One in order that all may be free from oppression; as Holy Spirit, God continues the work of liberation. The Holy Spirit is the Spirit of the Creator and the Redeemer at work in the forces of human liberation in our society today. In America, the Holy Spirit is black persons making decisions about their togetherness, which means making preparation for an encounter with whites.[26]

21. Ibid., 59–61.
22. Ibid., 55.
23. Ibid., 59; see also 62.
24. Ibid., 63.
25. Ibid., 63–64.
26. Ibid., 64.

The main qualities of God, as seen in black theology, are love and righteousness. Neither can be discussed in the abstract. God-talk must always be concrete.[27] How does black-talk about God relate to traditional theological language?

BLACK-TALK ABOUT GOD AND TRADITIONAL THEOLOGICAL LANGUAGE

With regard to the statement that God is Creator, black theology is not interested in speculations concerning "aseity" (God's independence from creation). Claiming God as Creator is, rather, a statement about God's relationship with his creatures, especially those under oppression. This statement is not about individuals, as in white theology, but primarily a political and social affirmation.

What about the immanence and transcendence of God? The immanence of God means that God always encounters humans in a situation of historical liberation. "The immanence of God is the infinite expressing itself in the finite."[28] The transcendence of God, no more than his immanence, is not a spatial statement. Rather, it refers to human purpose as defined by the infinite in the struggle for liberation. There is transcendental value in blackness, Cone argues.

The providence of God relates directly to how we think of suffering in God's world. Black theology cannot accept any view of God that even indirectly places divine approval on human suffering. "The death and resurrection of Jesus does not mean that God promises us a future reality in order that we might tolerate present evil."[29] God cannot be the God of blacks and will their suffering. Providence, therefore, is not a statement about the future; it is a statement about present reality. It is in this context that God's omnipotence must be defined. God's providence does not refer to his absolute power to accomplish what he wants but rather, Cone concludes, "the power to let blacks stand out from whiteness and to be."[30]

The Ungiven God: James H. Evans

To introduce his theology, James H. Evans mentions "two stubborn facts of African-American existence," namely, that God has revealed himself to the black community and that this revelation is inseparable from the historic struggle of black people for liberation. He sees these two convictions reflected in the biblical narrative about the call of Moses (Exod. 3:1–17) and the missiological declaration of Jesus (Luke 4:16–30). In other words, there is an integral connection between God's self-disclosure and the manifestation of

---

27. Ibid., 66–74.
28. Ibid., 76.
29. Ibid., 80–81.
30. Ibid., 81.

God's liberating intentions in the context of an oppressed people yearning for freedom. In the call of Moses, God does not reveal new knowledge but situates his appearance in the context of the fight for freedom. The Old Testament term *dabar*, usually translated "word," does not mean "the disembodied utterance of a distant Deity, but rather . . . the active engagement of God in bringing about what God proclaims."[31] God's self-revelation is thus dynamic and takes place in history. It is not an abstract, timeless event but the manifestation of the will of a living God.[32]

Evans encapsulates the meaning of *God* in African American theology as "the ungiven God" (the title of chap. 3). He argues that in spite of the common assumption that African Americans are inherently a religious people, the idea of God among black Christians is problematic, as expressed in Evans's somewhat ambiguous term *ungiven*. There are two main reasons for this. One has to do with the history of victimization and despoilment by white "Christians." The centuries-long subordination to the white race is related to racist judgments about the theological capacity—*in*capacity—of people of African descent; theirs is a "primitive" way of talking about God. The other reason has to do with the African origins of much African American God-talk,[33] namely, the mythopoetic description of the divine-human relationship that is universal among African traditional religions. According to this tradition, God and humanity, once living in close proximity, became distanced from each other because of an act of disobedience. Thus, African peoples live with the sense of both the presence and the absence of God. Related to this is the fact that, living in a world of injustice in which their identity was defined in terms of "otherness," African Americans began to conceive of God as the One beyond this corrupted world. God was seen as the Other in a world of oppression.[34]

According to Evans, three interrelated themes are crucial to any African American conception of God.[35] First, God is impartial, "no respecter of persons" (Acts 10:34). In a world of injustice, African Americans have put their faith in the One who deals justly with both blacks and whites. This affirmation not only prevents oppressors from claiming a divine mandate for their wrongdoing but also protects God's freedom. It dissociates God from the unjust structures of racist culture. This is one way of affirming God's transcendence: God is not limited to one's experience, white or black, but is beyond it.

Second, African American Christians claim that God is impartial and also partisan. He is on the side of the oppressed, as in the exodus story. This con-

31. Evans, *We Have Been Believers,* 11.

32. Ibid., 13.

33. There is no scholarly consensus concerning the amount and nature of the African origins of African American theology. See ibid., 56–57, with basic bibliographical guides.

34. Ibid., 54–58.

35. Ibid., 67–76.

viction is based on the love of God as the essence of God's being: "In traditional theological terms the partisanship of God is the political and historical manifestation of God's love."[36] God cares, God protects, God nurtures. The traditional term used to express the loving presence of God is *immanence.* God's freedom in his transcendence and God's loving involvement in his immanence must be kept in a dynamic relationship.

Third, God is personal. Personhood is not a limitation to God (as Tillich maintained, thereby refusing to call God a "person"), when, in Evans's view, one is careful about the personal concepts applied to God. In African American faith, concrete, personal images are the most common, yet God as spirit is also embraced, not as something contrary to the personal God but rather as something complementary.

Hispanic American/Latino Theologies

A Border Theology

North Americans of Hispanic/Latino origin—most of whom are *mestizos,* persons of mixed race—are often looked down on by the dominant white population in North America for not being American enough and by South Americans and Mexicans for not being true Latino/as.[37] Yet the Catholic Virgilio Elizondo maintains that the dynamic and lively tradition of *mestizo* Christianity carries much potential to enrich both Protestant and Catholic understandings of God.[38]

Hispanic/Latino theology in North America shares with other immigrant theologies the struggle of marginalization and identity formation. Even though Hispanics/Latinos are not newcomers to North America—Justo L. González chidingly remarks that the Anglo-American, not the Hispanic American, is the newcomer[39]—and as a significant minority population represent a growing Christian presence, they have had to struggle to establish their own theology over against Latin American theology in general and liberation theology in particular. This is not to say that many of the Hispanic/Latino theologians in North America do not share the basic agenda of liberation theologies. Often, however, their approach and methods differ significantly from their Latin American counterparts. Hispanic American/Latino theology has been called

---

36. Ibid., 70.

37. See Virgilio Elizondo, *Christianity and Culture* (Huntington, Ind.: Our Sunday Visitor, 1975); and idem, *Galilean Journey: The Mexican-American Promise* (Maryknoll, N.Y.: Orbis, 1983).

38. Virgilio P. Elizondo, foreword to Justo L. González, *Mañana: Christian Theology from a Hispanic Perspective* (Nashville: Abingdon, 1990), 13–14.

39. González, *Mañana,* 31; for the background concerning Hispanics in North America, see chap. 2.

a "border theology."[40] Elizondo urges his younger Latino colleagues not to limit their "understanding of God to the ways of knowledge of the Western World" but to come to the knowledge "of a far greater God by knowing God also through the categories of thought of . . . [their] own *mestizo* world of Iberoamerica."[41]

The rise of distinctively Hispanic voices in America in the 1950s was connected to the Hispanic *movimiento* for civil rights in society and the church, especially the Roman Catholic Church. The formative phase of Latino theology in North America began in the latter 1960s under the leadership of Elizondo, whose *Galilean Journey: The Mexican-American Promise* focused on the popular piety of Hispanic Catholics as a powerful theological resource. He also rehabilitated the story of Our Lady of Guadalupe as a key to Mexican American identity.[42] The early 1980s saw several crucial developments, such as the founding of a theological journal, *Apuntes,* which until the 1993 appearance of the *Journal of the Hispanic/Latino Theology* was the only scholarly venue for this type of theology. The emergence of the Academy of Catholic Hispanic Theologians in the United States (ACHTUS) was also a major event at that time. Women, who constitute roughly one-fourth of all American Latino theologians, participated in the development of *mujerista* theology and other feminist Hispanic views (to be studied below).[43]

The most noted American Hispanic/Latino theologian is Justo L. González, a church historian, theologian, and author of *Christian Theology from a Hispanic Perspective.* Virgilio Elizondo, Enrique Dussel, and Orlando Costas, among others, represent senior voices. A new generation of Hispanic theologians is now coming of age, with a number of women among them.

A Mañana *View of God: Justo L. González*

A Legitimately Biased Theology

Justo L. González, who became famous with his widely used textbook, *History of Christian Thought,* admits that his theology, like any other theology, is not unbiased. Even the Bible, he argues, is biased in that God is carrying out his particular purposes. "God has certain purposes for creation and is moving the world and humankind toward the fulfillment of those purposes. This

---

40. Yolanda Tarango and Timothy Matovina, "US Hispanic and Latin American Theologies: Critical Distinctions," *Catholic Theological Society of America: Proceedings* 48 (1993): 128. See also M. Shawn Copeland, "Black, Hispanic/Latino, and Native American Theologies," in *The Modern Theologies: An Introduction to Christian Theology in the Twentieth Century,* 2d ed., ed. David F. Ford (Cambridge, U.K.: Blackwell, 1997), 367.

41. Elizondo, foreword, 19.

42. See Allan Figueroa Deck, ed., *Frontiers of Hispanic Theology in the United States* (Maryknoll, N.Y.: Orbis, 1992), xii–xiii.

43. See Copeland, "Black, Hispanic/Latino, and Native American Theologies," 367–72.

means that, in a sense, God is biased against anything that stands in the way of those goals, and in favor of all that aids them."[44] The biased nature of the Bible is accentuated by its "preferential option for the poor," a model to be followed when "reading the Bible in Spanish."[45] Thus, the task of theology is not to produce some sort of neutral, "and therefore inane," interpretation of the nature of God and the universe but rather to discover the purposes of God.[46] The way God is presented in the Bible implies a "political agenda"; God is not interested only in "spiritual salvation" but also in life here and now.[47]

González himself experienced a twofold marginalization, first as a Protestant in Latin America in a predominantly Catholic culture—yet as a Protestant theologian, González fully embraces his Catholic background as a Hispano[48]—and later as an immigrant theologian in North America. He belongs to the people in exile, "by the waters of Babylon."[49] It is out of this "border experience" that his *Mañana* interpretation of God emerged. González finds here a parallel to Martin Luther's approach to God. It is not the "theologian of the glory" who finds God but the "theologian of the cross."[50]

THE LIVING GOD OF THE BIBLE AND DEAD IDOLS

For González, the crucial question about God is not whether God exists—he is not interested in attempting to offer proofs of God's existence; to a large extent faith is *faith*—but who or what this God is whose existence is either affirmed or denied. He is not sorry for the death of many gods who deserved to die—for the good of humankind. In fact, the starting point for González is this: "Any God whose existence can be proved is an idol." Any human creation that is raised to the level of the divine is an idol. By saying that, González is not contesting the right of Christian theology to speak of God using anthropomorphic language. In fact, all language about God must necessarily be anthropomorphic, in that it must be human language. "We have no ultra-human categories with which to refer to God." When we try to describe God, we either speak of God as greater than humans—God as *omni*potent, *omni*scient, and *omni*present—or we have to resort to the apophatic approach and define what God is not, God as *im*passible or *in*finite. But the apophatic cannot be the only way of speaking; to say what God is not like presupposes at least some knowledge of what he is. Anthropomorphism, therefore, is nothing to be scared of. The Bible talks about God's wanting to reveal himself in a way that, at least to some extent, can be understood.[51]

---

44. González, *Mañana*, 21.
45. The title of chapter 5 in ibid.
46. Ibid., 22.
47. Ibid., 83–85, quotations on 84.
48. See ibid., 55–66; for new horizons in Latino ecumenism, see 73–74.
49. Ibid., 41–42.
50. Ibid., 50.
51. Ibid., 90.

According to González, the way we should speak of God—and which would make sense to people who are marginalized—is how Scripture speaks of God. Clearly, the Bible never attempts to speak of God in Godself but rather in relation to humans. God is not depicted in Scripture as the Unmoved Mover of Aristotelian/Thomism or as the "pure actuality" of classical theism. When the Bible speaks of God, it speaks of creation and redemption, God for us.

The Bible does not describe God as impassible. On the contrary, there are repeated references to divine anger, love, and even repentance.

> God wrestles with Jacob and haggles with Abraham. God is like a stern judge who will be moved by the impertinence of a widow. God is love. Thus if there is any sense in which the God of the Bible can be described as "immutable," this has nothing to do with impassibility or ontological immobility, but rather with the assurance that God's "steadfast love endureth forever."[52]

The God of the Bible is both an active participant in the affairs of the world, such as by calling out a nation and leading them to a land, and also the object, even the victim, of history. "God does not rule the world with an iron fist, as Pharaoh ruled over Egypt or Pinochet ruled Chile." God does not destroy all opposition "with a bolt from heaven," nor is the opposition something God created, "like the military dictator who sets up an opposition party in order to claim that his rule is democratic." Does this view compromise the power of God? No, says González. "The Crucified is also the Risen One, who shall come again in glory to judge the quick and the dead. What it denies is an easy jump from creation to resurrection, with no cross." The cross is indispensable; it is "the supreme instance of the manner in which God's power operates." Yet some may claim that this view denies God's omnipotence. González responds that Scripture nowhere claims that God is omnipotent in the sense of being able to do "whatever strikes the divine fancy."[53]

In the same way, taking into account the way Scripture talks about the living God, González advises us to consider other so-called attributes of God, such as infinity, to see whether there is enough biblical material to issue such a claim. González takes a critical look at the "idols" brought about by the encounter between early Christianity and Greco-Roman philosophical religions. The early theologians' efforts to contextualize and defend the gospel in that environment are not the target of this Latino historian but rather the unfortunate subsequent developments. Theologians took Greek philosophy as the norm and measure of biblical statements, as an extracanonical yardstick. This takes us to the heart of González's politically sensitive reading of the history of theology. A God who is omnipotent, impassible, and divorced from the happenings of the world clearly helped to support earthly powers in both ecclesiastical and political

52. Ibid., 92.
53. Ibid., 93.

realms. The Yahweh of the Old Testament, who freed slaves from oppression and led them to the Promised Land, was replaced by the Supreme Being, the Impassible One, "who saw neither the suffering of the children in exile nor the injustices of human societies, and who certainly did not intervene in behalf of the poor and the oppressed."[54]

A TRINITARIAN CRITICISM OF THE TRINITARIAN DOGMA

One of the most creative sections of González's *Mañana: Christian Theology from a Hispanic Perspective* is his critical reading of the political implications of the way Christian theology expressed faith in "the One who lives as three" (the title of chap. 7). The basic dilemma of the orthodox doctrine of the Trinity, in González's view, is the idea of God as the absolute immutable. That view led to the problem of how such a God can relate to the world of transitory experience. Arianism was one way to negotiate this problem. González does not believe that Arius was more concerned about reaffirming Jewish monotheism than was the orthodox party (Athanasius and others). Rather, both parties were influenced by Greek philosophy's idea of God as one who is unable to relate to the mutable world; an intermediary was needed. For Arius, if the intermediary were God, that would make God mutable, which would destroy the idea of God as the Supreme Being and make Christian doctrine less suitable in service of Constantinian politics. In González's view, the "Arian impassible God . . . was more supportive of imperial authority than the living God of Scripture, even in the mitigated Nicene form."[55]

González considers it significant that it was not Arianism but rather patripassianism that appealed to the masses. Patripassianism, the modalistic idea that God in fact suffered in the Son, showed

> clearly that God was one of their number. God was not like the emperor and his nobles, who had an easy life in their lofty positions. God had toiled and suffered even as they must toil and suffer every day. On this point, it would seem that the Patripassianist had an insight into the nature of the biblical God that the more powerful leaders of the church had begun to lose.[56]

Even though González regards the rejection of patripassianism a correct choice, he believes that the underlying motifs behind its appeal, namely, asserting the suffering of God, must not be ignored. Theologically, the modalistic idea behind patripassianism does not do justice to biblical salvation history, and it makes incarnation only a passing moment. Christian theology, with the doctrine of the ascension, makes humanity a permanent quality of the Godhead. González summarizes the implications of these early theological disputes:

54. Ibid., 98; see also 96–100.
55. Ibid., 108–9; for the entire argument, see 101–9.
56. Ibid., 109.

The triumph over Arianism ensured that even amid the majority church of the Middle Ages and of modern times, the voice could be heard of the minority God who was made flesh in a humble carpenter belonging to an oppressed nation. The victory over Patripassianism assured Christians of all ages that suffering, oppressions, and despair do not have the last word, for behind the suffering Son and suffering humankind stands the One who vindicates the Son and all those who, like him, suffer oppression and injustice; that at the right hand of the throne of glory stands the Lamb of God, in representation of all those who are like lambs taken to the slaughter. But the profound insight of this Nicene faith was often overshadowed by the fact that Christians had now become a powerful body and would soon be literally a majority.[57]

González argues that the God of the Bible, a dynamic, living God, is a particular God. This "God does indeed speak Spanish, not in the sense of speaking this language in preference to others but in the biblical sense that the oppressed who speak Spanish—like those who speak black English—are given special hearing." González guesses that in Peru God speaks Quechua rather than Spanish, the language of a significant minority on the borders and margins of the society.[58]

Asian American Theologies

The Potential of an Autobiographical Theology for the People at the Margins

The fact that Asian American theology is less known in academic circles than even African American and Hispanic American theology is well illustrated by the fact that even the most recent (1997) version of the widely used globally representative textbook, *The Modern Theologians,* which offers an introduction to Christian theology in the twentieth century, does not include a section on this North American perspective, even though African, Hispanic, and Native American voices are given a fair treatment.[59] According to Peter C. Phan, there are a number of reasons for this lack of attention, such as the short time that Asians have been in the United States and their general lack of interest in academic disciplines other than the empirical and the scientific.[60] Yet the Asian

57. Ibid., 110.
58. Ibid., 111.
59. For a comparison of African, Hispanic, and Asian American theologies, see Peter C. Phan, "Contemporary Theology and Inculturation in the United States," in *The Multicultural Church: A New Landscape in the U.S. Church,* ed. William Cenkner (New York: Paulist, 1996), 109–30, 176–92.
60. Peter C. Phan, "Introduction: An Asian-American Theology: Believing and Thinking at the Boundaries," in *Journeys at the Margin: Toward an Autobiographical Theology in American-Asian Perspective,* ed. Peter C. Phan and Jung Young Lee (Collegeville, Minn.: Liturgical Press, 1999), xii.

American community is a rapidly developing immigrant community with a highly active church life and a steady growth in the number of ministerial students entering all varieties of North American divinity schools. A specifically Asian American theology is still in its beginning stages, but since the 1970s, influential voices have offered suggestions as to the development of an Asian theology in the North American context. They include Choan-Sen Song (Taiwan), Jung Young Lee (North Korea), Peter C. Phan (Vietnam), Anselm Kyongsuk Min (South Korea), Andrew Sung Park (South Korea, originally North Korea), Paul M. Nagano (Japan), and David Ng (China).[61]

Jung Young Lee argues that marginality is the key to multicultural theology, to follow the title of one of his works. His theology takes seriously both the Asian origin of Asian American theology and its marginal status in the North American context. It is not purely Asian nor purely American but both. Most, if not all, Asian American theologians received their education in the West and thus are quite familiar with the Western tradition. Ironically, many of them have devoted less time to their Asian roots. As Lee argues, being an immigrant means being "in-between."[62] To Americans, they are outsiders; to Asians back in their homelands, they are Americanized. When they return to Asia, it is a "foreign home."[63]

However, being "in-between"—what Phan also calls being "betwixt and between"[64]—and at the margins is not altogether negative. Out of that struggle comes new perspectives on and interpretations of God. Asian Americans, "being '*in-beyond*' the two worlds . . . help reconcile the two worlds and centers of power by creating a new world with its own center. But this new world does not marginalize anyone because of race, ethnicity, gender, or class. Rather, the circle of the new world is all-inclusive, enabling both natives to be immigrants and immigrants to be native."[65]

An appropriate theology for the people at the margins is autobiographical theology. Of course, this is not a new concept. The late James McClendon, a white ecumenical theologian of Fuller Theological Seminary, developed this

---

61. For the background of these peoples in the United States, see Jung Young Lee, *Marginality: The Key to Multicultural Theology* (Minneapolis: Fortress, 1995), 7–27. Terminology is still in the making, but in a recent compendium titled *Journeys at the Margin*, xi n. 1), the term "Asian American" includes Chinese, Japanese, Korean, Taiwanese, and Vietnamese but excludes, for example, Indian and Filipino. In the U.S. census, the category "Asians and Pacific Islanders" denotes any of the indigenous peoples of the Far East, Southeast Asia, the Indian Subcontinent, or the Pacific Islands. That category is significantly larger, including peoples from China, Japan, Korea, the Philippines, American Samoa, India, and Vietnam.

62. Jung Young Lee, "A Life In-Between: A Korean-American Journey," in *Journeys at the Margin*, 23–39.

63. For vivid illustrations of this dilemma, see Julia Ching, "The House of Self," in *Journeys at the Margin*, 41–62.

64. Peter C. Phan, "Betwixt and Between: Doing Theology with Memory and Imagination," in *Journeys at the Margin*, 113–33.

65. Phan, "Introduction," xx.

approach in his *Biography as Theology: How Life Stories Can Remake Today's Theology*.[66] But for Asians, this is the most natural way to do theology since Asian cultures cherish stories, narratives, poems, myths, and folklore. As David Ng once put it, "One's life story becomes a lifestory, a way of relating the events to providence."[67] This type of theology was attempted in a recent compendium by a number of seasoned Asian American theologians called *Journeys at the Margin: Toward an Autobiographical Theology in Asian-American Perspective*. Autobiography, however, as important as it is for theology, is not all that theology is. "Theology is not reducible to autobiography, personal or collective. . . . Autobiography shows the particularity of a theology in all its concreteness, but it does not show the dialectic of that particularity in its tensive interaction with other particularities in an increasingly universalizing, interdependent world," notes Anselm K. Min.[68]

The theologian who has worked hard to develop a genuinely Asian doctrine in the North American context is the late Korean Jung Young Lee, whose *Trinity in Asian Perspective* represents a lifetime of reflection on the possible convergences.[69] Much earlier he produced *God Suffers for Us: A Systematic Inquiry into a Concept of Divine Passibility*[70] in critical dialogue with Western theologies. Other Asian theologians currently teaching in the United States who have also labored in the field of the doctrine of God are the Japanese Kosuke Koyama and the Taiwanese Choan-Sen Song. Their contributions are highlighted in the section on Asian theology since both of them did their earlier work while still in Asia and do not specifically address the Asian *American* context.

The Trinity in Asian Perspective: Jung Young Lee

Yin-Yang as the Principle of Asian Thought

According to Jung Young Lee, Western and Asian ways of doing theology are different not only in terminology and topics but also in the underlying thought forms and approaches to reality. The distinctively Asian way of looking at reality uses the famous yin-yang symbolic way of thinking.[71] The cosmology of Asian people is encapsulated in the bipolarity of nature, which operates cyclically in terms of growth and decline. Everything in the world has its opposite, and

66. James McClendon, *Biography as Theology: How Life Stories Can Remake Today's Theology* (Nashville: Abingdon, 1974).

67. David Ng, "A Path of Concentric Circles: Toward an Autobiographical Theology of Community," in *Journeys at the Margin*, 82.

68. Anselm K. Min, "From Autobiography to Fellowship of Others: Reflections on Doing Ethnic Theology Today," in *Journeys at the Margin*, 158.

69. Jung Young Lee, *The Trinity in Asian Perspective* (Nashville: Abingdon, 1999).

70. Jung Young Lee, *God Suffers for Us: A Systematic Inquiry into a Concept of Divine Passibility* (The Hague: Martinus Nijhoff, 1974).

71. Lee, *Trinity in Asian Perspective*, chap. 2 provides the basic orientation to the yin-yang principle and its background in Asian thought.

these opposites are necessary and also complementary. Thus, the organizing principle of the cosmos is yin and yang.

> Yang is the essence of heaven, while yin is that of the earth. Yang moves upward, and yin moves downward. Yang is the masculine principle, while yin is the feminine principle. Yang is positive, yin is negative; yang is activity, and yin is quiescence; yang is motion, and yin is rest; yang is life, but yin is death.[72]

Although yin and yang are opposite in character, they are united. Yin is not only yin but also yang; yang is not only yang but also yin.[73]

What is highly significant is that yin and yang are relative because they are relational symbols. They are not primarily ontic or substantive symbols, as are those of classical theism. In other words, because classical theism focuses on "substance," it is more static than Asian thinking, which is more dynamic and elusive. Day is day because it is brighter than night; night is night because it is darker. But day can be day only in relation to night and vice versa. A husband is yang in relation to his wife but yin in relation to his father. It is, therefore, relationship that determines whether something is yin or yang.[74] Thus, relationship is a priori to an entity.[75]

Yin-yang includes contradictions and opposites yet also inclusions. It is, therefore, both-and and either-or. Lee takes up the example of the transcendence of God. Because God is transcendent—even in classical theism—he is also understood to be immanent.[76] Whereas in the West it is taken for granted that "an intelligent man must choose: *either* this *or* that,"[77] the Asian mind-set holds together both either-or and both-and at the same time. This is related to the fact that yin-yang symbolic thinking is based on the idea that change is the foundation of all existence.[78]

AN APOPHATIC ASIAN APPROACH TO GOD

Lee begins his reflections on God from the Asian yin-yang perspective by affirming, in the spirit of Eastern Orthodoxy's apophatic theology, that God is an unknown mystery and unknowable to us directly. God transcends our knowing and cannot be categorized in our finite expressions. Echoing the teaching of Tao Te Ching, Lee says that the "Name that can be named is not the real

---

72. Ibid., 25.

73. See Jung Young Lee, *Patterns of Inner Process* (Secaucus, N.J.: Citadel, 1976), 193–205.

74. Lee, *Trinity in Asian Perspective*, 30–32.

75. Ibid., 53; see also 52.

76. Ibid., 33–34; Lee has also developed theological implications in his "Yin-Yang Way of Thinking: A Possible Method for Ecumenical Theology," *International Review of Mission* 51, no. 239 (1971): 363–70.

77. Wilfred Cantwell Smith, *The Faith of Other Men* (New York: New American Library, 1963), 72, italics in text.

78. See Lee, *Trinity in Asian Perspective*, 53–54.

Name."[79] Creatures can never describe in an exhaustive way who the Creator is. To be more precise, theology represents a limited human understanding of God, a symbolic expression of God. God in himself is not identical with this symbolic human talk. Thus, Lee argues, theology always begins with human experience rather than with a propositional statement.[80]

Although the symbol of the Trinity transcends various human contexts, its meaning does not. It is expressed differently in different contexts. For example, the third- and fourth-century West looked at it differently than we do in our current multicultural context. Thus, the meaning of the Trinity is relative to its context. For a theological statement—a symbol—to be meaningful, it needs to be contextual. Lee believes that even if the Trinity as the core of the Christian faith is mystery and its meaning is relative to its context, the symbol itself transcends historical and cultural boundaries. His purpose is to offer it a new meaning through an alternative interpretation based on an Asian context.[81] Lee maintains that the only way to talk about God, the Unknowable, is to refer to trinitarian language.

Yin-Yang Symbolic Language as a True Trinitarian Language

Whereas Western theology has struggled with the notion that God is one yet three (persons), Lee takes this as the starting point not to be explained away. If Western logic makes it difficult to capture the meaning of this seeming paradox, the "rules" of logic need to be revised, not trinitarian language. The problem of conceiving that "one includes three" or "three includes one" has to do with an exclusive way of Western thinking, the logic of the exclusive middle. Therefore, yin-yang thinking as inclusive and relational is true trinitarian language. He explains further:

> When two (or yin and yang) include and are included in each other, they create a trinitarian relationship. Since yin and yang are relational symbols, yin cannot exist without yang or yang without yin. Moreover, yin and yang are related to each other because they include each other. This inclusiveness can be simply symbolized by the proposition "in," the inner connecting principle of yin and yang. When Jesus said, "Believe me that I am in the Father and the Father is in me" (John 14:11), he was in fact making a trinitarian statement. The Father and the Son are one in their "inness," but also at the same time, they are three because "in" represents the Spirit, the inner connecting principle which cannot exist by itself. In the inclusive relationship, two relational symbols such as yin and yang are trinitarian because of "in," which not only unites them but also completes them.[82]

79. Ibid., 13.
80. Ibid.; see also 50.
81. Ibid., 14–15.
82. Ibid., 58.

Lee doubts whether exclusive either-or thinking can ever be both mono-theistic and trinitarian. Yin-yang symbolic thinking is trinitarian, not only because of "in" but also because of "and." Yin cannot exist without yang or yang without yin; they presuppose rather than exclude each other. In the words of the Johannine Jesus (10:30), "The Father and I are one."[83]

Lee refers to the principle of the Chinese Trinity or Asian Trinity, namely, heaven as the Father, earth as the mother, and humanity as their children, including other creatures as companions. Lee summarizes:

> That is, to me, the very nature of the Christian idea of *oikoumene,* the household of God. Moreover, using familial symbols to personify the cosmos is very close to the Christian idea of the Trinity: the Father, the Holy Spirit, and the Son. The Father is closely related with the heavenly realm, and, therefore, is called the heavenly Father. The Holy Spirit is closely related with the earth as the sustainer and with feminine orientation, and, therefore, is the symbol of mother. The Son is closely identified with children or people, who are products of the father and mother. This is one of the paradigms most useful in relating an Asian trinitarian perspective to the Christian concept of the Trinity.[84]

83. Ibid., 58–59.
84. Ibid., 64.

24

Feminist, Womanist, and Latina Theologies

Feminist Theology

Does Naming God Make a God? The Problem of God Language

At a "Women's Liberation Day" rally in New York City in 1970, Betty Friedan said that the question of the decade was "Is God He?" That question is still pertinent in theological discussions.[1] Feminist debate about God boils down to the question of an appropriate language regarding God. Put simply, the debate is about whether language about God is symbolic/metaphorical or "realist" and whether another rendering of God should be found to replace the traditional masculine—even sexist, according to many—language about God.

The evangelical Donald G. Bloesch, who represents the traditionalist viewpoint, puts the issue in perspective: "Two decades ago [written in 1985] the principal issue in the church was whether the Bible should be demythologized (Bultmann) or deliteralized (Paul Tillich). Now the main issue is whether the Bible should be resymbolized."[2] The term *resymbolization* means the same as

1. Quoted in Margo G. Houts, "Language, Gender, and God: How Traditionalists and Feminists Play the Inclusive Language Game" (Ph.D. diss., Fuller Theological Seminary, Pasadena, California, 1993), 1.
2. Donald G. Bloesch, *The Battle for the Trinity: The Debate Over Inclusive God-Language* (Ann Arbor, Mich.: Vine Books, 1985), 1.

metaphorical or symbolic over against "real knowledge" of the eternal God.[3] According to Bloesch, the difference between feminist and traditional ways of addressing God is that the former emphasizes metaphorical language and sees language as opaque in regard to revelation; meaning, therefore, is equivocal and knowledge of God tacit (not real). Over against this, traditional theology emphasizes either analogical or propositional language. Even if knowledge is partial, the reference point of God-language (what God-language refers to) is univocal. Thus, language is translucent in regard to revelation.[4]

For Bloesch, as a representative of the traditionalist position, to reformulate biblical imagery is to transform the meaning of the term *God*. Thus, "the debate over sexist language is ultimately a debate concerning the nature of God."[5] This is indeed what feminists argue. In the words of Janet Martin Soskice, "The implications of one metaphor are very different from those of another. . . . Metaphor is not a neutral or ornamental aspect of speech."[6] Feminists disagree with the position that the God of the Bible, even if God transcends sexuality, "chooses to relate to us in the form of the masculine—as Father, Son, and Holy Spirit."[7] The right-wing traditionalists maintain that Scripture wants us to think of God as Lord and of lordship as authority.[8] But most traditionalists, let alone feminists, do not agree with this interpretation of Scripture. In his controversial book *The Language of Canaan and the Grammar of Feminism,* Vernard Eller sets forth a thesis that there is a hidden agenda behind the inclusive language movement of feminism, which is to avoid subjecting oneself to authority.[9]

Elizabeth Achtemeier, a leading female anti-feminist theologian in North America, campaigns against the adoption of feminine language in addressing God. She rejects not only the replacement of masculine imagery by feminine—with which the majority of traditionalists would feel comfortable at least to some extent—but also the inclusion of feminine imagery along with masculine. Achtemeier's reason is that "the Bible's language for God is masculine" so that God "will not let himself be identified with his creation."[10] She

---

3. Ibid., 11–12.

4. Ibid., 62–63; and Houts, "Language, Gender, and God," 11.

5. Donald G. Bloesch, *Is the Bible Sexist? Beyond Feminism and Patriarchalism* (Westchester, Ill.: Crossway, 1982), 66.

6. Janet Martin Soskice, *Metaphor and Religious Language* (Oxford: Clarendon, 1985), 62–63.

7. Donald G. Bloesch, *A Theology of Word and Spirit: Authority and Method in Theology* (Downers Grove, Ill.: InterVarsity, 1992), 91.

8. John M. Frame, "Men and Women in the Image of God," in *Recovering Manhood and Womanhood: A Response to Evangelical Feminism,* ed. John Piper and Wayne Grudem (Wheaton: Crossway, 1991), 229–30.

9. Vernard Eller, *The Language of Canaan and the Grammar of Feminism* (Grand Rapids: Eerdmans, 1982).

10. Elizabeth Achtemeier, "Exchanging God for 'No Gods': A Discussion of Female Language for God," in *Speaking the Christian God: The Holy Trinity and the Challenge of Feminism,* ed. Alvin F. Kimel Jr. (Grand Rapids: Eerdmans, 1992), 8.

sees the danger of pantheism lurking behind any use of feminine language, which for her necessarily implies "images of birth, of suckling, or carrying in the womb, and, most importantly, the identification of the deity with the life in all things."[11]

So how do feminists respond to traditional God-talk, and what options do they propose? No one has written more on this topic than Sallie McFague, with her ideas of "metaphor" and "model" as appropriate ways to solve classical theism's problem. We will discuss her view of God-language first, then survey some other proposals by feminist theologians on how to talk about God. Next there is a brief consideration of an important aspect of God-talk that feminist theology has brought to attention in recent years, namely, the relationship between ecology and God-talk: ecofeminism. Finally, two sections deal with women's theologies among non-white women: womanist theology among black women and *mujerista* theology among Hispanic women/Latinas in North America.

Metaphorical Language for God: Sallie McFague

Sallie McFague first developed her idea of an inclusive God-talk in *Metaphorical Theology: Models of God in Religious Language* and further refined it in her widely acclaimed *Models of God.*[12] Foundational for McFague is the distinction between two types of religious language: metaphorical and conceptual. For her, all God-talk is necessarily metaphorical, indirect. No words or phrases ever refer directly or literally to God; rather, they point toward God. Yet this indirect, nonliteral speech nevertheless conveys real knowledge about God. The difference between metaphor and model is that a model is an established usage of a metaphor, a conventional way of speaking about something; a model is a metaphor with "staying power."[13]

McFague sets her position over against two extreme positions. On the one hand, she opposes what she calls fundamentalism's refusal to accept the metaphorical character of God-language in its identification of the Word of God with human words. The essence of metaphorical theology is, on the contrary, the refusal to identify human constructions with divine reality.[14] On the other hand, she criticizes those who fail to see that naming something significantly influences how we view it, "what it is to us."[15] How we name

---

11. Elizabeth Achtemeier, *Nature, God, and Pulpit* (Grand Rapids: Eerdmans, 1992), 108–9.

12. Sallie McFague, *Metaphorical Theology: Models of God in Religious Language* (Philadelphia: Fortress, 1982); and idem, *The Models of God: Theology for an Ecological, Nuclear Age* (Minneapolis: Fortress, 1987).

13. McFague, *Models of God*, 31–36 succinctly summarizes the basic viewpoints; see also chap. 2, "Metaphorical Theology"; and *Metaphorical Theology*, chap. 3.

14. Ibid., 22.

15. Ibid., 3.

God to a large extent determines how we view God. "The dominance of the patriarchal model . . . excluded the emergence of other models to express the relationship between God and the world, and so the model had become idolatrous and had rendered the tradition's imagery anachronistic."[16] What is needed is both deconstruction of patriarchal language and reconstruction of complementary, more adequate models of speaking about God. That kind of attempt may be called "metaphorical" or "heuristic" theology. In that sense, theology is fictional, but McFague underlines the fact that some "fictions" are better than others, and so it matters which one we use.[17] The question that has to be asked—by every generation of theologians—is whether our metaphors are right for our time.[18]

According to McFague, when a metaphor is used for God—such as God as friend, a favored one for McFague—God is not identified with that particular metaphor. Rather, we can understand God in light of some of its characteristics.

On the basis of her metaphorical approach, McFague suggests alternative ways of addressing God that challenge the traditional "monarchial model."[19]

- God as mother introduces sexuality into God. Sexuality is also reflected in man and woman, who are created in God's image. The model of God as mother also speaks of love and creation.

- God as lover introduces the concept of *eros,* which traditionally has been described as the desire for union with what one wants. God's love also includes saving aspects, including the saving of the earth and the healing of individuals, societies, and the earth.

- God as friend signifies three perspectives, namely, love as *philia,* an open-ended bonding free from jealousy; the work of sustaining a friend's life; and companionship.

She Who Is: Alternative Ways of Addressing God

In addition to McFague's metaphorical approach, there are other routes taken by feminist theologians regarding God-talk.[20] Some want to exalt the feminine symbol over the masculine, an approach illustrated in the title *Changing of the*

16. Ibid., ix.
17. Ibid., xi–xii, 25–26.
18. Ibid., 30–31.
19. On the "monarchial model," see ibid., 63–69; on her alternatives, see chaps. 4–6.
20. Two broad classifications are suggested by Ted Peters, *God—The World's Future: Systematic Theology for a Postmodern Era* (Minneapolis: Fortress, 1992), 113–14: "revolutionary," which wants to replace traditional Christian language about God with polytheistic or nontheistic language, and "reformist," which, while criticizing the perils of traditional Christian God-talk, attempts to revise it to make it inclusive.

Gods: Feminism and the End of Traditional Religions.[21] Some want to dispense with all anthropomorphic language of God, especially the term *father,* as in Mary Daly's "After the Death of God the Father."[22] The majority, however, are content to retain anthropomorphic language as long as its sexist and exclusive perils are exposed and corrected. For example, Daly opposes the image of the Father God because it makes the "mechanisms for the oppression of women appear right and fitting"; the father image, in her opinion, has legitimized male domination in society.[23] Even more critically, "If God is male, then male is God."[24]

Elizabeth A. Johnson's *She Who Is,* a massive study in Scripture, Christian tradition, and other traditions, suggests that there are basically three ways to deal with sexist language if one wants to stay within the Christian theological tradition.[25] One is to add feminine traits to God such as nurture and care. In itself, this approach is limited because it still implies that God is Father yet with some "milder traits." The second way is to seek a more ontological footing for the existence of the feminine in God; here the main route has been to speak of the Spirit in feminine terms (the Hebrew *ruach* is feminine). The Spirit is often linked with events and features typical of women such as protecting and bringing forth life. Even this approach is limited because it maintains the duality of male-female in the divinity. A third approach, favored by Johnson, is to seek equivalent images of God as male and female. "The mystery of God is properly understood as neither male nor female but transcends both in an unimaginable way."[26] On the basis of Christian tradition, including Scripture, Johnson looks for female ways of speaking about God to balance the masculine and ends up with these three: Spirit-Sophia, Jesus-Sophia, and Mother-Sophia.[27]

The late Catherine M. LaCugna, a moderate Catholic trinitarian feminist theologian, suggested that "father" is not a proper name as much as a specific and personal way to identify God. "The total identification of God with Jesus the Son, even unto death on a cross, makes it impossible to think of

21. Naomi R. Goldenberg, *Changing of the Gods: Feminism and the End of Traditional Religions* (Boston: Beacon, 1979). See also Judith Plaskow and Joan Arnold Romero, eds., *Weaving the Visions: New Patterns in Feminist Spirituality* (San Francisco: HarperCollins, 1989); and Carol P. Christ, "What Are the Sources of My Theology?" *Journal of Feminist Studies in Religion* 1 (1985): 120–23.

22. Mary Daly, "After the Death of God the Father," in *Womanspirit Rising: A Feminist Reader in Religion,* ed. Carol P. Christ and Judith Plaskow (San Francisco: Harper & Row, 1979), 52–63. Note that in her *Beyond God the Father: Toward a Philosophy of Women's Liberation* (Boston: Beacon, 1973), Daly still cautiously supported a divine androgyny. See also Daphne Hampson, *Theology and Feminism* (Oxford: Basil Blackwell, 1990).

23. Daly, "After the Death of God the Father," 54.

24. Daly, *Beyond God the Father,* 19.

25. Elizabeth A. Johnson, *She Who Is: The Mystery of God in Feminist Theological Discourse* (New York: Crossroad, 1992), 47–57.

26. Ibid., 55.

27. Ibid., part 3.

God as the distant, omnipotent, monarch who rules the world just as any patriarch rules over his family and possessions."[28] What is most distinctive about naming God Father is that God is seen in relation, first to Son and Spirit and then to the world. LaCugna notes that even if addressing God as creator, redeemer, and sustainer (or sanctifier) is appropriate *ad extra* (in relation to the world), it is not fitting *ad intra* (God in inner-trinitarian relations). She suggests several analogies appropriate for that purpose such as Mother-Daughter, Father-Daughter, Mother-Son, Lover-Beloved, and Friend-Friend.[29] Several other feminist theologians have suggested relational metaphors.[30] Ruth C. Duck proposes source, Christ, and Spirit, developing images of fountain, offspring, and wellspring, respectively, which avoid both gender and subordination and imply relatedness.[31] Mary Rose D'Angelo suggests "God, source of being, Christ, channel of life, and Spirit of Living Water."[32]

Some feminist theologians, when revising God-talk, also pay attention to eschatology, to the future of God, not in an escapist sense but as a source of hope. The idea is illustrated in a recent festschrift for a senior American feminist theologian, Letty M. Russell, titled *Liberating Eschatology*.[33] Russell, who borrows from Moltmann's theology of hope, calls her approach "thinking from the end."[34] It is not only about Christians hoping for final victory of liberation but also about all humans, even all creation, being "God's utopia," God's future.[35]

Not all feminist theologians are content with these kinds of revisions. Some have suggested more radical renderings. Rosemary Radford Ruether's approach to sexism and God-talk is one of the best-known, more radical ones.

---

28. Catherine M. LaCugna, "Baptismal Formula, Feminist Objections, and Trinitarian Theology," *Journal of Ecumenical Studies* 26 (spring 1989): 243.

29. Ibid., 244–45.

30. See Gail Ramshaw Schmidt, "Naming the Trinity: Orthodoxy and Inclusivity," *Worship* 60 (November 1986): 491–98; Mary Collins, "Naming God in Public Prayer," *Worship* 59 (July 1985): 291–304; and Letty Russell, "Inclusive Language and Power," *Religious Education* 80 (fall 1985): 582–602.

31. Ruth C. Duck, *Gender and the Name of God: The Trinitarian Baptismal Formula* (New York: Pilgrim, 1991), 186.

32. Quoted in Houts, "Language, Gender, and God," 158.

33. Margaret A. Farley and Serene Jones, eds., *Liberating Eschatology: Essays in Honor of Letty M. Russell* (Louisville: Westminster John Knox, 1999).

34. Letty M. Russell, *Human Liberation in Feminist Perspective* (Philadelphia: Westminster, 1974), 27–28; and idem, *Future of Partnership* (Philadelphia: Westminster, 1979), 51–53. See also Anne E. Carr, *Transforming Grace: Christian Tradition and Women's Experience* (San Francisco: Harper & Row, 1988), 153.

35. Rosemary Radford Ruether, *New Woman New Earth* (New York: Seabury/Crossroad, 1975), 74.

God/ess: Rosemary Radford Ruether

Rosemary Radford Ruether notes that most images of God in religions are modeled after the ruling class of society, and therefore the biblical patriarchal image of God "allows the king and patriarchal class to relate to women, children, and servants through the same model of domination and dependency." Ruether offers an important qualification, however, with reference to Jesus' teaching, in which the idea of God as father is not based on a hierarchical relationship but rather supports the equality of all Christians as brothers and sisters.[36]

To break down the dualism of traditional God-talk—men/women, spirit/body, immanence/transcendence, and so on—Ruether, applying Paul Tillich's concept of God as the Ground of Being, suggests terms such as "primal Matrix" or "God/ess." For Ruether, God/ess is not a transcendent, personal being but the "transcendent matrix of Being that underlies and supports both our own existence and our continual potential for new being."[37] God/ess is no more identified with spirit, transcendence, or maleness than with matter, immanence, and femaleness. God/ess embraces duality.[38] Ruether identifies God/ess with the liberated self of the feminist woman: "The liberating encounter with God/ess is always an encounter with our authentic selves resurrected from underneath the alienated self."[39] Ruether clearly tests the boundaries of theism. Many think she has stepped over the boundaries.[40]

Ruether's pantheistically oriented approach leads to a consideration of the relationship between God (talk) and creation. This is a rapidly developing area of not only feminist studies but also a new area of Christian theology often called either ecological theology or green theology. It is so integral to the argumentation of much of feminist theology that it cannot be ignored in a survey of feminist theology and God-talk.

The Body of God: An Ecological Theology

Sallie McFague's *Models of God* is subtitled *Theology for an Ecological, Nuclear Age*. In revising God-talk, she calls for "a new sensibility"[41] toward our earth, especially in regard to the threat of nuclear catastrophe. The peril of patriarchal language for God is that it is imperialistic, triumphalistic, and may work against

---

36. Ibid., 65–66.
37. Quoted in Mary Hembrow Snyder, *The Christology of Rosemary Radford Ruether* (Mystic, Conn.: Twenty-Third Publications, 1988), 107.
38. Rosemary Radford Ruether, *Sexism and God-Talk: Toward a Feminist Theology* (Boston: Beacon, 1983), 193–94.
39. Ibid., 71.
40. See, for example, Stanley J. Grenz and Roger E. Olson, *Twentieth-Century Theology: God and the World in a Transitional Age* (Downers Grove, Ill.: InterVarsity, 1992), 233.
41. Title of chap. 1 in McFague, *Models of God*.

the continuation of life on this planet.[42] An important remedy is to revise God-language and make it more holistic, nondualistic, and sensitive. McFague's call for a new sensibility includes a holistic or ecological evolutionary view of reality; acceptance of human responsibility for nuclear knowledge; and an awareness of the constructive character of all human enterprises.[43] Metaphorical God-talk based on a holistic, nondualistic, nonhierarchical view of reality is the center of McFague's program. It resonates with Elisabeth Schüssler Fiorenza's brilliant statement, "Not the holiness of the elect but the wholeness of all is the central vision of Jesus."[44] In contrast to many secular feminists[45] and some feminist theologians, such as Mary Daly,[46] McFague claims not to promote a monistic view of reality in which all distinctions between human beings and other forms of life are leveled but a view of reality based on a model of the world as God's body. This model enhances mutuality and interdependence and envisions "resurrection" and "ascension" as Jesus' body.[47] This metaphor—again McFague reveals the metaphorical and thus the heuristic nature of her theology—makes the immanence of God the focus of her view of God.

McFague continued her reflections on the topic with a subsequent work, *The Body of God: An Ecological Theology.* Whereas in her earlier works McFague constructed models such as God as mother, lover, and friend, which focus on the immanence of God, this work sees "God's transcendence in an immanent way—that 'the world is our meeting place with God.'"[48] The focus is on God as embodiment, a theme quite strange to the classical tradition.

In *The Body of God,* McFague refines her idea of a mutual, interdependent relationship between God and creation in light of an impending eco-crisis. One of the key theses is that the traditional doctrine of incarnation has to be expanded to "include all matter. God is incarnated in the world."[49] At the same time, the idea of the world as God's body is also a radicalization of divine immanence, for God is not present in just one place, as Jesus of Nazareth, but in and through all bodies, "the bodies of the sun and moon, trees and rivers, animals, and people."[50] Yet for McFague, this is neither

42. Ibid., xi.

43. See ibid., chap. 1.

44. Elisabeth Schüssler Fiorenza, *In Memory of Her: A Feminist Theological Reconstruction of Christian Origins* (New York: Crossroad, 1983), 121, quoted in McFague, *Models of God,* 7.

45. See, for example, Ynestra King, "Making the World Live: Feminism and the Domination of Nature," in *Women's Spirit Bonding,* ed. Janet Kalven and Mary I. Buckley (New York: Pilgrim, 1984); and Susan Griffin, *Woman and Nature: The Roaring Inside Her* (New York: Harper & Row, 1978).

46. Mary Daly, *Pure Lust: Elemental Feminist Theology* (Boston: Beacon, 1984); and idem, *Gyn/Ecology: The Metaphysics of Radical Feminism* (Boston: Beacon, 1979).

47. McFague, *Models of God,* chap. 3.

48. Sallie McFague, *The Body of God: An Ecological Theology* (Minneapolis: Fortress, 1993), vii.

49. Ibid., xi; chap. 5 is devoted specifically to the doctrine of God.

50. Ibid., 133.

idolatry nor pantheism: The world, creation, is not identified or confused with God. It is the place where God is present to us. "Everything can be a metaphor for God, because no *one* thing *is* God."[51] Referring to the Exodus 33 narrative, in which Moses is allowed to see God's back but not his face, McFague says, "All bodies are reflections of God, all bodies are the backside of divine glory."[52] McFague sees her own model of God as a needed corrective to classical theism.[53]

Similarly, Susan B. Thistlethwaite, another noted feminist, talks about "God and her survival in a nuclear age."[54] She argues that American rightist theologies, whether political or those of fundamentalist apocalypticism, what she calls "theologies of salvation by the bomb," are an evisceration of the doctrine of God. While giving credit to theologians who are sensitive to the eco-crisis, such as Gordon Kaufman,[55] she argues that neither Protestant nor Catholic tradition has succeeded in speaking of God in terms relevant to a nuclear age. "That is, God of liberalism is above the hassle of human history. The liberal's God does not care whether we rule the world and hence has nothing at stake." However, she says, the "God of nuclearism has everything at stake."[56] Thistlethwaite sympathizes with Mary Daly, who argues that patriarchy is another word for *biocide* (biological suicide). *Biophilia* (love of creation) is the counterforce found in women but only when they are in touch with what Daly describes as the "elements" of the cosmos. Whereas patriarchy changes "elements" into the "elementary," feminism embraces elements, which could be described as the interconnections of spirit and matter in all of nature. That is the thrust of Daly's *Pure Lust: Elemental Feminist Philosophy.* Daly takes it as no coincidence that Oppenheimer, the main architect of the nuclear bomb, named the fatal device "Trinity." Traditional theology, with its masculine emphasis, has caused the use of force. On the contrary, the holistic goddess language of feminist theology—in the opinion of Daly and many others[57]—is the symbol of reintegration of the radical disconnections between mind and body, spirit and matter, transcendence and immanence that are symptoms of patriarchy.[58]

51. Ibid., 134, italics in text.

52. Ibid.

53. Ibid., 136; see 136–41 for a consideration of major models of God in the classical tradition.

54. Susan B. Thistlethwaite, "God and Her Survival in a Nuclear Age," in *Constructive Christian Theology in the Worldwide Church,* ed. William R. Barr (Grand Rapids: Eerdmans, 1997), 127–42.

55. Gordon Kaufman, *Theology for a Nuclear Age* (Philadelphia: Westminster, 1985).

56. Thistlethwaite, "God and Her Survival," 133.

57. Ibid., 135; and Carol P. Christ, "Why Women Need the Goddess: Phenomenological, Psychological, and Political Reflections," in *Womanspirit Rising,* 273–87.

58. Daly, *Pure Lust,* 73.

As mentioned, the development of an ecological theology or green theology is not the task of feminist theologians alone. Many others have joined this enterprise, most recently Mark I. Wallace with his *Fragments of the Spirit.*[59]

Womanist Theology

The Agenda of Womanist Theology

The 1983 groundbreaking book by Alice Walker, *In Search of Our Mothers' Gardens,* makes a powerful statement about the right and the need of black women to develop their own response to sexism.[60] The expression "womanist theology"[61] is the name used by black women in various theological and religious circles to denote two things. First, it emphasizes the positive experiences of African American women, created in the image of God, as a basis for doing theology and ethics. Second, it calls attention to the experiences of sexism black women have encountered—and continue to encounter—in society and the church.[62] Another motive for the rise of womanist theology is the perceived failure of black theology and black liberation movements to address the issue of inequality in the midst of the black community, namely, the marginalized position of their women.[63] Black women, like Hispanic Americans, do not want to identify themselves with white feminists, since the agenda of whites is not the same as that of blacks or Latinas. This confrontation is clearly illustrated in the title of Jacquelyn Grant's *White Women's Christ and Black Women's Jesus.*[64]

Womanist God-Talk

Based on their everyday life of oppression, black women speak of God as both "strength of life" and "empowering spirit": "God is neither simply the ultimate

---

59. Mark I. Wallace, *Fragments of the Spirit: Nature, Violence, and the Renewal of Creation* (New York: Continuum, 1996); for a brief discussion, see my *Pneumatology: The Holy Spirit in International, Ecumenical, and Historical Perspective* (Grand Rapids: Baker Academic, 2002), 159–64.

60. A helpful, up-to-date introduction to the topic is offered in Stephanie Y. Mitchem, *Introducing Womanist Theology* (Maryknoll, N.Y.: Orbis, 2002).

61. Alice Walker, *In Search of Our Mothers' Gardens: Womanist Prose* (New York: Harcourt Brace Jovanovich, 1983).

62. Dwight N. Hopkins, *Introducing Black Theology of Liberation* (Maryknoll, N.Y.: Orbis, 1999), 129. See also Teresa L. Fry, "Avoiding Asphyxiation: A Womanist Perspective on Intrapersonal and Interpersonal Transformation," in *Embracing the Spirit: Womanist Perspectives on Hope, Salvation, and Transformation,* ed. Emilie M. Townes (Maryknoll, N.Y.: Orbis, 1997), chap. 6.

63. Jacquelyn Grant, "Black Theology and the Black Woman," in *Black Theology: A Documentary History, Volume One: 1966–1979,* ed. James H. Cone and Gauraud S. Wilmore (Maryknoll, N.Y.: Orbis, 1979), 423.

64. Jacquelyn Grant, *White Women's Christ and Black Women's Jesus: Feminist Christology and Womanist Response* (Atlanta: Scholars Press, 1989).

ground of being by which we are grasped in moments of mystical experience nor some ultimate point of reference whom we come to understand primarily by reason."[65] Human talk about God is by definition limited; this is the first step toward nonidolatrous imaging of God. However, even though limited, it is not simply human talk. "Faith in God must emerge from something deeper and more ancient, . . . the divine ground of all creation, of all that is and all that will be—God Godself."[66]

Womanist theology sees several weaknesses in traditional North American (and other Western) discourse on God. Influenced by Greco-Roman philosophies, they make sharp distinctions between body and soul, give preference to the spiritual/mental over the physical, and believe that a universal, one-size-fits-all theology is possible.[67] This has led to despising the body and ordinary life, which is seen as being in opposition to the spirit and the "spiritual." Western Christianity, in the womanist perspective, has also been "uniquely paranoid-schizophrenic and obsessive-compulsive" in approaching different cultures.[68] Womanist theologians desire to develop a God-talk that takes as its starting point the specific situation of black women.

Sisters in the Wilderness: Delores S. Williams

Jacquelyn Grant, a systematic theologian, poses the question, Where do God and humanity meet each other? Her answer is twofold: On the one hand, God makes himself known by direct communication to poor African American women. On the other hand, God's revelation appears in the Bible, but it has to be received in a people's own context. Recently, feminist and womanist Bible hermeneutics has helped African Americans read the Bible from their own perspective; one example is Delores S. Williams's 1993 book, *Sisters in the Wilderness: The Challenge of Womanist God-Talk.*

In contrast to her male counterparts, Williams takes the wilderness experience of Hagar rather than the exodus event of Israel as a theological paradigm. Whereas in the exodus narrative liberation stands in the forefront, in Hagar's story survival is the key; God participates in Hagar's and her child's survival. God meets the runaway slave girl in the wilderness and tells her to go back to Sarah, to bondage, not for bondage's sake but for the sake of survival, since Hagar could not give birth in the wilderness.[69] What is most instructive in this story—and paradigmatic for black women—is that Hagar is the only person

65. Karen Baker-Fletcher and Garth Baker-Fletcher, *My Sister, My Brother: Womanist and Xodus God-Talk* (Maryknoll, N.Y.: Orbis, 1997), 27.

66. Ibid., 28.

67. Mitchem, *Introducing Womanist Theology,* 35.

68. Ibid., 37.

69. Delores S. Williams, *Sisters in the Wilderness: The Challenge of Womanist God-Talk* (Maryknoll, N.Y.: Orbis, 1993), 5.

in the Bible attributed with the power of naming God (Gen. 16:13). She uses the designations for God used by Abraham and Sarah, her oppressors, but she also gives God a new name, *El Roï,* "God of seeing." This God also promises to take care of her son, Ishmael, even though Sarah does not want to give Hagar an inheritance (Gen. 21:9–10).[70]

In her reading of the Hagar story, Williams challenges not only white feminist theology but also black male theology. She argues that it is doubtful that God is the liberator of *all* the oppressed, a claim made by James H. Cone and other black male theologians. There is also a non-liberative facet to the God of the Bible with regard to many non-Hebrew females and male slaves ("the oppressed of the oppressed"). God seems to be "partial and discriminating."[71] Williams also takes examples from the covenant code (Exodus 20–23) and the holiness code (Leviticus 19), where commandments given by God do not treat equally male and female slaves or free and slave women. Williams concludes that womanist theology, unlike Cone's and other male liberationists' theologies, cannot take exodus and election themes as paradigmatic without qualifications.[72] This is also the basic difference between the white feminist "liberation lens" and the black womanist "survival lens"; even if sharing common concerns, their approach is different because of different contexts.[73] The fact that black male theologians are beginning to dialogue with and listen to their female counterparts is illustrated in works such as Garth Kasimu Baker-Fletcher's *Xodus: An African-American Male Journey,* which offers an inclusive agenda.[74]

Latina Theology

The book that brought the agenda of Latina/Hispanic American women to public notice was *Hispanic Women: Prophetic Voice in the Church* edited by Ada Maria Isasi-Diaz and Yolanda Tarango.[75] This was the first attempt to gather together leading ideas of Latina theology, called *mujerista* theology. "A *mujerista* is someone who makes a preferential option for Latina women, for our struggle for liberation."[76] The *locus theologicus,* therefore, is the *mestizaje* (mixed white and native people in Latin America) and *mulatez* (mixed black

70. Ibid., 20–27.

71. Ibid., 144–45.

72. Ibid., 144–46; chap. 6 is devoted to the consideration of the relationship between womanist God-talk and black liberation theology.

73. Ibid., 197; chap. 7 is devoted to this topic.

74. Garth Kasimu Baker-Fletcher, *Xodus: An African-American Male Journey* (Minneapolis: Fortress, 1996).

75. Ada Maria Isasi-Diaz and Yolanda Tarango, eds., *Hispanic Women: Prophetic Voice in the Church* (San Francisco: Harper & Row, 1988).

76. Ada Maria Isasi-Diaz, *Mujerista Theology: A Theology for the Twenty-First Century* (Maryknoll, N.Y.: Orbis, 2001), 61.

and white people) and their condition as racially and culturally mixed people.[77] Out of that struggle emerges a knowledge of God, a "theology from below" as opposed to "academic and churchly" theology, which provides knowledge of God that is "fragmentary, partisan, conjectural, and provisional."[78] In contrast to the dominant North American theology, which generally regards popular religion as primitive, *mujerista* theology "recognizes popular religion as a credible experience" of the divine.[79] Thus, *mujeristas* participate in the holiness of God; they, too, are made in the image and the likeness of the divine.[80] Furthermore, *mujeristas* claim for themselves religious authority, as "the image of God, as a metaphor for the divine."[81]

Mujerista theology, therefore, gives voice to North American Hispanic women, who are uneasy about identifying themselves fully with mainline feminist theology, perceived as an enterprise of white women. In her *En la Lucha: A Hispanic Women's Liberation Theology*, Isasi-Diaz, currently the leading thinker of the movement, focuses on "grassroot Latinas' religious understanding and the way those understandings guide their daily lives": "We firmly believe that those religious understandings are part of the ongoing revelation of God, present in the midst of the community of faith and giving strength to Hispanic Women's struggle for liberation."[82]

Many other women theologians in the Latina/Hispanic community have developed a liberation theology. Maria Pilar Aquino, author of *Our Cry for Life: Feminist Theology from Latin America*,[83] has developed a theology that is not limited to North America but extends to the liberation of all Latin American women. Aquino and others, such as Jeanette Rodriguez,[84] do not identify themselves as *mujerista* theologians, even if their work has much in common with that of Isasi-Diaz and her colleagues. Aquino and Rodriguez rely on sociological and demographic studies combined with theological and religious analysis.

Isasi-Diaz's latest work, *Mujerista Theology* (2001), attempts to offer a comprehensive view of the current status of Latina theologizing on the North American scene. According to her, *mujerista* theology is a liberative praxis done by activist-theologians. Even if its focus is the context and struggle of Latinas,

77. Ibid., 62–63.

78. Ibid., 71–72.

79. Arturo Bañuelas, "U.S. Hispanic Theology," *Missiology* 20, no. 2 (1992): 290–91, quoted in ibid., 75.

80. Isasi-Diaz, *Mujerista Theology*, 174.

81. Ibid., 198.

82. Ada Maria Isasi-Diaz, *En la Lucha [In the Struggle]: A Hispanic Women's Liberation Theology* (Minneapolis: Fortress, 1993). See also her *Mujerista Theology*, 1–2.

83. Maria Pilar Aquino, *Our Cry for Life: Feminist Theology from Latin America* (Maryknoll, N.Y.: Orbis, 1993).

84. Jeanette Rodriguez, *Our Lady of Guadalupe: Faith and Empowerment among Mexican-American Women* (Austin, Tex.: University of Texas Press, 1994).

it is not a theology exclusively for them but a "theology *from* the perspective of Latinas."[85]

La lucha, "struggle," is the mode of God-talk in Latina theology. Jesus' suffering is the model, but Isasi-Diaz does not believe that Jesus suffered more than all other human suffering or that God, whom Jesus called Father, demanded that Jesus suffer to fulfill his mission on earth. Suffering may be inevitable, but in itself it is not good, nothing to be desired.[86]

A biblical story *mujeristas* use frequently is the story of Shiphrah and Puah, two midwives (Exod. 1:15–21). The "main moving force and motivating principle of their action was the fear of God," not in terms of fear of punishment but a sense of *mysterium tremendum.* This sense of terror is not merely negative. It "is also an expression of faith, trust, love, and communion, based on God's unmerited, gratuitous, unearned love." This makes these two women "mother, life-givers of the Hebrew people."[87]

A highly appreciated value in *mujerista* theology is solidarity. Solidarity means participating in the ongoing process of liberation, and it is a significant positive force "in the unfolding of the 'kin-dom' of God."[88] Salvation comes from God, but it is worked out between God and each human being and among human beings.

85. Isasi-Diaz, *Mujerista Theology,* 1.
86. Ibid., 129–30.
87. Ibid., 163.
88. Ibid., 89.

25

Reflections on the
North American Scene

Two interrelated questions occupy us at the end of this survey of views about God in contemporary North American theologies: What are some of the common features and differences among these various approaches? How do these views challenge classical theism?

As mentioned at the beginning of this section, the North American scene is extremely diverse, both culturally and ecclesiastically, and incorporates significant third world voices in various forms. Among "white" theologies, whereas the right wing of evangelicalism continues the tradition of classical theism, based on the authority of the inerrant Word of God (understood mainly, even if not exclusively, as propositional truths), the theological left wing, at least for a while, suggested the death of God. In between these two radically opposing views is a search for a dynamic, relational, more immanent doctrine of God. This is heralded most forcefully by process theology's understanding of God as an entity among other entities in the world. Its theologically more conservative version is Open theism, an attempt to revise classical theism in a way not unparalleled in the history of theology but also not typically used by more conservative Christians.

The other strand of North American theologies of God, called contextual or minority-voice theologies, have advanced the dialogue between culture and theology in dramatic new ways, especially since the 1960s. Women theologians—feminists, womanists, Latinas, and to a lesser degree women from Asian backgrounds—have raised the most serious criticism against the biblical, historical, and contemporary tradition of talking about God in masculine and thus—in their interpretation—sexist terms. Though much of the impetus for feminist-oriented theology has come from feminist movements outside the church, women theologians have bravely taken up the challenge of re-creating God-talk with regard to not only classical theism but also the theological academy, which is still dominated by their male counterparts. A proliferation of women's voices has also taken place along cultural lines, which has helped give minority groups (African American, Asian, and Latina women) a distinctive voice. Womanist theology has perhaps had the hardest time finding an identity among black (male-dominated) theologies, white feminists, and classical traditions. Theologians from Latin American backgrounds, whether male or female, have also had to struggle to gain their own identity. Many textbooks routinely lump them in with liberation theologies.

The main dialogue partners for North American theologians have been European theologies. One obvious reason is that Europe has provided not only much of the theological tradition but also the mentors under whom many North American theologians received at least part of their education. Overall, the thinking about God in North America is far less dependent on theological giants and much more related to schools of thought; this is a major difference from Europe, where few if any schools have arisen since Karl Barth and Paul Tillich (and even they did not so much attract disciples as invite critical dialogue).

The relationship between culture and theology—God-talk and a particular context—intensifies as we enter the last part of this survey, which covers views of God among African, Asian, and Latin American theologies in their respective contexts.

Part 6

God in Non-Western Perspective

Jung Young Lee, the theologian from Korea whose views on God were considered in chapter 23, reminds us how the radical changes in Christianity affect theology and theological education:

> As the demographical picture of Christianity shifts from the First World to the Third World countries, Christianity is no longer exclusively identified as a Western religion. In fact, Christianity is already not only a world religion but a world Christianity. This means Christianity cannot be understood exclusively from a Western perspective. Likewise, theological education must also take a global perspective, for our theology is also a world theology.[1]

A transformation of the Christian church is taking place so rapidly that even specialists have a hard time keeping track of it. According to Philip Jenkins's *Next Christendom,* the most recent attempt to take stock of the changes, the typical Christian in the first decade of the third millennium is a non-white, nonaffluent, non-northern person who is more often female. "If we want to visualize a 'typical' contemporary Christian, we should think of a woman living in a village in Nigeria or in a Brazilian *favela.*"[2] Or as the Kenyan theologian John Mbiti put it, "The centers of the church's universality

1. Jung Young Lee, *The Trinity in Asian Perspective* (Nashville: Abingdon, 1999), 11.
2. Philip Jenkins, *The Next Christendom: The Coming of Global Christianity* (Oxford: Oxford University Press, 2001), 2.

[are] no longer in Geneva, Rome, Athens, Paris, London, and New York, but Kinshasa, Buenos Aires, Addis Ababa, and Manila."[3] The Hispanic scholar Justo L. González speaks of the "Reformation of the twentieth century."[4] Jenkins calls this phenomenon "Christianity going south"[5] and describes it as "one of the transforming moments in the history of religion—not only of Christianity—worldwide."[6]

Statistics are staggering: By 2050, only roughly one-fifth of the world's three billion Christians will be non-Hispanic whites. Thus, terms such as "the third church" have emerged based on the analogy of the third world.[7] Andrew Walls, the leading scholar on African Christianity, argues that a distinctively new tradition—"a new church"—is in fact arising in Africa, the center of the rapid growth of world Christianity. This new church, which combines elements of older traditions, new Pentecostal/charismatic spiritualities, and emerging independent, often locally colored, beliefs and practices, represents a fourth major force next to Catholicism, Protestantism, and Orthodoxy. Walls points to this as "the standard Christianity of the present age."[8]

What is the significance of these developments for the doctrine of God? To begin with, Lee illustrates the need for a genuinely cross-cultural interaction in contemporary theology:

> An Asian perspective complements a Western or an American perspective because Christianity belongs to both Asia and the West simultaneously. If Christianity is a Western religion only, non-Western perspectives on Christianity should be regarded as subsidiaries to the Western perspective. Even today [in 1999] many traditional theologians view most Third World theologies, including liberation and indigenous theologies, as subsidiaries of traditional Western theologies. As long as Third World theologies continue to attempt to validate their work according to the views of Western theologies, they will continue to be supplementary to Western theologies. . . . My work intends not to supplement the traditional idea of the Trinity but to complement it by presenting a new interpretation of the Trinity from an Asian perspective.[9]

3. Quoted in Kwame Bediako, *Christianity in Africa* (Maryknoll, N.Y.: Orbis, 1995), 154.

4. Justo L. González, *Mañana: Christian Theology from a Hispanic Perspective* (Nashville: Abingdon, 1990), 48.

5. This is the basic thesis of Jenkins, *Next Christendom.* He explains his choice of North-South as the dominant pattern especially in chap. 1, which also includes good bibliographical references. The basic statistical source is David B. Barrett, George T. Kurian, and Todd M. Johnson, *World Christian Encyclopedia,* 2d ed. (New York: Oxford University Press, 2001); for global statistics, see 12–15.

6. Jenkins, *Next Christendom,* 1.

7. Walbert Buhlmann, *The Coming of the Third Church* (Slough, U.K.: St. Paul, 1976).

8. Christopher Fyfe and Andrew Walls, eds., *Christianity in Africa in the 1990s* (Edinburgh: Centre of African Studies, University of Edinburgh, 1996), 3. See also Andrew Walls, *The Missionary Movement in Christian History* (Maryknoll, N.Y.: Orbis, 1996).

9. Lee, *Trinity in Asian Perspective,* 12.

Does this mean, then, that European and North American theologies of God, including the tradition of classical theism, need to be replaced? Not quite. Even though nobody denies the urgency of developing culturally relevant doctrines of God, it is also true that even in Africa, Asia, and Latin America, much of what is happening theologically is still a response to the past two millennia of Christian tradition. The Christianity of the Southern Hemisphere is mainly if not exclusively a Christianity imported from Western missionaries. The doctrine of God as taught in two-thirds world Bible colleges, many theological seminaries, and the churches owes much more to Augustine and Aquinas than to secular theologies of the West. Thus, theologically, two-thirds world churches partially live in a "pre-Enlightenment" era. By this comment, I am not suggesting that these churches are "primitive."

In addition—as Jenkins argues—the "new Christianity" in the Southern Hemisphere, rather than being "fervently liberal, activist, and even revolutionary," as liberal, secularly oriented Western academicians have predicted since the 1960s, seems to be conservative and traditionalist.[10] Most of these churches read the Bible literally, take the "supernatural" as "natural," and look upon God as the one who intervenes. Most of them perceive reality as consisting of God and his opponents—Satan and demonic forces. Classic Christian events such as dreams, visions, prophecies, and miracles, especially healings, are everyday phenomena to the majority of African, Asian, and Latin American Christians. This "new Christianity" is not otherworldly in the sense of being escapist; it differs from the liberal, secular West in that faith in God is supposed to bear on everyday life situations such as despair, poverty, sickness, childbirth, drug abuse, and so on. What is said of Brazilian Pentecostals applies as well to most other Christians from the Southern Hemisphere: "Their main appeal is that they present a God that you can use. . . . The Pentecostal groups have the kind of God that will solve my problems today and tomorrow. People today are looking for solutions, not for eternity."[11]

What follows is a discussion of African, Asian, and Latin American views of God as represented by some leading theologians.

---

10. Jenkins, *Next Christendom*, 6–8.
11. Quoted in ibid., 77.

26

God in African Theologies

The African Context for God-Talk

Even though Andrew Walls has recently claimed that "anyone who wishes to undertake serious study of Christianity these days needs to know something about Africa,"[1] systematic theological reflection on God has not paid much attention to how African theologies and spiritualities have challenged classical theism and contemporary God-talk.[2] John Pobee has argued, "If there is to be a serious and deep communication and rooting of the gospel of Christ, the African stamp will have to replace the European stamp."[3]

Can anything in general be said about the African worldview as a background to God-talk in the midst of literally thousands of ethnic groups and languages? Understandably, scholarly assessments vary. Yet it seems reasonable to accept some basic orientations underlying most African cultures, which have shaped and been shaped by traditional religions and have in turn shaped Christian interpretations of God. Features routinely assigned to the African context include the following:[4]

1. Andrew Walls, "Eusebius Tries Again," *International Bulletin of Missionary Research* 24, no. 3 (2000): 105.
2. See Kwesi Dickson, "African Theology: Origin, Method and Content," *Journal of Religious Thought* 30, no. 2 (1975): 37.
3. John Pobee, *Toward an African Theology* (Nashville: Abingdon, 1979), 17.
4. For a concise survey, see William Dyrness, *Learning about Theology from the Third World* (Grand Rapids: Zondervan, 1990), 43–52.

- Perhaps most characteristic of the African worldview (as well as much of Asian and Hispanic cultures) is that religion permeates all of life. In the words of John S. Mbiti, "There is no formal distinction between the sacred and the secular" or between "the spiritual and material areas of life."[5]

- A sense of harmony and well-being is reflected in the African focus on the order of creation. Seasons of nature as well as human life exemplify order. Harmony is affirmed even when facing life's fears, ambiguity, and many threats.

- To the African mind, the world of the spirits is as real as the visible world, perhaps even more real. The visible world is "enveloped in the invisible spirit world."[6]

- Life and world are believed to be governed by God, the ancestors, and (other) spirits. In a study by Mbiti of over three hundred peoples in Africa, all had some notion of God as the supreme being.[7]

- Living in a close relation to God are the spirits, including ancestors. Called by various names, these real powers were created by God to mediate his power and occupy a status lower than that of God. According to the contemporary scholarly assessment, often explicit worship of the spirits does not compromise the basically monotheistic orientation of most African religions. Among the spirits, ancestors, who live closer to the living community, are a central feature of all African religiosity.

- A this-worldly orientation, including a focus on the human community and its well-being, is a well-known feature of African religiosity. This orientation does not exclude the other-worldly reality; rather, religions are brought to bear on this life and these particular people.[8]

- Conversion is often understood as an encounter between two or several systems of salvation, a kind of power encounter. The God who is believed to be the strongest is given allegiance.[9]

What complicates study of African conceptions of God is that much of the theology is in oral form. Africans are not less "theological" about their faith in God;[10] they merely employ different forms of theologizing.

---

5. John S. Mbiti, *African Religions and Philosophy* (London: Heinemann, 1969), 2.

6. Tokunboh Adeyemo, "Unapproachable God: The High God of African Traditional Religion," in *The Global God: Multicultural Evangelical Views of God*, ed. Aída Besançon Spencer and William David Spencer (Grand Rapids: Baker, 1998), 130–31.

7. Dyrness, *Learning about Theology*, 44; and Mbiti, *African Religions and Philosophy*, 29.

8. See Cyril C. Okorocha, "Religious Conversion in Africa: Its Missiological Implications," *Mission Studies* 9.2, no. 18 (1992): 168–81.

9. See Cyril Okorocha, "The Meaning of Salvation: An African Perspective," in *Emerging Voices in Global Christian Theology*, ed. William A. Dyrness (Grand Rapids: Zondervan, 1994), 59–92.

10. Kwesi Dickson, *Theology in Africa* (London: Darton, Longman & Todd, 1984), 13.

What about the theme of liberation—economic, social, and political? Mbiti claims that African theology begins more often with a shout of joy and an affirmation of life than with a cry for deliverance.[11] Routinely, African theology is divided into two categories: African and black theology. The latter usually denotes black liberation theologies, especially from the South African context; the former refers to African theology in general. Yet some liberation theologies are not South African, and several African theologians are politically active.[12]

Another feature of the context for God-talk in Africa is the tension between the persistent and growing influence of traditional religious beliefs and the conservative, often fundamentalist, version of Christianity brought by Western missionaries.[13]

The following study focuses first on four African theologians who address African doctrines of God: Kwesi Dickson, a Methodist from the Akan cultural context in West Africa; John Pobee, an Anglican theologian from Ghana; Charles Nyamiti, a Roman Catholic originally from Tanzania who has written extensively on the Gikuyu theology from Kenya; and the expatriate A. Okechukwu Ogbonnaya, who now resides in the United States and whose work focuses on the concept of communitarian divinity and its relation to the Trinity. These theologians know European and international theology well and have studied in the West; they have also written extensively in English. Yet they all have attempted to offer a genuinely African doctrine of God in their own contexts. After highlighting these theologians, the chapter briefly discusses views of God among African Independent Churches, a rapidly growing indigenous force in African Christianity; contributions of liberation theologies; and theologies of African women. First, however, we begin by discussing the extent to which traditional African concepts of God have provided the background for specifically Christian doctrines of God.

The Christian Concept of God and the African Concept of God

Few if any theologians would contest the influence of traditional African beliefs in God on contemporary Christian views of God. Bolaji Idowu, among

11. Quoted in Dyrness, *Learning about Theology,* 36.

12. See John Parratt, *Reinventing Christianity: African Theology Today* (Grand Rapids: Eerdmans, 1995), 25–28. See also Alfred T. Hennelly, *Liberation Theologies: The Global Pursuit of Justice* (Mystic, Conn.: Twenty-Third Publications, 1995), 160–94, which discusses Bénézet Bujo. See Mercy Amba Oduyoye and Deane William Ferm, *Third World Liberation Theologies: An Introductory Survey* (Maryknoll, N.Y.: Orbis, 1986), chap. 3, which lists more than ten names under the category African liberation theology, most of them from outside South Africa.

13. See Dickson, "African Theology," 34–45; and Parratt, *Reinventing Christianity,* chap. 1. The harshest pronouncement of the irrelevancy of traditional Christian theology to the African context has come from F. Eboussi Bolanga. See his *Christianity without Fetishes* (Maryknoll, N.Y.: Orbis, 1984); and idem, "The African Search for Identity," in *The Churches of Africa: Future Prospects,* ed. C. Geffre and B. Luneau (New York: Seabury, 1977), 26–34.

others,[14] has emphasized their continuity rather than their discontinuity and has argued that African traditional religions are basically monotheist. He resists the Western perception that the idea of a "High God," with each tribe having its own deity, implies polytheism.[15] Kwame Bediako qualifies Idowu's passionate appeal by noting that for the purposes of "establishing African identity," Idowu has blurred the genuine differences between these two conceptions of God.[16] John Kibicho, another advocate of the principle of continuity, describes the Kikuyu concept of God as follows:

> The Kikuyu concept of God (Ngai or Mugai) is basically monotheistic. The names of God in Kikuyu express the belief that he is owner of all things (Nyene), source of all mysteries (Mwene-Nyaga) and omnipotent (Murungu); he is also the Great Elder (Githuri) and Father (Baba). It is believed that God is invisible, spiritual and omnipresent, transcendent and immanent, sustainer and controller of all things, benevolent towards humans. He was addressed not only in times of need but also in thanksgiving and for guidance. This traditional idea . . . continued after the christianization of the Kikuyu and still remains the basic concept of Kikuyu.[17]

Western missionaries, however, failed to recognize the true character of Ngai and concluded that the Kikuyu were ignorant of the true God. Hence, the missionaries demanded a radical abandonment of the traditional concept of God.[18] Gabriel Setiloane not only endorses Kibicho's view but also argues that in a sense the traditional African concept of God is a "wider, deeper and all-embracing concept," more so than that of the "western theological tradition." Setiloane refers to the fact that the Western "Christian theologians' 'God' could easily die because he is so small and human" in contrast to the African unlimited, "immense, incomprehensible, wide, tremendous and unique" God.[19] Thus, he encourages African Christians to "Africanise the western Christian concept of God and thus raise it to the level of Modimo [the Great God of African tribal religions], which is much higher."[20]

14. See also John Kibicho, "The Continuity of the African Concept of God into and through Christianity: A Kikuyu Case-Study," in *Christianity in Independent Africa,* ed. E. Fashole-Luke, R. Gray, A. Hastings, and G. Tasie (London: SCM, 1978), 370–88; and Gabriel Setiloane, "How the Traditional World-View Persists in the Christianity of the Sotho-Tswana," in ibid., 402–11.

15. See K. A. Dickson and S. Torres, eds., *Biblical Revelation and African Beliefs,* papers from the Consultation of African Theologians, Ibadan, 1966 (Maryknoll, N.Y.: Orbis, 1979), 13–17; and Bolaji Idowu, *African Traditional Religions: A Definition* (London: SCM, 1973), 62–65.

16. Kwame Bediako, *Theology and Identity* (Oxford: Oxford University Press, 1990), 352; see also 267–302.

17. As summarized in Parratt, *Reinventing Christianity,* 69.

18. Kibicho, "Continuity of the African Concept of God," 379.

19. Gabriel Setiloane, "Where Are We in African Theology?" in *African Theology en Route,* ed. K. Appiah-Kubi and S. Torres (Maryknoll, N.Y.: Orbis, 1979), 60.

20. Ibid., 63.

John Parratt, in his widely acclaimed *Reinventing Christianity: African Theology Today*, takes the middle position. He admits that the criticism of Setiloane has to be heeded because it reveals the one-sided picture of the Christian God who was introduced to Africans. He also wonders whether misgivings by some African theologians target aspects of classical theism rather than the dynamic, powerful picture of God in the Bible.[21] Setiloane's view of a "weak God" in Christianity is a misrepresentation of the biblical idea of God, the Powerful, who nevertheless allows himself to participate in the pain of the world.[22] Charles Nyamiti picks up on this:

> What is new to the Africans is the fact that God's power is manifest in weakness: in Christ's humility, meekness, forgiveness of sins, and—most astoundingly—in his suffering, his death on the Cross, and its glorious consequences in Christ himself and the whole of creation.[23]

Parratt's and Nyamiti's approaches attempt to overcome twin perils: ignoring the obvious connections between the traditional African concept of God and Christianity's concept of God and uncritically emphasizing their continuity. There is both continuity and discontinuity. Nyamiti, for example, suggests that any genuinely Christian concept of God in Africa should take seriously traditional elements such as dynamism, solidarity, participation, anthropocentrism, and the place of the supernatural. He also notes that Christian theology needs to acknowledge the ways African religions name God, for example, God as mother.[24] At the same time, African theologians should be aware of aspects of traditional religions that are unacceptable to Christianity, such as an emphasis on the immanence of God to the exclusion of his transcendence, or an emphasis on his transcendence to the detriment of his concern for humankind. What Nyamiti regards as the major difference, however, is that the Christian concept of God is Christ-centered. This is the real dividing line even in the midst of similarities.[25]

The God in Akan Context: Kwesi Dickson

A Contextual Theology for Africa

Kwesi Dickson[26] has distinguished himself as one of the leading biblical scholars, especially of the Old Testament, and has argued for the importance of

21. Parratt, *Reinventing Christianity*, 72.

22. Ibid., 73.

23. Charles Nyamiti, *African Tradition and the Christian God* (Eldoret, Kenya: Gaba, 1976), 57.

24. Ibid., 15. On the significance of names for God, see John Mbiti, *Concepts of God in Africa* (London: SPCK, 1970), 327–36.

25. Nyamiti, *African Tradition and the Christian God*, 6–8.

26. I am heavily indebted to the detailed, balanced survey and assessment of Dickson, John Pobee, and Charles Nyamiti in Peter Fulljames, *God and Creation in Intercultural Perspective:*

the Old Testament for African Christianity and an African view of God. He has shown that much of Christianity in Africa, especially among the independent churches, reveals a considerable predilection for the Old Testament.[27]

The book that brought Dickson international recognition was his 1984 *Theology in Africa*. He believes that a genuine African theology must be relevant to the culture and possess a methodology suitable for its context. Both would free Africans from doing "theology in terms of areas of thought defined in the West." He fears that the Western "methodological straitjacket" compels Africans to think along Western lines and thus hampers originality of thought.[28] A significant portion of African theology is found in prayers, songs, hymns, and liturgy of the common people, and Dickson believes this must not be dismissed. Scripture and culture are the two pillars that provide the foundation for theology.[29]

The God of the Old Testament and the God of the Akan

The starting point for Dickson's doctrine of God for Africa is that religion in general plays a crucial role in African life. He defines religion as "an acknowledgment of God's rule over mankind."[30] He believes it is possible to establish that "there is one God of the whole earth, and that every religion is to a certain measure an embodiment of the drama of God meeting man."[31]

To understand the significance of these statements for his view of God in Africa, we need to note Dickson's approach to the Old Testament, which sees both continuity and discontinuity between Israel and Africa. The Old Testament is a particular story for a chosen people (exclusivism), but it is also "an invitation to those outside the Israelite tradition to see themselves as sharing their traditions" (universalism).[32] One aspect of this universalism is that in the Old Testament God is seen as the Lord of the whole earth and is concerned with all peoples, not only with the people of Israel. Dickson also highlights the religiocultural continuities between Israel and Africa, such as their views of nature, spirit possession, and sense of community.[33]

Dialogue between the Theologies of Barth, Dickson, Pobee, Nyamiti, and Pannenberg (New York: P. Lang, 1993).

27. Dickson, *Theology in Africa*, 141–43.

28. Ibid., 119; and Kwesi Dickson, "The African Theological Task," in *The Emergent Gospel*, ed. S. Torres and V. Fabella (Maryknoll, N.Y.: Orbis, 1978), 119.

29. Dickson, *Theology in Africa*,14.

30. Ibid., 30.

31. Ibid., 36.

32. Kwesi Dickson, "Continuity and Discontinuity between the Old Testament and African Life and Thought," *Ghana Bulletin of Theology* 4, no. 4 (1973): 99, quoted in Parratt, *Reinventing Christianity*, 60.

33. Dickson, *Theology in Africa*, 168–70.

Dickson, along with several colleagues,[34] laments the fact that the Bible brought to Africans by missionaries has been read from the perspective of literal fundamentalism. Therefore, there has been a tendency to limit biblical studies on the continent.[35] Parratt makes an interesting point here, namely, that the literalist interpretation is surprising in light of the similarities between the mythological language used in the Old and New Testaments and the language used in African oral literature.[36]

Akan Views of God as an Example of an African Theology

Dickson has done much of his theological work in the Akan context (Akan is the major tribe and a national language of Ghana). Yet his purpose is to develop an African theology that is suitable for other contexts on the continent as well, since he believes there is an underlying united core in African Christianity and its doctrine of God.[37] At the same time, he is also quick to point to differences between the biblical (mainly Old Testament) and Akan concepts of God.

The various names for deities in the Akan context reveal that God is understood as the ultimate reality, on whom all things depend:

> God is the supreme being, the creator, the originator, the power that sustains all things, the infinite, the one who endures from ancient times and forever. Everything is from God and ends up in God, who himself is uncaused.[38]

As an African theologian, Dickson emphasizes the importance of ancestors in representing a sense of community and the "concept of corporate personality," not unknown in Israel.[39] The ancestors are regarded as part of the community, and by their presence they express the solidarity of the community. The spirits of the ancestors use their power for the well-being of the community; this is consistent with the fact that not all the dead become ancestors, only those who lived a good, virtuous life or served as leaders of the community. Ancestors are certainly lower in status than God but higher than humans.[40] They are called

---

34. E.g., E. Fashole-Luke, "The Quest for African Christian Theology," *Journal of Religious Thought* 32, no. 2 (1975): 78.

35. Dickson, *Theology in Africa*, 16–17. For an opposite view in defense of a North American fundamentalism with regard to the African context, see Nigerian B. H. Kato, *Theological Pitfalls in Africa* (Kisumu, Kenya: Evangel Publishing House, 1975).

36. Parratt, *Reinventing Christianity*, 63.

37. Dickson, *Theology in Africa*, 9. For the discussion, with bibliographical notes, see Fulljames, *God and Creation in Intercultural Perspective*, 39–40.

38. Fulljames, *God and Creation in Intercultural Perspective*, 41, with reference to Kwesi Dickson, "Introduction to Second Edition," in J. B. Danquah, *The Akan Doctrine of God* (London: Cass, 1968).

39. Dickson, *Theology in Africa*, 170.

40. Fulljames, *God and Creation in Intercultural Perspective*, 47.

on at the important moments of life.[41] The concept of ancestors in Dickson's view is in many ways similar to the Old Testament view of community.[42]

Dickson notes that in the Akan theology of God there is also a distinctive theology of nature, even though the specific term *nature* is missing from the language (the closest term means "God's created things"). The Akan view perceives nature as a vital, dynamic part of the reality created by God. The principle "kinship with nature" is an affirmation of the interconnectedness of everything. "The universe is for him [African] a living universe, and he is part of it."[43]

God and nature are close to each other in the Akan context. Yet Dickson maintains that Christian theology cannot equate God and nature any more than the Israelites could, in agreement with Canaanite beliefs, see the land as "infused with divinity."[44] The land, however, was significant to the Israelites as a premier gift from God, as it is also to the Akans. The land is not divine; it is a gift from God.[45] Akan culture, however—and much of African cultural-religious thought, which does not have a concept of eschatology or an expectation of an end[46]—does not share with Christian theology the view that the fulfillment of nature will take place in the eschatological coming of the kingdom of God.[47]

Another theme relevant to all African religions is spirit possession. Dickson notes that in the Old Testament several prophets were taken hold of by the Spirit of God to communicate the word of God to the people. Similar kinds of prophetic experiences are familiar in the Akan context. The main difference is that whereas in Akan society the prophets are usually depicted as the guarantors of harmony, the prophets of Israel were often called to challenge the status quo. Another difference is that whereas in the Old Testament the experience is attributed directly to God/God's Spirit, in the Akan context possession is by lesser divinities and other spirit powers.[48]

God and Community: John Pobee

John Pobee's method of approaching the doctrine of God in the African context is similar to Dickson's. He takes into consideration both the biblical teaching and the cultural context; he has also worked mostly with the Akans

---

41. Dickson, *Theology in Africa*, 69.
42. Ibid., 172–74.
43. Ibid., 52; see also 49–51.
44. Ibid., 166.
45. Ibid., 165.
46. See the significant discussion in John Mbiti, "Eschatology," in *Biblical Revelation and African Beliefs*, ed. K. A. Dickson and S. Torres (Maryknoll, N.Y.: Orbis, 1979), 159–84.
47. Dickson, *Theology in Africa*, 166.
48. Fulljames, *God and Creation in Intercultural Perspective*, 53–54.

of Ghana. One of the ways he contributes to a distinctively African theology of God is by utilizing African proverbs and other folk wisdom.

For Pobee, the leading theme from the Akan context is the sense of community.[49] He illustrates the critical role of the community in African theology with a reference to René Descartes: "Whereas Descartes spoke for Western man when he said, 'cogito ergo sum,'—I think, therefore I exist—Akan man's ontology is 'cognaturs ergo sum'—I am related by blood, therefore I exist, or I exist because I belong to a family."[50] This is reminiscent of John Mbiti's statement, "I am because we are, and since we are, therefore I am."[51]

The concept of community helps to explain the meaning of God and the incarnation in the Akan context. In that culture, human personality is considered to consist of three components, two of which are related directly to family lineage: soul (or destiny, *kra*) is received from God, life-blood *(mogya)* from the mother, and spirit (or character, *sunsum*) from the father. The humanity of Jesus comes from a woman (Gal. 4:4), and he belonged to the lineage of David (Rom. 1:3).[52] The concept of community is also the basis for affirming the humanity of the Son of God. Sin in Akan society is essentially an antisocial, anti-community act. Jesus' life was that of perfect love; he did not commit sin against other people or the community.[53]

One of the choice depictions for Jesus in the Akan community is Jesus as the healer. Jesus' acts of healing are signs of the power of God: "Jesus has the power of God and wields it. He could not have wielded that power unless he had been 'ensouled' with God."[54] The theme of healing, as already mentioned, is a typical part of African spirituality and the doctrine of God.

God is viewed as great and powerful in the Akan context. The power seen in the work of healers is traditionally understood to come from God and is associated with the power of God as creator. The Akans illustrate this by speaking of Jesus as having a "heavy *kra*." A person's *kra* is received directly from God and represents the presence of God in that person.[55] God is present in every human being, as is expressed in the saying "all people are God's children, none is the earth's child."[56]

The Akans also speak of the Son of God as the spokesman of the chief.[57] By these and other parallels between the African worldview and biblical faith in

49. See especially Pobee, *Toward an African Theology,* chap. 3.
50. Ibid., 49.
51. Mbiti, *African Religions and Philosophy,* 106.
52. Pobee, *Toward an African Theology,* 83, 88; and Fulljames, *God and Creation in Intercultural Perspective,* 72–73.
53. Pobee, *Toward an African Theology,* 92.
54. Ibid.
55. Fulljames, *God and Creation in Intercultural Perspective,* 74.
56. Pobee, *Toward an African Theology,* 94.
57. Ibid., 94–98.

God, Pobee develops a theology based on the model of John 1:14, the Word, *Logos,* "dwelling" (Greek, *skēnōsis*) in a particular culture.[58]

God and Ancestors: Charles Nyamiti

Toward a Systematic Theology for the African Context

Charles Nyamiti is best known for his extensive work on the theme of ancestors, as illustrated in his widely acclaimed work *Christ as Our Ancestor.*[59] One of his earlier works, *African Tradition and the Christian God* (1976), also focuses on the role of ancestors in the Gikuyu context in Kenya and beyond. Furthermore, he has written extensively on the need to develop an African theology.[60]

What makes Nyamiti's approach to African theology different from those of Dickson and Pobee is that he is not ashamed to call for a more systematic approach to the doctrine of God and other Christian doctrines. He is well aware of the presence of African theology mainly in prayers, hymns, and other forms of spirituality, but he believes theologians need to move beyond these. One reason is that Africa is rapidly moving from its "traditional mode of life to the technological and scientific age."[61] Nyamiti notes that Christian theology has always tended to be systematic and to use existing philosophical and other means for presenting a coherent account of its beliefs; he mentions Aquinas as an example here. He also calls for a more systematic approach because he proposes an interaction between the African cultural context and the tradition of the Catholic Church and its interpretation of the biblical message. Of course, many have criticized him for suggesting that Africans use categories from other cultures,[62] but he responds by saying that the systematization of the Christian doctrine in the African context has to be done critically and with necessary modifications.[63]

Nyamiti is also open to the possibility of developing an African philosophy as a tool for elucidating Christian faith, similar to the use of Aristotelianism in the medieval era.[64] This task would require both affirmation of those traits

58. John Pobee, "Mission, Paternalism, and the Peter Pan Syndrome," in *Crossroads Are for Meeting: Essays on the Mission and Common Life of the Church in a Global Society,* ed. Philip Turner and Frank Sugeno (Sewanee: SPCK/USA, 1986), 95–96.

59. Charles Nyamiti, *Christ as Our Ancestor* (Gweru, Zimbabwe: Mambo Press, 1984).

60. Charles Nyamiti, *The Scope of African Theology* (Eldoret, Kenya: Gaba, 1973).

61. John Pobee, "Approaches to African Theology," in *Emergent Gospel,* 35.

62. For a moderate, constructive dialogue with Nyamiti, see Bénézet Bujo, *African Theology in Its Social Context* (Maryknoll, N.Y.: Orbis, 1992), 56.

63. Nyamiti, *Scope of African Theology,* 33; see also Fulljames, *God and Creation in Intercultural Perspective,* 98–99.

64. Pobee, "Approaches to African Theology," 35.

that are in harmony with Christian faith and critical scrutiny of those that are not. This is what Christian theology has always done, Nyamiti argues.[65]

God as Parent-Ancestor

Several African theologians have used ancestor imagery. Nyamiti uses the category of ancestor in three interrelated ways:

1. God as ancestor[66]
2. Christ as ancestor[67] or brother ancestor[68]
3. the communion of saints as ancestors[69]

The last usage is probably the most widespread application of the ancestor concept in African Christianity.

What is the significance of the ancestor theme for the African context? Nyamiti summarizes it in five points. Ancestors:

1. offer kinship between the dead and the living king
2. have sacred status, usually acquired through death
3. serve as an example of behavior in community
4. have regular communication with the living through prayer and rituals
5. mediate between God and humans (applies mostly to Christ as ancestor)[70]

One of the distinctive features of Nyamiti's view of God is the way he uses the theme of parent-ancestor. The parent-ancestor to whom prayer and sacrifice is offered by a family at a time of sickness or at key points in the agricultural cycle is the parent of the oldest living member of a family. Thus, Nyamiti's application of the category of ancestor to God differs from those who perceive of God as the Great Ancestor, the original progenitor of the human species.[71] Even though the blood relationship of parent and child is basic to Nyamiti's view (and this does not, of course, apply to God-human relations), he suggests that God may be understood analogically as a parent-ancestor because the emphasis in the definition above is on the reflection of the parent's character

---

65. Ibid., 38.

66. Nyamiti, *African Tradition and the Christian God,* chap. 8.

67. Nyamiti, *Christ as Our Ancestor.*

68. This usage comes occasionally in Nyamiti, *African Tradition and the Christian God.*

69. See, for example, Charles Nyamiti, "Uganda Martyrs: Ancestors of All Mankind," *African Christian Studies* 2, no. 1 (1986): 37–60.

70. As summarized in Fulljames, *God and Creation in Intercultural Perspective,* 116.

71. This is the view of J. B. Danquah, *The Akan Doctrine of God,* 2d ed. (London: Cass, 1968).

by the child. God is the source of all things, but he also wants to enter into personal relationship. What is significant is that parent-ancestors may be either fathers or mothers and that God shows qualities of both fatherhood and motherhood.[72]

In addition to the ancestor theme as a way to link biblical faith and the African context, Nyamiti notes several others:

- God as the power and life
- God as communion and sharing
- God as the one who is holy, numinous, and mysterious[73]

A Trinitarian View of the Ancestor Theme

Nyamiti applies the ancestor theme to Christ based on his role as the mediator between God and humanity. Christ as brother ancestor is the means by which God communicates with humanity. Within the Trinity there is an eternal ancestral relationship between the Father and the Son, who are therefore described as ancestor and descendent. As humans are incorporated into the descendency of Christ, they come to share in his relationship with God as ancestor.[74]

The Holy Spirit as part of the Trinity is introduced here: "The Ancestor and the Descendent communicate with one another in and through the Spirit, and seen from this perspective, the Spirit appears to be the expression of their mutual love—in as much as love is expressed by the mutual giving to each other of the divine gift, that is, the Holy Spirit." Thus, according to Nyamiti, the Holy Spirit is needed to secure the sacred communication between ancestor and descendent: "Since in God, this sacred communication can only be made through the Holy Spirit, divine ancestorship and descendency demand by their very nature the presence of the Holy Spirit."[75]

For Nyamiti, Christ's redemptive activity can be understood only in terms of the incarnation of one who is in eternal relationship with the Father, the parent-ancestor. He thus understands redemption as the bridging of the gap between God and humanity caused by sin.[76] Such an understanding is appropriate in the African context because many African societies tell stories of God withdrawing to heaven after his friendship with humans was broken. Nyamiti also notes that his view of incarnation is close to that of the Greek fathers, for

72. Fulljames, *God and Creation in Intercultural Perspective,* 115.
73. See ibid., 106–12.
74. Ibid., 116.
75. Nyamiti, *African Tradition and the Christian God,* 49.
76. Nyamiti, *Christ as Our Ancestor,* 74–76.

whom "Christ saved the totality of mankind by assuming human nature and uniting it . . . to God."[77]

What about the death of Jesus? Nyamiti echoes Jürgen Moltmann's idea that Christ's death had to do primarily with the inner-trinitarian relations. Thus, "the crucifixion of the Son is the sacred communication and ritual self-giving of the Descendent to his divine Ancestor, whereas the glorification of the Son by the Father through the Spirit is the divine ancestral answer."[78]

The Communitarian Divinity: An African Approach to the Trinity

The purpose of the work titled *On Communitarian Divinity: An African Interpretation of the Trinity* by A. Okechukwu Ogbonnaya is to explore the idea of the Trinity in Africa on the basis of the North African church father Tertullian. The study, therefore, is a wonderful comparison of classical theism and African theologies. Ogbonnaya wants to correct those who have attempted to fit traditional African thought into Western models and also those who have failed to see the integral link between community and Trinity.[79]

Ogbonnaya laments that even African theologians still carry on theological discourse as though a monotheistic conception of the divine were fundamental. One of the side effects is that many oppressed people in Africa fail to see the relevance of a liberating communitarian concept of God. African concepts, which major in community, have to be taken as the point of departure for God-talk in general and the Trinity in particular, he argues. Tertullian's work as an African, Ogbonnaya contends, leans in the direction of conceiving of the Trinity as a community of equal persons—with a temporal rather than an ontological functional subordination among the persons.[80]

Ogbonnaya's starting point is obvious: Communality is foundational to the African worldview.[81] In Africa, while face-to-face encounter is of vital importance, the sense of community goes beyond actual physical encounters; spiritual ties to the community always exist. "In the context of Africa, people are surrounded not by things but by beings—the metaphysical world is loaded with beings."[82] The ancestors and persons yet to be born are part of the community. It is thus a community that reaches into the past, respects the present,

77. Ibid., 73.

78. Ibid., 46.

79. A. Okechukwu Ogbonnaya, *On Communitarian Divinity: An African Interpretation of the Trinity* (New York: Paragon House, 1994), ix.

80. Ibid., xii–xix.

81. Ibid., 1.

82. Ibid., 8, quoting Gerhardus Cornelis Oosthuizen, "The Place of Traditional Religion in Contemporary South Africa," in *African Traditional Religion in Contemporary Society*, ed. Jacob K. Olupon (New York: Paragon House, 1991), 40.

and looks into the future. Therefore, Ogbonnaya argues, God's revelation in African Christian theology should not be seen as something giving objective data but something happening within the community.[83]

The principle of communality also applies to the divine: "Communality is the essence of the gods."[84] This takes us to the heart of the debate concerning the understanding of God in African traditional religion: whether it is monotheistic or polytheistic. For Ogbonnaya, these two views are not the only options; he prefers the idea of the divine as a community of gods.[85] Gods are connected with family, generativity, and proliferation. Ogbonnaya summarizes that "the concept of *the One* is present in African religions, but so also is the concept of *the Many*," and this cannot be called either monotheism or polytheism but communalism.[86]

When developing his doctrine of the Trinity, Tertullian took biblical passages such as "Let us make man in our image" (Gen. 1:26) and "Let us go down and confuse their language" (Gen. 11:7) as a guide to help him expand the monotheism of Judaism. These kinds of biblical orientations in Ogbonnaya's interpretation underscore "the community of persons within the Divine One."[87]

The Trinity for Tertullian was connected to creation and salvation and thus to community, both human community in general and the church community in particular. He liberally used terms from nature to speak of the plurality in the Godhead such as roots-branch-fruit, source-river-rivulet, and sun-ray-tip. He used not only cosmological but also relational concepts from society. One was family, a concept crucial to African cultures. When contemplating the immanent Trinity, Tertullian believed that the one God was not alone: "Even in the beginning before the creation of the universe God was not alone, since he had within himself both Reason [*Logos*] and inherent in Reason, His Word, which He made second to himself by agitating it within himself."[88] There is also intersubjectivity in the immanent Trinity, since the "Word . . . is both always in the Father" and "I and the Father are one."[89]

Ogbonnaya believes that by taking clues from Tertullian, African theology can construct a communal doctrine of the Trinity. "This communality of the Divine is a community of equality. This equality is based on the fact that all share in one nature." Relationality, he summarizes, is also a basic characteristic of the divine community.[90]

83. Ogbonnaya, *On Communitarian Divinity*, 9–11.
84. Ibid., 13, quoting Edmund Ilogu, *Christianity and Igbo Culture* (New York: NOK Press, 1974), 201.
85. Ogbonnaya, *On Communitarian Divinity*, 23. For the consideration of the monotheistic and polytheistic options, see 14–23.
86. Ibid., 27.
87. Ibid., 55.
88. Ibid., 61–62, quoting Tertullian, *Adversus Praxeas* 5.
89. Ogbonnaya, *On Communitarian Divinity*, 62, quoting Tertullian, *Adversus Praxeas* 8.
90. Ogbonnaya, *On Communitarian Divinity*, 89.

The Dynamic View of God among the African Independent Churches

The main reasons for the dramatic growth of Christianity in Africa are Pentecostal/charismatic movements and African Independent Churches (AIC).[91] The AIC and other independent churches have numerically outdistanced their mother churches.[92] Already in the early 1980s, David B. Barrett reported that the AIC claimed thirty-one million adherents throughout the African continent; the current number is significantly larger.[93] This is what Kwame Bediako has recently called the "new centers of universality."[94] Many believe that the AIC has the potential to embody a type of Christian spirituality and faith that does not merely contextualize superficial elements of the Western interpretation of Christianity but rather represents a legitimate version of the Christian faith, a non-Western religion. Being rooted in African soil, the theological mode of the AIC is different from its Western counterparts. Its oral and narrative style is also prevalent elsewhere outside the West.[95] African Independent Churches are also significant in that they highlight the place of spirituality within the community and generally place less emphasis on doctrinal orthodoxy than do established churches.[96]

As far as doctrine is concerned, it is difficult to say anything conclusive about African Independent Churches because little of their beliefs has been put into written form. The spectrum of theological opinion within them is wide, "stretching from the solidly orthodox at the one extreme to the avowedly nativistic at the other."[97] AIC spiritualities illustrate the lack of relevance of much of the traditional Christian doctrine of God in the African context. F. Eboussi Boulaga contends that this, in addition to the rationalism and historicism of typical Western-inherited theology, has been the main reason for the emergence of a new kind of Christian spirituality. "Christianity has its formulae and ideals, but these are not brought down from heaven to earth in

91. W. J. Hollenweger, foreword to *African Initiatives in Christianity: The Growth, Gifts, and Diversities of Indigenous African Churches—A Challenge to the Ecumenical Movement*, ed. John M. Pobee and Gabriel Ositelu II (Geneva: WCC Publications, 1998). The acronym AIC stands for several interrelated titles: African Indigenous Churches, African Initiated Churches, or African Independent Churches. The last name is gaining more following in recent theological literature.

92. An up-to-date introduction to the AIC is provided in Allan H. Anderson, *African Reformation: African Initiated Christianity in the Twentieth Century* (Trenton, N.J.: Africa World Press, 2000).

93. David B. Barrett, *Schism and Renewal in Africa: An Analysis of Six Thousand Contemporary Religious Movements* (New York: Oxford University Press, 1982), 815.

94. Kwame Bediako, *Christianity in Africa* (Maryknoll, N.Y.: Orbis, 1995), 111.

95. See Allan H. Anderson, "Pluriformity and Contextuality in African Initiated Churches"; http://artsweb.bham.ac.uk/aanderson/index.htm (September 1997).

96. Parratt, *Reinventing Christianity,* 6.

97. Ibid., 7.

any practical way." These ideals remain, he says, "the invisible no-place where souls gather."[98]

While all African churches acknowledge the reality of the spirit world,

> it is the independents who help us to see the overriding African concern for spiritual power from a mighty God to overcome all enemies and evils that threaten human life and vitality, hence their extensive ministry of mental and physical healing. This is rather different from the Western preoccupation with atonement for sin and forgiveness of guilt.[99]

In the AIC and African Pentecostalism, the religious specialist or the "person of God" has the power to heal the sick and ward off evil spirits. This holistic function, which does not separate the physical from the spiritual, is emphasized, and indigenous peoples see Christianity as a powerful religion to meet human needs.

Liberation Theologies in the African Context

While not classified as a liberation theologian, John Pobee has "argued that because of the non-negotiable tenet of the sovereignty of God over all life, Christian involvement in politics is also non-negotiable."[100] Pobee understands theology as a practical discipline that should guide economic policy making and political action. He has shown great sympathy for many of the aims of liberation theologies, in particular black theology in Southern Africa.[101]

Charles Nyamiti, however, while agreeing with the need to address social and political issues such as racism and oppression, warns about the danger of building one's theology on a particular case. He is concerned that these and related problems remain linked to the root problem of sin and alienation from God.[102]

According to Bénézet Bujo, African theology is by nature liberation theology, since the idea of liberation is inherent in the concept of life in Africa. This is accentuated by the this-worldly orientation of the African mentality, which focuses on the now rather than the future. "Though God is present implicitly in every situation, the African outlook is essentially anthropocentric."[103]

98. Boulaga, *Christianity without Fetishes,* 63, as paraphrased in Parratt, *Reinventing Christianity,* 108.

99. H. W. Turner, *Religious Innovation in Africa* (Boston: G. K. Hall, 1979), 210.

100. John Pobee, "Political Theology in the African Context," *African Theological Journal* 11 (1982): 170.

101. John Pobee, "Church and Politics," *Bulletin of African Theology* 6 (1984): 124–40.

102. Nyamiti, *African Tradition and the Christian God,* 26–43; and idem, "Approaches to African Theology," 42–44.

103. For details, see Parratt, *Reinventing Christianity,* 122–25.

South Africa has become the center of liberation theologies in Africa, which is understandable in light of the history of apartheid. Allan Boesak popularized the term "black Consciousness," which, though echoing concerns similar to those of American black theology under James H. Cone, has distinctive elements.[104] For Boesak, as for other black theologians, theology is about liberation. "Black Theology believes that liberation is not only 'part of' the gospel or 'consistent with' the gospel; it is the content and framework of the gospel of Jesus Christ."[105] He also champions the idea of a black Messiah and focuses on the historical Jesus.[106] But he is suspect of Cone's methodology because it seems to identify black power with the gospel and one-sidedly emphasizes racism solely as the experience of blacks. Furthermore, Boesak and many other South African black theologians, especially Desmond Tutu, champion the idea of reconciliation and repentance.[107]

John W. de Gruchy's *Liberating Reformed Theology* is another South African contribution, one that harkens back to John Calvin to glean resources for a liberating view of God. In his view, Calvin's theology is "best understood as a liberating theology that is catholic in its substance, evangelical in its principle, and socially engaged and prophetic in its witness." Yet he mentions that there is ambiguity in Reformed tradition: "For while they may be liberating in intent, they have also been guilty of legitimating oppression in practice."[108] De Gruchy argues that Calvin, Barth, and recent Catholic theologies of liberation have much in common. The call to promote justice is a task given to the entire ecumenical church. The Christian "is called to respond in faith, active in hope and love, to God's redemptive activity, so that the whole of creation can be liberated by grace from the bondage of sin and oppression and can be restored to full life in Jesus Christ, through the Spirit, to the glory of God."[109]

African Women on God

Feminist theologies of African women share the following with those of the third world.[110]

104. See Basil Moore, "What Is Black Theology?" in *The Challenge of Black Theology in South Africa,* ed., Basil Moore (Atlanta: John Knox Press, 1974), 1–10.

105. Allan Boesak, *Farewell to Innocence: A Socio-Ethical Study on Black Theology and Black Power* (Maryknoll, N.Y.: Orbis, 1977), 9.

106. Ibid., 41–42.

107. Ibid., 92. After examining both Cone's and Boesak's views, Volker Küster (*The Many Faces of Jesus Christ: An Intercultural Christology* [Maryknoll, N.Y.: Orbis, 2001], 147–52) concludes that Cone is closer to Boesak in his theology than the majority of scholarship thinks.

108. John W. de Gruchy, *Liberating Reformed Theology: A South African Contribution to an Ecumenical Dialogue* (Grand Rapids: Eerdmans, 1991), xii.

109. Ibid., 281.

110. Ursula King, introduction to *Feminist Theology from the Third World: A Reader,* ed. Ursula King (Maryknoll, N.Y.: Orbis, 1994), 16–19.

- doing theology rather than speculating on topics unrelated to the real world
- using the depth of oppression, suffering, and struggle as the starting point for doing relevant theology
- valuing dreaming, not as a way of escape but as a way of empowerment and creativity
- cherishing the theme of church-as-community as the appropriate framework for relevant theologizing[111]
- focusing on the need for liberation at all levels as the guiding principle

Mercy Amba Oduyoye of Ghana, the most noted African feminist theologian, notes that in our attempts to be one and at peace with people, we too often forget that God put an end to the ideology of the tower of Babel, replacing it later with the more meaningful and community-building diversity of Pentecost: "life in the Spirit of God as opposed to the mentality of 'let us . . . make a name for ourselves' (Gen. 11.3–4)." She notes that we are indeed united in our reading of biblical motifs and imagery, the exodus, the Magnificat, the proclamation from Isaiah that Jesus read at Nazareth, and so on.[112]

Black women theologians ask questions such as, Where is God in our lives, at home, at work? What does it mean to be fully human in the image of God? How are we being called to serve God?[113] They acknowledge the special situation of oppression and subjugation in most African countries. Yet at the same time they uphold the value of black women and their trust in God. Oduyoye writes hopefully:

> Happy and responsible in my being human and female, I shall be able to live a life in doxology in the human community, glorifying God for the gifts I receive in others and the possibility I have of giving myself freely for the good of the community while remaining responsible and responsive to God. It is only thus that I can say I am fully human.[114]

Black women theologians from South Africa have joined their male colleagues in developing a liberating theology appropriate to that context. They criticize the beginnings of black theology for being insensitive to the liberation

111. See Mercy Amba Oduyoye, "The Value of African Religious Beliefs and Practices for Christian Theology," in *African Theology en Route,* 111.

112. She calls this "beings-in-relation" notion an integral component of the African context. See Mercy Amba Oduyoye, "Reflections from a Third World Woman's Perspective: Women's Experience and Liberation Theologies," in *Feminist Theology from the Third World,* 24.

113. Roxanne Jordaan and Thoko Mpumlwana, "Two Voices on Women's Oppression and Struggle in South Africa," in *Feminist Theology from the Third World,* 163.

114. Mercy Amba Oduyoye, *Hearing and Knowing: Theological Reflections on Christianity in Africa* (Maryknoll, N.Y.: Orbis, 1986), 137.

of black women.[115] They join black theology in maintaining that "God is no neutral God." Yet they are not willing to say that God is on the side of black woman only or that God is a black woman. Oduyoye argues that feminism in the African context is not the world of the female; it is the world of all "who are conscious of the true nature of the human community."[116] In Roxanne Jordaan and Thoko Mpumlwana's words, "Above all, Black women are prepared to accept God's granting dominion to all people over the earth."[117] Black women liberationists also maintain that the call to communion with God comes "on the soil of Africa." But how do they have that communion when the soil is taken away? This is the struggle of black feminist theologians as they try to make "God relevant to all people."[118]

115. Jordaan and Mpumlwana, "Two Voices on Women's Oppression," 152.
116. Oduyoye, *Hearing and Knowing,* 121.
117. Jordaan and Mpumlwana, "Two Voices on Women's Oppression," 152–53.
118. Ibid., 155–56.

27

God in Latin American Theologies

The Latin American Context for God-Talk

The story behind the popular cult of Guadalupe reveals much about the Latin American context. The Virgin appeared to Juan Diego, a poor and unlearned Indian, and gave him certain instructions to pass on to the bishop of Mexico. The bishop, of course, did not want to listen to the man until a miracle assured him that the Virgin had indeed manifested herself to the poor man. "Thus the Virgin of Guadalupe became a symbol of the affirmation of the Indian over against the Spanish, of the unlearned over against the learned, of the oppressed over against the oppressor."[1]

It has been said that whereas African theology begins with a shout of joy, Latin American theology begins with a cry of despair. One could also say that while African theologians are drawn to issues of culture and identity, many Latin American theologians wrestle with social and political issues.[2]

Theologians agree that liberation is the major impetus of theology in Latin America. But what is behind the appeal of the theme of liberation? Poverty is one candidate. Most likely, what makes the issue of poverty critical in the Latino context is the historical background. The leading historian of liberation theology, Enrique Dussel, makes the perceptive comment that Latin Americans

---

1. Justo L. González, *Mañana: Christian Theology from a Hispanic Perspective* (Nashville: Abingdon, 1990), 61.
2. William Dyrness, *Learning about Theology from the Third World* (Grand Rapids: Zondervan, 1990), 71–72.

have always been outsiders to writing their own history; others have written it for them.[3] In other words, theirs has been a history written by their conquerors.

Ronaldo Muñoz, a Chilean theologian who lives and works in the working-class barrio of Santiago, has analyzed various uses of God-talk as the key to developing a proper doctrine of God from the liberation perspective. He speaks of the "God of the Poor," who is at the same time the God of all people, not only the poor. According to Muñoz, the main question for Christians today is not whether we are believers or atheists; the fundamental issue is which God we believe in and which gods we deny. He notes that in the churches of Latin America, the topic of God is approached from many different angles:

- The privileged minorities use the name of God as they fight with all the weapons of power and technology to defend their property and rights.
- The underprivileged minorities resign themselves to their destitution in the name of God, though a growing number is awakening to a struggle for liberation.
- Those who are politically oriented use the name of God to call for social reconciliation.
- For some, the most important thing about the doctrine of God is orthodoxy and right belief, and they try to convert others to their own particular understanding.
- Finally, some use the name of God to urge solidarity with the impoverished masses, "making taking their side in the struggle for a more just world the all-important task."[4]

Muñoz finds fault with two reductionist approaches to God: One relates God only to the salvation of the individual after death. According to the other, the "utopistic" Marxist interpretation, salvation comes as a result of collective efforts.[5]

God's Self-Revelation among the Poor

The Latin American bishops who met in Puebla in 1979 made a significant theological-methodological observation: They identified the poor as the locus of God's revelation. According to them, the proper subjects of liberation theology are

---

3. Enrique Dussel, *The History of the Church in Latin America: An Interpretation* (San Antonio, Tex.: Mexican-American Cultural Center, 1974), 3; see also ibid., 75.
4. Ronaldo Muñoz, *The God of Christians* (Maryknoll, N.Y.: Orbis, 1990), 9, 11.
5. Ibid., 8.

young children, struck down by poverty before they are born . . . indigenous peoples . . . living marginalized lives in inhuman situations . . . the peasants; as a special group they live in exile almost everywhere on our continent . . . marginalized and overcrowded urban dwellers, whose lack of material goods is matched by the ostentatious display of wealth by other segments of society.[6]

This human reality—what it is to be the poor, the despised, the marginalized—is understood by Latin American theologians to be the "praxis" of theology. This term has three interrelated facets. First, human beings are heavily shaped by political-historical reality. Second, human reality is intersubjective: "Human beings are not first ahistorical 'I's' that express their unique essences in relations to others through language. . . . All subjectivity arises out of intersubjective relations between human beings." Third, humans must and can intentionally create history, "transforming and shaping reality for the improvement of human flourishing."[7]

Pablo Richards summarizes much of the agenda of Latin American liberation theology: The "mystery of the presence of God in the world of the poor" is that "God personally comes to meet us and to bestow a self-revelation. The world of the poor is now seen for what it is: the privileged locus of the presence and revelation of God." Furthermore, "God is revealed as the life, strength, hope, gladness, and utopia of the very poorest and most oppressed."[8]

Various liberation theologians have made contributions to the doctrine of God. Gustavo Gutiérrez of Peru, though not a founder of Latin American liberation theology, has become its embodiment, especially in North America and Europe. Juan Luis Segundo of Uruguay, while less known outside theological circles, is a representative liberation theologian, especially in regard to theological method and its implications for the doctrine of God. Leonardo Boff of Brazil, who was silenced by his superiors, distinguished himself in several areas, especially Christology, ecclesiology, and the doctrine of the Trinity. Other names that could be added include Robert Muñoz of Chile, who wrote a major study on the doctrine of God from the liberation perspective;[9] Jon Sobrino, a premier Christologist from a liberation perspective; José Comblin, a pneumatologist; and José Míguez Bonino, who popularized liberation theology with his *Doing Theology in a Revolutionary Situation.*[10]

6. John Eagleson and Philip Scharper, eds., *Pueblo and Beyond: Documentation and Commentary* (Maryknoll, N.Y.: Orbis, 1979), 32–39.

7. Rebecca S. Chopp, "Latin American Liberation Theology," in *The Modern Theologians,* 2d ed., ed. David F. Ford (Cambridge, U.K.: Blackwell, 1997), 412.

8. Pablo Richards, "Theology in the Theology of Liberation," in *Mysterium Liberationis,* ed. Ignacio Ellacuria, S.J., and Jon Sobrino, S.J. (Maryknoll, N.Y.: Orbis, 1993), 150–51.

9. Muñoz, *God of Christians.*

10. José Míguez Bonino, *Doing Theology in a Revolutionary Situation* (Philadelphia: Fortress, 1975).

The God Who Saves History: Juan Luis Segundo

The Hermeneutic Circle as the Starting Point for Doing Theology

All liberation theologies tend to be critical of the existing world order and the subjugation of the marginalized by the powerful. Juan Luis Segundo, however, has made the notion of being critical one of the building blocks of his theology and God-talk. He presents his methodology using a hermeneutical circle:

1. Our way of experiencing reality leads to ideological suspicion.
2. We apply our ideological suspicion to the ideological superstructure in general and to theology in particular.
3. A new way of experiencing theological reality leads to exegetical suspicion, namely, that the prevailing interpretation of the Bible has not taken important pieces of data into account.
4. The final result is a new hermeneutic, a new way of interpreting Scripture with the new elements at our disposal.[11]

This hermeneutical circle—or perhaps, spiral—"keeps on moving on to an ever more authentic truth that is to be translated into an ever more liberative praxis."[12] There is a mutual relationship between theory and practice, each of which constantly informs the other.

This methodology is not a secondary issue to Segundo. He makes the famous statement, "It is the fact that the one and only thing that can maintain the liberative character of any theology is not its content but its methodology."[13]

Faith and Ideology

Echoing the approach to knowledge (how we understand what knowledge is) currently known as the sociology of knowledge, Segundo engages in a critical scrutiny of existing theologies. This is called ideology critique, and the doctrine of God is the main target of his ideological criticism.[14] He maintains that the typical Christian (Catholic) conception of God is that God is more interested in timeless values than in efforts to solve historical problems in this world. This is the heritage of classical theism. He finds the same world-distancing tendency in Catholic sacramental theology, which serves the "interests of the ruling classes and is one of the most powerful ideological factors in sustaining the status quo."[15]

---

11. Juan Luis Segundo, *The Liberation of Theology* (Maryknoll, N.Y.: Orbis, 1976), 9.
12. Ibid., 97.
13. Ibid., 39–40.
14. Juan Luis Segundo, *Faith and Ideologies* (Maryknoll, N.Y.: Orbis, 1982).
15. Segundo, *Liberation of Theology*, 41.

Segundo refers to "ideological suspicion," or a "hermeneutic of suspicion"—terms now widely used in liberation discourse—and seeks to expose the latent assumptions and interpretations that guide theology and views of God. Both terms refer to approaches to theology that seek to uncover the hidden agenda or motifs in theology and biblical interpretation. According to him, traditional Western theology is a textbook example of a theology adapted to the particular ideological interests of the dominant social classes. Such theology is not ideology-free; no theology is. Therefore, it can never hide behind the label of "an academic discipline in the security of some chamber immune to the risks of the liberation struggle."[16]

Segundo considers this challenge to ideology in light of his view of the Bible, the source of revelation. His guiding principle is that Scripture contains both faith and ideology, but there is a distinction: "One element is permanent and unique: faith. The other is changing and bound up with different historical circumstances: ideologies."[17] Christians can proceed in two ways. They can search the Bible for situations that are closest to present situations and then accept the ideology in the Bible as the correct response of faith for today. The second one, preferred by Segundo is this:

> To invent an ideology that we might regard as the one which could be constructed by a gospel message contemporary with us. What would the Christ of the Gospels say if he were confronting our problems today? If the faith is one amid the diversity of history, then there must be some ideology that can build a bridge between that faith and our present-day situation even as there were such ideologies in the past.[18]

Segundo does not believe that revelation has ended; it is a continuing process. He believes John teaches this when he talks about the "Spirit of truth" leading Jesus' followers into "all the truth."[19] Exegeting John 16:16, "many things which Jesus himself had not spoken," Segundo suggests that "ideologies" could be substituted for "things": Jesus knew that new historical situations would emerge about which he could not yet speak. But later, when "they are spoken by the Spirit . . . they will automatically be converted into ideologies associated with a specific historical situation that renders them comprehensible and useful."[20] Thus, there is a dynamic relationship between faith and ideologies. On the one hand, ideologies spring from faith. On the other hand, without ideologies, faith is "as dead as a doornail."[21]

---

16. Juan Luis Segundo, *Our Idea of God* (Maryknoll, N.Y.: Orbis, 1973), 27.
17. Segundo, *Liberation of Theology*, 116.
18. Ibid., 117.
19. Ibid., 120.
20. Ibid., 121.
21. Ibid., 122. For this section, I am indebted to the careful analysis in Alfred T. Hennelly, *Liberation Theologies: The Global Pursuit of Justice* (Mystic, Conn.: Twenty-Third Publications, 1995), 32–35.

The Danger of Idolatry

In *Our Idea of God,* Segundo draws theological conclusions from his ideological criticism. He seriously doubts whether traditional discussions about the existence and attributes of God have meaning for modern believers. Segundo also faults the death-of-God theologians for worrying about God's existence rather than trying to find an appropriate way to speak of God to oppressed people.[22] He is convinced that Christians and atheists have much more in common than most Christians realize, because the God atheists reject is not necessarily the God of the Bible but a God created by ideological theology. In his own words, "Our notion of God must never cease to retravel the road which runs from atheism to faith."[23] In fact, the danger of idolatry—the worship of false gods, gods who do not exist apart from the imagination of the ruling classes—is far greater than the threat of atheism.

Segundo's foundational observation is that various images of God serve different purposes:

> One person pictures a God who allows dehumanization whereas another person rejects such a God and believes only in a God who unceasingly fights against such things. Now those two gods cannot be the same one. So a common faith does not exist within the church. The only thing shared in common is the formula used to express the faith. And since the formula does not really identify anything, are we not justified in calling it a *hollow* formula vis-à-vis the decisive options of history?[24]

God as a Society of Persons

What, then, is Segundo's proposal for a more appropriate view of God? His guiding idea is this: God is a society of persons, encountered only within the history of this world. The doctrine of the Trinity is trying to explain how God is related to history and humanity. In Segundo's terminology, the Father is "God before us"; the Son, "God with us"; the Spirit, "God within us." Both as the creator, who set the stage for history, and as the God of the promise, giving history its goal, Yahweh revealed himself as "God before us." God showed his commitment to history and humanity, thus fulfilling his promise, in the person of the Son, "God with us." Jesus promised to his disciples his ongoing presence, the presence of God, in the person of the Spirit, "God within us." Thus, in Segundo's view, the biblical portrayal of God is tied to salvation history.[25] On the basis of how God was perceived by the first Christians to relate to history and humanity, there arose from the soil of Jewish monotheism a

---

22. Segundo, *Our Idea of God,* 4.
23. Ibid., 182.
24. Ibid., 43, italics in text.
25. Ibid., 21–31, 37–42.

view of the trinitarian God as a society of persons. They were unified for the sake of the common goal but were distinct "persons."[26]

Why did this picture of God fade into the background during the history of theology? Segundo does not believe it had to do with a changing mind-set from Hebraic modes of thought to Greco-Roman ones, which were needed for Christian apologetics. On the contrary, he "suspect[s] that there must be something deeper and more decisive at work here, because these speculative influences were already around when the Church was elaborating the correct and clearcut formulation about a God who is a society."[27] That "something deeper" for Segundo is the Western cultural emphasis on the "private," also illustrated in the way capitalistic economy is set up to protect an individual's rights. Thus, God was looked to as the "private" par excellence. Segundo even wonders whether "Christians evince a persistent tendency to reject, in practice, the notion of an incarnate God; and reduce it to the notion of an inaccessible God who is perfectly happy *in se* [in himself]." This, in turn, is nothing other than "shift[ing] onto God the features wherewith the individual feels he can find self-fulfillment in a society based on domination."[28]

This "monotheistic" notion tends to deny God-with-us in history and major on the "God of reason" or the divine nature.[29] But that kind of God, unlike the Father of Jesus Christ, has little to do with the world and human beings. Further, since such a God has immutable perfection, to whom nothing can be added, human liberty is an empty concept because God is unmoved by what happens in history. These false ideas of God both nurtured the notion of society and derived partly from it because there is a mutual relationship between theology and society.[30] These false ideas also, in the final analysis, oppose the biblical revelation. To confess Jesus Christ as God-in-the-flesh is to recognize that God has chosen this world and its history as the locus of his revelation and work. "Thus, to devalue the world and history was to defy God."[31]

Another unfortunate implication of the idea of a "rational," "perfect" God, a "de-personalized" God-as-divine-nature, is that it gives human beings freedom to depersonalize or dehumanize one's fellow beings. Ironically, the fear of attributing too human elements to God has led theology to "'purify' the notion of God by stripping all historical realism from it." But this is the most radical anthropomorphism, Segundo notes.[32] Therefore, the stakes are high

---

26. Ibid., 66.

27. Segundo, *Our Idea of God,* 66.

28. Ibid., 68.

29. Ibid., 101.

30. Ibid., 105.

31. As paraphrased in Stanley David Slade, "The Theological Method of Juan Luis Segundo" (Ph.D. diss., Fuller Theological Seminary, School of Theology, Pasadena, California, 1979), 361; see especially Segundo, *Our Idea of God,* 157.

32. Segundo, *Our Idea of God,* 114–15.

concerning the doctrine of God, for it has implications for views of society and anthropology.

God's Option for the Poor: Gustavo Gutiérrez

Without doubt, Gustavo Gutiérrez is the most well-known figure in Hispanic liberation theology,[33] and his book *A Theology of Liberation* is its main textbook (originally published in Portuguese in 1971). For Gutiérrez, theology is a "critical reflection on Christian praxis in light of the Word."[34] As such, it criticizes the one-sided approaches of "theology of wisdom" and "theology of rational knowledge." These are not to be dismissed but corrected in light of the historical and social contexts of the church.

A Theocentric Foundation for the Option for the Poor

According to Gutiérrez, the reason for giving the poor preferential treatment is that God has chosen to reveal himself among the poor. Preference for the poor, in other words, is not an invention of liberation theology but accords with the way God is revealed in the Bible: "The ultimate reason for a commitment to the poor and oppressed does not lie in the social analysis that we employ, or in our human compassion, or in the direct experience we may have of poverty."[35]

In response to his critics, Gutiérrez clarifies the meaning of the term *preferential:* It does not mean exclusivity (as if God's revelation were limited to his presence among the poor) but rather primacy.[36] According to Gutiérrez, the "whole Bible, from the story of Cain and Abel onward, is marked by God's love and predilection for the weak and abused of human history."[37] A preferential option for the poor was also at the heart of Jesus' preaching concerning the reign of God. Several parables make it clear that "the last shall be first" (Matt. 20:16).[38]

This brings us to another, related emphasis in Gutiérrez, namely, God's love. For Gutiérrez, the "love of God is a gratuitous gift." Thus, "Loving by

33. For a recent assessment of Gutiérrez's theology by a number of international liberationists, see Marc H. Ellis and Otto Maduro, *Expanding the View: Gustavo Gutiérrez and the Future of Liberation Theology* (Maryknoll, N.Y.: Orbis, 1998).

34. Gustavo Gutiérrez, *A Theology of Liberation: History, Politics, and Salvation,* rev. ed. (Maryknoll, N.Y.: Orbis, 1988), 11; see 3–12 for basic orientations in his method of theology.

35. Gustavo Gutiérrez, "Option for the Poor," in *Mysterium Liberationis,* 240. See also Gustavo Gutiérrez, *The Truth Shall Make You Free: Confrontations* (Maryknoll, N.Y.: Orbis, 1990), 155–68.

36. Gutiérrez, "Option for the Poor," 239.

37. Ibid., 240.

38. See ibid., 241–44.

preference the poor, doing that, God reveals this gratuity. And by consequence as followers of Jesus Christ, we must also do this preferential option for the poor."[39] This theocentric, biblical preference for the poor is the driving force for doing liberation theology: "If faith is a commitment to God and to human beings, it is not possible to believe in today's world without a commitment to the process of liberation."[40]

Consequently, "to know God is to do justice." An important route to encountering God takes the form of concrete action for others, especially the poor. Similarly, Christ is to be found in one's neighbors as one reaches out to them and their needs. Thus, Gutiérrez speaks of the "human mediation to reach God." For Gutiérrez, it is "not enough to say that the love of God is inseparable from the love of one's neighbor. It must be added that love for God is unavoidably expressed through love of one's neighbor."[41]

God Transcendent and Material

Liberation theology emphasizes that we encounter God in history and that "humanity [is the] temple of God." The active presence of God in the midst of people is one of the oldest and most enduring biblical promises, Gutiérrez maintains.[42] The prophets extended the concept of the presence of God so that it was not limited to the temple, since "God dwells everywhere." This is the biblical idea of transcendence and universality. The incarnation of God in Jesus brought the biblical promise of the presence of God to fulfillment.[43]

Jesus Christ, and the incarnation of God in his person, is the key to discovering the dynamic relationship between God's transcendence/universality and its "spiritual" (wrought by the Spirit) manifestation in believers. Jesus Christ is the temple of God and God's presence. In addition, not only the church but also human beings are temples, that is, the locus of God's presence. Finally, through the reception of the Spirit, an "internalization" of God's presence occurs in the hearts of individual believers, what Gutiérrez also calls "an integration" of God's presence. Having described this manifold presence of God, Gutiérrez emphasizes that even following the Christ event and the reception of the Spirit by individual believers, God's presence is not limited to the "spiritual." It is also present "materially."

39. Gustavo Gutiérrez, "Theology and Spirituality in a Latin American Context," *Harvard Divinity Bulletin* 14 (June–August 1984): 4.
40. Quoted in Hennelly, *Liberation Theologies,* 11.
41. Gutiérrez, *Theology of Liberation,* 110–15, quotation on 114–15.
42. Ibid., 106–7. The biblical passages he refers to are Exod. 29:45–46; Ezek. 37:27–28; among others. Note that chapter 4 is appropriately titled "Encountering God in History."
43. Ibid., 108.

God is even more "material." God is no less involved in human history. On the contrary, God has a greater commitment to the implementation of peace and justice among humankind. God is not more "spiritual," but is closer and, at the same time, more universal; God is more visible and, simultaneously, more internal.[44]

These considerations have profound implications for an understanding of the nature of salvation brought about by God. For Gutiérrez, salvation in liberation perspective—which he regards as the biblical perspective—is a wider concept than that of classical theology. Salvation is not something otherworldly, in regard to which "the present life is merely a test." Salvation, the communion of human beings with God and others, is something that embraces all human reality, transforms it, and leads it to its fullness in Christ. Gutiérrez says that salvation as "fulfillment embraces every aspect of humanity: body and spirit, individual and society, person and cosmos, time and eternity."[45]

This "material" side of God is accentuated by the biblical emphasis on the integral relationship between creation and salvation: Creation is "the first salvific act." Therefore, biblical faith is "faith in God who gives self-revelation through historical events, a God who saves in history."[46] In other words, the "God who makes the cosmos from chaos is the same God who leads Israel from alienation to liberation."[47]

The God of Life

The biblical God shows himself to be *The God of Life*.[48] The basic thesis of that book, a biblical study of the doctrine of God, is this: "Our starting point is our faith: we believe in the God of life. We aim to think through this faith by going ever deeper into the content of biblical revelation. And we do this while taking into account the way in which the poor feel God. Faith and reflection on God feed each other."[49]

Gutiérrez agrees with Pascal that the God of Abraham, Isaac, and Jacob, the God of Jesus Christ, is not the same as the god of the philosophers. In fact, Gutiérrez acknowledges that philosophy has a hard time trying to capture who the God of revelation is. Philosophical theology is imprisoned in Greek and Aristotelian concepts and therefore, for example, the idea of God's love does not match the biblical sense. According to the Greek mentality, love as *pathos* ("passion") implies a need and thus seems to compromise the perfec-

44. Ibid., 109–10.
45. Ibid., 85.
46. Ibid., 86–87.
47. Ibid., 89.
48. Gustavo Gutiérrez, *The God of Life* (Maryknoll, N.Y.: Orbis, 1991).
49. Ibid., xvii.

tion attributed to God. In the Bible, God is a mysterious yet concrete love. Love is always turned to communion, to relations. The only way to know anything about the biblical God is through the Son, God made man. This accords with the foundational insight Gutiérrez never tires of emphasizing: Human beings believe in God in the context of a particular historical situation. It is here that God can be confronted. "From the experience of death of the poor, a God who liberates and gives life is nevertheless affirmed." He is a God who manifests himself in weakness yet overcomes death.[50] "God is God who saves us not through his domination but through his suffering. . . . And it is thus that the cross acquires its tremendous revelatory potential with respect to God's weakness as an expression of his love for a world come of age."[51]

There is a dual theme of God's absence and presence in the Bible. The God of the Bible is the God who comes to the people: "I have come down to rescue them from the hand of the Egyptians" (Exod. 3:8). Yet God also departed his dwelling place. Prophets saw the temple empty of God's presence, and Jesus had to empty the temple because of the oppression of the poor. Gutiérrez notes that the reason God had to depart over and over again was the lack of true worship; worship is not only about rituals and rites but also about how we treat the poor, the blind, the outcasts. The *shekinah*, the presence of God, while found in the entire cosmos, is also found within history. It is God's choice, Gutiérrez claims, to be present and active in the historical movement of human society and its happenings.[52]

Human Society as the Image of the Trinity: Leonardo Boff

Leonardo Boff, a Franciscan priest from Brazil, was silenced by the Vatican because church officials believed he was championing the cause of liberation theology in a way that threatened the hierarchy and because of his views of Mary as an expression of the "humanity" (if not the incarnation) of the Holy Spirit. What is interesting about Boff's highly acclaimed *Trinity and Society,* however, is that it is not a controversial book. It is a tightly argued, warmly written treatise on the doctrine of God, especially the Trinity, based on the best of biblical, historical, and contemporary traditions. Boff sets forth a powerful proposal for a view of the trinitarian God as a communion of equal persons. This social doctrine of the Trinity serves as a critique of oppressive, inequitable political and social models and as an archetype for a new human society—including the church, which tends to be hierarchical—in the "image and likeness of the

---

50. Ibid., xiii–xiv.
51. Gustavo Gutiérrez, *Essential Writings,* ed. James B. Nickoloff (Minneapolis: Fortress, 1996), 39.
52. See Gutiérrez, *God of Life,* 69–91.

Trinity,"[53] based on an equal, loving fellowship among sisters and brothers.[54] For his social program of the Trinity, Boff gleaned from the works of several contemporary theologians, especially Karl Rahner, Jürgen Moltmann, and John Zizioulas. Rahner's view, according to which God-in-himself is identical to how he relates to humans in salvation history, is the guide for Boff's study of God; Moltmann's insistence on the social analogy with a view to equality is the motivation; and Zizioulas's communion theology serves as the contemporary tool to rehabilitate ancient patristic communion theology.

For Boff, the leading aim is to take the doctrine of God "from the solitude of one to the communion of three," as the opening title of *Trinity and Society* puts it. In the spirit of Moltmann, Boff offers a critical reconstruction of the kind of monotheism that sees God as unrelated to the world and its pain, perfect in his fullness of being. To speak of "love" in regard to that kind of God is unfounded. Rather, for Boff, God is "the Trinity as a mystery of inclusion."[55] Boff starts with a principle of "richness of unity" on the way to a social doctrine that "avoids solitude, overcomes separation and surpasses exclusion."[56] Thus, another chapter in his book is titled "In the Beginning Is Communion."[57] God exists in a loving, mutual relationship. This kind of communion in the Godhead "can be seen as a model for any just, egalitarian (while respecting differences) social organization. On the basis of their faith in the triune God, Christians postulate a society that can be the image and likeness of the Trinity."[58]

According to Boff, most societies in Latin America and throughout the third world have lived under the stigma of dependence, which has produced a deep dualism between rich and poor, privileged and underprivileged, powerholders and oppressed. Christian faith has had an ambiguous role in this. Often the Christian message has served the purposes of the oppressors. Boff mentions several "disintegrated understandings" of God that have served counterpurposes in society. Paternalistic or patriarchal depictions of God make people objects of help and create an atmosphere of dominance. Depictions of God as an oppressive, dominant, and tyrannical figure give rise to "pathological expressions" of power. These are, in Boff's terminology, "political dangers of an a-Trinitarian monotheism."[59]

Communion theology, as opposed to classical trinitarian approaches that operate with categories of "substance" or "person" and are unrelated to salvation

---

53. Leonardo Boff, *Trinity and Society* (Maryknoll, N.Y.: Orbis, 1988), 50.
54. Ibid., 119.
55. Heading in ibid., 2.
56. Heading in ibid., 3.
57. See Boff, *Trinity and Society*, 128–48. Pay careful attention to Boff's titles. Unlike in current English-speaking literature, in which titles are appreciated for their capacity to elicit excitement, Boff often summarizes his main thesis in the title. Thus, the titles are often boring but helpful in comprehending the argument.
58. Ibid., 11.
59. Heading in ibid., 11–16, 20–23.

history and human society, is a needed corrective. Human society is not irrelevant to the doctrine of God; in fact, there is a mutual, reciprocal relationship between God and society: "So human society is a pointer on the road to the mystery of the Trinity, while the mystery of the Trinity, as we know it from revelation, is a pointer toward social life and its archetype."[60] We should speak of the trinitarian God using the ancient language of *perichōrēsis,* mutual interpenetration:

> Speaking of God must always mean the Father, Son and Holy Spirit in the presence of one another, in total reciprocity, in immediacy of loving relationship, being one for another, by another, in another and with another. No divine Person exists alone for its own sake; they are always and eternally in relationship with one another: the father is Father because he has a Son; the Son is Son only because he has a Father; the Spirit is Spirit only because of the love in which the Father begets the Son and the Son gives back to the Father.[61]

In this perichoretic unity, "each [person of the Trinity] is itself, not the other, but so open to the other and in the other that they form one entity, i.e., they are God."[62] *Perichōrēsis,* in other words, represents the principle of both union and difference, unity-in-diversity or diversity-in-unity.[63] Conceived as loving communion, the Holy Trinity is "good news to men and women, especially to the poor."[64] It is the proper model for human and ecclesial society, even if no human person is able to live in total *perichōrēsis* with another person. This is also a corrective to misguided paternalism. Fatherhood in the Bible is not patriarchalism but the basis of universal fellowship. The Father is dependent on the Son and the Spirit for his fatherhood. And once the Father created the world, the world began the process of becoming the "body of the Trinity" in the sense that humanity and all creation will be "inserted into the very communion of Father, Son, and Holy Spirit."[65]

One aspect of liberation dear to Boff's heart is overcoming sexism. His trinitarian vision of God holds to a "trans-sexist theology of the maternal father and paternal mother." The dynamic, living, biblical doctrine of God, Boff claims, can be expressed by the symbols of either father or mother or by a combination of them. Boff notes that this is not contrary to the classical tradition; the Council of Toledo (675) spoke of the "Father's womb," in which the Son was conceived.[66]

---

60. Ibid., 119.

61. Ibid., 133. Clearly, Boff appropriates here the ancient rule of Athanasius and insights similar to Wolfhart Pannenberg (as discussed above), even though he does not give explicit references.

62. Boff, *Trinity and Society,* 32; the biblical references are to John 10:30 and 17:21.

63. Ibid., 148–54.

64. Ibid., 156.

65. Ibid., 108. Thus, it is important to note that for Boff talk about the world as God's body has a different meaning than for Sallie McFague, studied above.

66. Boff, *Trinity and Society,* 120–21. For the feminine character of each of the trinitarian persons, see 170–71 (Father), 182–83 (Son), and 196–98 (Spirit).

Latin American Women on God

Since we have looked at some leading themes of Latina God-talk in the North American context and at third world women's approaches in the discussion of African feminist voices, this section highlights only those perspectives that are more visible among women in Mexico and South America. Ivone Gebara of Brazil outlines some characteristics of the way Latin American women do theology:

- Theological reflection begins with the living realities and shared experiences of women in Latin America.
- Re-creating, but not simply repeating, tradition in a way that makes sense to the particular context of Latin American women is a leading principle.
- The theological work reflects an ability to view life as the locus of both oppression and liberation, grace and a lack of grace.
- The contributions of disciplines other than theology, such as anthropology, psychology, and other social sciences, are used in order to relate to the whole tapestry of life.
- Major loci for doing theology are the basic ecclesial communities, the grassroots ecclesial units.[67]

Rather than trusting male-dominated philosophical, ideological, and analytical concepts of God, Latina feminists go back to a biblical way of talking about God that relates to their specific situation. The frequent listening to stories and testimonies is evident, for example, in the anthology *Through Her Eyes* edited by Elsa Tamez, a leading Latina theologian from Mexico.[68] The God of Latina women is a living, dynamic, relational God:

> From our perspective the Presence of Creative-Recreative Spiritual Force, the source of Life and Love, is like an ongoing movement, an ebb and flow that moves in growing waves that wash over everything. It is like throwing a rock into a still pond; the ripples spread out wider and wider until they reach the shore where they seem to bounce back toward the spot from which they started; it affects the whole surface of the pond.[69]

On the predominantly Catholic continent, one aspect of re-creating tradition involves inquiring into the role of Mary, the mother of God, as the archetype for being a woman:

---

67. Ivone Gebara, "Women Doing Theology in Latin America," in *Feminist Theology from the Third World,* ed. Ursula King (Maryknoll, N.Y.: Orbis, 1994), 55–59.
68. Elsa Tamez, ed., *Through Her Eyes: Women's Theology from Latin America* (Maryknoll, N.Y.: Orbis, 1989).
69. Alida Verhoeven, "The Concept of God: A Feminine Perspective," in *Through Her Eyes,* 54–55.

Mary was Mother of God, virgin, immaculate, and was assumed into heaven. . . .
The mystery of Mary leads back to the greater mystery, the mystery of God, and
it opens a unique and original perspective for viewing this mystery: the feminist
perspective. The tradition of faith has concentrated on the feminine in Mary,
the Mother of Jesus. It has viewed all women's potentialities as realized in her.
. . . To recognize in Marian dogmas the traces of the feminine as revealed by
God, the theological face of the feminine element of God, God's face as seen
from a feminist perspective, is something that we will be constantly striving to
keep in mind here.[70]

Latina theologians have tried to re-create God-talk to make it more inclusive
and liberating.[71] The divine mystery that creates, saves, and sanctifies cannot
be identified primarily with one of the two sexes.[72]

Many Latinas also think the doctrine of the Trinity has a lot of potential for
their purposes.[73] The Trinity is about the mystery of the communion of the
three divine persons. To say that God is Father, Son, and Spirit does not have
to do with God being male. Thus, God the Father can also be called Mother, or
Maternal Father, or Paternal Mother. Some Hispanic women wonder whether
the term *rahamim* ("womb"), whose usage has biblical precedent, can be used
of the love of God. "This divine female womb, pregnant with gestation and
birth, identified with the Father, appears also in the incarnate Son." With regard to the Spirit, Maria Clara Bingemer offers this image: "The Spirit is sent
like a loving mother to console the children left orphaned by Jesus' departure
(John 14:18, 26) and to teach them patiently to pronounce the Father's name,
Abba (Rom. 8:15)."[74]

In the context of Latin America, the doctrine of God is approached from
the perspective of liberation. In the next chapter, which focuses on conceptions
of God in Asia, the theme of liberation reappears, but it takes a new focus in
this context of rich religious and cultural traditions.

70. Ivone Gebara and Maria Clara Bingemer, "Mary—Mother of God, Mother of the Poor,"
in *Feminist Theology from the Third World,* 280.

71. See Ana Maria Tepedino and Margarida L. Ribeiro Brandão, "Women and the Theology
of Liberation," in *Mysterium Liberationis,* 222–31.

72. Maria Clara Bingemer, "Women in the Future of the Theology of Liberation," in *Feminist
Theology from the Third World,* 314–15.

73. See Maria Clara Bingemer, "Reflections on the Trinity," in *Through Her Eyes,* 81–95.

74. Bingemer, "Women in the Future of the Theology of Liberation," 315.

28

God in Asian Theologies

The Asian Context for God-Talk

Only in the last part of the twentieth century did a distinctively Asian Christian theology emerge. Despite the small number of Christians in most parts of Asia, its Christian tradition is rich.[1] Three Christian traditions are present in Asia. First, according to the oldest tradition, the apostle Thomas evangelized the Middle East and the western and southern coast of India. The second tradition concerns the vital Catholic missionary influence after the discovery of the sea route to India and the rest of Asia in the later Middle Ages. This proliferation of Christian churches spread all over Asia. The third and more recent tradition is largely attributed to the modern missionary movement of European (and later American) origin, which was mainly Protestant.[2]

Today, the continent on which more than half of the world's population lives is not easily divided into theological centers.[3] Perhaps the most fertile soil has been India and Sri Lanka. Because of the long tradition of English-speaking education in these countries, they have contributed significantly to the

---

1. The number of Christians in Asia ranges from less than 1 percent to a few percent at most, with the exception of the predominantly Roman Catholic Philippines (about 85 percent Christian), South Korea (less than one-third Christian), and China (estimations vary widely).

2. George Gispert-Sauch, S.J., "Asian Theology," in *The Modern Theologians: An Introduction to Christian Theology in the Twentieth Century,* 2d ed., ed. David F. Ford (Cambridge, U.K.: Blackwell, 1997), 455.

3. I am making use of and adapting the classification in ibid., 456.

emerging international theologizing. Theologians such as Raimundo Panikkar, Swami Abhishiktananda, M. M. Thomas, Stanley J. Samartha, and Aloysius Pieris are well-known figures within and outside Asia. A rising center of theological thinking is Korea, with its phenomenal church growth. Korean theology ranges from conservative evangelical theology that cuts across denominational boundaries to a more liberal strand of Asian pluralism and Minjung theology. Some Japanese theologians such as Kosuke Koyama have made headway into the international theological academy, as has the Taiwanese Choan-Seng Song.

Asian Christian theology is still emerging and distinguishing itself after a long hegemony of Western influence.[4] Understandably, Asian theologians show no lack of criticism of Western theology and its view of God. Tissa Balasuriya of Sri Lanka laments that Western theology is ethnocentric, ecclesiocentric, clerical, patriarchal, pro-capitalistic, devoid of socioeconomic analysis, and nonpractical.[5] Asian liberation theologians, under the leadership of Aloysius Pieris, another Sri Lankan, have complained about the lack of relevance of Western approaches to the social and political context of Asia.[6] Choan-Seng Song faults Western theology for rationalism and a lack of imagination.[7] His dream is to develop a *Theology from the Womb of Asia.*[8] Jung Young Lee criticizes the Western approach for being captive to Aristotelian logic, which is in opposition to the inclusive yin-yang thinking of Asia.[9] Masao Takenaka of Japan concurs and issues a call for a distinctively Asian approach to God-talk that utilizes means such as art and drama rather than the argumentative method of the West. In his delightful yet incisive *God Is Rice,* he calls the Western approach to theology a *ya-ya* method. "Whenever two or three Western theologians are gathered together, there is argumentation about God," he chidingly remarks.[10] As an alternative he recommends the "Ah-hah!" method, which he sees as the approach of the Bible. People did not come to know God by discussion or argument but by experiencing him. Thus, he says, we "must awaken in ourselves the appreciation of the living reality who is God. In the Bible we have many surprising acknowledgments. . . . 'Ah-hah! In this way, God is working in our world, in a way I did not know.'"[11]

---

4. A helpful discussion is offered in Merrill Morse, *Kosuke Koyama: A Model for Intercultural Theology* (Frankfurt am Main: Peter Lang, 1991), chap. 5.

5. Tissa Balasuriya, "Toward the Liberation of Theology in Asia," in *Asia's Struggle for Full Humanity: Toward a Relevant Theology,* ed. Virginia Fabella (Maryknoll, N.Y.: Orbis, 1980), 26. See also Tissa Balasuriya, *Planetary Theology* (Maryknoll, N.Y.: Orbis, 1984), 2–10.

6. Aloysius Pieris, *An Asian Theology of Liberation* (Maryknoll, N.Y.: Orbis, 1988), 81–83.

7. Choan-Seng Song, *Third-Eye Theology,* rev. ed. (Maryknoll, N.Y.: Orbis, 1990), 19–23.

8. Choan-Seng Song, *Theology from the Womb of Asia* (Maryknoll, N.Y.: Orbis, 1986).

9. Jung Young Lee, *Marginality: The Key to Multicultural Theology* (Minneapolis: Fortress, 1995), 64–70; and idem, *Trinity in Asian Perspective* (Nashville: Abingdon, 1996), chaps. 2–3.

10. Masao Takenaka, *God Is Rice: Asian Cultures and Christian Faith* (Geneva: World Council of Churches, 1986), 8.

11. Ibid., 9.

According to Peter C. Phan, Scripture and tradition serve as the foundation for a distinctively Asian theology and doctrine of God,[12] but the Bible and tradition are far from the only resources. Phan mentions several others. The first resource is made up of the billions of Asian people themselves with their daily "stories of joy and suffering, hope and despair, love and hatred, freedom and oppression."[13] This collective memory includes women's stories. The second resource is the sacred texts and ethical and spiritual practices of Asian religion and philosophy. In Asia, religion and philosophy are inextricably joined, not unlike in medieval Christendom. Phan's own "Christ of Asia: An Essay on Jesus and the Eldest Son and Ancestor" is an example of utilizing Asian sacred texts to interpret theology.[14] The third resource is Asian monastic traditions with their rituals, ascetic practices, and social commitment. The fourth consists of Asian cultures in general, which include myths, folklore, symbols, poetry, stories, songs, visual art, and dance.[15]

To capture the essence of Asian distinctiveness, whether in regard to Christian or non-Christian spirituality, the words of Aloysius Pieris are often quoted: "The Asian context can be described as a blend of a profound religiosity (which is perhaps Asia's greatest wealth) and an overwhelming poverty."[16] Asian religiosity, far from being marginalized or waning, is alive and well. With all the rapid developments in technology and education, Hinduism, Buddhism, Confucianism, and a host of other religions, most of them manifested in forms that used to be called "animistic" (having to do with spirits) and permeating all of life, continue shaping the worldview and everyday life of Asian men and women. Religion is visible and a part of everyday life. Therefore, talk about God/gods can be carried on everywhere, from the street markets to luxurious hotels to desperate slums to exotic restaurants. Everywhere in Asia, Christian theology dialogues with and is shaped by encounters with other living religions.[17] The challenge of pluralism is nowhere stronger than here.

The following surveys the doctrine of God in various Asian contexts as represented by some leading Asian theologians: Stanley J. Samartha of India has championed a theocentic pluralism; Raimundo Panikkar, also of India,

12. Peter C. Phan, "Introduction: An Asian American Theology: Believing and Thinking at the Boundaries," in *Journeys at the Margin: Toward an Autobiographical Theology in American-Asian Perspective,* ed. Peter C. Phan and Jung Young Lee (Collegeville, Minn.: Liturgical Press, 1999), xv, italics in text. See R. S. Sugirtharajah, ed., *Voices from the Margin: Interpreting the Bible in the Third World* (Maryknoll, N.Y.: Orbis, 1991).

13. Phan, "Introduction," xvi.

14. Peter C. Phan, "The Christ of Asia: An Essay on Jesus and the Eldest Son and Ancestor," *Missionalia* 45 (1996): 25–55.

15. Phan, "Introduction," xii–xviii, quotation on xvi. I have modified Phan's categorization.

16. Aloysius Pieris, "Western Christianity and Asian Buddhism," *Dialogue* 7 (May–August 1980): 61–62.

17. For the significance of the encounter with other religions to emerging Christian theology in Asia, see Morse, *Kosuke Koyama,* 100–102.

has produced a unique understanding of the trinitarian God as a theandric mystery; Choan-Seng Song of Taiwan has provided a narrative theology of God utilizing various Chinese and other Asian philosophical and religious sources; and Kosuke Koyama of Japan offers a contextualization of the doctrine of God in the Buddhist context of Thailand. This chapter also addresses the poverty of the Asian context in a survey of Asian liberation theologians and provides a sample of Asian female contributors to the doctrine of God.

Theocentric Pluralism: Stanley J. Samartha

The challenge of religious pluralism pervades all of Asia, particularly India. A number of theologians from India have responded to this challenge from a Christian perspective. One of the most prolific is Stanley J. Samartha, who issues a powerful call to reconsider Christian doctrine, especially of God and Christ, in relation to other world religions.[18]

Samartha agrees with Christian tradition that knowledge of God is mediated through Christ. But, especially in his later main work, *One Christ—Many Religions: Toward a Revised Christology*,[19] Samartha argues that Christocentrism is applicable only to Christians. It can never be considered the only way to the mystery of the divine. Instead of the traditional "normative exclusiveness" of Christ, he suggests the "relational distinctiveness" of Christ. Here *relational* means that the Christian doctrine of God, especially Christology, is not unrelated to neighbors of other faiths. The word *distinctiveness* points to the fact that the great religious traditions are different responses to the mystery of God.

According to Samartha, the key to an authentic doctrine of God is honoring the distinctive worldview and patterns of thinking of Asian people. This involves the concept of mystery. The acceptance of a sense of mystery and the rejection of an exclusive attitude provide the tools for constructing an Asian theology of God. The notion of mystery provides the ontological basis for tolerance, which would otherwise run the risk of becoming uncritical friendliness. The emphasis on mystery is not meant to be an escape from the need for rational inquiry. Rather, it reveals that rational inquiry is not the only way to do theology. Samartha believes that mystery lies beyond the dichotomy of theistic versus nontheistic religions.[20]

This view can be called a theocentric pluralism, and it is based on a distinctive understanding of God and how God is related to Christ. Samartha's reluctance to regard Jesus Christ as an exclusive revelation of God is not based

---

18. See Stanley J. Samartha, "The Cross and the Rainbow: Christ in a Multireligious Culture," in *Asian Faces of Jesus*, ed. R. S. Sugirtharajah (Maryknoll, N.Y.: Orbis, 1995), 104.

19. Stanley J. Samartha, *One Christ—Many Religions: Toward a Revised Christology* (Maryknoll, N.Y.: Orbis, 1991).

20. Samartha, "Cross and the Rainbow," 111.

on a desire to lessen Christ's significance but—ironically—on his understanding of God: "The Other [God as the Mysterious Other] relativizes everything else. In fact, the willingness to accept such relativization is probably the only real guarantee that one has encountered the Other as ultimately real."[21] In other words, those who recognize God alone as absolute will recognize all religions as relative. This kind of theocentric pluralism, therefore, is different from the naïve understanding of classical liberalism: God as the Father of all and Jesus (of history) as an enlightened teacher about his Father. It is also vastly different from John Hick's version of pluralism in which the doctrine of God has lost its transcendence and has little if anything to share with Christian tradition.

The Trinitarian God and the Cosmotheandric Mystery: Raimundo Panikkar

Raimundo Panikkar said he "left" Europe as a Christian, "found" himself as a Hindu, and "returned" as a Buddhist, without ever having ceased to be a Christian.[22] This Catholic thinker was born in Spain to a Spanish Roman Catholic mother and a Hindu father. After living in Europe and Asia—and completing three doctorates and mastering a number of languages—he did his most significant work in California. Because Panikkar is one of the most creative and difficult to understand theologians of our time, the most we can do here is highlight some crucial aspects of his doctrine of God.[23]

The Cosmotheandric Structure of Reality and Trinity

Even though Panikkar's theological vision is multidimensional and embraces topics ranging from God to Christ to the church to sacraments to salvation, the various strands come together in his notion of "cosmotheandrism." The term *theandrism* comes from two Greek terms meaning "God" and "human person," and it has roots especially in Eastern theology (Dionysius the Areopagite and Maximus the Confessor). The neologism "cosmotheandrism" has a technical sense in Panikkar's thought, though he does not always use the term in the same way. Panikkar says that "the cosmotheandric principle could be stated by saying that the divine, the human and the earthly—however we may prefer

21. Stanley J. Samartha, *Courage for Dialogue: Ecumenical Issues in Inter-Religious Relationships* (Maryknoll, N.Y.: Orbis, 1982), 151.

22. Raimundo Panikkar, *The Intrareligious Dialogue* (New York: Paulist, 1978), 2.

23. A fine, up-to-date discussion of Panikkar's thought by a number of leading scholars from various persuasions is Joseph Prabhu, ed., *The Intercultural Challenge of Raimon Panikkar* (Maryknoll, N.Y.: Orbis, 1996). Francis X. D'Sa, S.J., "The Notion of God," 25–45, offers a fine introduction to Panikkar's doctrine of God; Ewert H. Cousins, "Panikkar's Advaitic Trini-tarianism," 119–30, highlights his trinitarian vision.

to call them—are the three irreducible dimensions which constitute the real, i.e., any reality inasmuch as it is real."[24] Or, "There is no God without Man and the World. There is no Man without God and the World. There is no World without God and Man."[25] In other words, the cosmotheandric principle expresses Panikkar's fundamental structure of reality, an intimate interaction of God, humankind, and the world or cosmos. There is no hierarchy, no dualism; one of the three does not dominate or take precedence.

From this vision Panikkar constructs his view of God in his small yet important book *The Trinity and the Religious Experience of Man.*[26] He regards the term *trinitarian* as synonymous with cosmotheandric.[27] There is also a correspondence of cosmos with the Spirit, the immanent; theos with the Father, the transcendent; and anthropos with Man, the Son.

But why does Panikkar resort to trinitarian language in his wide and inclusive religious vision? The reason is that the notion of trinitarian—like cosmotheandric—genuinely reflects the structure of reality. The doctrine of the Trinity is not a forced concept.

Such an exercise in recognizing the trinitarian structure of the world goes back to ancient Christian theologians, especially Augustine. But before explicating the application to Father, Son, and Spirit, we must pay attention to Panikkar's use of the Hindu notion of *advaita,* which means "non-duality" (literally, "not two"), a cherished Asian way of thinking. According to Panikkar, there "are not two realities: God and man (or the world), as outright atheists and outright theists are dialectically driven to maintain. Reality is theandric; it is our way of looking that causes reality to appear to us sometimes under one aspect and sometimes under another because our vision shares in both."[28] The pair yin-yang points in the same direction. Thus, Ewert H. Cousins calls Panikkar's trinitarian view "advaitic trinitarianism."[29] When applied to the ancient problem of unity and diversity in the trinitarian God, the advaitic principle implies that Father and Son are not two but also not one. The Spirit unites and distinguishes them.[30]

The advaitic, theandric vision also accentuates relationality as opposed to the "substance" approach of classical theism. Panikkar notes that if "being" can be

24. Quoted in D'Sa, "Notion of God," 34–35.

25. Quoted in Kajsa Ahlstrand, *Fundamental Openness: An Enquiry into Raimundo Panikkar's Theological Vision and Its Presuppositions,* Studia Missionalia Upsaliensia 57 (Uppsala: Uppsala University, 1993), 134. The term *man* here includes male and female.

26. Raimundo Panikkar, *The Trinity and the Religious Experience of Man: Icon-Person-Mystery* (Maryknoll, N.Y.: Orbis Books, 1973). The book is also known as *The Trinity and the World Religions.*

27. Ibid., 71.

28. Ibid., 75.

29. Cousins, "Panikkar's Advaitic Trinitarianism," 119–30; for the term *advaitic,* see 120.

30. Panikkar, *Trinity and the Religious Experience of Man,* 62.

ascribed to each of the trinitarian members, this leads to tritheism; if "being" is ascribed only to God as a single being, then modalism is inevitable.[31]

The Silence of God: An Answer of the Buddha

Panikkar's cosmotheandric trinitarian vision goes beyond his attention to classical Christianity. This becomes clear when he exposits the role of members of the Trinity. The Father is "Nothing." What can be said about the Father is "nothing." This is the apophatic way, the way to approach the absolute without name.[32] There is no "Father" in himself; the "being of the Father" is "the Son." In the incarnation, *kenōsis,* the Father gave himself totally to the Son. Thus, the Son is God.[33]

Panikkar believes this understanding is the needed bridge between Christianity and Buddhism as well as between Christianity and advaitic Hinduism. What *kenōsis* ("self-emptying") is for Christianity, *nirvana* and *sunyata* are for these two other religions. This is the theme of his book *The Silence of God: An Answer of the Buddha.* "God is total Silence. This is affirmed by all the world religions. One is led towards the Absolute and in the end one finds nothing, because there *is* nothing, not even Being."[34]

"It is the Son of God who is, and so is God," Panikkar affirms.[35] In that sense, the Son is the only "person" of the Trinity. For this statement to make sense, Panikkar notes that the term *person,* when used of the internal life of the Trinity, is an equivocal term that has different meanings in each case. Since the Father is a different kind of "person" compared to the Son, and the Spirit differs in nature from both, it is not advisable to use the term *person* for these different meanings.[36] In that qualified sense, it is also understandable when Panikkar says that there is in fact "no God" in Christian theology in the generic sense of the term. There is only "the God of Jesus Christ." Therefore, the God of theism is always the "Son," the only one with whom human beings can establish a relationship.[37]

What about the Spirit? The Spirit is "immanence." Making this meaning of the Spirit more concrete is challenging: "Immanence is incapable of revealing itself, for that would be a contradiction of terms; an immanence which needs to manifest itself, is no longer immanent." Panikkar uses images to say something more about the Spirit: The Father is the source of the river, the Son

31. Raimundo Panikkar, *The Silence of God: An Answer of the Buddha* (Maryknoll, N.Y.: Orbis, 1989), 141.

32. Panikkar, *Trinity and the Religious Experience of Man,* 46.

33. Ibid., 45–47.

34. Ibid., 52.

35. Ibid., 51.

36. See ibid., 51–52.

37. Ibid., 52.

is the river that flows from the source, and the Spirit is the ocean in which the river ends.[38]

In his desire to build bridges, Panikkar searches for analogies in Hinduism and Buddhism. The Spirit can be described as Hinduism's "Divine *Sakti* penetrating everything and manifesting God, disclosing him in his immanence and being present in all his manifestation."[39] Panikkar is convinced that Hinduism and Christianity are not antagonistic in the final vision: "It is Christianity and Hinduism as well that belong to Christ, though in two different levels."[40]

Theology from the Womb of Asia: Choan-Seng Song

Third-Eye Theology

Storytelling is characteristic of the theology of Choan-Seng Song, who moved from Taiwan to teach in the United States and was at one time the president of the World Alliance of Reformed Churches. In the narrative method of theology (theology based primarily on stories), he sees parallels to God's own story.[41] Theology, therefore, is "a humble effort on our part to grapple with God's storytelling."[42] In one of his earlier works, *Tell Us Our Names: Story Theology from an Asian Perspective*,[43] Song issues a call for an authentic story theology. He challenges traditional theological categories such as essence and substance, especially for God's work and mission in the world, based on folktales, myths, and parables. Song's latest major work, *The Believing Heart: An Invitation to Story Theology*, inquires into the nature of God-talk as part of story theology. He notes that theology is commonly understood as discourse on God, study of the nature of God, exploration into the mystery of God. All things are related to God. But Song asks, is this an appropriate way of looking at theology and God-talk? For him, a more suitable way involves approaching theology from the vantage point of wrestling with God. Theology is not so much our God-talk as God's talk to us. We must distinguish between talking about God and God talking to us. These can never be equated.[44]

---

38. Ibid., 63.

39. Raimundo Panikkar, *The Unknown Christ of Hinduism: Toward an Ecumenical Christophany* (Maryknoll, N.Y.: Orbis, 1981), 57.

40. Ibid., 58–61.

41. Choan-Seng Song, "Five Stages toward Christian Theology in the Multicultural World," in *Toward an Autobiographical Theology*, 2.

42. Ibid., 3.

43. Choan-Seng Song, *Tell Us Our Names: Story Theology from an Asian Perspective* (Maryknoll, N.Y.: Orbis, 1984).

44. Choan-Seng Song, *The Believing Heart: An Invitation to Story Theology* (Minneapolis: Fortress, 1999), 23–30.

A landmark in Song's contribution to an authentic Asian theology is his *Third-Eye Theology: Theology in Formation in Asian Settings.* In Song's view, theology should begin with the heart, which transcends reason and is a window to the mystery of Being (God). The heart serves as a "third eye," an image that he borrows from the Japanese Zen master Daisetz Suzuki:

> Zen . . . wants us to open a "third eye," as Buddhists call it, to the hitherto unheard-of region shut away from us through our own ignorance. When the cloud of ignorance disappears, the infinity of heavens is manifested where we see for the first time into the nature of our own being.[45]

Heart theology faces the challenge of a double darkness: the darkness surrounding the heart of Being (God) and the darkness separating Christian spirituality from Asian spiritualities. When this double darkness is lifted, a true "heart-to-heart" communication can happen and people can see "the love and compassion of God for the world in a fuller and richer light."[46] This kind of theology is far removed from rational, "scientific" theology as an academic discipline that often treats God as a "rational" Being to be investigated.[47] Third-eye theology, heart theology, is better suited to the "Asian intuitive approach to reality."[48] The intuitive approach also makes room for the "irregularities" in God's work; Song does not believe in a "straight-line God" or "straight-line theology."[49]

A contextual Asian theology could also be called a *Theology from the Womb of Asia,* another title of his. A theology from the womb is a liberation theology that involves new life struggling to come into existence:

> As a mother commits herself totally to bringing into fruition the seed of life within her, so Christians must be committed to the emergence of a new world in which light prevails over darkness, love overcomes hate, and freedom vanquishes oppression.[50]

God's Love-Pain

According to Song, the beginning of theology is not human rationality but God's heartache: "God's heart aches. God's heart aches because of an immediate danger to creation," as the creation story implies.[51] Creation is

---

45. Choan-Seng Song, *Third-Eye Theology: Theology in Formation in Asian Settings,* rev. ed. (Maryknoll, N.Y.: Orbis, 1979), 26–27, quoting from Daisetz Suzuki, *Essays in Zen Buddhism,* First Series (London: Luzac, 1927), 1.

46. Song, *Third-Eye Theology,* 38.

47. Ibid., 59–60 criticizes classical theology as represented by Thomas F. Torrance for its desire to be a "scientific," "objective" discipline.

48. See Song, *Third-Eye Theology,* 62–64.

49. Choan-Seng Song, *The Compassionate God* (Maryknoll, N.Y.: Orbis, 1982), 25–27.

50. Song, *Third-Eye Theology,* 137.

51. Ibid., 51.

God's response to the cosmic groaning produced by the forces of disorder and confusion. Redemption points to the new creation at the eschaton, when God will wipe away every tear and end all death and pain (Rev. 21:4). This integral connection between creation and redemption is also a "prototype of doing theology":

> Theology begins with God's heartache on account of the world. God does not theologize in a vacuum or in the midst of God's glorious splendor and light but in confrontation with the power of *tehom* ["abyss"], the darkness that poses a real threat to the birth, growth, and fruition of life. Creation redemptively carried out is God's theology in action.[52]

Song gleaned from the late Japanese theologian Kazoh Kitamori, whose *Theology of the Pain of God* was released in 1946, just following World War II. In that formative work, Kitamori describes God as suffering pain. Even though Kitamori wrote in the aftermath of the destruction of his homeland, he emphasizes that the idea comes primarily from the Bible; it is also rooted in Buddhist tradition, which focuses on suffering. For Kitamori, the main impetus for divine suffering does not come from involvement in history but from internal conflict within God's own nature. God is a God of love, but he is also a God of wrath. Pain comes out of this dilemma. Theology of pain describes "the heart of God most deeply," following Jeremiah and Paul.[53]

According to Song, Kitamori's emphasis on pain brings depth to an understanding of God and God's relationship to the world. "It challenges a cheap interpretation of the Gospel as all joy, happiness, and success in the world to come. And it does strike sympathetic cords in Asian spirituality, particularly the one fostered by the Buddhist tradition."[54] While Song greatly appreciates Kitamori's work, he is also critical of the fact that by placing the pain of God in conflict with God's own self, Kitamori is within the theological tradition of the West. That tradition is illustrated both by Martin Luther and the contemporary Reformed theology of Jürgen Moltmann.[55] Song is also not happy that Kitamori makes pain "the essence of God."[56] The implication is that in the final analysis pain reigns over God. Kitamori's God "is not only the God who has pain but the God who is pain." Song also notes that if the pain of God is only about conflict within God between God's love and wrath, then it has little to do with humanity. "An internal struggle of God between love and wrath may be part of God's salvation for humanity. But more importantly,

---

52. Ibid., 56–57.
53. See Kazoh Kitamori, *The Theology of the Pain of God* (Richmond, Va.: John Knox Press, 1965), 19–21.
54. Song, *Third-Eye Theology*, 75–76.
55. Ibid., 77.
56. Kitamori, *Theology of the Pain of God*, 47.

salvation is the external event in which God's pain-love succeeds in locating homeless people and winning them back to God."[57]

Song's preferred way of talking about God's pain is in relation to God's love. He refers to the "pain-love" of God, noting that when speaking Chinese, one says the two words *love* and *pain* in the same breath *(thun-ai)*. The pain-love of God is expressed in the Old Testament with the term *hesed* and in the New Testament with the word *agapē*, Jesus Christ being the prime example of the latter.[58] Song sympathizes with process theology, which eschews the immutable, unmovable God and talks about God as someone acted upon and who feels the world. This is the God presented in the Bible, especially in the Old Testament, Song argues.[59]

Song highlights the importance of "the humble theology of the suffering servant" as the model for theology of God. Jesus is the "light to the nations" and the bringer of salvation to all (Isa. 49:6). Song comments on Isaiah 52–53, which describes the innocent suffering of the servant of Yahweh:

> In this tragic end of the Servant, God's love and compassion comes to its full expression. The God of the Servant is the God of all those who suffer, the God of those regarded as the refuse of humankind. . . . It shows us that God does not behave according to our theological principles.[60]

Three Mile an Hour God: Kosuke Koyama

Waterbuffalo Theology

Kosuke Koyama of Japan, while serving as a missionary to Thailand before becoming the dean of the Southeast Graduate School of Theology, began to develop his distinctively Asian "countryside theology."[61] What finally drove Koyama to the task of developing an authentically Asian theology, first presented in his widely read *Waterbuffalo Theology*, was his pastoral experience with the Thai mountain farmers: "On my way to the country church, I never fail to see a herd of waterbuffaloes grazing in the muddy paddy field. The waterbuffaloes tell me that I must preach to these farmers [with] objects that are immediately tangible . . . 'sticky rice' . . . 'rainy season,' 'leaking house.'"[62] Thai farmers are not concerned about metaphysical problems related to God, but they are

---

57. Song, *Third-Eye Theology,* 84–85.
58. Ibid., 84.
59. Ibid., 85–86.
60. Song, *Compassionate God,* 49.
61. For a recent appraisal of Koyama's theology by a number of international scholars, see Dale T. Irvin and Akintunde E. Akinade, eds., *The Agitated Mind of God: The Theology of Kosuke Koyama* (Maryknoll, N.Y.: Orbis, 1996).
62. Kosuke Koyama, *Waterbuffalo Theology* (Maryknoll, N.Y.: Orbis, 1974), vii.

interested in hearing that the "monsoon rain cannot make God wet! God is the Lord of monsoon rain. He sends his monsoon for his purpose."[63]

Taking seriously the context for doing theology is more complicated than it might appear. Thailand is a good example. According to Koyama, there are two Thailands. "Thailand One" is a traditional Thailand shaped by Buddhism and other ancient values originally from India and Ceylon. This Thailand is characterized by *apatheia* ("no passion") anthropology and *apatheia* history based on the "withdrawal" mentality of Buddhism. "Thailand Two" is linked to Western colonialism, modernization, and Christianity. It is characterized by *patheia,* a passion that can be traced back to the special love and concern of a personal God in the Bible. These two Thailands confront each other and live side by side.[64] Koyama sees that behind this confrontation lies "a theological friction" caused when contemporary Thailand and ancient Israel meet.[65]

> God's pathos is at work in Thailand as it was in Israel, and both traditionalism and modernization are making their contributions to his working. The tension points are creative in that they prepare Thai spirituality for a realization of the new creation in Jesus Christ.[66]

For Koyama, theology is always a second-order reflection.[67] "There is a difference between God and theology. This is as obvious as the difference between wife and wife-ology. . . . God can neither be equated with theology nor contained in theology. . . . There is the sovereign God but there cannot be the sovereign theology." In the final analysis, theologies are "very humble human attempts to say something about God because God has first spoken to us."[68] Put another way, "theology is man's understanding of God on the basis of God's understanding of man. It is as a child understands his mother only by way of his mother's far more intense and profound understanding of the child."[69]

Like Song, Koyama mainly writes in a narrative theological style. Many of his writings are devotional in nature and dialogue extensively with the biblical materials. In the most delightful yet theologically perceptive book *Three Mile an Hour God,* Koyama speaks of the God who is in no hurry, a God suited to the Thai context with its mentality of *maiphenrai* (meaning something like "It does not matter" or "It is okay"). In the desert, God took forty years to teach

---

63. Ibid., 41.
64. See especially Kosuke Koyama, "Thailand: Points of Theological Friction," in *Asian Voices in Christian Theology,* ed. Gerald H. Anderson (Maryknoll, N.Y.: Orbis, 1976), 65–86.
65. Ibid., 75.
66. As paraphrased in David J. Hesselgrave and Edward Rommen, *Contextualization: Meanings, Methods, and Models* (Grand Rapids: Baker, 1989), 81.
67. For a helpful discussion, see Morse, *Kosuke Koyama,* 119–26.
68. Kosuke Koyama, *Fifty Meditations* (Maryknoll, N.Y.: Orbis, 1979), 176.
69. Ibid., 55.

a lesson to the Israelites (Deut. 8:1–4). Comments Koyama, "Mind you, forty years for one lesson! How slow and how patient! No university can run on this basis."[70] This is a lesson that cannot be learned in the classroom but in the wilderness, in an open space. In this space both danger and promise are present. The Bible does not speak simply about danger; that would reduce faith to a "protection-from-danger-religion." Neither does the Bible speak only about promise; that would make faith a "happy-ending-religion." The Bible speaks about a crisis situation, the coexistence of danger and promise. This leads us to trust in God, Koyama says.[71] Consequently, Koyama criticizes the heritage of the Western missionary enterprise, which presented to Asians a God with a "predictable finger," thus making God subservient to human interests.

> I count it to be a great misfortune that this God with the predictable finger was preached far more forcefully and universally in Asia than the God with the unpredictable finger. The God of the predictable finger (the answer-God) in truth looked too cheap to be true to the eyes of the Asians whose hearts are much more receptive to the message of the unpredictable finger of God (the invitation-God).[72]

Koyama often reminds us of the danger of domesticating God. People expect the God of the predictable finger to change the world with the flick of a finger, as it were. But that kind of God is like an idol made for human purposes.[73] Biblical faith rejects such a view of God. Koyama notes that the Apostles' Creed says, "I believe in God. It does not say: 'I believe in what God brings to me if I believe in God.'"[74]

The Story-God in History

For Koyama, history is story. Consequently, the God of the Bible is a "story-God, not a theory-God."[75] This God surveys the story of humankind in all its complexity and addresses it personally by becoming involved in it. The biblical God personally experiences history.[76]

The biblical image of the covenant is a powerful reminder of the real involvement of God in history. This contrasts with the passivity of Buddhism and its depreciation of history. For Koyama, one way to talk about God's involvement

---

70. Kosuke Koyama, *Three Mile an Hour God: Biblical Reflections* (Maryknoll, N.Y.: Orbis, 1979), 3.

71. Ibid., 3–4.

72. Kosuke Koyama, *No Handle on the Cross: An Asian Meditation on the Crucified Mind* (Maryknoll, N.Y.: Orbis, 1977), 77.

73. Ibid., 69–71.

74. Koyama, *Fifty Meditations,* 170.

75. Koyama, *No Handle on the Cross,* 99.

76. Koyama, *Waterbuffalo Theology,* 52.

with history is to talk about God's wrath: "The wrath of God is provoked by the historical violation of God's 'holiness and love.' . . . History is the locus of God's perturbation of soul." This view of God differs drastically from classical theism's emphasis on God as "the highest good, the tranquil non-pathos." "God can be moved to wrath because he is God in history."[77]

The loving and suffering involvement of God with the world came to focus in the incarnation and the cross. Koyama emphasizes that the crucifixion took place in history. "And precisely there man sees God's covenantal triumph!"[78] Koyama admits that this is a strange picture of God, a picture rejected by many. "It is an unfamiliar concept that there is a God who is the Creator of all and the Visitor to prisons, who 'neither slumbers nor sleeps,' who is moved to burning wrath against man, who yet promises hope ('but of you I will make a great nation')."[79]

According to Koyama, the Judeo-Christian tradition contributes the unique and enduring spiritual insight "that the personal God, the one who creates, preserves, and consummates all things, does not 'handle' history."[80] This crucial insight comes to focus in Koyama's idea of the "crucified mind" and the crucified God.

The Crucified Mind and the Crucified God

Koyama, like Song, appreciates the contribution of Kitamori's *Theology of the Pain of God*.[81] Yet Koyama does not locate God's pain in the inner life of God but rather in his feelings for the world. In this, he is indebted to Martin Luther's theology of the cross. The heart of Koyama's theology is his vision of the crucified mind,[82] the prism through which he looks at the work and the presence of God in the world. The crucified mind takes as its source and model Christ's crucifixion. Koyama also refers to the apostle Paul, who wrote much of his correspondence from prison in the midst of suffering.[83]

The meaning of the crucifixion rests in the limitless love of God demonstrated through the utter abandonment of Jesus on the cross. Koyama highlights the importance of the theme of Jesus' rejection at the crucifixion. Jesus was judged to be a sinner. But that is not the whole story. From Genesis through the history of Israel and culminating in Jesus Christ, God personally took on humanity's rejection of God and turned it into redemption.[84] Only

---

77. Ibid., 103–4.
78. Ibid., 152.
79. Koyama, *Theology in Contact* (Madras: Christian Literature Society, 1975), 50.
80. Koyama, *No Handle on the Cross*, 13.
81. See Koyama, *Waterbuffalo Theology*, chap. 11.
82. Ibid., chap. 19; see also Morse, *Kosuke Koyama*, 145.
83. Koyama, *Waterbuffalo Theology*, 219.
84. Ibid., 175–78.

those who are loved can be rejected—and then taken back by God. "No one is ever so forsaken as Jesus Christ since no one is ever so close to God. The cry upon the cross came from the same man who said: 'I am not alone, for the Father is with me' (John 16:32)."[85]

God's love enters the human situation, taking risks and paying the price for this painful encounter. This is the pattern to be followed by those who have the crucified mind. It is also what distinguishes God from idols:

> God carries us. Any "god" we can carry is . . . an idol. That which we can carry is subject to our control. . . . But in trying to carry the living God of Mount Sinai, the God of Abraham, Isaac and Jacob, we insult him and we destroy ourselves.[86]

Liberation Theology in the Asian Context

Bishop Julio Xavier Labazan of the Philippines has described the unique nature of Asian suffering in four ways. One concerns the sheer magnitude of poverty, oppression, and injustice. Second, Asian suffering is centuries old, even ancient. Third, Asian suffering is unique in that it has inspired religiosity, leading to the question, How can we explain and escape suffering? Fourth, Asian suffering is "non-Christian" (most Asians who suffer are not Christian), and it poses the following question to Christianity: How can Christianity reveal God's presence in suffering to those who have never known the God of the Bible?[87]

Two names tower above the other distinctively Asian contributions to liberation theology: M. M. Thomas of India and Aloysius Pieris of Sri Lanka.

Salvation and Humanization: M. M. Thomas

M. M. Thomas, a lay theologian from the Mar Thoma Church in India, has made the struggle for the humanization of Asia the cornerstone of his theology.[88] Thomas's gateway to theology involved the emergence of his political and social consciousness;[89] at one time he even became a member of the communist party while

---

85. Koyama, *Three Mile an Hour God*, 26.

86. Ibid., 34–35.

87. T. K. Thomas, ed., *Testimony amid Asian Suffering* (Singapore: Christian Conference of Asia, 1977), 19–20. See also Virginia Fabella, ed., *Asia's Struggle for Full Humanity* (Maryknoll, N.Y.: Orbis, 1980), 152–60; and *Report of the Catholic Bishops' International Conference on Mission in Manila, 1979.*

88. See M. M. Thomas, "My Pilgrimage in Mission," *International Bulletin of Missionary Research* 13, no. 1 (1989): 28–31.

89. See M. M. Thomas, "The Absoluteness of Jesus Christ and Christ-Centered Syncretism," *Ecumenical Review* 37 (1985): 390–91.

seeking ordination as a pastor. The title of his main book, *Salvation and Humanization*,[90] sets forth the thesis that the validity of religion in general and Christianity in particular is based less on its doctrinal orthodoxy than on its contribution to the human quest for a better quality of life and social justice. In *Risking Christ for Christ's Sake*,[91] Thomas attempts to develop a "Christ-centered humanism" that is based on a syncretistic view of religions. Thomas's view is that all religions, not only Christianity, are supposed to contribute to the alleviation of social problems. He believes that even the atheistic secular ideologies of India have been "drawn to the crucified Jesus and what it means for tortured humanity." Consequently, Thomas criticizes Christian liberation movements for their inability to recognize the liberative force of other religions. Naming Christianity a specifically liberationist religion too easily leads to the implication that other religions are not, thus fostering unhealthy isolation of Christianity from other religions.[92]

At the same time, there is no doubt about Thomas's strong Christian commitment. His view of God is Christocentric and focuses on his idea of a "cosmic Christ." The Christian God in the form of Christ as the cosmic Lord of history is present wherever poverty, injustice, and oppression are opposed. Therefore, every attempt to better creation and the life of creatures is related to Christ, whether or not acknowledged by the agents of change.[93]

Thomas's cosmic Lord of history is not related to the mystery of the divine as much as to the historical plane, the struggle for equality, justice, and peace. "[T]he cosmic lord of history becomes the meeting point of religions as they struggle for justice. Christ is present not so much in ahistorical mystery as in the human quest for a better life. Therefore, for Thomas, the cosmic lord of history and the historical Jesus, who labored among the poor, are one and the same, sharing an identical purpose."[94]

God or Mammon: Aloysius Pieris

Aloysius Pieris, a Sri Lankan Jesuit and director of a research institute that promotes Christian-Buddhist dialogue, is the leading Asian liberation theologian. His *Asian Theology of Liberation* is comparable in significance to Gustavo Gutiérrez's works in the Latin American context. For Pieris, what is essential about religions in general and Christian faith in particular is liberation, yet he

90. M. M. Thomas, *Salvation and Humanization* (Madras: Christian Literature Society, 1971).

91. M. M. Thomas, *Risking Christ for Christ's Sake: Toward an Ecumenical Theology of Pluralism* (Geneva: World Council of Churches, 1987).

92. See, for example, M. M. Thomas, "Uppsala 1968 and the Contemporary Theological Situation," *Scottish Journal of Theology* 2 (1970): 49.

93. Cited in Volker Küster, *The Many Faces of Jesus Christ: Intercultural Christology* (Maryknoll, N.Y.: Orbis, 2001), 84.

94. Priscilla Pope-Levison and John R. Levison, *Jesus in Global Contexts* (Louisville: Westminster John Knox, 1992), 73.

never tires of emphasizing the uniqueness of the Asian context and its mul-
tifaceted religiosity.[95] Thus, Asian poverty can never be reduced to a purely
"economic" or "social" problem.[96]

Asian religiosity is distinctive, according to Pieris, in its integration of
cosmic and metacosmic soteriology. Here *cosmic*—often pejoratively called
animistic—relates to the cosmic forces (heat, fire, wind, and so on), which are
regarded with an attitude of awe and fear. In Asia, however, unlike in Africa
and Oceania, the cosmic religions have been domesticated and integrated
into the main "metacosmic soteriologies," namely, Buddhism, Hinduism, and
Taoism. These religions represent the "Transphenomenal Beyond," to be realized through *gnōsis*. Therefore, a certain spiritual elite is needed as "personal
embodiments of the *mysticomonastic* idealism held out as the climax of human
perfection. They serve as models and the symbols of 'liberated persons.' "[97] To
address this unique Asian context, Pieris argues, a distinctively Asian theology
of liberation is needed, which he calls "the Asian sense in theology."[98]

Pieris maintains that in the Asian context, God-talk must be made relative to
God-experience. But since the common thrust of religion in Asia is a concern for
liberation (variously named *vimukti, moksha, nirvana,* and so on), all religions
should be seen as catalysts for liberation.[99] The same relates to God-experience
and concern for humanity: One is not prior to the other. Pieris is convinced
that the Asian face of God can be found only in the "abyss where religion
and poverty seem to have the same common source: God, who has declared
mammon to be the enemy (Matt. 6:24)." But where is the locus of this kind
of liberating activity? For Pieris, it is not Christian life within the church but
rather the God-experience of God's people living beyond the church.[100]

According to Pieris, Calvary brought Jesus' cause for the poor to its culmination in that he awakened the consciousness of the poor "to their unique
liberative role in the totally new order God is about to usher in." There is no
middle ground here: "Religion and politics must go together—whether for
God or against God."[101] There is an "irrevocable covenant" between God and
the poor, just as there is an "irreversible antagonism" between God and mammon.[102] Even though what Christ did at Calvary is defining, Christian faith

95. Aloysius Pieris, "Toward an Asian Theology of Liberation: Some Religiocultural
Guidelines," in *Asian Christian Theology: Emerging Themes,* ed. Douglas Elwood (Philadelphia:
Westminster, 1980), 240.

96. Ibid.

97. Ibid., 242–43.

98. Ibid., 245–50. See also Pieris, *Asian Theology of Liberation,* 69.

99. See Vinoth Ramachandra, *The Recovery of Mission: Beyond the Pluralist Paradigm* (Downers
Grove, Ill.: InterVarsity, 1996), 48.

100. Pieris, *Asian Theology of Liberation,* 86.

101. Aloysius Pieris, *Love Meets Wisdom: A Christian Experience of Buddhism* (Maryknoll,
N.Y.: Orbis, 1988), 49.

102. Pieris, *Asian Theology of Liberation,* 120–21.

should not turn its back on Buddhism in its effort for liberation. These two religions represent two complementary "core experiences": *gnōsis,* "liberating knowledge," in Buddhism and *agapē,* "redemptive love," in Christianity.[103]

The Voice of Asian Women Theologians

Imagining God in a New Key

The emergence of feminist theology in Asia began in the early 1980s. This movement has sought to use Asian myths, stories, and other cultural means to express Christian theology in more meaningful terms. One of the first books to present an Asian women's theology was Marianne Katoppo's *Compassionate and Free.*[104] The journal *In God's Image* has been the main paper for Asian women's publications since the 1980s.[105]

Many Asian women, living under not only poverty but also oppression, marginalization, abuse, and pervasive prostitution,[106] side with their African and Latin American colleagues and create new, fresh images of God suitable for their specific context.[107] They include:

- God as community: As Elizabeth Dominguez from the Philippines says, "To be in the image of God is to be in community."[108]

- God as Creator in nature and in history: Asian women experience God in their own "creativity as a woman who gives birth, as a cook, gardener, communicator, as a writer, as a creator of the environment, atmosphere, life."[109] This same God sides with the oppressed, as witnessed in the exodus and Jesus' life.

- God as life-giving Spirit: Whereas neo-orthodox theology promotes a transcendent, absolute-other God, Asian women speak of God as a life-giving Spirit whom they can encounter within themselves and in everything that fosters life.

---

103. Pieris, *Love Meets Wisdom,* 110–11. See also Alfred T. Hennelly, *Liberation Theologies: The Global Pursuit of Justice* (Mystic, Conn.: Twenty-Third Publications, 1995), 209–11.

104. Marianne Katoppo, *Compassionate and Free: An Asian Woman's Theology* (Maryknoll, N.Y.: Orbis, 1980).

105. See Gispert-Sauch, "Asian Theology," 457–58; Chung Hyung Kyung, *Struggle to Be the Sun Again: Introducing Asian Women's Theology* (Maryknoll, N.Y.: Orbis, 1990), chaps. 1–2; and Kwok Pui-Lan, "The Future of Feminist Theology: An Asian Perspective," in *Feminist Theology from the Third World,* ed. Ursula King (Maryknoll, N.Y.: Orbis, 1994), 63–75.

106. See Marianne Katoppo, "The Church and Prostitution in Asia," in *Feminist Theology from the Third World,* 114–22.

107. Kyung, *Struggle to Be the Sun Again,* 48–52.

108. Quoted in ibid., 48.

109. Rita Monteiro, "My Image of God," *In God's Image* (September 1988): 35.

- God as mother and woman: Since God is the source of life, God can be portrayed as mother and woman. This portrayal challenges the traditional concept that emphasized, along with other attributes, God's immutability. This image also criticizes the dominant patriarchal picture of God.[110]

Much of Asian women's theology—similar to the theology of many male Asian theologians—can be found in the form of narratives, poems, stories, and testimonies. Lee Sun Ai's pictures of God are typical of this theology:

> God is movement
> God is the angry surf
> God is like mother
> God is like father
> God is like friends
> God is power of being
> God is power of living
> God is power of giving birth.[111]

Han-pu-ri Theology: Chung Hyun Kyung

Chung Hyun Kyung, a leading Asian woman theologian from Korea, received much controversial attention at the 1991 World Council of Churches Canberra Assembly because of her stirring plenary address. In that presentation, the Holy Spirit was depicted in the image of Kuan Yin, the Chinese female bodhisattva symbol of compassion who is revered in various parts of Asia beyond China.[112] According to Kyung, for Asian women to develop an authentically Asian theology, "we have to touch something really real among and around us in order to meet God." This means doing theology based on "God's revelations in our ordinary everyday experiences." It is not enough to try to articulate Korean women's God-experiences using biblical or other traditional theological sources apart from their experiences within their cultural context of suffering and life giving.[113] In addition, "By discerning the presence and action of God in our midst, I want to empower my own liberation process as well as that of my community."[114]

110. See Katoppo, *Compassionate and Free*, 65–76; and Ranjini Rebera, "The Feminist Challenge," in *The Power We Celebrate*, ed. Musimbi R. A. Kanyoro and Wendy S. Robins (Geneva: World Council of Churches, 1992), 37–50.

111. Lee Sun Ai, "Images of God," *In God's Image* (September 1988): 37.

112. The full text can be found in Michael Kinnamon, ed., *Signs of the Spirit* (Geneva: World Council of Churches, 1991), 37–47.

113. Chung Hyun Kyung, "'Han-pu-ri': Doing Theology from Korean Women's Perspective," in *We Dare to Dream: Doing Theology as Asian Women*, ed. Virginia Fabella and Sun Ai Lee Park (Kowloon, Hong Kong: Asian Women's Resource Centre for Culture and Theology, 1989), 136.

114. Kyung, *Struggle to Be the Sun Again*, 1.

A cultural resource Kyung uses for her theology of God is the concept of
han-pu-ri. The term *han* in Korean culture has several meanings ranging from
the experience of oppression to a sense of unresolved resentment to people's
"root experience," which "comes from the sinful interconnectedness of classism,
racism, [and] sexism."[115] While both men and women in Korean society have
suffered from the curse of *han,* women's lot has been more severe. A release from
han is the main purpose of women's theology in Korea. The term *han-pu-ri*
comes from Korean shamanistic religion, in which the *kut* ritual eliminates or
overpowers ghosts. This is what the good news of the gospel is all about:

> For us, the gospel of Jesus means liberation (Han-pu-ri) and life-giving power.
> In that sense we are Christians. Where there is genuine experience of liberation
> (Han-pu-ri) and life-giving power, we meet our God, Christ, and the power of
> the Spirit. That is good news.[116]

A "good" theology, one relevant to and "born out of Asian women's tears and
sighs and from their burning desire for liberation and wholeness," challenges
God about his silence. Asian women are asking, "Where were you when we
were hungry? Where were you when we called your name as our bodies were
raped, mutilated, and disfigured by our husbands, policemen, and the soldiers
of colonizing countries? Have you heard our cries?"[117]

Asian women's theology also challenges the picture of classical theism. Asian
women no longer believe in an omnipotent, sovereign God who takes care
of every agony in their lives, like a father or a big brother caring for a help-
less little girl. That God, like the God of their colonizers and the God of the
dominant institutional church, did not give Asian women life-giving power.
"Instead, 'he' accentuated their feelings of abandonment and helplessness like
a judgmental father or brother who wanted to set an example for a bad girl:
'See, as I told you, you should have been quiet, obedient, and dead!' "[118] Asian
women are now searching for the God who gives birth to their dignity and
nourishes and empowers them, the God with whom they can share their tears
and sighs, "a God who weeps with our pain."[119]

---

115. Kyung, "'Han-pu-ri,'" 138.
116. Ibid., 144–45.
117. Kyung, *Struggle to Be the Sun Again,* 22.
118. Ibid., 22–23.
119. Ibid., 23, quoting from Kwok Pui-lan, "God Weeps with Our Pain," in *New Eyes for
Reading Biblical and Theological Reflections by Women from the Third World,* ed. John S. Pobee
and Barbel von Wartenberg-Potter (Geneva: World Council of Churches, 1986), 90.

29

Reflections on Non-Western God-Talk

Perhaps the best way to take stock of the various interpretations of God among African, Latin American, and Asian theologians is to discern the common orientations and emphases of these otherwise different theologies. A related task involves assessing their significance in relation to classical theistic traditions.

First, these theologians have a genuine desire to relate Christian God-talk to their local religious and cultural heritages. For example, African theologies harken back to the variegated tapestry of traditional religions. Thus, several African theologians have adopted perspectives such as God as Ancestor. It is not enough to add something exotic to the otherwise predominantly Western God-talk. Rather, these theologians seek a genuinely Asian, African, or Hispanic interpretation of God. Opinions vary regarding how much traditional classical theological language can be retained in a contextualized approach; compare, for example, the approach of Charles Nyamiti, who wants to build on the classical Thomist foundation, with that of Kwesi Dickson, who builds his doctrine of God on the basis of biblical tradition yet within the Akan context.

Second, these theologians use a theological method that differs from the Western method. Most often they use a type of narrative theology, such as that of Choan-Seng Song of Asia. They approach the theological task from the heart rather than from a detached analytical perspective. This narrative approach makes use of folktales, myths, and poems.

Third, as a result of their theological method and consideration of context, their doctrine of God is dynamic, concrete, and "tangible." The emphasis in contextual Christian interpretations of God is God's presence in the world—in creation, human beings, human struggles.

Fourth, community—God as community and human beings as a community relating to God—is a crucial category in most third world theologies of God. The communal, corporeal emphasis of many non-Western cultures will certainly help Western theologies rehabilitate the biblical communion theology.

Fifth, Latin American theologians, under the leadership of Gustavo Gutiérrez, have been at the forefront of focusing the doctrine of God on society, politics, and economics. Asian liberationists have appropriated the category of liberation to their specific context, relating it not only to social and political concerns but also to Asia's pervasive religious context. In the African context, the South African fight against apartheid set the precedent for a genuinely black theology of liberation.

Sixth, third world theologies contain the distinctive voices of women. Speaking from their positions of marginalization, poverty, oppression, and abuse, Hispanic, Asian, and African women theologians have advocated not only feminine images of God, such as mother or parent, but also images associated with birth and nature. While learning from their European/North American colleagues, third world feminists have also adopted their own agenda.

Seventh, the all-pervasive challenge of other religions shapes the doctrine of God. Religious pluralism will undoubtedly be a major challenge—if not *the* major challenge—to the Christian doctrine of God in the third millennium. Western discourse on pluralism will benefit immensely from third world theologians' extensive dealings with the issue.

Finally, although the doctrine of the Trinity has not been the focus of third world interpretations of God—perhaps because third world theology has been less speculative and philosophical in nature—some exciting developments regarding the Trinity have taken place. Leonardo Boff's idea of God as "equalitarian community" speaks powerfully for social and ecclesiastical equality; A. Okechukwu Ogbonnaya's view of the Trinity as "communitarian divinity" is a needed reminder of the primacy of community in human and divine life; and Raimundo Panikkar's mystical, advaitic vision of the Trinity as cosmotheandric mystery invites Christian theologians to engage theology of religions from trinitarian foundations.

How do these orientations of third world interpretations of God relate to their contemporary European and North American counterparts? Contextual differences aside, several common features appear:

- a focus on the immanence of God and God's presence in the world instead of on his transcendence; an emphasis on the attributes of God that have to do with his love, responsiveness, and dynamism
- an emphasis on salvation history, including social and political realities, as the proper locus of the doctrine of God
- a rehabilitation of the category of community

- an effort to speak inclusively of God and thus make the discourse meaningful to both sexes and all classes
- a growing interest in relating God-talk to other religions

What contributions do third world interpretations of God make to classical theistic traditions? Not surprisingly, they have helped theologians acknowledge the biblical dynamism and narrative form of God-talk. They also point to the need to reassess God's relation to the world in terms of God's active involvement. Furthermore, they reveal the contextuality of all God-talk, already visible in the Bible's variety. Rather than a universal "world theology of God," a locally contextual, salvation-historical, and socially as well as politically relevant interpretation of God is emerging to challenge more sterile, academic traditions.

Epilogue

The Future of God-Talk in the Third Millennium

The major challenges—and inspirations—to Christian theology at the beginning of the third millennium do not come from atheism but from three related sources: the dramatically changed philosophical and religious ethos of the Western world since the Enlightenment, the radical transformation of Christianity as it moves south and east, and the pervasive influence of religious pluralism and the interchange among religions. The future of Christian theology to a large extent depends on how it tackles these three challenges.

As should be evident from this survey, the conditions for talking meaningfully about God changed dramatically after the Reformation. What the Enlightenment started, postmodernism pushed to the extremes.

It is becoming increasingly clear that a palpably different understanding of God and his relationship to the world is steadily pressing itself upon the modern consciousness. A new immanentalism is displacing the transcendentalism that has hitherto characterized both Catholic and Protestant theology. The emphasis today is not on the almightiness of God but on his vulnerability. Attention is given to God's empathy with the world rather than his majesty, his pathos rather than his infinite beatitude. The idea of a suffering God is supplanting the idea of an impassible God, vigorously defended in Christian tradition. God is no longer the infinite supreme being beyond world history but now "the Infinite in the

303

finite" (Schleiermacher). God is no longer a static Infinite but now a dynamic Infinite that "emerges" out of the void but also "rushes" in (Sri Aurobindo).[1]

The basic categories of classical theism are being revised in light of recent philosophical and worldview trends as well as biblical scholarship. Radical changes in biblical scholarship that accompanied the demise of the historical-critical paradigm have given systematic theologians a new appreciation for the dynamism and relevance of the biblical narratives.

The second major influence on the doctrine of God comes from third world theologies and other contextual voices. Whereas respected schools seek to hire scholars from third world contexts, amazingly little has changed in the way textbooks are written and classes taught. Yet theology at the international level must give proper attention to these contextual voices and offer opportunities for patient dialogue between Western and non-Western theologies in light of biblical and historical traditions.

Religious pluralism and other religions constitute the third major challenge to the theology of God. In the words of John Habgood, "Other faiths used to belong to other lands. At home rival religious claims could safely be ignored. Or if not ignored, patronized."[2] But not anymore. Other gods no longer reside only in exotic lands. They are among our neighbors and in our schools, our workplaces, and sometimes our families through intermarriage.[3] Yet contact with other religions is nothing new to Christianity. A major impetus for the emergence of the classical theistic traditions was the struggle to make the biblical faith in Yahweh, the Father of Jesus Christ, understandable to followers of other religions. Alan Race, in his widely used textbook *Christian and Religious Pluralism,* claims that "the future of Christian theology lies in the encounter between Christianity and other faiths."[4]

Christian theology in general and the doctrine of God in particular have a twofold task in light of these challenges. It is crucial, but not enough, to study the context in which Christian theology confesses its faith in Yahweh, the Father of Jesus Christ. Much work needs to be done not only in Africa, Asia, and Latin America but also in the West, for example, among women and others whose voices have not been properly heard in the discourse. In addition, a critical, appreciative rereading of Christian tradition—both biblical and historical—is needed. The historical survey indicated that the various

1. Donald G. Bloesch, *God the Almighty: Power, Wisdom, Holiness, Love* (Downers Grove, Ill.: InterVarsity, 1995), 17.

2. John Habgood, Archbishop of York, preface to *Many Mansions: Interfaith and Religious Tolerance,* ed. Dan Cohn-Sherbok (London: Bellew, 1992), vii.

3. On the challenge of religious pluralism to Christian theology, see Veli-Matti Kärkkäinen, *An Introduction to Christian Theology of Religions: Biblical, Historical, and Contemporary Perspectives* (Downers Grove, Ill.: InterVarsity, 2003).

4. Alan Race, *Christians and Religious Pluralism: Patterns in the Christian Theology of Religions* (Maryknoll, N.Y.: Orbis, 1982), xi.

traditions of classical theism include more variety, dynamism, and creativity than is often acknowledged. Of course, there is no denying the limitations of the classical traditions. They are, after all, time-bound theological traditions, nothing more than human words about God for a particular situation. Yet as mentioned, the purpose of this book is not to argue for (or against) classical theistic traditions but to highlight the story of Christian interpretations of God, past and present, in light of the dynamic relationship between classical theism and its challengers.

No doubt, discourse about God will occupy the minds—and hearts—of theologians at the international and the ecumenical level in the third millennium. In this endeavor, we need one another's help and wisdom from the God we are talking about. While writing this book on God, more often than not I shared the feeling of Dante, who at the end of his masterpiece, *The Divine Comedy*, acknowledged, "My own wings were not enough for that—except that my mind was illumined by a flash through which its wish was realized. For the great imagination here power failed."[5]

5. Dante, *The Divine Comedy*, trans. H. R. Huse (New York: Holt, Rinehart & Winston, 1954), 481.

Subject Index

Scripture Index